# The Poetics of Decadence

*SUNY* series in
Chinese Philosophy and Culture

David L. Hall and Roger T. Ames, editors

# The Poetics of Decadence

---

## Chinese Poetry of the Southern Dynasties and Late Tang Periods

Fusheng Wu

STATE UNIVERSITY OF NEW YORK PRESS

Production by Ruth Fisher
Marketing by Patrick Durocher

Published by
State University of New York Press, Albany

© 1998  State University of New York

For information, address the State University of New York Press,
State University Plaza, Albany, NY  12246

**Library of Congress Cataloging-in-Publication Data**

Wu, Fusheng, 1959–
    The poetics of decadence : Chinese poetry of the Southern
  dynasties and late Tang periods / Fusheng Wu.
        p.   cm. — (SUNY series in Chinese philosophy and culture)
    Includes bibliographical references and index.
    ISBN 0–7914–3751–5 (alk. paper). — ISBN 0–7914–3752–3 (pbk. :
  alk. paper)
      1. Chinese poetry—T'ang dynasty, 618—907—History and criticism.
    2. Chinese poetry—Northern and Southern dynasties, 386–589—History
  and criticism.   3. Hsiao, Kang, 503–551—Criticism and
  interpretation.   4. Wen, T'ing-yün, 812–ca. 870—Criticism and
  interpretation.   5. Li, Ho, 790–816—Criticism and interpretation.
  6. Li, Shang-yin, 813–858—Criticism and interpretation.
  7. Decadence in literature.  I. Title.  II. Series.
  PL2321.W82   1998
  895.1'1309—dc21                                            97–37507
                                                                CIP

10 9 8 7 6 5 4 3 2 1

*To Xiaolian, and our son, Jeremy Hao Wu*

# Contents

# Acknowledgments

This book evolved from my dissertation. I should like to first thank the members of my dissertation committee, Professors Dore Levy, David Lattimore, and Edward Ahearn of Brown University, for their guidance. I am especially grateful to Professor Dore Levy, who brought this wonderful topic to my attention in my preliminary examination and encouraged me to pursue it afterward. During my five-year study at Brown she constantly challenged me with intellectual rigor, while at the same time looking after me with personal concerns—I feel very fortunate to have had the opportunity to study with her. Li Qiancheng, my former colleague and old friend at Nankai University, China, proofread the manuscript; his meticulous attention helped to eliminate many technical errors. Deborah Porter, my colleague at the University of Utah, read part of the manuscript and offered helpful comments. Ilene Cohn's editorial remarks helped to improve the style of the book. The expert help from Nancy Ellegate, Ruth Fisher, and other editorial staff at the SUNY Press not only made the publication of this book an exciting event in my life, but also greatly reduced the level of anxieties involved. Thanks to Professor Roger Ames, whose interest in the book was the first step in making it available to the public, and to the three anonymous readers at SUNY Press, for their sympathetic reports.

Very often the completion of an academic project entails the help and understanding of those who are not directly involved in the project itself. My parents first introduced Chinese literature to me and always

hoped that I would become an accomplished scholar in their fields—
Chinese literature and history. The publication of this book will fulfill
their dream. My wife, Deng Xiaolian, provided me with constant love
and understanding that helped to carry us together through several
difficult stages of our life. The members of the Engelhart family have
been extremely generous in offering their love and support; Carl and
Margaret, in particular, have been guiding my life with their parental
affections, integrity, and intellectual curiosity since they picked me
up at the J. F. K. airport, New York, on the night of July 28, 1990—a
night that will forever remain in my memory. Finally, a deep bow to
my grandmother, Liu Shude. She brought me up but did not live to
share my joy today. This is a rare moment when I wish I could believe
in the existence of spirit.

Chapter 2 was originally published under the title "Decadence in
Chinese Literature: Xiao Gang's Palace Style Poetry" in *Chinese Studies*
XV, no. 1 (1997): 351–95; part of Chapter 1 was originally published
under the title "The Concept of Decadence in the Chinese Poetic Tradition" in *Monumenta Serica* XLV (1997): 39–62. I would like to thank
*Chinese Studies* and *Monumenta Serica* for their permissions to reprint
the aforementioned articles in the present study.

This book is an intertextual[1] study of decadent (*tuifei* 頹廢) poetry in the Chinese literary tradition. It considers specifically work from the periods of the Southern Dynasties and Late Tang,[2] when decadent poetry was produced in great quantity. It focuses on the works of four poets, namely, Xiao Gang蕭綱 (503–51) or Emperor Jianwen of Liang dynasty 梁簡文帝 Li He 李賀 (790–816), Wen Tingyun 溫庭筠 (812?–66), and Li Shangyin 李商隱 (813–58). Its goal is to demonstrate that decadent poetry is among other things a poetic agenda that deliberately challenges and subverts the canonical concept and practice of poetry. It constituted a poetic genre with its own unique, complex, and self-reflexive verbal system. In taking such an intertextual approach I aim to demystify decadent poetry and disentangle it from its lurid overtones and sensational associations. By situating decadent poetry within the context of a conventional system of signs, we can for the first time use *tuifei* or decadence as a neutral critical term, rather than as a term of moral and political opprobrium, as it has been used in the Chinese tradition. Such an approach also provides us with an insight into the textual/intertextual nature of decadent poetry that traditional criticism, with its exclusive emphasis on subject matter, tends to neglect.

Indeed, the word *decadence* has evoked lurid associations. In the context of English and French literature:

The word "decadence" is at once a sobriquet for the historian, a reproach for the moralist, a condemnation for the literary purist. There immediately emerges the cliché of the superannuated aesthete, the dandy twirling his gold-headed cane, as he leers over his absinthe at a voluptuous woman strolling down the boulevard. Hence in the popular mind the literature of the decadence, exuding decay, is superficially preoccupied with the exotic and the erotic.[3]

In the Chinese literary tradition the mention of *tuifei* 頹廢, the closest Chinese equivalent of decadent, calls to mind the night-long drinking party of Chen Houzhu 陳後主 (553–604), the last emperor of Chen dynasty. Drunken and surrounded by singing girls, the emperor and his court poets composed one erotic poem after another even as his enemies were on the verge of capturing the city.[4] Or the term suggests the poet/dandy Wen Tingyun, who, after dissipating all his financial resources and his official career while visiting brothels, then gets into a brawl with the police and receives a sound beating.[5] The association is so strong that it has become a powerful myth, a myth that not only lends an aura of sensationalism to decadent literature, but has also generated a particular scholarly approach.

This approach is often marked by a tendency to take the part for the whole and to see all decadent literature as a single cultural and ideological entity, thus overlooking its textual and artistic richness and diversity. For instance, the erotic poetry of Xiao Gang and other court poets is often used to represent all Palace Style poetry, and Late Tang poetry is not infrequently typed as being preoccupied with the subtle, feminine mentality of disillusioned and delicate literati in an age of decline.[6] This is compounded by the fact that in the Chinese literary tradition ideology and morality are often adopted as the standards of judgment. Specific literary analysis is frequently sacrificed for the coherence of a general intellectual picture. The following chapters will show that this approach often blinds us to other features—especially textual and generic features—that reveal the true nature of decadent poetry.

To achieve a more balanced understanding of decadent poetry we must first distance ourselves from the myth surrounding it. We begin by examining the original meanings of *tuifei* 頹廢 and its Western counterpart, *decadence*. Although they belong to two otherwise very different cultures, the meaning and evolution of these two terms are strikingly similar. Despite its sensational associations, the Chinese compound *tuifei* was first employed by the historian Fan Ye 范曄 (398–444) in a very concrete sense, to refer to the decay of school buildings.[7] Similarly in the West "decadence" (*decadentia*) was first defined by Peter Du Cange (1610–88), the lexicographer of late Latin, to describe farms and hills that had fallen into ruin.[8] As time went on both *tuifei* and *decadence* came more and more to describe a moral, spiritual, and political state, such that their original association with material breakdown was completely obliterated by the newer metaphorical application. By now a *tuifei* or decadent building is a totally incomprehensible concept. The origins of the two phrases are lost.

Based on the etymology of "decadence," the *New Princeton Encyclopedia of Poetry and Poetics* defines decadent literature to be "a 'falling away' (L.: *de-cadere*) from previously recognized conditions or standards of excellence."[9] This definition evokes the most important aspects of the original meaning of decadence, namely, the inevitable physical breakdown of farms, slopes, school buildings, and other objects.[10] Decadence in literature is also envisaged as an inexorable and hence "natural" process in the development of literary history. Literature inevitably becomes decadent at some stage, precisely as nature and human construction are bound to decay with the passage of time. For a physical object decadence is a falling away from its solid foundation and construction. For literature decadence is a falling away from "previously *recognized* conditions or standards of excellence" (my emphasis) which, because of their "recognized" status, have been conventionalized or upheld as canonical.

I will problematize this definition through a close examination of theoretical and poetic texts from the Chinese tradition in the following chapters. First, to use the literary works of a certain age, however revered they are by later writers, as the ultimate criterion against which all subsequent writings are judged is essentially ahistorical, although ironically decadence makes sense only in a historical context. Moreover, decadent poetry in the Chinese tradition sets out to challenge the canon; it is a deliberate deviation from the norm. To be a "falling away" constitutes its very locus of significance. Thus, it is by no means natural or inevitable.

To begin, I delineate how what is not decadent, or what is healthy in literature, is dependent upon a set of conventional presumptions as to what literature is or ought to be. These presumptions are the background against which decadent literature operates. A deviation like decadent literature can therefore only be understood fairly by relating it to the norm and the canon from which it is considered as to have fallen away.

This is where the first chapter of this work begins. It will establish a theoretical framework for the following four chapters, which are devoted to close textual and intertextual analysis of the works of the four aforementioned poets. It aims to define for the first time the concept of decadence in the Chinese literary tradition. I begin with the fundamental principle that "poetry expresses one's will" (*shi yanzhi* 詩言志) and try to demonstrate through a close analysis of this maxim and other related documents from the classical tradition that this canonical principle, with its emphasis on spontaneity, naturalness, transparency of expression, and sociopolitical responsibility and moral seriousness of content, actually condemns any subsequent development of Chinese poetry to a state of decadence.

These canonical standards simply cannot accommodate the work of later poets who are more concerned with the artfulness of their works or who view poetic production not simply as a means to express one's feelings and thoughts but also as a craft that can be learned through repeated, sometimes mechanical, practice. The poets in the Southern Dynasties court, for example, did not write their poetry to express their will; for them poetic production was a public game in which each poet was merely a player. Therefore they did not need a straightforward, transparent verbal medium as demanded by the above maxim and the Great Preface to *The Book of Songs*. Instead, they needed a highly sophisticated and artificial style that could make their game technically challenging and entertaining. But since the standards spelled out by these two documents had become ultimate values in the Chinese tradition, deviation from them is inevitably viewed as decadent.

Xiao Gang and Palace Style poetry (*gongtishi* 宮體詩), which are considered in the second chapter, illustrate the point. The project of Palace Style poetry is a deliberate attempt to undermine the canonical concept of poetry by carefully separating the aesthetic quality and concerns of poetry from its social and political obligations. In turning poetry into clever verbal play, it removes it from its exalted position as a state instrument for administering its people. Palace Style poetry attends to artfulness of expression at the expense of depth of meaning, and thus has been considered as anathema in the Chinese tradition, having violated both the Confucian concept of literature and the Daoist idea of language. Confucianism regards social and political values of poetry as indispensable, and Daoism valorizes the function of language to communicate a profound meaning, rather than to ignore such communication by foregrounding itself, as Palace Style poetry does. But the significance of Palace Style poetry is not merely negative, because it demonstrates by its own practice the vulnerability of many presumptions in the Chinese tradition. For instance, before the Southern Dynasties period the dominant view of poetry had been the rigid Confucian notion that the sole function of poetry was to serve the state. The Daoist concept of language as a fishnet to be discarded as soon as the fish is caught was given new emphasis in the *xuanxue* 玄學 (dark and subtle learning) discussions of the Wei and Jin eras.[11] Had these principles actually held sway, the development of Chinese poetry would have been hindered. In particular, the structurally complex and technically demanding poetry of the Tang period would have been an impossibility. Consider, as an example, regulated verse (*lüshi* 律詩), which is regarded by many as the tour de force of Tang poetry. This highly sophisticated and technical poetry would have been unthinkable if poetry were intended solely to "express one's will" or if poets disdained their poetic language. Tang poetry, by contrast, employs complicated metrical patterns and formal rules that suggest the poet's fascination and even obsession with the formal quality of his work, and this quality often tends to overwhelm the expressive function of poetry. One readily finds such instances in the works of Li He and Li Shangyin, and they even exist in the oeuvre of Du Fu. Palace Style poetry, in experimenting with tonal patterns, laid the groundwork for regulated verse. In challenging the fundamental assumptions of the Chinese literary tradition, such as the overemphasis on poetry's sociopolitical role and the refusal to regard it as a complex linguistic craft, it broadened the view of literature and language, and made possible the emergence of a more imaginative and sophisticated poetry.

The next three chapters deal with three Late Tang poets whose poetry shows a noticeable continuity from the Palace Style convention. One of the clichés in the history of Chinese poetry is that the vitality of the Chinese poetic tradition (as represented by *The Book of Songs* and the poetry of the Han, Wei, and Jin periods) was lost in the frivolous and artificially ornate works of the Southern Dynasties poets. But such vitality was regained on an even higher level during the High Tang period, only to be lost again in the Mid and Late Tang eras, when Chinese poetry was once more haunted by the ghost of the decadent Southern Dynasties poetry.[12] Li He, Wen Tingyun, and Li Shangyin are usually regarded as the most prominent representatives of this reassertion of the values and characteristics of the Southern Dynasties poetry, particularly the Palace Style poetry.[13] I debunk these clichés surrounding Late Tang poetry. Through a careful reading of their poetic works, I will show that they all to a great extent transformed the impersonal, rigid, and superficial Palace Style poetry and formed their own distinctive characteristics. This is so even though the three self-consciously wrote in the Palace Style convention, which itself signifies a defiance of the canonical tradition because by Late Tang, Palace Style poetry had already become an archetype of decadence, and even though Southern Dynasties poetry often served as historical and artistic image for them to meditate upon. In each case— the baffling complexity of Li He, the tantalizing elusiveness of Li Shangyin, and the sensual indulgence of Wen Tingyun—the poet has transcended Palace Style poetry. One might still call their works "decadent," but in this context the word no longer designates a single writing style applied to the works of poets who are little more than a group of interchangeable names. Rather, it has acquired new qualities and connotations that vary with the poet.

Decadence as a poetics in Chinese poetry has never been studied, certainly not thoroughly and systematically, and not by scholars inside China nor by those outside China. Recently works on the poets referred to above all concentrate on the poetry of individual poets, rather than considering them together under a unifying subject. The present study—the first attempt to define "decadence" systematically in the Chinese poetic tradition—will provide a much needed critical apparatus for a neglected yet important subject. By relating an often condemned poetic genre to the canonical tradition for the first time, I demonstrate that the so-called decadent poetry is a critique of the canon and convention. Removed from its sensational associations, it is better understood as an attempt on the part of a group of poets to find their own places in an already well established literary convention. The often violent denunciations hurled at them by traditional criticism and the pervasive influences of decadent poetry on Chinese poetry suggest that they have achieved their goal.

As I stated at the beginning of the introduction, the main thesis of this study is that Chinese decadent poetry challenges the canonical tradition. It is pointless to argue now whether the poets actually "intended" this challenge. The best way to avoid this fallacy of intentionality is to look closely at what is in the text and see what it evokes in certain historical and cultural contexts. The context that I try to establish is that of the canonical tradition, particularly the canonical tradition vis-à-vis decadent poetry. Apart from examining theoretical documents such as the Great Preface to *The Book of Songs*, the most effective way to do this, I believe, is by investigating how decadent poetry was received during the various stages of the classical tradition. Thus, in conducting this intertextual analysis, I have studied readings and commentaries on decadent poetry by critics of different periods, particularly the critics of the Qing dynasty. While by no means do I regard the traditional poetic theory and criticism as a seamless whole, I have chosen to emphasize Qing criticism in establishing this context, for two reasons. First, we simply do not possess detailed contemporary readings and commentaries of the poetic texts used in this study. And second, the readings and commentaries by Qing critics are not only the most detailed, the most systematic, and the most sophisticated in the classical tradition, they are also the ones most helpful to our understanding the traditional exegetical convention because many of them were closely guided by the canonical views of poetry. As a contemporary Chinese scholar pointed out, Qing studies of poetry represent the most mature stage of poetry criticism in the classical tradition. They compensate for their lack of innovation by their exhaustive inclusion of nearly every aspect of the Chinese canon.[14] Therefore, it is justifiable to use them as illustrations of canonical theory and criticism of poetry.[15]

Finally, I should point out that while this study touches upon some general cultural issues, these are treated mainly within the framework of literature in the sense of belles lettres. It will therefore tend to ignore some larger issues such as the sociopolitical history and significance of decadent poetry, although passing remarks on these issues will be made. The very breadth of decadence as a topic makes it possible and almost necessary to study it from many different approaches. One can trace the evolution of the word, as Richard Gilman did in his *Decadence, The Strange Life of an Epithet*. One can study the topic from a philosophical point of view, as C. E. M. Joad's *Decadence: A Philosophical Enquiry*.[16] One can investigate the intellectual and cultural history of a period in which decadent literature is produced in abundance, as in A. E. Carter's *The Idea of Decadence in French Literature 1830–1900* and Holbrock Jackson's *The Eighteen Nineties: A Review of Art and Ideas at the Close of Nineteenth Century*.[17] The researcher on any topic must focus on those aspects that suit his or her interests and ability best, but in doing so he or she necessarily sacrifices features that would look essential to someone else. This cannot be avoided, and in our age of specialization this is a lesser sin than it might have been in an age like the Renaissance, when the scholar seemed able to master all human knowledge available to him. That time is gone forever—we have "fallen away" too far from that golden era. Living in a decadent age, I can proceed with peace of mind on a decadent study of a decadent topic.

## Chapter 1

# Defining Decadence
# in the Chinese Poetic Tradition

s has been indicated in the Introduction, the concept of decadent literature as a "falling away" from "previously recognized" conditions and standards of excellence is predicated upon a set of conventional presumptions about the nature of "canon"[1] in a literary tradition. The canon is the background against which decadent literature operates. Therefore, let us begin our discussion with the canonical concept of literature. Such a concept was formed very early in the Chinese tradition, and the single most important statement about the nature of poetry[2] is the one recorded in *Shang shu* 尚書 (*The book of historical documents*):

> Poetry expresses one's will; song prolongs one's words; sounds correspond to melody; instruments accord with sounds; when the eight tones are all balanced and do not encroach upon one another, spirits and human beings will be in harmony.

> 詩言志，歌永言，聲依永，律和聲，八音克諧，無相奪倫，神
> 人以和。[3]

Unlike Aristotle's mimetic theory, which locates poetry at an external source,[4] this expressive theory defines poetry as a movement from the internal to the external. Its origin is unequivocally located in the poet's heart or mind (*xin* 心).[5] It also establishes the important role that poetry is expected to play in regulating human affairs, hence the close link between the quality of poetry and certain social conditions. This view of poetry is further elaborated by another key document, the Great Preface to *The Book of Songs* (詩大序):

> Poetry is where one's will goes. In mind [or heart] it is will; coming out in language, it is poetry. The emotions are stirred within and take on form in words. When words alone are inadequate, we speak them out in sighs. When sighing is inadequate, we sing them. When singing them is inadequate, unconsciously our hands dance them and our feet tap them.

> 詩者，志之所之也，在心爲志，發言爲詩。情動於中而形于言，言之不足故嗟嘆之，嗟嘆之不足故永歌之，永歌之不足，不知手之舞之，足之蹈之也。[6]

The assumption is that poetry flows from one's inner response to an external stimulus. It is a "natural"—that is, automatic—product of the stimulus-response process. Poetry is conceived as a physico-biological need of the human being, essential for maintaining the balance and health of mind and body. Not only does this formulation imply that spontaneity and sincerity are the most essential qualities in poetry, since any response that is forced or faked is not natural and hence cannot bring about the desired therapeutic result (of physical or mental health). It also implicitly mandates the linguistic style best equipped to fulfill such a task. Only the most straightforward, the most transparent, verbal medium can articulate one's feelings and thoughts effectively and spontaneously unleash one's mental and physical tensions. The complete absence of any discussion on technical aspects of poetic production in this preface[7] indicates that poetry is not viewed as a craft to be mechanically pursued. To the contrary, tinkering with and polishing the product can only betray insincerity on the part of the poet, impede the process of communication, and deny the raison d'être of poetry. But as we will see later, it is precisely with such tinkering and polishing that decadent poetry is associated.

This view echoes Confucius's distrust of sophisticated speech. A passage in the *Analects* records that when someone criticized one of his students as being "truly virtuous, but not ready with his tongue," Confucius defended him with the following words:

10

What is the good of being ready with tongue? They who argue in sophisticated speech only make themselves despised. I do not know whether he is virtuous, but why should he show readiness of the tongue?

焉用佞？禦人以口給，屢憎於人。不知其仁，焉用佞？[8]

Confucius seems to be suggesting that sophisticated speech is incompatible with a virtuous personality. Similarly, the Great Preface indicates that in poetry an artificial and intricate verbal medium obstructs rather than enhances the communication of heartfelt thoughts and emotions. That is, only a spontaneous verbal medium can express a spontaneous reaction.

In the previously quoted passage from *Shang shu* there is another element that enormously influenced the Chinese attitude toward poetry—the belief that poetry can and should play a role in maintaining harmony between humankind and spirits or nature. Later, when Chinese society had evolved from its primitive state, when the functions of gods and spirits had been replaced by civil government, this semireligious mandate to maintain a harmony between humankind and spirits was transformed into a political mandate: poetry must help government to administer its people. It must help society to maintain order. It must, as Confucius says, serve to "stimulate [the will] (*xing* 興), observe [social customs] (*guan* 觀), hold together [members in a community] (*qun* 群), and voice grievance [about social injustice] (*yuan* 怨)."[9] The Great Preface misses no opportunity to elaborate this concept:

Feelings are expressed in sounds; when sounds form in pattern, it is music. The music of a peaceful world is leisurely and happy, its politics is in order; the music of a disordered world is full of grievance and anger, its politics is in chaos. The music of a defeated country is sad, and its people are in trouble. Therefore, to uphold what is just, to correct what is wrong, to move heaven and earth, to reach the gods and spirits, nothing comes close to poetry. This is why the ancient kings use it to regulate husband and wife, to establish filial piety among people, to make their morality honest, to make their customs beautiful, and to improve the milieu in society.

情發於聲，聲成文謂之音。治世之音安以樂，其政和；亂世之音怨以怒，其政乖；亡國之音哀以思，其民困。故正得失，動天地，感鬼神，莫近於詩。先王以是經夫婦，成孝敬，厚人倫，美教化，移風俗.[10]

Throughout history the consensus has been that the texts we have been considering so far lay the foundation of the canon in the Chinese literary tradition. Xu Shen 許慎 (30–124), the author of the first Chinese dictionary, *Shuowen jiezi* 說文解字, takes poetry (*shi* 詩) and will (*zhi* 志) to be synonyms because "poetry is the will expressed in words".[11] Zhu Ziqing 朱自清 refers to the statement that "poetry expresses one's will" as "the founding principle of Chinese poetic theory."[12] Stephen Owen regards the Great Preface to be:

> the most authoritative statement on the nature and function of poetry in traditional China. Not only was it to be the beginning of every student's study of the *The Book of Songs* from the Eastern Han through the Sung, its concerns and terminology became essential part of writing about poetry and learning about poetry. It was the one text on the nature of poetry that everyone knew from the end of Han on, and even when the Great Preface came under harsh attack in later ages, many positions in it remained almost universally accepted.[13]

Perhaps no one will dispute that any subsequent development in Chinese literature had to take into account of the two "recognized" conditions and standards of excellence advanced by these texts: (1) the spontaneity, sincerity, and naturalness of expression, and (2) "political correctness" of content. Together they constitute the cornerstone of Confucian poetic theory. However, in Confucius's own or putative works we find some tensions that undermine this theory and its implied criteria.

It is clear that Confucius emphasizes the subject matter and practical function of poetry; for him poetry is an important means of achieving his social and political ideal. He once says that if one cannot use poetry in diplomatic missions—even though one could recite *The Book of Songs* in its entirety—there was no point in learning it.[14] But in fact Confucius is never totally pragmatic, as evidenced by the tremendous emphasis he lays on the role and aesthetic appeal of ritual.

Ritual keeps social regulations from becoming tyrannical because it encourages people to act spontaneously and willingly. When filial piety becomes a ritual act, for instance, the son acts not only out of a sense of obligation and responsibility but also out of a sense of personal satisfaction, because the aesthetic elements of ritual transform the very act into artistic play.[15] This is why Confucius expressed distaste for any "substance without form": "When substance (*zhi* 質) overwhelms the form (*wen* 文, or pattern), it is vulgar; when form overwhelms substance, it is extravagant. Only when one can achieve a balance between form and substance can one become a gentleman."[16] Besides abhorring its vulgarity, Confucius also disliked the naked expression of content because it could never achieve effectively the goal it aims at. In another often cited remark he says "words without *wen* do not go very far."[17]

These words in praise of embellished linguistic expression seem to contradict the condemnation of sophisticated speech uttered by a ready-tongued person; or at least the difference between embellished words and sophisticated speech is not obvious. Moreover, the balance between form and content that Confucius seems to advocate is a delicate one, because compared with content, form is of a much more unstable nature. One can try to establish authority over the content of writing by relating it to the statement of one's intentions. In the Chinese tradition this endeavor carries enormous weight because of the *zhiren lunshi* 知人論世 exegetical habit that was implied in the canonical concept of poetry[18] and elevated to a principle by Mencius. It stipulates specifically that to understand the meaning of a text, one must explore the author's life and his time.[19] But this is not easy to accomplish since one must work with impersonal linguistic signifiers that operate in a context extending far beyond the control of their user. Form, therefore, can easily elude the attempt at containment by its specific user and acquire a meaning that often undermines and even contradicts the author's intentions.

This is exactly what happens to Confucius with regard to his view of poetry. The delicate equilibrium he sets up between the sociopolitical function of poetry as a sheer instrument of social and political purpose and its formal aesthetic appeal as the artistic expression of the rectifying political will can be upset. Because the canon of Chinese poetry is based essentially on the presumed but precarious balance between the two aspects of this tension, although different periods seem to have emphasized one or the other,[20] it is highly unstable. As we shall see, any later developments in Chinese poetry or literature are inevitably attempts to redefine or redraw this subtle equilibrium. The moralists advocate the overriding importance of content and try to contain poetry as an instrument of their political agenda. Artistically minded writers, however, aim to give form a larger role in their literary production. The so-called decadent poetry in Chinese tradition is nothing but such an effort on the part of a group of poets to rethink and redefine the poet's relationship to this canon. And thus the emphasis on the aesthetic appeal of form can be seen as a self-conscious critique and reshaping of an orthodox principle.

The Great Preface sows other seeds of potential disruption of the Confucian canon that it upholds because it considers the process of decline as ineluctable. The poems in *The Book of Songs* were considered to be the ultimate examples of Chinese poetry, yet as the Great Preface would have it, even in these poems—said to have been selected by Confucius himself—such a process of decline had already begun:

> When the kingly way declined rites and moral principles were abandoned; the government lost its power to instruct; the political structure of the states changed; the customs of the family were altered: at this point the mutated poems were written.

至於王道衰，禮義廢，政教失，國異政，家殊俗，而變風、變雅作矣。[21]

The decline of poetry, then, is seen as the necessary result of the decline of a political and social reality, because, in this view, poetry is inherently connected to the quality of society. Of course, when belief in the inherent connection between poetry and sociopolitical life is shattered in later ages, the basis for the belief in the decline of poetry is undermined as well.[22] Zhu Ziqing points out that the word *bian* 變 (to change, changed, or "mutated" as in Owen's rendering), can have two very different connotations, depending on the context. In political and social history, it is a negative term, indicative of a deviation from a norm. In philosophy, particularly the cosmological philosophy established in *The Book of Changes*, it represents a vital force in the movement of the universe and hence is a positive word.[23] The Great

Preface seemed to have used it exclusively in its moral and historical sense. Still, it considers the mutated poems in *The Book of Songs* to be the proper models because in any event they are thought to have "emerged from feelings and stopped at rites and morality."[24] In other words, as long as poetry expresses what is deeply felt and conforms to the moral and political principles of government, it is good poetry. But there is a subtle contradiction in this phrasing, because "emerging from feelings" (*fahu qing* 發乎情) implies a spontaneity and naturalness that are undercut by "stop at rites and morality" (*zhihu liyi* 止乎禮義), which suggests a deliberate, artificial imposition of controls. Therefore, the canonical notion of poetry is problematic because these two basic demands are potentially irreconcilable, and the balance between them is at best precarious.

As we will see throughout the following chapters, artistic control is a prominent feature of Chinese decadent poetry. However, such control is not exercised for moral and political reasons as is demanded by the Great Preface. Instead, it has been radically transformed into something purely aesthetic.

We might call this way of thinking "a decline mentality." Confucius himself is the earliest authority of such a mentality.[25] He is obsessed with the notion that he lives in an era of decadence, a time that has fallen from the old glory of the Western Zhou dynasty (1045–711 B.C.). He looks back nostalgically to that lost golden age: "How beautiful [are the ways of Zhou]; I am a follower of Zhou!"[26] He laments the loss of political and cultural unity and the invasion of barbarian culture. He instructs his students to "abandon the music of Zheng (*zhengsheng* 鄭聲), distance themselves from villains; for the music of Zheng is lascivious, and villains are dangerous."[27] But in Confucius's strongest lament about the decline of his age, he metaphorically fuses his own personal decline and historical decadence: "How far I have declined (*shuai* 衰); it has been a long time since I dreamed of the Duke of Zhou!"[28] This touching statement will bear heavily upon the minds of Chinese literati as it comes to be linked to the fate of culture and literature. Not just politically and socially is their age a decadent one, but their writing too represents a decline from the achievement of our ancestors. Although some writers did try to discredit this self-effacing mentality, it remained influential throughout Chinese classical tradition.[29]

On the significance of the Great Preface, especially the part on "mutated poems" (*bianfeng bianya* 變風變雅) in *The Book of Songs*, Stephen Owen comments:

> Chinese literary historical process was often described in terms of movement between "proper" (*zheng* 正) and "mutated" (*bian* 變). These terms are replete with value judgment and in this context are firmly linked to issues of moral history. *Zheng* describes the stability of a government and society functioning properly, a stability that is manifest in the "tone" of poems of the age. *Bian* appears in this context as a falling away, a "devolution," in which the growing imbalances in society manifest themselves in poetry. These terms never became entirely free of value judgments that were ultimately rooted in moral history; in later ages, however, there was some attempt to use them in a purely literary sense. In this context *zheng* might represent the norm of some genre, the *bian* would be a falling away from that norm; these processes of attaining a norm and subsequent devolution might operate independently from the moral history of dynasties.[30]

We may of course argue that the very separation of literature from its moral and sociopolitical environment represents a decadent step on the part of later writers and critics, a *bian*, falling away, from *zheng*, the proper, the norm.[31]

In Chinese tradition the theoretical model for decadence is provided not only by Confucius and the Great Preface, but also by the reputed founder of Daoism, Laozi 老子. He situates his Dao (道 the Way) in a state of utter innocence in which there is no differentiation, no language; all is in an organic harmony:

> Dao is eternal, nameless. Though the uncarved block seems small, it may be subordinated to nothing in the world. If kings and barons can preserve it, all creation would of itself pay homage, heaven and earth would unite to send sweet dew, and people would of themselves achieve peace and harmony.
> Once the block is cut, names appear. When names begin to appear, know then that there is a time to stop. It is by this knowledge that danger may be avoided.

道常無名，樸。雖小，天下莫能臣。侯王若能守之，萬物將自
賓。天地相和，以降甘露，民莫之令而自均。
始制有名，名亦既有，夫亦將知止，知止可以不殆。[32]

Laozi describes Dao as an "uncarved block"—a metaphor of profound and rich implications. In his writings it represents an ideal
state that incorporates all elements, human and nonhuman, into an
organic harmony through its negative quality. Because it is *not* carved,
it paradoxically remains open to everything and can include everything. The values implied by the metaphor of the uncarved block are
opposed to craftsmanship and any connections with craftsmanship.
Naturalness is the ideal, so is simplicity as opposed to artificiality and
elaboration. The Great Preface dooms Chinese poetry to perpetual
decline by claiming that the process is already evident even in the
very book that it sets up as the canon. But the author of the Great
Preface saw the reasons for such decline as social and political, and
somehow manageable, at least theoretically under enlightened rulers.
Nevertheless, neither Confucius nor the author of the Great Preface
seem to have felt much real optimism. Laozi is more unrelenting. For
him, any effort at shaping human life is tantamount to carving the
uncarved block, and therefore decadent. And this refers not just to
literature, but to the whole of human culture.

However, it is precisely with the metaphor of carving that literature is later associated. The Eastern Han philosopher Yang Xiong 揚
雄 (53 B.C.–A.D.18) gave up his career as a writer of rhyme-prose (*fu*
賦) because he regarded it contemptuously as "a petty skill of insect
carving" and therefore is not worthy of a gentleman.[33] As Yang Xiong
lived in a time when Confucius's thought had recently been made
into an orthodoxy and thus still held sway over people's thinking,[34] it
is not surprising that he abandoned his rhyme-prose writing on Confucian grounds. He thought it did not have a moral and political function.
Later, in the Southern Dynasties period, when orthodox Confucianism suffered a major decline in almost every aspect of Chinese culture,[35]
the values implied by the metaphor of carving changed dramatically.
The Southern Dynasties critic Liu Xie 劉勰 (c. 465–520) incorporated
the metaphor into the title of his monumental work on literary theory
and criticism: *Wenxin diaolong* 文心雕龍 (*The literary mind and the
carving of dragons*).[36] Although the image of carving remains the same,
the object of carving has been changed.

Laozi's uncarved block symbolizes the undifferentiated state of harmony between humankind and its world. In Yang Xiong the insect speaks for itself as trivial; but in Liu Xie what is carved is the fanciful, extravagant dragon, which, with its rich associations of grandeur and power in Chinese culture,[37] evokes feelings of awe and respect. No longer condemned as by Laozi and Yang Xiong, carving for Liu Xie is to be celebrated. The *Literary mind and the carving of dragons* is an important part of a critique of the established views of literature since Confucius's age, a critique that is reflected in numerous writings of the Southern Dynasties period. In many ways Liu Xie's work sums up the thinking and rethinking of the issues related to literature, its values, functions, and characteristics; hence it deserves a closer look.

I will touch on only those parts of Liu Xie's huge and complicated book that are directly relevant to our study of decadent poetry. First, in using the metaphor of carving in the title of his work, Liu Xie affirms the value of craftsmanship in literature (*wen* 文).[38] As has been shown, spontaneity and naturalness had always been highly prized in the writings of earlier periods. Confucianism and Daoism, however much they differ on other matters, converge on this. Confucian poetic theory disdains craftsmanship. It views the nature of poetry as a spontaneous, sincere response to an external event. Therefore, any attempt to polish the product betrays an insincerity in motivation and results in artificiality in style. The Daoist rejection of craftsmanship stems from a worldview that only the pristine state is able to retain the healthy harmony that civilization, with its differentiation and division, inevitably destroys. In this system craftsmanship is the typical evil of civilization. By contrast, there is Liu Xie, who in Stephen Owen's view, is trying to "dissociate his idea of craft from the pejorative associations that hover around all terms for craft in Chinese."[39] It seems that Liu Xie wants more than just a dissociation; rather, he actually rejects those pejorative associations.

Certainly there are many passages in Liu Xie's book that seem to support orthodox views of literature. In the first three chapters—entitled "Yuandao" 原道 ("On the origin of the way [of literature]"), "Zhengsheng" 徵聖 ("On following the ancient sages"), and "Zongjing" 宗經 ("On following the classics")—he systematically recounts the Confucian poetic theory. But even in these passages Liu Xie struggles, as Confucius had done before, to strike a balance between the content of literature and its form:

18

Yan He wrongly thought that Confucius painted on the already
colorful feathers of birds and that he vainly used florid language.
But his accusation against the Sage missed its point. The patterned writings [*wen*] of the Sage are full of elegance, but their
beauty is accompanied by solid substance. Although the Way of
Heaven is hard to know, we still try to investigate it. The beautiful patterns of literary works [*wenzhang* 文章][40] are not hidden
from us; how can we afford not to think about them?

顏闔以為：　"仲尼飾羽而畫，徒事華辭。"雖欲訾聖，弗可得
已。然則聖文之雅麗，固銜華而佩實者也。天道難聞，猶或鑽
仰；文章可見，胡寧勿思。[41]

In this passage Liu Xie rebuts the accusation against Confucius
using the Confucian argument that "words without *wen* (form or
pattern) do not go very far" and therefore cannot carry out their mission, which is the expression of the author's will. But like Confucius,
in giving so much weight to the function of *wen* in fulfilling a
sociopolitical task, Liu Xie inevitably slants toward one pole of the
Confucian golden mean and consequently risks disrupting it. This
tendency is further illustrated by the following paragraph on "Verbal
Parallelism" ("*lici*" 麗辭):

Therefore the beauty in verbal parallelism lies in artistry and
cleverness; but in factual parallelism appropriateness is the most
important. If in a couplet the two paralleled events are of un-
equal qualities, it is like using a steed to pull the left of a carriage while using a nag on its right. If an event is left alone
unmatched it is like the one-legged monster *kui* that hobbles
and limps. If [a literary work] does not have a unique spirit, or if
its patterns [*wen*] lack outstanding colors, then even if it uses
parallelism its dullness can only make us drowsy. The important
thing is to make one's thinking coherent and the factual parallelism complexly pertinent, and to make the colors of the paired
jade match. One should alternate single and coupled elements,
and harmonize the brilliance [of the writing] by adopting various kinds of pendants: this is the most important. If one pon-
ders hard along this line, the secret [of verbal parallelism] will
be shown of itself.

是以言對爲美，貴在精巧；事對所先，務在允當。若兩事相
配，而優劣不均，是驥在左驂，駑爲右服也。若夫事或孤立，
莫與相偶，是夔之一足，趻踔而行也。若氣無奇類，文乏異
采，碌碌麗辭，則昏睡耳目。必使理圓事密，聯璧其章。迭用
奇偶，節以雜佩，乃其貴耳。類此而思，理自見也。[42]

We have here a technical manual of parallelism. The emphasis on
"artistry and cleverness" (*jingqiao* 精巧) is unmistakable, although
Liu Xie also warns his readers to avoid mere cleverness—creating
beautiful patterns devoid of a vital content. The images of jewelry
(jade, pendants) are signatures of such emphasis. He also points out
that dull style, no less than dull content, can put people to sleep. Style
is at least as important as content. Here he rejects Confucius's presumption that "those who have virtue will have words [that is, know
how to express their virtue in words]; those who have words do not
necessarily have virtue."[43] He can not accept Confucius's claim that
inner virtue will inevitably produce graceful expression. Good writing,
says Li Xie, comes from painstaking practice.

We have already remarked that Laozi's worldview leads him to the
condemnation of human culture, of which *wen* is an essential part.
But one of the Confucian classics, *Zhou yi* 周易 or *The Book of Changes*,
offers another worldview. It elevates the status of *wen* by linking it to
the structure of the universe and the creation of human language. It
regards the *wen* of humankind as having a correspondence to the *wen*
of the universe and believes that they illuminate one another:

> [The ancient sages] observe the patterns (*wen*) of heaven to
> investigate the changes of seasons; they observe the patterns
> (*wen*) of human kind to accomplish the transformation of the
> world.

觀乎天文以察時變，觀乎人文以化成天下。[44]

By following closely the correspondence between them, the sages of
ancient times were able to create a unique human culture by providing humankind with a language:

> In ancient times, when Pao Xi ruled over the world, he lifted his
> head to observe the signs of heaven; he bent down to observe

the orders of the earth. He observed the patterns (*wen*) of birds and beasts, and the appropriateness of the earth. He obtained [ideas] from his own person, and from objects afar. Thereupon he invented the Eight Trigrams.

古者包犧氏之王天下也，仰則觀象於天，俯則觀法於地，觀鳥
獸之文與地之宜，近取諸身，遠取諸物，於是始作八卦。[45]

Later, when *wen* was linked to writing and identified with literature, the implications of such theory could be enormously rich. Writers with an aesthetic bent were only too eager to use this classic authority to advocate their own views of literature. In the opening chapter of *Wenxin diaolong*, Liu Xie elaborates on this:

Human patterns (*wen*) originated in the Ultimate Origin. The symbols in the *The Book of Changes* are the earliest manifestations of this divine light. Pao Xi started it by drawing [the eight trigrams], and Confucius offered his explanations by writing the "Wings" [explanations]. The chapter "Patterned Words" was written especially by him to explain the *qian* and the *kun*. The patterns (*wen*) of words are indeed the heart of Heaven and Earth!

人文之元，肇自太極，幽贊神明，易象惟先。庖犧畫其始，仲
尼翼其終。而乾坤兩位，獨制文言。言之文也，天地之心哉！[46]

The literary and aesthetic arrangement of writing, or "patterns of words" (*yanzhiwen* 言之文) in Liu Xie's phrasing, is presented as the manifestation of the structure of the universe. It is no surprise that in the following passage Liu Xie argues that the aesthetic quality of patterns, *wen*, physical and human, is natural (*ziran* 自然):

With the emergence of mind/heart, language is created, and when language is created, its patterns (*wen*) become manifest: such is the way of nature. This applies to myriad of things in the universe, because both animals and plants have their patterns (*wen*). Dragons and phoenixes portend wondrous events through the picturesqueness of their appearances, and tigers and leopards display their graceful manners through the colorful stripes on their bodies. The sculptured brilliance of clouds surpasses the painters' works in their artistry, and the blossoms of plants depend on no embroideries of the craftsmen for their marvelous grace. How could one say that they rely on external adornment? They are natural, that is all.

心生而言立，言立而文明，自然之道也。傍及萬品，動植皆文：龍鳳以藻繪呈瑞，虎豹以炳蔚凝姿；雲霞雕色，有逾畫工之妙；草木賁華，無待錦匠之奇；夫豈外飾，蓋自然耳。[47]

Liu Xie here seems to be engaging in the debate over the relative merits of the natural and the artificial, and in this passage he clearly inclines toward the natural, in his regard for the beautiful patterns of the objects of the universe as spontaneous manifestations of nature's wonder and therefore surpassing by far the work of any human craftsman. But in the same chapter he also recounts the past literary glory of the ancient sages like Confucius:

When birds' marks replaced knotted ropes, writing first emerged. . . . Lord Shun was the first to compose songs and use them to express his will, and the suggestions put forward by his ministers Bo Yi and Hou Ji set a precedent for future memorials. Then the House of Xia arose, with its lofty achievements and great merits. The nine elements and orders are in perfect harmony and were celebrated in songs, and the House became still richer in attainment of virtue. By the time of Shang and Zhou, literary form (*wen*) surpassed the substance. The "hymns" and "odes" [of *The Book of Songs*] shine fresher daily in flowery brilliance. When King Wen was in trouble, his oracular judgments glowed bright; couched in rich and cryptic language, they contain subtle meanings, solidly grounded and profound. And Dan, the versatile Duke of Zhou, further glorified these achievements by composing poetry and compiling the "hymns" [in *The Book of Songs*], polishing with ax (*fuzao* 斧藻) [the literary qualities] of all kinds of writings. Our Master [Confucius], standing without peer among the early sages, continued this glorious tradition. The Six Classics, after he has cast and molded (*rongjun* 鎔鈞)

them, ring out the resonant music of bronze and jade. He carved and chiseled (*diaozhuo* 雕琢) human feelings, and interweaved the diction and style [of these works].

自鳥跡代繩，文字始炳。…元首載歌，既發吟詠之志；益稷陳謨，亦垂敷奏之風。夏後氏興，業峻鴻績，九序惟歌，勛德彌縟。逮及商周，文勝其質，雅頌所被，英華日新。文王患憂，繇辭炳曜，符采復隱，精意堅深。重以公旦多才，振其徽烈，剬詩緝頌，斧藻群言。至夫子繼聖，獨秀前哲，鎔鈞六經，必金聲而玉振；雕琢情性，組織辭令[48]

This is an extremely revealing but also puzzling passage. Liu Xie holds that a golden age in Chinese literature was realized in the writings of a group of sages who are presented as extraordinary craftsmen. He judges their success in terms of technical accomplishment, which is ironic to say the least because this chapter, which opens Liu Xie's entire discussion, is supposed to trace the ultimate origin of literature.[49] Not only are their writings described as having a strong sensual and formal quality, to the extent that "literary form (*wen*) surpassed the substance," but the activities of these ancient sages are described in language and imagery usually used to describe the activities of craft workers: to polish with ax (*fuzao* 斧藻), to cast and mold (*rongjun* 鎔鈞), to carve and chisel (*diaozhuo* 雕琢), to interweave (*zuzhi* 組織). These images, with their echoes of craftsmanship, completely undermine Liu Xie's previous statement that human *wen* is, like the *wen* of the physical world and animals, natural, and that natural beauty surpasses artificial ornaments. Most significantly, Liu Xie's phrase to describe Confucius's activity of editing and compiling ancient classics, *diaozhuo* (to carve, to chisel), is to become the standard term to describe an ornately decadent literary style.[50] This puzzling, self-contradictory passage highlights again the tension between form (*wen* 文) and content (*zhi* 質), a phenomenon that was well established even in Confucius's time. Liu Xie may want to achieve the equilibrium between the two poles, but his own language and metaphors speak to a different position.

By Liu Xie's time, then, literary theory had undergone immense changes. Critics were increasingly more concerned with form and other technical aspects of writing. Literature, particularly poetry, was no longer conceived solely as a natural, spontaneous response to a historical event but instead began to be regarded as a craft. This trend is reflected in the critical discourse of the time, which is filled with the vocabulary of craftsmanship. This important shift signals that poetic production was beginning to be removed from the author's mind/ heart as stipulated by canonical documents like the Great Preface. The separation between the poet's personality and his work, which was to be boldly and unequivocally announced by Xiao Gang, is already taking shape here.

The vigorous rethinking of literature and its values during the late period of Southern Dynasties was encouraged by royal figures like Xiao Tong, Crown Prince Zhaoming 昭明太子蕭統 (501–31) and his brother Xiao Gang who later became the Emperor Jianwen of the Liang dynasty. Yet another example of using the classic link between *wen* of the universe and *wen* of humankind to elevate the status of literature is found in Xiao Tong's preface to *Wen xuan* 文選, the first comprehensive literary anthology of China:

| | |
|---|---|
| 式觀元始 | Let us examine the primordial origins of civilization, |
| 眇覿玄風 | And distantly observe the customs of the remote past. |
| 冬穴夏巢之時 | Times when men dwelled in caves in winter, nests in summer, |
| 茹毛飲血之世 | Eras when people consumed raw meat and drank blood. |
| 世質民淳 | It was a pristine age of simple people, |
| 斯文未作 | And our culture (*siwen*)[51] had not yet been invented. |
| 逮乎伏羲氏之 王天下也 | Then when Fu Xi ruled the empire, |
| 始畫八卦 | He first Drew the Eight Trigrams, |
| 造書契 | Created writing (*shuqi*), |
| 以代結繩之政 | To replace government by knotted ropes. |
| 由是文籍生焉 | From this time written records came into existence. |
| 易曰: "觀乎天文 | The *Changes* says, "Observe the patterns (*wen*) of the sky, |
| 以察時 | To ascertain the seasonal changes. |
| 觀乎人文 | Observe the patterns (*wen*) of man, |

24

以化成天下。" To transform the world."
文之時義遠矣哉![52] The temporal significance of patterned writing (*wen*)
is far-reaching indeed!

Xiao Tong states that it is culture (*siwen* 斯文) that single-handedly
rescued us from the primitive, animallike state, and that writing,
especially writing with aesthetic qualities (*wenji* 文籍), is the most
essential part of this culture. This effort to eulogize literary writing
and its functions tends also to result in privileging belles lettres over
other genres. Thus Xiao Tong excluded the works of pre-Qin philos-
ophers from his anthology on the grounds that "the main purpose [of
these writings] is to formulate ideas, not to establish [beautiful tex-
tual] patterns (*wen*)" (蓋以立意爲宗，不以能文爲本).[53] Although
Xiao Tong still adhered to the Confucian poetic doctrine that poetry
expresses one's will,[54] his criterion for selecting and categorizing texts
clearly reflects a tendency toward aestheticism. As David Knechtges
puts it, Xiao Tong has come "close to conveying the idea of pure literature."[55]

This aesthetic tendency in the literary theory of the Southern
Dynasties produced an intense awareness of the formal, especially
musical, qualities of poetry. In the past Chinese poetry had relied for
its musical quality on natural, unanalyzed word sounds. Moreover,
rhyme and metrical pattern, though always important in Chinese
poetry, had not been studied separately and independently. This was
to be expected, because before the Southern Dynasties period poetry
had never been considered an independent subject of learning, but
instead had always been related to a larger sociopolitical and moral
context. But by the Southern Dynasties many poets and scholars were
drawn to the study of the metrical pattern.[56] This study in turn laid
the foundation for the metrical pattern of regulated verse that would
reach its consummation in the hands of Tang poets like Du Fu. The
leading advocate of this so-called *yongming* 永明 poetry was Shen
Yue 沈約 (441–513), whose "Biographical Sketch of Xie Lingyun" 謝
靈運傳 in *Song shu* 宋書 (*The History of [Liu] Song Dynasty*) offers a
most complete statement of this metrical theory:

Now, if I were to bare my breast and speak from the heart in
evaluating the skill or awkwardness of former writers, it seems

that there is something more to be said. Take the five colors that complement each other or the eight musical timbres that sound harmoniously in concert. They are just like the shades dark and yellow or the *yin* and *yang* pitch pipes, each of which is suited to its appropriate object. One would want to have the notes *gong* and *shang* alternating with each other or the lowered and raised pitches tempering each other. Whenever there is a floating sound in the first line of the couplet, it must be followed by a cut-off echo in the corresponding syllable of the second line. Within a single line the sounds and rhymes should all be unique, and between the two lines of a couplet the patterns of light and heavy should be completely different. It is only with those who subtly understand these general principles that one can begin to talk about refined writing (*wen*).

若夫敷衽論心，商榷前藻，工拙之數，如有可言。夫五色相宜，八音協暢，由乎玄黃律呂，各適物宜。欲使宮羽相變，低昂互節，若前有浮聲，則後須切響。一簡之內，音韻盡殊；兩句之中，輕重悉易，妙達此旨，始可言文。[57]

Even without delving into the details of Shen Yue's view of metrical pattern in poetry, this quotation demonstrates that during the Southern Dynasties poetry was liberated from its previous dependence on politics and morality to become an independent subject of learning, with its own principles, its own values, and its own logic of development. This is an enormous step, especially in the context of a culture in which sociopolitical and moral values have always overwhelmed other concerns.[58] However, it was precisely these sociopolitical and moral values that was ignored by Shen Yue in his essay. He concentrated instead exclusively on the technical and aesthetic aspects of poetry. If this "decadent" attitude is implied here by the assiduous exclusion of the traditional values associated with poetry, it was made explicit by Xiao Gang in that bold statement that "the principle of one's personal cultivation is different from the principle of literary composition. In personal cultivation one should be prudent, but in literary composition one should be unrestrained."[59]

What a novel and radical separation of literary production from moral cultivation, unquestionably a deliberate refutation of the canonical view that literature, especially poetry, is the externalization of one's will or moral character and that it reflects a political and social reality. For how can we know the character of the author through his writing, as Yang Xiong assumed we could,[60] or how can we discern the sociopolitical background of the author and his time, which was considered as essential by Confucius and the Great Preface, if there is a disjunction between the writing and its author? Obviously a virtuous author is capable of composing very unprincipled poetry, and vice versa. This view of disjunction actually invalidates the cherished notions about the moral and sociopolitical functions of poetry, which form the cornerstone of the Chinese poetic tradition.

On other occasions Xiao Gang still espoused the orthodox view that poetry expresses one's feelings. For example, in a letter to his cousin Prince Xiang Dong (與湘東王書) Xiao Gang complains that the literature produced at the capital at that time was "shallow, superficial and totally silly" because the writers never bothered to "chant their feelings" (*yinyong qingxing* 吟詠情性).[61] By implication, if those poets had tried to express their feelings, their poetry would not have sunk to its lamentable state. But how should one reconcile this claim for the analogy of personal feeling and the quality of literary production with the precisely opposite view that there is absolutely no connection between one's personal character and one's writing? In fact, Xiao Gang's own poetry, especially those in decadent line, expresses very little of his feelings; nor is it meant to do so. His espousal of the canonical concept of poetry is therefore either mere lip service or politically motivated.[62]

Xiao Gang's name has always been associated with Palace Style poetry (*gongtishi* 宮體詩).[63] Ever since its flowering in the court of the Southern Dynasties, it was an embarrassment, an anathema, to orthodox literati and was condemned for its decadent style and subject matter. A detailed study of the stylistic features of Palace Style poetry will be the subject of the next chapter. For the moment, let us consider the theoretical assumptions behind it and why it offended conventional taste.

The literary agenda of Palace Style poetry is fully represented by *Yutai xinyong* 玉台新詠 (*New songs from a jade terrace*), an anthology of love and amorous poetry compiled by the court poet Xu Ling 徐陵 (507–83) under the commission of Xiao Gang.[64] Xu Ling's half-joking preface can be considered as a manifesto for the new, decadent trend in the poetry of the time. Since it is crucial to our study of poetic texts in the following chapters, I will quote this long preface in some detail:

| | |
|---|---|
| 夫凌雲槪日 | There were palaces that reach clouds and obstruct the sun— |
| 由余之所未窺[65] | These are what You Yu[65] had never seen. |
| 千門萬戶 | One thousand gates, ten thousand houses— |
| 張衡之所曾賦[66] | These are what Zhang Heng[66] once wrote about. |
| 周王璧台之上 | On the jade terrace of the King of Zhou, |
| 漢帝金屋之中 | In the gold house of the Emperor of Han, |
| 玉樹以珊瑚作枝 | There are jade trees with coral boughs, |
| 珠簾以玳瑁爲押 | And pearl blinds with tortoiseshell pendants. |
| 其中有麗人焉 | Within were found beautiful women. |
| 其人也五陵豪族 | They are ladies from the aristocratic houses of Wuling, |
| 充選掖庭 | Who were chosen for the imperial harem. |
| 四姓良家 | They are girls of the best families of Four Clans, |
| 馳名永巷 | Renowned throughout the long streets. |
| 亦有穎川新市 | There are also beauties from Yingchuan and Xinshi, |
| 河間觀津 | [Lovely girls from] Hejian and Guanjin. |
| 本號嬌娥 | One of them was originally called "Delicate Fair," |
| 曾名巧笑 | Another was once named "Dainty Smile." |
| 楚王宮里 | In the palaces of Chu |
| 無不推其細腰 | There was none who did not admire their slender waists; |
| 衛國佳人 | The fair women of Wei |
| 俱言訝其纖手 | All marveled at their delicate hands. |
| 閱詩敦禮 | They are well versed in *The Book of Songs* and *Rites*, |
| 豈東鄰之自媒[67] | Quite different from the east neighbor[67] who did her own matchmaking! |
| 婉約風流 | Their charming, romantic airs |
| 異西施之被教[68] | Are not different from those of Xi Shi after she had been trained. |

The list of beautiful women, their graceful behaviors, and precious ornament continues for another three pages in Birrel's English translation. How far the subject matter of this "new" poetry has strayed from the classical tradition! Gone is the noble sociopolitical and moral function, to be replaced with tales of the entertainment quarters of the court and the opulent bedrooms of aristocratic women and their lovers. It is noteworthy that the women listed in the preface are not merely from aristocratic families, but are also highly skilled in music and literature. Xi Shi 西施, the traditional archetype of female beauty, had first to be "trained" before she could be admitted into the court where Xu Ling and other poets composed their works. Artifice and craftsmanship have replaced naturalness and innocence as the new aesthetic.[69] The language of this preface is the embodiment of this narrow, refined view of poetry. Besides the elaborate *pianwen* 駢文 style with its balanced and intricate metrical pattern, Xu Ling employs artificial, precious, and sensual imagery to describe the beauties and their environment: jade, jewelry, ornament, cosmetics, colors, and slightly unveiled flesh. Indeed these will become standard tropes for later poets writing in this style. Anne Birrel says in her introduction to *New Songs from a Jade Terrace* that such style, with its "ambiance of boudoirs, cosmetics, pillows, and palace ladies is a world apart from the solemnities of exegetical scholarship. It is an urbane acknowledgment that art is lightly to be pursued for art's sake." [70]

The very locus of this poetry, with its suggestion of sexual escapades, was enough to raise the eyebrows of the Confucian literati. Xu Ling, aware of the possible criticism that would greet his work, offers the wry justification that the poems collected in his book "could feel no shame beside the 'Odes' and 'Hymns'; for they come from the 'Airs'" (無忝於雅頌，亦靡濫於風人). Odes, hymns, and airs are the poems collected in *The Book of Songs*. The first two are often marked by a solemn, even religious, tone and a deep concern with social issues. The airs are mostly folk songs, many on the subject of love, written in simple, straightforward style. In connecting the "new poems" in his anthology with these canonized works, Xu Ling betrays an anxiety, or at least an awareness, that his poems actually signal a deviation from the earlier tradition. In a culture where tradition confers authority, he must justify his project by linking it to a "previously recognized standard of excellence." But surely no one could take this connection seriously, not only because of the enormous gap between the two—one is marked by profound sociomoral concerns and straightforward style, the other is characterized by mild eroticism and artificial mannerism—but also because of the jesting tone in which this connection is made. Xu Ling dismisses even this far-fetched claim later in his preface, also in tongue-in-cheek tone. He tells us that reading his book is "certainly different from Empress Deng's study of *The Spring and Autumn Annals*, / For a scholar's attainments are hard to acquire" (豈如鄧學春秋，儒者之功難習).[71]

Here again is why Palace Style poetry is so offensive to traditional taste in China: it lacks seriousness as its practitioners treat poetry as a game, an artistic display. Cao Pi 曹丕 (187–226) once said that "literature is the grand cause by which the country is governed; it is eternal."[72] Because rationalism in Confucian philosophy discredited any possibility of obtaining an afterlife through religion, literature is regarded as one of the chief means of passing one's name on to posterity and hence of achieving immortality.[73] Since Confucius's age there has always been something akin to a religious awe with regard to poetry. To joke about it as Xu Ling does in his preface is tantamount to a sacrilege. By demoting literature from its sublime place as a locus of national spirit to a mildly erotic and courtly environment, Xu Ling launches a bold challenge to the canonical tradition.[74]

Even though the "new poetry" enjoyed the patronage of royal figures like Xiao Gang and other members of the Xiao clan, it was condemned, along with its theory, already in Xu Ling's own time. Pei Ziye's 裴子野 (469–530) essay "On insect carving" ("*Diaochong lun*" 雕蟲論) is considered as a classic example of this condemnation because it is based entirely on conservative orthodoxy. It is illuminating to study this essay alongside Xu Ling's preface, because no other writings demonstrate so sharply the wide gap between this new literary trend and the orthodox tradition that it aims to critique.

"On insect carving" was not written as a direct response to the challenge embodied in Xu Ling's preface. Since Pei Ziye lived from 469 to 530, and *Yutai xinyong* was not compiled until about 545, Pei's essay cannot be a direct rebuttal to Xu Ling's theory of the new poetry. But *Yutai xinyong* actually represents the culmination of this new literary trend, which was well under way during Pei's time. Therefore, Pei was certainly attacking the literary theory and practice represented by Xu Ling's preface and the anthology:[75]

In ancient times poetry consisted of Four Beginnings (*sishi* 四始)[76] and Six Principles (*liuyi* 六藝).[77] It formed the [moral and political] atmosphere in the whole nation and displayed the will of gentlemen. It [taught people to] cultivate virtue and punish evil. It was what a kingly transformation depended upon. Writers of later ages paid attention only to the leaves and branches [of poetry]; they adopted florid style to please themselves. *Chuci* started the melancholy, fragrant style, which was closely followed by Sima Xiangru's charm and ease. From then on writers followed only the sound and shadow and gave up the correct model. Cai Yong 蔡邕 (132–92) compared the numerous poems of such kind to the works of clowns, Yang Xiong regretted [his early rhyme-prose writings] and regarded them as from the hand of child. Since there is no sage to appear in our time, who can tell the difference between what is graceful and what is lascivious? As for five- character-line poetry, it originated from Su Wu 蘇武 (140–60 B.C.) and Li Ling 李陵 (?–74 B.C.); its grand power was enhanced by Cao Zhi 曹植 (192–232) and Liu Zhen 劉楨 (?–217); Pan Yue 潘岳 (247–300) and Lu Ji 陸機 (261–303) consolidated its leaves and branches. By the time of Eastern Jin people valued embellished writings of Xie Lingyun 謝靈運 (385–433) and Yan Yanzhi 顏延之 (384–456), that had no use in the court. From early [Liu] Song to Yuanjia period (420–53) [the poetry written] was mostly like classical and historical documents. By the time of Daming (457–64) the taste for embellished writing took hold. No more to be found were the extraordinary talent and the graceful tone of the ancient sages. Now this trend is still increasing. Youths of noble families give up the Six Principles and sing what they feel. The scholars seek only metaphors in writing and take studies of classics to be boorish. They use their uninhibited writings to refute the classics, and take pride in doing so. Their works are not set to music, and never "stop at rites and morality." They are obsessed with flowers and plants, and with all their efforts seek after wind and clouds. The evocative power of their work is shallow, and their will is weak. Their writing is clever and unprincipled, obscure and not profound. If we trace the origin of this trend, we will find that it is the fashion of [Liu] Song. If Jizi heard this he would not have regarded it as the music of a thriving nation;[78] and Confucius would never have taught such poetry to his son. Xun Qing 荀卿 (fl. 298 B.C.–238 B.C.) once said that "in a chaotic time the writing is obscure and florid." Isn't this [writing of our time] close to that?!

31

古者四始六藝，總而爲詩，既形四方之風，且彰君子之志，勸
美懲惡，王化本焉。後之作者，思存枝葉，繁華蘊藻，用以自
通。若悱惻芳芬，楚騷爲之祖，靡漫容與，相如扣其音。由是
隨聲逐影之儔，棄指歸而無執。賦詩歌頌，百帙五車，蔡邕等
之俳優，揚雄悔爲童子。聖人不作，雅鄭誰分。其五言爲
家，則蘇、李自出，曹、劉偉其風力，潘、陸固其枝葉。爰及
江左，稱彼顏、謝，箋繡鞶帨，無取廟堂。宋初迄於元嘉，多
爲經史，大明之代，實好斯文。高才逸韻，頗謝前哲，波流相
尚，滋有篤焉。自是閭閻年少，貴游總角，罔不擯落六藝，吟
詠情性。學者以博依爲急務，謂章句爲專魯。淫文破典，裴爾
爲功，無被於管弦，非止乎禮義。深心主卉木，遠致極風雲，
其興浮，其志弱。巧而不要，隱而不深，討其宗途，亦有宋之
風也。若季子聆音，則非興國，鯉也趨庭，必有不敢。荀卿
有言，“亂代之徵，文章匿而采。”斯豈近之乎?[79]

Pei starts by repeating the canonical view of poetry established in
the Great Preface, that poetry originates from the poet's will and
performs a sociopolitical function. He then proceeds to recount another
classic story of how poetry began to decline after the ages of the ancient
sages until it became mere frivolity in his own time. What upsets Pei
most about this "new" poetry is that its undisciplined style obliterated the deep social and moral concern that had once been considered
the sine qua non of poetry. The precarious balance between form and
content that had been drawn by Confucius was disturbed.

The story of the gradual decline of literature is not new. It has also
been told by Liu Xie in *Wenxin diaolong*:

A careful analysis will show that the literary productions during
the times of the Yellow Emperor and the Tang Yao are pure and
substantial; during the Yu and Xia, substantial and eloquent;
during the Shang and Zhou, beautiful and graceful; during the
Chu and Han, hyperbolic and alluringly charming; in the times
of the Wei and Jin, superficial and ornamental; and at the beginning of the [Liu] Song, pretentious and novelty-ridden. Decline
from the simple to the pretentious, literary style becomes more
and more insipid as it approaches our own time.

摧而論之，則黃唐淳而質，虞夏質而辨，商周麗而雅，楚漢侈
而艷，魏晉淺而綺，宋初訛而新。從質及訛，彌近彌淡。[80]

Like the Great Preface, Liu Xie's version of literary decadence—
the falling away of literature from its origin, the classics—seems to
be based on an abstract principle of inevitable decline, that decadence
results from temporal remoteness from the source. But this is something that people of later generations cannot help. Therefore although
Liu Xie tries to link literary decadence to a corresponding political
and moral decay, his effort looks jejune because it is not presented as
working on a historical level. Pei Ziye's attack on the new poetry of
his time conveys a sense of urgency because he believed it heralded
imminent political and social catastrophe.

It is noteworthy that Pei Ziye adopts the metaphor of carving to
describe the poetry of his age. He suffuses it with negative values and
connotations: that such poetry is trivial and not worth the pains lav-
ished on it by the youths of the time; that it contains the seeds of
sociopolitical disaster because its excessive concern for form ("leaves
and branches" as opposed to root) is a sign of a perverse social reality.
The echo of Yang Xiong is unmistakable. In again choosing the insect
as the object of carving, Pei also indirectly criticized Liu Xie, who had
tried to vindicate the values of craftsmanship in literature by replacing
Yang Xiong's tiny insect with a powerful dragon.

Pei Ziye's denunciation of Palace Style poetry, together with the
theory of the ineluctable decline of literature in the Great Preface
and *Wenxin diaolong*, established a pattern of criticism of decadent
literature that is repeated time and again by critics of later generations. However, the later critics enjoyed a historical advantage over
both Liu Xie and Pei Ziye: the political and social catastrophes pre-
dicted by Pei Ziye have been realized. The Southern Dynasties in whose
courts the decadent Palace Style poetry flourished first were destroyed
by each other and finally were conquered by their northern enemies.
History, that is, had vindicated the canonical view that a frivolous,
extravagant literature would bring about disasters. For scholars and
statesmen of Sui and Tang dynasties, more than for their counter-
parts of earlier generations, Palace Style poetry evokes not just a lascivious, ornate, frivolous poetry, but also one after another short-lived
dynasties. Their understanding of the Southern Dynasties poetry is
therefore justifiably tinged with a strong sense of mission and reflection. As Wei Zheng 魏徵 (580–643), the early Tang statesman, poet,
and author of "Preface to the Biographical Sketches of Literati" 文學
傳序 in *Sui shu* (*History of Sui dynasty*) says of Palace Style poetry:

After the Datong period of the Liang Dynasty, the grand ways of the ancient times declined and social customs became increasingly opposed to the norms. The literature of that period strove after what was new and clever. Emperor Jianwen and Prince Xiangdong started this trend of extravagance; Xu Ling and Yu Xin 庾信 (513–81) developed it in their own manners. The meaning of such literature is shallow and fastidious; its style [*wen*] is obscure and florid; its diction aims at being superficial, and its feeling is mostly sad. If judged by the ear of Yan Ling 延陵 [i.e., Jizi], it would surely be regarded as the tone of a lost nation.

梁自大同之後，雅道淪缺，漸乖典則，爭馳新巧。簡文、湘東啓其淫放，徐陵、庾信分道揚鑣。其意淺而繁，其文匿而彩。詞尚輕險,情多哀思。格以延陵之聽，蓋亦亡國之音乎！[81]

Compared with Pei Ziye, Wei Zheng had the historical advantage: he denounces Palace Style poetry with greater knowledge and in a much more self-assured tone. He closes his passage with a rhetorical question not about how close (*jin* 近) this new poetry comes to the writings of a disorderly world, but about whether it *is (gaiyi . . . hu* 蓋亦... 乎) such writing. What is more, in Wei Zheng's preface the country represented by such poetry is not simply "disorderly" (*luan* 亂), but it has already been lost or defeated (*wang* 亡), as it had been under Southern Dynasties. It is this historical reflection and sense of mission that prompted Yu Shinan 虞世南 (558–638), a former writer of Southern Dynasties Palace Style poetry, to dissent from the order of Emperor Taizong of Tang 唐太宗 (r. 627–49) to match the emperor's poem in Palace Style style:

His Majesty wrote a poem in the Palace Style and ordered Yu Shinan to match it. Yu Shinan answered: "Your Majesty's poem is indeed artful, but its style is not proper. When a monarch likes certain things, his subjects below will like them in the extreme. I fear that if this poem is passed around, the customs of the entire empire will become decadent. Thus I dare not accept your command."

帝嘗作宮體詩，使賡和。世南曰： "聖作誠工，然體非雅正，上之所好，下必有甚者。臣恐此詩一傳，天下風靡，不敢奉詔。" [82]

By this time the image of Southern Dynasties poetry (especially Palace Style poetry) as the representative of a decadent literature that had brought down a nation was already part and parcel of the literary convention,[83] so much so that for Chinese poetry to regain its vitality it had to break away from it. It is not surprising then that the first authentic Tang poetry has often been considered a sharp departure from Southern Dynasties poetry, a step finally taken by Chen Zi'ang 陳子昂 (c. 659–700) after early Tang poetry had for nearly a century remained in that much cursed shadow.[84] Chen Zi'ang's letter to his friend Dongfang Qiu 東方虯 reiterated the common wisdom about Southern Dynasties poetry:

The way of literature has been in decline for five hundred years. The strong style [*fenggu* 風骨, wind and bone] of the Han and Wei was not passed on in the Jin and [Liu] Song, but it is evidenced in historical documents. In leisure hours I have carefully examined poems of Qi and Liang, works of garish beauty that strove after ornateness, but which were utterly lacking in deeper significance. Always then I would sigh, brooding on the ancients, in constant fear that they will be lost in their distance from us and perish, and that the Airs and the Odes [of the *The Book of Songs*] will not be written—I am deeply troubled.

文章道弊五百年矣。漢、魏風骨，晉、宋莫傳，然文獻有可徵者。僕嘗暇時觀齊、梁間詩，彩麗競繁，而興寄都絕，每以永嘆。思古人常恐逶迤頹靡，風雅不作，以耿耿也。[85]

Chen Zi'ang made it his mission to stop the process of decline that had reached its climax during Qi and Liang, and to restore the "deeper significance" (*xingji* 興寄) that had characterized classical writings like *The Book of Songs* and the poetry of the Wei and Jin period but that had been abandoned by decadent poets in the courts of the Southern Dynasties. Chen's letter did not offer any fresh ideas on the subject. Even his eulogy of Han and Wei poetry was modeled after Liu Xie's concept of *fenggu* 風骨 (wind and bone, or "strong style" in Owen's translation). But Liu Xie had not explicitly contrasted the masculine writing of the Jian'an 建安 period (196–219) to the feminine style of Qi and Liang Palace Style poetry. Chen Zi'ang, however, stated explicitly that the poetry of Qi and Liang represented a decline not only from the ancient classical tradition, but also from the more recent literature of the period just past. In other words, the strong style of Han and Wei is presented as yet another canon by which the poetry of other times is to be judged.

This canonization of texts other than the classics deals yet another blow to the Southern Dynasties Palace Style poetry. Ancient classics, after all, represent the ultimate in the Chinese tradition and all later literature suffers beside them. Therefore to call a particular litera- ture decadent because it departs from the ancient models is actually idle talk: has not the Great Preface pointed out that even in *The Book of Songs* this move toward decadence has already been taken? By this standard we are all decadent, only to different degrees. As has been observed before, this concept of decline has become an abstract and jejune principle because it is often not rooted in a concrete historical context. But it is much more powerful to argue that the writings of a particular and less remote period are canonical and others are not, because the comparison or contrast is made on a solid historical basis and on an equal footing. Here we should take a close look at Liu Xie's concept of strong style *fenggu* 風骨, its application to the literature of Wei and Jin, and its implications for our discussion of Southern Dynas- ties and Late Tang decadent poetry.

The concept of *fenggu* was recounted in detail by Liu Xie in his *Wenxin diaolong*:

*The Book of Songs* contains Six Principles, and of these, *feng* (wind)[86] stands at the head of the list. It is the source of trans- formation, and the proof of emotion and vitality. Therefore he who wishes to express melancholy emotions must begin with the wind, and to organize language in chanting he must above all emphasize the bone. Phrases and diction are conditioned by the bone in much the same way as the standing posture of a body is conditioned by its skeleton; feelings contain wind in the same way as forms embrace breath. When expressions are orga- nized on the right principles, literary [*wen*] bone is there; and when the emotion and vitality are powerful and clear, there we find the pure literary [*wen*] wind. If a literary piece has nothing but rich and brilliant colors, without wind and bone to keep it air-borne, then one shaking is enough to destroy its splendor, lacking as it does the vigor that supports its beautiful pattern. Therefore, to organize one's thought and design one's composition one must nourish one's vitality; for when one is strong and full, his writing will shine with fresh brilliance.

詩總六義，風冠其首，斯乃化感之本源，志氣之符契也。是以 怊悵述情，必始乎風，沈吟鋪辭，莫先于骨。故辭之待骨，如 體之樹骸，情之含風，猶形之包氣。結言端直，則文骨成焉； 意氣駿爽，則文風清焉。若豐藻克瞻，風骨不飛，則振采失 鮮，負聲無力。是以綴慮裁篇，務盈守氣，剛健既實，輝光乃 新，[87]

In this passage *feng* (wind) refers to the spiritual and emotional quality of literature. Though invisible, it should be strong and full of vitality so that it can transform society. *Gu* (bone) refers to the diction and language that embodies the aforementioned spiritual and emotional quality. It is visible and concrete. Liu Xie's *fenggu* is actually a redrawing of the Confucian balance of form and substance. *Feng* is *de* 德, the virtue; *gu* is what makes virtue manifest and holds it together, like the bone of a human body which gives it shape and holds its flesh together. If either of these mutually supportive elements is lacking, the balance is upset: without *feng* the affective power of literature will be weakened and dry; without *gu* will collapse the structure of a literary work. This is not a new notion, but Liu Xie conducts his discussion on a more sophisticated and more technical level, reflecting the enormous progress and changes in knowledge of and attitudes toward literature since Confucius's age. *Fenggu* is also a much more appropriate metaphor, because it evinces an acute recognition of the dual, but inseparable, parts of literature: the invisible affective power and its visible material embodiment.[88]

Liu Xie did not relate this concept of *fenggu* directly to the literature of Wei and Jin. But his definition of the former and his characterization of the literature of the latter imply a qualitative connection between the two. In the chapter entitled "Temporal Orders of Literature" ("Shixu" 時序) in *Wenxin diaolong*, Liu Xie discusses the characteristics of the writings of some most renowned authors of the Jian'an period[89] and then praises the literature of the era:

If we examine the writings of the time we will find that they are full of vigorous spirit. This is because their authors lived in a world of disorder and separation, and at a time when morals declined and the people were complaining. They felt all this deeply in their hearts, and this feeling was expressed in a profoundly moving style. For this reason their works teem with vitality and strength.

觀其時文，雅好慷慨，良由世積亂離，風衰俗怨，並志深而筆長，故梗概而多氣也。[90]

This eulogy is apparently based on the canonical views that I have recounted: that literature is solidly rooted in the sociopolitical background of the time; that it is inextricably bound up with the fortunes of the country; and that it is able to situate the expression of an individual's will in such larger context. Hence, not only does this literature express the author's personal feelings and thoughts, but it also represents an active participation in the nation's struggle to regain peace. What is more, all these noble feelings and thoughts are manifest in a masculine literary style marked by vigor and vitality.

The effort to canonize this straightforward, heroic quality of Han and Wei literature began before Liu Xie. Zhong Rong 鐘嶸 (?–518) spoke of the loss of the *fengli* 風力 (wind and vigor) of Han and Wei in the poetry of the early Southern Dynasties period.[91] Pei Ziye also used the term *fengli* to describe the poetry of Cao Zhi and Liu Zhen.[92] The most powerful influence in this effort is without question Chen Zi'ang's letter, quoted earlier. In that letter he contrasts the *fenggu* of Han and Wei with the very different quality of Southern Dynasties poetry, which is considered a falling away from the former. This view is echoed often in the writings of later poets and critics. The High Tang poet Li Bai 李白 (701–62) praised the poetry of Jian'an as having *gu*.[93] In another poem he applauded the poetry of Jian'an at the expense of the Southern Dynasties poetry, spelling out again the sharp contrast between them.[94] *Wenjing mifulun* 文鏡秘府論, a collection of literary criticism and instructional manuals compiled during Mid Tang by Kukai 空海 (774–835), explicitly charges that Southern Dynasties poetry is decadent (*tuihui* 頹毀).[95] Later, the Song critic Yan Yu completed this process by placing the poetry of Han and Wei side by side with the poetry of High Tang as the orthodox standard (*zheng* 正) of Chinese poetic tradition, relegating poetry of other periods to the category of *bian* 變, the deviant or decadent.[96]

By early Tang, then, a decadent trend in Chinese poetry is already clearly perceived as part of a well-established critical and literary convention. Specifically, it is a poetry that has abandoned the lofty, moral, social, and political function, a function that the poems in *The Book of Songs* were said to have fulfilled in the past. The scope of the subject matter of decadent poetry is also noticeably narrower than that of the ancient classics and the poetry of the Han and Wei period. It is concerned less and less with the issues of society and more and more with the private, often unconventional, aspects of the poets' lives and their environment. Thus, the description of the bedroom life of court ladies and their aristocratic patrons, once unworthy of mention, has mostly replaced the presentation of life in the larger context. It has disrupted the classical balance between form (*wen*) and content (*zhi*) by devoting excessive attention to the technical aspects of poetry. It has abandoned the noble simplicity of ancient style to adopt a fastidiously refined mannerism. In lieu of the masculine vigor of the earlier literature, it adopts a style of marked femininity. In sum, it has degraded literature from the sublime position it occupied in ancient tradition to a trivial skill of insect carving.

The archetype of this decadence is the poetry of the Southern Dynasties. This is because all the above qualities are readily found in the Palace Style poetry of the period, which has proved the ultimate principle of the canonical theory of literature: that literary works inevitably reflect a certain sociopolitical and moral state of a society. The corrupt, decadent society of Qi, Liang, and Chen found expression in the corrupt, decadent poetry written by those corrupt, decadent rulers and poets they patronized in their courts.

For all that this may be true, it is not the end of the story. As we have seen, many aspects of the decadent concept of poetry had already been presaged by the tensions within the classical tradition itself. Its florescence in the Southern Dynasties period is the result of a long, gradual process of reflection by many writers, both traditional and decadent. This conventional, and often emotional, view of decadent poetry has also neglected one of its crucial aspects: that it is a critique of the canonical standards of excellence and canonical standards of meaning. Further, the Southern Dynasties period was a critical stage in the development of the Chinese poetic tradition, because it was the sine qua non for the glorious achievement of Tang poetry. The irony is that, far from signaling a setback for the tradition, decadent literature actually marks an advance for the tradition, a step forward in expanding its capacity to deal with new experiences and in its technical innovations.

Chapter 2

# Xiao Gang
# and Palace Style Poetry

Xiao Gang's connection with Palace Style poetry is well known and well documented. As was shown in the preceding chapter, Palace Style poetry is probably the most notorious representative of decadence in the Chinese literary tradition. Although it is debatable whether Palace Style poetry started with Xiao Gang or with his literary mentor Xu Chi 徐摛 (474–551),[1] Xiao Gang is certainly the most important early promoter and author of such poetry. Of the 779 poems collected in *Yutai xinyong*, over 100 were written by Xiao Gang, by far the largest contribution by a single author. One might of course regard this as the editor's flattery of Xiao Gang, who was the patron of this project. But the very fact that such a large number of Xiao Gang's poems fit into the category of Palace Style poetry is indicative of the remarkable affinity between them.

One must begin with Xiao Gang's views on literature because to a great extent his poetry was guided by them. Xiao Gang's letter to his brother Xiao Yi offers his most extended comment on the subject; in it he voices his unhappiness with the literary tendencies in the writings of his contemporaries:

Recently I have studied the literary styles of the capital. They are all exceptionally dull and pedantic. Writers compete in frivolity and superficiality, and contend in producing melodious tunes.

I have tried to think about it throughout the long winter nights; still I cannot figure out the reason for this. These works have strayed from the principles of comparison (*bi* 比) and evocation (*xing* 興), and are diametrically opposed to "Airs" (*feng*風) and "Encountering Sorrow" (*sao* 騷). Under certain circumstances one may use "Six Codes"[2] and the "Three Canons of Rites,"[3] because in predicting auspicious and inauspicious events and entertaining noble guests there is a proper function for them. But I have never heard that anyone who aims to express his feelings in song should copy the "Rules for Women"; or someone who takes up his pen to articulate his will should imitate the "Injunction against Drunkenness!" In describing "the Spring days linger"[4] they imitate "Guizang" [a chapter in *The Book of Changes*]; in portraying "the rivers roll on"[5] they adopt "Da-zhuan" [another chapter from the same book].

比見京師文體，懦鈍殊常，競學浮疏，爭爲闡緩。玄冬修夜，思所不得，既殊比興，正背風騷。若夫六典三禮，所施則有地；吉凶嘉賓，用之則有所。未聞吟詠情性，反擬內則之篇；操筆寫志，更摹酒誥之作；遲遲春日，翻學歸藏，湛湛江水，遂同大傳。[6]

Xiao Gang's main complaint, then, is that his contemporaries have confused literature, particularly poetry, with historical documents and philosophical works. To the contrary, he argues, poetry has a unique function that separates it from other genres: to "express in song one's feelings" (*yinyong qingxing* 吟詠情性).This authoritative statement is taken from no other source than the Great Preface to *The Book of Songs*. But in adopting this phrase, Xiao Gang has altered it to suit his own agenda.

To understand how far Xiao Gang's adaptation has departed from its original context, we need to examine the relevant part of the Great Preface:

When the kingly way declined, rites and moral principles were abandoned; the government lost its power to teach; the political structure of the states changed; the customs of the family were altered. And at this point the mutated poems were written. The historians of the states understood clearly the marks of success

42

and failure; they were pained by the abandonment of proper human relations and lamented the severity of punishments and governance. They expressed their feelings in song (*yinyong qingxing* 吟詠情性) to criticize those above, understanding the changes that had taken place and thinking about former customs. Thus the mutated poems emerge from the feelings, but they go no further than rites and moral principles. That they should emerge from feelings is human nature; that they go no further than rites and principles is the beneficent influence of former kings.

至于王道衰，禮義廢，政敎失，國異政，家殊俗，而變風變雅作矣。國史明乎得失之跡，傷人倫之廢，哀刑政之苛，吟詠情性，以風其上，達于事變而懷其舊俗者也。故變風發乎情，止乎禮義。發乎情，民之性也，止乎禮義，先王之澤也。[7]

Poetry is situated in the grand context of national history and social customs. It is quite clear in this passage that the maxim "to express one's feelings in song" (*yinyong qingxing* 吟詠情性), which was later canonized as the most authoritative statement on the characteristic generic function of poetry, is deeply rooted in a social and political context. It is both the origin of poetry and the ultimate standard by which poetry must be judged. In other words, the value of poetry derives from its combining personal experience with concerns about a political and social reality. The poet's personal feelings must be integrated into a larger social and political background. These two aspects of *qingxing* 情性 (feelings), the personal and the sociopolitical, constitute another source of tension and delicate balance in Chinese poetic theory. Xiao Gang set out to subvert this balance, to undermine the pragmatic, moralistic attitude toward literature that had dominated the literary theory up to his time. In another letter he expressed his outrage at Yang Xiong and Cao Zhi, who had both said that literary production was a trivial skill and not worthy of a gentleman's effort:

I began to love writings when I was very small, and now it is over twenty-five years. I once considered that even sun, moon, stars, and the patterns on the fiery dragon are evidenced in natural portents and reveal themselves in human affairs, how can we stop producing literary works and chanting songs? Yang Xiong once said [literary composition] is not worthy of a man: this is to use petty words to explain the Way; Cao Zhi once said [literary composition] is not for gentlemen: this is also to use petty argument to explain writing. In terms of meting out punishment, their crime can never be pardoned.

綱少好文章，於今二十五載矣。竊嘗論之，日月參辰，火龍黼黻，尚且著于玄象，章乎人事，而況文辭可止，詠歌可輟乎？不爲壯夫，揚雄實小言破道；非謂君子，曹植亦小辯破言。論之科刑，罪在不赦。[8]

As was shown in chapter 1, it was a common practice during the Southern Dynasties period to defend and glorify literature by relating it to the inherent structure of the universe. Xiao Gang does not offer anything new in this matter. What is new here is the belligerence of the rhetoric directed against two authors so well respected in his age, particularly Cao Zhi, who was ranked by Zhong Rong as one of the first class poets in his *Classification of Poetry* (*Shi pin*).[9] Xiao Gang rails against their narrow, utilitarian views of literature.[10] On another occasion he redefines the ancient dictum that poetry must "express one's feelings." While the Great Preface demands that personal feelings be integrated into a sociopolitical context, Xiao Gang seeks to separate them, because he considers moral cultivation and literary production to be totally different matters. Xiao Gang's theory removes poetic occasions from larger sociopolitical contexts and from situations that might produce a spontaneous, emotional response. In another letter on poetry he offers a revealing definition of what he regards to be the proper "feelings" that poetry is supposed to express in song:

[Her] twin temples face the [candle] light, displaying her absolute grace and beauty; [her] hair ornaments shake as she walks, in a way that would emulate those of the ancients. In a high pavilion she laments her fate, knitting her eyebrows; she weeps in Changmen Palace,[11] ruining the makeup on her face. There are also those slender-waisted ladies in pictures who make you feel that they are real, or pretty faces in mirrors that equal the paintings: all this embodies extraordinary feelings and has exquisite novelty.

雙鬢向光，風流已絕；九梁插花，步搖爲古。高樓懷怨，結眉
表色；長門下泣，破粉成痕。復有影里細腰，令與眞類；鏡中
好面，還將畫等。此皆性情卓絕，新致英奇。[12]

Xiao Gang's letter breaks with the Great Preface in situating its
poetic occasion in a highly artificial, ornate, and mildly erotic setting—
namely, the entertainment quarters of the court. Its focus is entirely
on the sensual, playful, and affected performance of singing girls or
court women. Several erotic aspects of such a woman are described:
her hairstyle (*shuangbin* 雙鬢), hair ornaments (*jiuliang chahua* 九
梁插花, *buyao* 步搖), and her physical features (*xiyao* 細腰). Her gestures are portrayed as amusingly affected and artificial, particularly
since (as we will see later in the discussions of poetry) all of the phrases
are clichés of the Palace Style convention—such as lamenting by a
high pavilion (*gaolou huaiyuan* 高樓懷怨), knitting eyebrows (*jiemei*
結眉), weeping by the Changmen Palace (*Changmen xiaqi* 長門下泣).
Such description alerts us that what is being described is a theatrical
and lighthearted performance.

The passage makes no mention of political and moral function of
poetry. Instead, poetry has been transformed from an instrument of
the state into a personal entertainment, a transformation that troubles
Xiao Gang not at all. Quite the contrary, he praises these poetic occasions and proudly calls them "outstanding" (*zhuojue* 卓絕). Xiao Gang
also carries out his covert subversion of the canonical tradition on
the linguistic level, because the artificial diction and the playful tone
that he adopts in this passage stand in a sharp contrast to the straightforward style and solemn voice of the Great Preface. They demonstrate that like the performance of the singing girl, poetry produced
under such circumstance is also a carefully controlled game, nothing
like a poem spontaneously produced. Thus, although Xiao Gang uses
the phrase *xingqing* 性情 (feelings), he has thoroughly redefined it.
Instead of signifying a solemn engagement in social reality as it does
in the Great Preface, it refers to a detached game played in the court.

This passage evokes the category of *yan* 艷, which was used by Xu
Ling to characterize the poems collected in *Yutai xinyong*.[13] While Xu
Ling might have used this word proudly and positively, it later became
one of the most frequently used terms to criticize the frivolously ornate
nature of late Southern Dynasties poetry, particularly the poetry of

Chen Houzhu[14] and the poetry of Late Tang poets such as Wen Tingyun and Li Shangyin.[15] Originally *yan* was used to describe a women's physical beauty.[16] But later it was adopted by critics to describe a literary style marked by fastidious ornateness and mild eroticism.[17] There is little question that this trend was started by Xiao Gang and the poets at his court, particularly Xu Ling whose preface to *Yutai xinyong* was a manifesto of such a literature of femininity. Like Xu Ling's preface, Xiao Gang's letter also has a court lady at the center of poetic activity. However, it is important to bear in mind that the centrality of women in Palace Style poetry is only a superficial phenomenon.[18] My analysis of poems in the following pages will demonstrate that Palace Style poetry privileges women as the central topic because women, especially the court lady, fit perfectly with the court poets' notion of poetry that regards poetry as purely entertainment, as a game to satisfy their desire for artistic control. It is no coincidence that besides portraying women, court poets devote much of their attention to poetry on objects (*yongwushi* 詠物詩). The poet can write of women and objects however he wants, however frivolous, in ways that would be unthinkable for writing about weighty events. The latter are simply too solemn to be trifled with. Thus this "new"[19] concept of poetry inevitably needs a new type of subject matter, one that departs from the orthodox tradition. Femininity, with its associations with sensuality, eroticism, and frivolity, provides a ready alternative to the old preoccupation with such masculine qualities as social responsibility and moral seriousness.

This is not to say that women never occupied an important place in Chinese poetry. Ever since "Li Sao" 離騷 ("Encountering Sorrow") by Qu Yuan 屈原 (c. 339–278 B.C.),[20] the use of a beautiful woman as a symbol of a virtuous gentleman was an established convention. In fact, "On a Beautiful Woman" is a stock theme title in the poems of the *yuefu*, or "music bureau" (樂府詩),[21] originally folk poems collected by government officials for use by the state in governing the people. The establishment of the music bureau by Emperor Wu of Han 漢武帝 (156–87 B.C.) and the collection of folk songs were motivated by political concerns.[22] *Yuefu* poems have therefore always been characterized by a political and moral tendency. Later, with the appearance of literati *yuefu* poems—that is, poems written by literati in imitation of the original folk songs collected by the music bureau—this moral and political slant tended to weaken, but it was seldom in serious jeopardy before the late Southern Dynasties period because even if there were few political and social elements in literati *yuefu* poems, they could always be made to represent political and social issues by an allegorical reading, like the Han exegetes' reading of *The Book of Songs*.[23]

By the Southern Dynasties period, to read *yuefu* poems allegorically had become a generic requirement. This is particularly true during the earlier Wei and Jin era when *yuefu* poems were seriously studied, imitated, and composed by literati poets. Those who chose to write in this genre, particularly members of the Cao family and their followers, were usually willing to conform to these generic expectations. Even Cao Zhi, who to many had started the trend toward an ornate style, tried to adhere to the conventional rules. For this reason the *yuefu* poems, especially those by Cao Zhi, were generally regarded as models of this particular convention. Below I will examine two poems of the same title by Cao Zhi and Xiao Gang. Comparing the two, we will see how Xiao Gang subverted the established conventions.

| 美女篇 | ON A BEAUTIFUL WOMAN (BY CAO ZHI) | |
|---|---|---|
| 美女妖且閑 | That beautiful woman is charming and graceful, | |
| 采桑歧路間 | She is plucking mulberries at the crossways. | |
| 柔條紛冉冉 | Tender boughs bob up and down, | |
| 落葉何翩翩 | How elegantly the fallen leaves fly. | 4 |
| 攘袖見素手 | She pulls up her sleeves, revealing her white hands, | |
| 皓腕約金環 | Her snowy wrists are encircled with gold. | |
| 頭上金爵釵 | A golden swallow rests on her head, a hairpin, | |
| 腰佩翠琅玕 | Her waist is dressed in green agate. | 8 |
| 明珠交玉體 | Shining pearls adorn her body of jade, | |
| 珊瑚間木難 | Coral pearls alternate with emerald beads. | |
| 羅衣何飄飄 | Her silken robe flutters round about her, | |
| 輕裾隨風還 | Her light skirt floats with the wind. | 12 |
| 顧盼遺光彩 | A glance back—the light and color of her eyes! | |
| 長嘯氣若蘭 | A long exhalation—her breath smells orchid. | |
| 行徒用息駕 | Passing travelers halt their carts and horses, | |
| 休者以忘餐 | Those who are resting forget to eat their meals. | 16 |
| 借問女安居 | 'Lady, may I ask where you live?" | |
| 乃在城南端 | "At the southern end of the town. | |

| | | |
|---|---|---|
| 靑樓臨大路 | Our green mansion faces the big road, | |
| 高門結重關 | The high gate is locked with several bolts." | 20 |
| 容華耀朝日 | Her face graces the morning sun, | |
| 誰不希令顏 | Who can look, without longing, upon it? | |
| 媒氏何所營 | What are the matchmakers doing? | |
| 玉帛不時安 | Why is the silk not arranged by this time? | 24 |
| 佳人慕高義 | A fair woman will look for noble virtue, | |
| 求賢良獨難 | To find a virtuous man is no easy task. | |
| 眾人徒嗷嗷 | People vainly gossip and slander, | |
| 安知彼所觀 | How can they understand her aspirations? | 28 |
| 盛年處房室 | Though in her prime, she stays at home, | |
| 中夜起長嘆[24] | She rises at midnight, and sighs. | |

In a short editorial preface to this poem, Guo Maoqian writes that "the woman of beauty is a symbol of a gentleman. This poem is about a virtuous gentleman seeking an enlightened ruler to serve. However, if the time is not right for him to serve, even if he should be sought by others, he would never bend."[25] Cao Zhi's poem lends itself to this allegorical reading in several aspects. The image of a mulberry-picking woman goes back to the *The Book of Songs*. Although modern commentators prefer to disregard the Confucian exegesis of this book, the allegorical reading of its poems was already a convention by the Han dynasty.[26] By then this image was given another representation in the well known *yuefu* poem "The Mulberry Trees by the Road" (陌上桑).[27] In this poem the portrayal of the woman is vivid and dramatic. Not only is her beauty described in detail, but she delivers a long lecture to the arrogant official who is making unwanted advances to her. Such representation lends itself to an allegorical reading by combining physical beauty with a positive moral quality, a combination that the Confucian exegetes eagerly sought.[28]

Because structurally Cao Zhi's "On a Beautiful Woman" is modeled after "The Mulberry Trees by the Road," and because the beautiful woman in Cao Zhi's poem is presented as engaging in a highly allegorical act, picking mulberry leaves, it is not surprising that some critics devised allegorical readings of Cao Zhi's poem: these technical features of the poem are generic markers. They invite the readers to read this poem in the same way as they read "Mulberry Trees by the Road" and other poems dealing with women picking mulberry leaves in *The Book of Songs*. Huang Jie's 黃節 *Han-Wei yuefu fenjian* 漢魏樂

府風箋 contains several readings of this kind. The following is by the Yuan dynasty (1260–368) critic Liu Lü 劉履:

Zijian [i.e., Cao Zhi] was determined to help his monarch to rule. He wanted to establish himself in service in order to pass his name down to posterity. But he was unable to do so. Although he was enfiefed, in his heart he felt he was not serving [his monarch]. He therefore adopted the image of a virgin to convey his longing and frustration. Words like charm (*yao* 妖), grace (*xian* 閒), shiny (*hao* 皓), and white (*su* 素) are used to symbolize his beautiful talent and quality; the jewelry and dress is used to suggest his high virtue. Her brilliance brims over, her fragrant name spreads more widely as the days pass: this is why people are so envious of her. Moreover, she lives in a green mansion with a high gate, close to the southern end of the town and facing the big road. She is not residing in a remote place and therefore hard to know, but why is she not appreciated and offered a dowry in good time? Actually [Cao Zhi] was suspected by the monarch and consequently not given an important position. He blamed the matchmaker because he dared not speak out his frustration directly. Since ancient times virtuous gentlemen have always chosen a just state to serve; this is precisely like a beautiful woman choosing a noble-minded [man] to be her spouse. Zijian was an intimate member of the royal family of Wei and should have shared fortunes and misfortunes of the state. Even if he had other aspirations, how could he fulfill them? This is what is meant by "To find a virtuous man is no easy task"; but how can others understand his views? "She remains unmarried in her prime, and fears losing her opportunity in life"; this is why "She rises at midnight, and sighs."

子建志在輔君匡済，策功垂名，乃不克遂，雖授爵封，而其心猶爲不仕，故托處女以寓怨慕之情焉。其言妖、閒、皓、素，以喻才質之美，服飾珍麗，以比己德之盛；至于文采外著，芳譽日流，而爲眾所希慕如此。況謂居青樓高門，近城南而臨大道，則非疏遠而難知者，何爲見棄，不以時而幣聘之乎？其實爲君所忌，不得親用；今但歸咎于媒薦之人，蓋不敢斥言也。且古之賢者，必擇有道之邦，然後入仕，猶佳人之擇配而慕夫高義者焉。惟子建以魏室至親，義當與國同其休戚，雖欲他

求，豈可得乎?此所謂“求賢獨難，”而其所見亦豈眾人所能
知哉?夫“盛年不嫁，將恐失時，”故惟中夜長嘆而已。[29]

It is difficult to translate this passage into English without causing
confusion, because there are no pronouns in the Chinese text. Liu Lü
is clearly exploiting this linguistic peculiarity, since this reinforces
his point that the woman's story is an allegory of Cao Zhi's experience. Consequently, it is nearly impossible to separate them. This interpretation is an extreme example of this mode of reading because it
manages to incorporate almost every element of the poem into a neat
allegorical framework. Indeed, it looks excessive and far-fetched.[30] But
the fact that such a reading was done in the first place is what is
significant.

In many respects this reading is certainly encouraged by Cao Zhi's
poem itself, for, as mentioned earlier, the structure of that poem follows
that of "The Mulberry Trees by the Road," even though the narrative
section of Cao Zhi's piece is much shorter and its diction is noticeably
more polished. Both poems begin with the setting of an outside scene
in which the heroine appears. The middle sections of both poems are
detailed descriptions of the physical beauty and dress of the two
women. Their speeches take the form of an answer to a question. The
endings are different: while "The Mulberry Trees by the Road" ends
with the woman uttering a proud speech, Cao Zhi's poem closes with
the lonely woman arising from bed and sighing over her fate at midnight. But judged against the entirety of the poems, this difference is
minor. Moreover, the ending of Cao Zhi's poem performs the same
function as that of the "Mulberry Trees by the Road": both indicate a
similar mental state—the heroines' determination to remain loyal to
their ideal. Therefore, despite the tendency toward literary embel-
lishment in Cao Zhi's piece, it still retains the elements essential for
an allegorical interpretation.

The framework of this allegorical reading is built upon a long-stand-
ing exegetical convention that had its origin in Confucius's comments
on *The Book of Songs*[31] and was particularly reinforced by Han studies
of *The Book of Songs* and Qu Yuan's poetry. The two most influential
works in this exegetical convention are Zheng Xuan's 鄭玄 (127–200)
commentary edition of *The Book of Songs*, *Maoshi Zhengjian* 毛詩鄭
箋 and Wang Yi's 王逸 (fl. 110–20) edition of *Chuci*, *Chuci zhangju* 楚
辭章句.[32] Zheng Xuan finds an allegorical intent in every poem from

*The Book of Songs*, whether historical or topical. I have noted briefly that a poem describing a woman picking mulberry leaves was interpreted by him as "an allegory for the diligence [of the king]."[33] But it is Wang Yi who played a critical role in making a convention of the allegorical treatment of poetry about beautiful woman. In Qu Yuan's poetry, especially in "Encountering Sorrow," flowers and women are often used as a symbol of the poet's virtue and integrity. In the beginning of "On Encountering Sorrow," for example, after a brief account of his royal lineage, Qu Yuan asserts that:

| 紛吾既有此內美兮 | Having from birth this inward beauty, |
| 又重之以修能 | I added to it fair outward adornment. |
| 扈江離與辟芷兮 | I dressed in selinea and shady angelica, |
| 紉秋蘭以爲珮 | And twined autumn orchids to make a garland.[34] |

Wang Yi takes the image of the garland to be a symbol of virtue and interprets the act of dressing in selinea and other beautiful plants in the following words: "Orchid is a fragrant grass. . . . It is the symbol of virtue, which is why virtuous people wear flowers as decoration."[35] Convention connects flowers and women; so in two lines that are the source of both theme and imagery in Cao Zhi's poem, Qu Yuan says, "And I thought how the trees and flowers were fading and falling,/ And feared that the Fair One's beauty would fade too" (惟草木之零落兮，恐美人之遲暮).[36] We have seen that Qu Yuan has already established a link between himself and the flowers, and now through a metonymic transformation he has linked himself with the fair one whose beauty is as ephemeral as a flower's. If this shift of gender is still ambiguous in these two lines, it becomes less so in the next two lines, when Qu Yuan explicitly describes himself with a stock feminine image, moth-eyebrow (*e'mei* 蛾眉) and compares himself with a beautiful female who is the target of vicious attacks by other jealous women: "All those ladies are jealous of my moth-eyebrows,/ They spread slanders to accuse me of being lascivious"(眾女嫉余之蛾眉兮，謠諑謂余以善淫).[37]

The poet tells his readers unabashedly that his fate is like that of a beautiful woman: he has met with grief because his outstanding virtue arouses the antagonism of wicked men, precisely as a beautiful woman loses the favor of her lord because other court ladies resent her remarkable beauty. Thus in Qu Yuan's work the symbolic significance of the beautiful woman and flowers is firmly established, so much so that even as early as Wei and Jin its metaphorical and allegorical function had become a convention.

By the time Xiao Gang wrote his "On a Beautiful Woman," this convention already had a history of more than five hundred years. It is particularly strong in *yuefu* poetry, whose peculiar generic rules are further reinforced by the solid intertextuality within the genre. The titles of *yuefu* poetry are powerful signs that direct the reader's attention to a set of conventional prescriptions and expectations both inside and outside the poem. He/she expects certain technical characteristics with regard to imagery, language, and structure, because he/she has absorbed the traditional knowledge concerning poems that bear the title in question.

Related to this, knowledge about the technical features of the poem, too, provides signals for interpretation: the reader knows that a poem about a beautiful woman will begin in a certain way, will adopt certain imagery, and should be understood in a certain sense as well. Consequently, a poet who opts to write in the *yuefu* genre is deliberately engaging with all these aspects of the convention. As a contemporary critic points out, "citing or opposing conventions of genre brings about a change in the mode of reading."[38] Thus, in selecting a title from the *yuefu* repertory Xiao Gang is citing this convention. The reader is prepared for a reading that is richly informed by the conventions of the *yuefu* poems and other related works as those by Qu Yuan and Cao Zhi. Now let us turn to his poem:

| 美女篇 | ON A BEAUTIFUL WOMAN (BY XIAO GANG) | |
|---|---|---|
| 佳麗盡關情 | She is the supreme embodiment of romance, this pretty woman, | |
| 風流最有名 | Her charming manner makes her most famous. | |
| 約黃能效月 | Light yellow temples can imitate the moon, | |
| 裁金巧作星 | Gold hairpins cleverly form the stars. | 4 |
| 粉光勝玉靚 | Her bright face surpasses the beauty of jade, | |
| 衫薄擬蟬輕 | Her gauzy clothes resemble the wings of the cicada. | |
| 密態隨流臉 | An intimate air accompanies her glowing face, | |
| 嬌歌逐軟聲 | Alluring songs follow her soft voice. | 8 |
| 朱顏半已醉 | Her blushing face is already half drunk, | |

52

微笑隱香屏[39]    With a delicate smile she hides herself behind the
fragrant screen.

What strikes us first is that Xiao Gang's poem is much shorter
than Cao Zhi's (which in turn is shorter than the anonymous Han
*yuefu* poem "Mulberry Trees by the Road"). The narrative, dramatic
part of Cao Zhi's poem is completely cut out of Xiao Gang's version.
Recall that in Cao Zhi's poem the narrative section provides information about the status of the woman by telling of her background. More
importantly, she plays a very active role in the poem by offering this
information in her own proud voice. She makes it clear that she is not
someone to be trifled with, and that her extraordinary beauty is not
an invitation to flirtation but an external sign of inner virtue.[40] She
might not be appreciated by others, but this is quite another story,
and she remains unreconciled to the vulgar society.

The omission of this dramatic part in Xiao Gang's poem not only
deprives the woman of any opportunity to speak for herself, but it
also transforms her into an object, because what remains is only the
compact description of her makeup, dress, and manner. Liu Lü has
shown that in Cao Zi's poem such description can be read as reinforcing
the point made in the narrative section, for like the beautiful flowers
and ornaments in *Chuci*, what are described in this part can be viewed
as the external manifestations of inner virtue. But in Xiao Gang's
poem the descriptive section has gained total independence. Once
severed from the larger context, it loses any trace of its original allegorical function.

Indeed, whereas it is impossible to read Xiao Gang's poem allegorically, Cao Zhi's poem can easily be allegorized. The woman is given
the opportunity to convince the reader that she is a person of high
ethical standards. In a rhetorical gesture strongly evocative of *yuefu*
convention, like the woman's speech in "Mulberry Trees by the Road,"
the speech by the woman in Cao Zhi's poem also comes in the form of
an answer. The conventionality of this gesture, together with the descriptive images that recall the *Chuci* convention, works to persuade
the reader that like Qu Yuan and the woman in "Mulberry Trees by
the Road," the woman in Cao Zhi's poem is also a person of noble
character. The reader can then readily connect that information with
the exegetical tradition established in the study of *The Book of Songs*
and Qu Yuan's work, a tradition that had been particularly emphasized

in interpreting *yuefu* poems. This process of making connections is essential for our understanding of poetry dealing with beautiful woman, especially those that bear a *yuefu* title.

Let us now turn to Xiao Gang's poem, to see why it defies allegorical treatment. The poem begins with the general statement of the charm and fame of this pretty woman. With the second couplet it quickly moves into the mode of description. Lines 3 and 4 describe the woman's makeup and hair ornaments. The comparison of these manmade products with moon and stars creates a strong visual effect. It also introduces the artificial transformation of nature that is to become one of the most common themes in Palace Style poetry. In the next couplet the sensual appeal shifts from the visual to the tactile. Line 6 presents a highly erotic image: the woman's clothes as thin as cicada wings. The intent is obvious, even though the poet does not explicitly mention the transparency of her garb. Her flesh is all the more apparent because of this half-concealment. Then, the poet adds further erotic enticement, this time in the auditory realm: the alluring songs (*jiaoge* 嬌歌) and the soft voice (*ruansheng* 軟聲) of the woman enliven the atmosphere and increase the seductive power of the poem.

In line 7 we witness a significant difference between Cao Zhi and Xiao Gang's poems. In Cao Zhi's work, and for that matter in the anonymous "Mulberry Trees by the Road," the fair woman is viewed by others only from a distance. One can interpret this on two levels: on the literal level it shows that the woman observes the Confucian ethical norms by keeping a proper distance from the male members of society. Allegorically it symbolizes the poet's resolve to maintain his integrity in a corrupt and vulgar world. But in the glowing face of Xiao Gang's woman there is an "intimate air" (*mitai* 密態), a suggestion of flirtation on her part that violates the proper separation between herself and her male observers. The reader begins to suspect that his half-veiled woman is not the woman in Cao Zhi's poem, a feeling then confirmed by the next line: she turns out to be a singing girl! We are surprised to discover this, but our surprise becomes even greater when we reach the last two lines of the poem: the half-drunken woman is not just openly flirting, she is beckoning her guest to join her in the innermost realm of her boudoir. Seduction and sensuality close this carefully constructed poem as the half-concealed woman smiles alluringly at her audience, hidden behind a fragrant screen.

An allegorical reading eludes this poem. It remains stubbornly as it is, a poem of mild eroticism and seduction.[41] The tone is playful, indicating that Xiao Gang is teasing his Confucian-minded readers. First, he arouses their expectations by choosing a poetic title rich in generic associations, and then he deliberately frustrates them by turning the poem into one of completely different import.

Another distinctive character of Xiao Gang's poem is the striving toward refinement. It demonstrates the characteristic fascination in Palace Style poetry with precious diction and linguistic sophistication. We already noted that Xiao Gang's poem is much more compact than Cao Zhi's, preserving only those parts that serve his purpose and suit his taste. One cannot but marvel at his achievement. In just ten lines he manages to reveal the status of the woman, her physical and mental quality, her (and for that matter, the poet's) aesthetic taste, and a highly enticing act of flirtation. Xiao Gang has pruned the images of nature in Cao Zhi's poem and kept only the images of precious, colorful ornaments. He uses parallelism abundantly and effectively. In this poem of ten lines, there are three parallel couplets that highlight the most characteristic aspects of the woman, her ornaments, and her gestures. In the third couplet, for example, the described items are not only linked one to the other, but also help to emphasize each other: alluring songs (*jiaoge* 嬌歌) are both related to, and occasioned by her intimate air (*mitai* 密態); her glowing face (*liulian* 流臉) and soft songs (*ruansheng* 軟聲) lend force to one another, combining to produce both visual and auditory effects in an increasingly captivating description. All this develops smoothly into the climax of the final two lines.

Xiao Gang's revisionist effort to refine traditional *yuefu* poetry is a systematic one. Although he did produce a few ancient-sounding poems in this genre, the majority of his *yuefu* poems tend toward a fastidious refinement and artificiality. I now compare two pieces bearing the same title, one of Xiao Gang's *yuefu* poems and an anonymous *yuefu* song:

有所思 My Beloved (anonymous)

有所思 My beloved—
乃在大海南 He lives at the south of the great sea.
何用問遺君 What will I give you as a token of love?

| | |
|---|---|
| 雙珠玳瑁簪 | A tortoiseshell hairpin with two pearls |
| | at both ends, 4 |
| 用玉紹繚之 | Which I have encircled with a jade ring. |
| 聞君有他心 | Then I heard your heart has set on another |
| | person, |
| 拉雜摧燒之 | I took the hairpin out, broke it, and burned it! |
| 摧燒之 | And after that I let wind blow away its ashes. 8 |
| 當風揚其灰 | |
| 從今以往 | I swear that I will never think of you again, |
| 勿復相思 | |
| 相思與君絕 | My love for you is finished! |
| 雞鳴狗吠 | By dawn the cocks will crow, the dogs will bark, |
| 兄嫂當知之 | My elder brother and his wife will know all |
| | about this. 12 |
| 妃呼豨 | Alas! |
| 秋風肅肅 | The autumn wind is whistling by, |
| 晨風颸 | the pheasant cries, longing for its mate,[42] |
| 東方須臾 | Soon at daybreak I will let him know my |
| 高知之[43] | decision. |

This is a poem of a betrayed woman. The heroine is a young woman full of passion, both when she is in love and when she has lost that love. The highly colloquial diction, the irregular metrical pattern, and the straightforward syntax increase the spontaneity and emotional intensity of the poem. The poem's voice is that of a woman of determination, who has the will and ability to take control of her life in the face of an otherwise desperate situation. It is a folk song as one expects it to be: simple but effective.[44]

Xiao Gang's poem of the same title is of a very different character:

| 有所思 | MY BELOVED |
|---|---|
| 昔未離長信 | In the past before she left the Palace of |
| | Eternal Fidelity, |
| 金翠奉乘輿 | She rode in a carriage decorated with gold |
| | and emerald. |
| 何言人事異 | But how human affairs are full of changes, |
| 夙昔故恩疏 | Now the old favor is removed from her. 4 |
| 寂寞錦筵靜 | She is lonely on the silent brocade mat, |
| 玲瓏玉殿虛 | Her exquisite body is in the empty jade palace. |

| 掩閨泣團扇 | Closing the boudoir door she weeps over the "round fan," |
| 羅幌詠蘼蕪 | By the gauze curtain she sings "Uphill I picked fragrant herbs." 8 |

The speaker in the anonymous folk song reminds us of those strong-minded women in *The Book of Songs*.⁴⁶ The heroine in Xiao Gang's poem, however, is a court lady. The only connection between the two is that both are betrayed by their lovers, a telling transformation. It shows that Palace Style poetry is preoccupied with aristocratic life and evinces a distaste for rustic materials. The obscure woman in the anonymous folk is not a fit subject for Palace Style poetry.

The allusion to the Palace of Eternal Fidelity in the first line serves to announce the change. Not only does it indicate the locus of the poem, but it also demonstrates efficiently the taste for compactness and economy of expression in Palace Style poetry. The Palace of Eternal Fidelity was the residence of Han empresses. Since it was the place where the well-known, talented court poet Lady Ban (班婕妤 fl. 32–7 B.C.) lived after she fell out of favor with Emperor Cheng of Han, it has through a metonymic transfer become the metaphor for deserted court ladies. While the female persona in the folk song is indignant over her lover's betrayal, the court woman of Xiao Gang's poem expresses only a melancholy. Much stronger is her nostalgia for her past happiness. These two women speak in sharply contrasting voices: the voice of the one is passionate, assertive, the voice of the other barely speaks but is struck mute. She is seen from the point of view of an observer who is interested only in the despondent, erotic side of her experience. In the first instance the story recounts a heart-breaking event because the speaker is the victim of this desertion. In the second it is merely a poetic occasion for the poet who is removed from the woman's experience. The matter is of an interest to him only for providing an opportunity to exercise his poetic skill.

In lines 5 and 6 Xiao Gang directs our view to the most private part of the lady's bedroom, to the stereotypical image of Palace Style poetry: a longing, lonely woman in an empty, alienating environment. The fullness of her desire is set off by the emptiness of the surrounding; her loneliness is highlighted by the contrast between her small, exquisite body and the huge, deserted palace. Again Xiao Gang manipulates parallelism very effectively. The first two characters in both lines, *jimo* 寂寞 (lonely) and *linglong* 玲瓏 (exquisite), are adjective phrases describing the subjective condition of the court lady. The third and fourth characters, *jinyan* 錦筵 (silk mat) and *yudian* 玉殿 (jade palace), are noun phrases signifying an objective condition that directly contrasts the subjective one. This parallel structure is completed by the last word of each line, *jing* 靜 (silent) and *xu* 虛 (empty), two static verbs that further intensify the discrepancy between the lady's mental state and the alienating environment. The silence of her mat sets out the agitation and the heat of her longing, but the emptiness of the jade palace is a synecdoche of an empty, cold world.

Xiao Gang is manipulating familiar conventions. The deserted woman is a stock theme in both folk *yuefu* poems and court poetry, and Xiao Gang alludes to both in the last two lines. The "round fan" in line 7 refers to a poem by Lady Ban in which she compares herself to a fan that is laid aside when autumn comes.[47] Line 8 alludes to another anonymous ancient verse "Uphill I Pick Fragrant Herbs" 上山采蘼蕪, which is the first poem in *Yutai xinyong* and is called an "ancient poem" (*gushi* 古詩) by Xu Ling.[48] The relationship between these two poems is precisely like the relationship between Xiao Gang's "My Beloved" and the *yuefu* poem of the same title that I have just discussed: Lady Ban's piece is marked by precious ornament, puns, and erotic hints, while the ancient poem is straightforward and has several narrative sections. In juxtaposing the two, Xiao Gang transforms a largely folk tradition into a sophisticated literary composition that reflected life at court. Indeed, in Xiao Gang's poem all traces of the ancient verse are gone, leaving a work that is even more mannered than the one by Lady Ban.

Xiao Gang's rejection of the *yuefu* convention is even more striking in another poem bearing a *yuefu* title, "Plucking Chrysanthemum" 採菊篇. Here again Xiao Gang alludes to "Uphill I Pick Fragrant Herbs," as he had done briefly in the last line of "My Beloved." The poem alluded to describes a chance encounter between a deserted wife and her former husband. It begins with the following couplet:

| | |
|---|---|
| 上山採蘼蕪 | Uphill she picked fragrant herbs, |
| 下山逢故夫 | Downhill she met her former husband. |

The rest of the poem consists entirely of their dialogue, in which, using very colloquial language, they compare the qualities of his former

58

and present wives.[49] Again Xiao Gang cuts out the narrative part of
the old poem and changes it from a direct engagement in which the
woman plays an active role into a detached, refined description, thereby
greatly reducing its emotional impact:

月精麗草散秋株　Moonlight shines on the fair grass, disperses in
　　　　　　　　　autumn trees,
洛陽少婦絕妍姝　The young ladies of Luoyang display their supreme
　　　　　　　　　beauty.
相呼提筐採菊珠　Baskets on arms, they call upon each other to go pick
　　　　　　　　　chrysanthemum,
朝起露濕霑羅襦[50] While the dew at dawn dampens their silken robes.

The open rejection of the *yuefu* convention comes at the end of the
poem, when Xiao Gang playfully announces:

東方千騎從驪駒　In the east a thousand carriages pulled by sable
　　　　　　　　　steeds pass by,
更不下山逢故夫[51] They never come downhill to meet their former
　　　　　　　　　husbands.

The deliberate, humorous transformation of "Downhill she met her
former husband" 下山逢故夫 to *They never come downhill to meet
their former husbands* 更不下山逢故夫 speaks for itself. By placing
the emphatic negative phrase "never" (*gengbu* 更不) before a most
memorable line of a most memorable *yuefu* poem, Xiao Gang signals
his rejection of a well-respected tradition. This rhetorical gesture also
signals that unlike the *yuefu* poem which deals with a real life situation, his is a lighthearted parody.[52]

The playful use of allusions effectively quashes any possible emotional appeals in the poem. The statement about the loneliness of
court women consequently remains an empty trope separated from,
and even working against, the main body of the text. This mannerism
in Palace Style poetry—the emphasis on artistry at the expense of the
affective—is what draws the most criticism from the tradition-minded
scholars. In the Chinese tradition an overemphasis on the aesthetic
aspect of a literary work is often regarded as the reflection of a decadent
moral character. Thus the official biography of Xiao Gang in *Liang shu*
梁書 (*The history of Liang dynasty*), while giving a positive account of

his life, finds his poetry "not worthy of a gentleman."[53] It is understandable that some modern critics, fed up with what are often simplistic attacks on Palace Style poetry, may rise in its defense, but it is quite unnecessary to claim that it upholds canonical values when it clearly does not. One critic, for instance, says that Xiao Gang's poetry "aimed for the natural spontaneity of the folk song,"[54] a totally unfounded defense, albeit one that may have arisen from Xiao Gang's own words. In the previously quoted letter to his brother Xiao Yi, Xiao Gang does seem to be saying that the proper function of poetry is to "express one's feelings," thus affirming the canonical standard of *shi yanzhi*, that poetry is the expression of one's will. His poetic output, however, betrays a very different tendency. We saw in our comparison of the two poems called "My Beloved" that Xiao Gang is more interested in artistic control than expressing emotions. In the following poem by him this tendency is even more remarkable.

| 和徐錄事見 | MATCHING CENSOR XU'S POEM ON SEEING |
| 內人作臥具 | HIS WIFE MAKING BEDROOM FURNISHINGS |

| | | |
|---|---|---|
| 密房寒日晚 | Hidden boudoir in a late cold day, | |
| 落照度窗邊 | The rays of the setting sun cross the window sill. | |
| 紅簾遙不隔 | Red curtains are far away but do not block my view, | |
| 輕帷半卷懸 | Light drapes hang half rolled up. | 4 |
| 方知纖手製 | I then know her slender hands are making [furnishings], | |
| 詎減縫裳妍 | Who can say the beauty of her sewing is reduced? | |
| 龍刀橫膝上 | Dragon shears lie across her knees, | |
| 畫尺墮衣前 | The colorful ruler slips down in front of her skirt. | 8 |
| 熨斗金塗色 | The iron is covered with a sheen of gilt varnish, | |
| 簪管白牙纏 | The needle pool is cased with snow-white ivory. | |
| 衣裁合歡褶 | She cuts clothes into love-pleasure pleats, | |
| 文作鴛鴦連 | And designs the pattern of linked mandarin ducks. | 12 |
| 縫用雙針縷 | She sews with double-needle thread, | |
| 絮是八蠶綿 | The wadding she uses is the silkworm floss. | |
| 香和麗丘蜜 | Her perfume is a mixture of Liqiu nectar,[55] | |
| 麝吐中台煙 | Her incense-burner exhales Zhongtai smoke.[56] | 16 |
| 已入琉璃帳 | Already she has entered her lapis bed curtains, | |

| | |
|---|---|
| 兼雜太華氈 | The floor is covered by Taihua rugs.[57] |
| 且共雕爐暖 | "Let's enjoy together the warmth from our carved stove, |
| 非同團扇捐 | Certainly my fate is not like the rejected round fan. |
| 更恐從軍別 | Still I fear you would leave me to join the troops, |
| 空床徒自憐[58] | and that I would be left alone, lamenting vainly my fate on an empty bed. |

20

The poet's deliberation is demonstrated by the enticingly gradual disclosure of the poem. Lines 1 and 2 present a hidden boudoir bathed in the light of the setting sun. The invisibility of the heroine in this concealed world only enhances our desire to know something about her. *Mi* 密 (hidden, sealed) can also mean "intimacy," and in this line both meanings are equally present. Hence from the outset the poet has designed his work to allure us and direct our attention. But he must not keep the reader in the dark for very long, lest he lose the reader's interest. The reader needs some enticement to play along. So in lines 3 and 4 Xiao Gang begins to disclose the woman's world to his audience. This world is encircled by red curtains that are visible in the distance. The process of unveiling has begun, but only very frugally, for after the assurance in line 3 that the curtains do not block his view, the reader is informed in line 4 that the woman's world is only partly visible through the "half rolled up" light drapes. Our first glimpse of her is restricted to her hands. From there our attention is directed to the various luxurious pieces of bedding: dragon shears, a colorful ruler, a gilt pressing iron, an ivory needle case. Palace Style poetry, as we have seen, loves ornament.

The naming of the specific types of clothes that the woman is making in the next few lines is marked by erotic puns. In line 11 *hehuanzhe* 合歡褶 (love-pleasure pleats) hints at both conjugal and sexual union because in Chinese the word *he* 合 means to unite; the sexual overtones are unmistakable. The image of mandarin ducks in line 12 is a cliché for paired lovers because they almost never separate from each other. This veiled sexual allusion is again hinted at more directly by the last word *lian* 連 (literally, to link, to connect) in this line. Line 15 adopts another two highly allusive puns: *he* 和 (to mix, to be together) and *mi* 蜜 (literally it means "honey," but it is a homophone of *mi* 密, intimate),[59] both of which hint at the conjugal and sexual intimacy between the woman and her husband. The climax of this unveiling process comes in line 17 when the poet announces that his view has "already entered the lapis bed curtains," which is no doubt the most intimate part of an already very private world. But if the reader's expectation is aroused by this final penetration, it is quickly thwarted by the next line: our view is directed away from bed to the rugs on the floor. Bathos has set in. Having waited this long, one does not expect to enter the woman's bedroom to look at the rugs, even a particularly rare Taihua rug. However, we are given one more opportunity to see the woman in line 19, when she beseeches her husband to enjoy the warmth from the stove and not to desert her. But here her image becomes blurred, because when she is finally allowed to speak it is in the language of a cliché that has lost much of its referent: the deserted round fan became too common a metaphor for a deserted woman after Lady Ban wrote the poem in which she compared herself to a round fan. The same can be said about the last two lines, for by Xiao Gang's time a self-pitying woman in an empty bed had become a sheer conventional device to end a poem.

It is impossible to regard such a poem as aiming at the spontaneity of the folk song tradition. And it is equally impossible to consider it as an expression of deeply felt emotions and thoughts. Palace Style poetry is never meant to be a spontaneous or a powerful emotional response to an external stimulus as dictated by the Great Preface. What counts most for court poets is decorum,[60] an artistic practice that undermines the canonical notion of poetry that emphasizes the message, not the method, by which the message is communicated. In this mildly decadent atmosphere, poetic wit is the password, and an elegant improvisation or performance is the key to success. Hence, eroticism in Palace Style poetry never approaches pornography. To describe a sexual act openly would not only be distasteful, it would also threaten the poet's artistic control. This concept of control critiques the notion of spontaneity and sincerity which is at the core of the Chinese canon. It suggests an aloof dandy who is fastidious in his deportment. Those Chinese critics who find pornography in Palace Style poetry misunderstand its artistic agenda.[61] To clarify this issue, let us look at some other poems by Xiao Gang.

| 詠內人畫眠 | ON A WIFE'S DAYTIME NAP |
|---|---|
| 北窗聊就枕 | By the north window she leans on the pillow, |
| 南簷日未斜 | At the south eaves the sun is still high. |
| 攀鉤落綺障 | She removes the hook, lets down the silken curtain, |
| 插捩舉琵琶 | and inserts the plectrum, raises the *pi-pa*.   4 |
| 夢笑開嬌靨 | Her smiles in dream reveal a pair of lovely dimples, |
| 眠鬟壓落花 | Her hair in sleep presses the fallen flowers. |
| 簟文生玉腕 | Patterned mat enlivens the jade wrists, |
| 香汗浸紅紗 | Fragrant sweat soaks the red gauze.   8 |
| 夫婿恆相伴 | Her spouse all along has been accompanying her, |
| 莫誤是倡家 [62] | Do not mistake her for a woman of the pleasure houses. |

The opening couplet sets the scene. The first two lines, though not verbally parallel (as usually they are not), contrast inside (the woman's bedroom) with outside (the open sky), a contrast reinforced by the directional words "north" and "south." The second, third, and fourth couplets describe the woman's state before and after she goes to sleep. Significantly, all are written in neat, sophisticated parallelism. The couplet of lines 3 and 4 depicts her before sleep, with each line portraying two actions that are linked by a relation of cause and effect: she removes the hook to lower the silken curtain; similarly the purpose of installing the plectrum is to take up the *pi-pa* to play. Besides the grammatical parallelism in these two lines, there is a contrast in the two central verbs: *luo* 落 (to lower) and *ju* 舉 (to raise), which move in opposite directions. This careful construction creates a balance that reinforces the artificiality of the poem.

The third and fourth couplets describe the woman at sleep and are the center of the poem's eroticism. These four lines are the finest of Xiao Gang's use of parallel structure.[63] *Mengxiao* 夢笑 (dream smile), which begins line 5, and the first phrase *mianhuan* 眠鬟 (sleep hair) in line 6 are both unusual formations because the modifying word in each case *meng* 夢 (dream, to dream) and *mian* 眠 (sleep, to sleep) can be used ordinarily only as verbs and nouns. But in this instance Xiao Gang has twisted them to make them function as adjectives, with startling effect, as both bring a sense of action to a static description.

Instead of "her smiles in dream" and "her hair in sleep" as in my translation, the phrase *mengxiao* (dream smile) conveys both acts of dreaming and smiling. Similarly in *mianhuan* (sleep hair) the lifeless hair has been transformed into something alive, performing the same act as the woman does. The two verbs in this couplet again indicate a contrast in direction: while *kai* 開 (to open) in line 5 moves up and outward, *ya* 壓 (to press) in line 6 moves down and inward. The objects of these two verbs *jiaoye* 嬌靨 (lovely dimples) and *luohua* 落花 (fallen flowers) not only parallel each other in structure; they also imply one another in meaning: the dimples on the woman's face are compared with the flowers from the trees.

The fourth couplet continues the show of wit. In line 7 the white hands of the woman are described as being animated by the patterned mat. But what is most noticeable is another erotic climax in line 8, when the woman is described with the sexually charged image "fragrant sweat" (*xianghan* 香汗). In addition, the poet almost strips her naked with his suggestive language: we are told that the fragrant sweat "soaks" (*jin* 浸) her "red gauze" clothes (*hongsha* 紅紗), but the body under the semitransparent gauze is nevertheless marked by its absence from the scene. However, just as the scene is nearing its climax and the reader's desire is slightly aroused, in lines 9 and 10 Xiao Gang abruptly deflates the moment in a playful, anticlimactic tone. Desire is not to be satisfied—the woman in question is not a prostitute or singing girl but a married lady who is always guarded by her spouse. Not only is the thematic content of the last couplet banal, but its language too is very colloquial. The poem suddenly shifts from a highly elegant descriptive mode to ordinary address. The poet has again successfully played a game with his reader.

Works like this one are abundant in Palace Style poetry. It was written not to stimulate, let alone satisfy, sexual desire as pornography is. It was written instead to demonstrate how the clever court poet can transform an act of passion into an act to be contemplated with disinterest. To aestheticize, not to arouse, is the trademark of Palace Style poetry. Sexuality has to be aestheticized because it "implies abandoning the dandy's self-sufficiency, ceasing to be egocentric . . . and also it is natural, a denial of the cult of artificiality."[64] Sexual passion is too unpredictable; it upsets the artistic balance and control that the decadent poet like Xiao Gang strives to achieve.

The repeated use of the same imagery in poem after poem tends to erode the affective impact of Palace Style poetry. Many recurrent images in Palace Style poetry—a lonely woman on an empty bed, golden or carved utensils, ornate jewelry, an abandoned round fan, and so on—have become clichés even in the Southern Dynasties period. Like the loss of ethical, allegorical referents in Xiao Gang's version of *yuefu* poems, so Palace Style poetry more generally seems to have lost its ability to treat the poet's genuine personal experiences. Small wonder that most of Palace Style poetry consists of occasional poems (*yingjingshi* 應景詩) or poems on objects (*yongwushi* 詠物詩)—that is, poems typically composed or improvised at social gatherings—where conformity to set rules regarding metrical pattern, title, content, and so on, was much more important than personal response and originality of the individual poet. This situation very much resembles that of English Neoclassical poetry, which was equated with wit and had become purely "joke or repartee."[65] Fastidious propriety becomes the dominant concern, while profound thinking and feeling are outlawed because they tend to upset such propriety. So it was during the Southern Dynasties. As a result, when Xiao Gang actually composed works with a distinct personal tone, he had to break sharply with the Palace Style convention. Xiao Gang's oeuvre contains a small number of such works, for example, the following piece:

| 泛舟橫大江 | CROSSING THE BIG RIVER BY BOAT | |
|---|---|---|
| 滄波白日暉 | Blue waves glow under the white sun, | |
| 遊子出王畿 | A traveler departs from His Majesty's domain. | |
| 旁望重山轉 | He turns away to gaze at the mountain ridges as they whirl, | |
| 前觀遠帆稀 | He watches straight ahead as distant sails grow fewer. | 4 |
| 廣水浮雲吹 | Floating clouds are blown above the vast waterscape, | |
| 江風引夜衣 | River wind swirls his night clothes. | |
| 旅雁同洲宿 | Journeying geese together settle on the river isles, | |
| 寒鳧夾浦飛 | Cold ducks fly along its banks. | 8 |
| 行客誰多病 | Who is the traveler that suffers so many ills? | |
| 當念早旋歸[66] | He should remember to come back soon. | |

In contrast to the other poems that we have been studying, we feel refreshed from the very beginning because the setting of the poem is out in the open air, instead of in a woman's bedroom or entertainment quarters of court. Gone are the images of ornament and dress; gone are the minute descriptions of the indolent and flirting gestures of court ladies and singing girls; gone are the mawkish self-pity and unwarranted sadness that conclude many Palace Style poems. In short, gone is the poetic diction of Palace Style convention. Parallelism is used in the middle three couplets, but here it has been rid of traces of mannerism and therefore does not sound stilted. The vast landscape comes out effectively on its own, well structured by the parallelism but essentially retaining its character. Mountain ridges and distant sails not only set each other off, but they also very much belong to the same scene; hence their connection is a "natural" one. The same can be said of other parallel items in the poem: vast waters with river wind, traveling geese with cold ducks.

In Palace Style poetry the tension between the natural and the artificial is a key issue, as artificiality is characteristically valorized, and what is natural is usually transformed into something artificial. In this poem, however, artificiality is held at bay. Although artistic control is still a central concern as is indicated by the abundant use of parallelism, it is not the raison d'être of the poem. Instead, it is made to serve a much larger purpose, the expression of a deep personal feeling, the loneliness of an individual human being in the face of the vast, eternal universe.

What is surprising to a reader familiar with the complete poetic production of Xiao Gang is how much this expression accords with dictates of the Great Preface to *The Book of Songs*. This deeply felt loneliness and the related homesickness of the traveler comes from the powerful contrast between the vastness and eternity of the universe on the one hand and the tininess and transience of the human being on the other. But this contrast has been carefully built throughout the poem. The traveler is portrayed as leaving the city by boat in the first couplet; in the next three couplets nature is linked to the traveler either through shared action (lines 3 to 6), or through the implied connection between natural phenomena and his mental state (lines 7 and 8). The traveler's loneliness is particularly indicated by the parallelism in lines 7 and 8, where the geese nesting together on the river isles are contrasted with the cold ducks flying over the banks. They are conventional images used to set off in relief the contrasting homelessness and loneliness of the wanderer. Consequently when the speaker admonishes the traveler to return home in the last two lines the reader is ready for this shift.

Nevertheless, the ending of this poem is probably as conventional as the self-pitying women in Palace Style poetry, and our naturalization of this poem depends upon another convention.[67] We regard this poem as "natural" because it meets the expectations of the poetic convention established by *The Book of Songs*, "Nineteen Ancient Poems," and consolidated by the poets of the Wei and Jin eras. The lonely, homesick traveler had been a conventional motif since ancient times,[68] and as such had its own generic and linguistic requirements, such as a deep emotional involvement and a straightforward style. Since Xiao Gang's poem fulfills most of these requirements, those who regard these features as essential to great poetry would deem this poem successful. However, the very fact that Xiao Gang was able to produce a poem of this kind yet preferred to devote his talent to the production of Palace Style poetry serves to highlight his reaction against the canonical tradition.

Poems like "Crossing the Big River by Boat" are very rare in Xiao Gang's oeuvre.[69] It seems that he had little interest in landscape and natural imagery, although right until his time landscape poetry had been in vogue, led by the diligent practice and abundant production of poetry in this genre by Xie Lingyun (謝靈運 385–433), and Xie Tiao (謝朓 464–99). This is to be expected, because Palace Style poetry is mostly concerned with the refined and artificial aspects of court life. When Xiao Gang did choose to write of an outdoor activity, he often could not help being confined by the diction of Palace Style poetry and geographical boundaries of court life:

| 晚景出行 | TAKING A WALK IN LATE SUNLIGHT |
|---|---|
| 細樹含殘影 | Slender trees take in the lingering sunlight, |
| 春閨散晚香 | A spring bedroom sends out late perfume. |
| 輕花鬢邊墮 | Light flowers hang down her curls, |
| 微汗粉中光 | Faint sweat glistens on her makeup. |
| 飛鳧初罷曲 | She has just sung the "Flying Ducks" tune, |

4

| | |
|---|---|
| 啼鳥忽度行 | And abruptly begins another called "Chirping Crows." |
| 羞令白日暮 | She is upset by the darkening white sun, |
| 車騎鬱相望 [70] | And anxiously watches for the horse and carriage.    8 |

The title of the poem promises a late afternoon outing, but except for the last line, which mentions carriages and horses, the poem is mostly suggestive of indoors. This is because the language used in the poem to describe a putative outdoor activity is essentially language for the boudoir. The setting is technically outdoors, but it ends there. The first line features two images from nature, trees and lingering sunlight, yet what is natural is immediately transformed into a highly artificial courtly convention: trees are modified by the feminine and erotic word "slender" ($xi$ 細), which is often used to describe the waist of court women.[71] The verbs of this couplet again portray two neatly contrasted movements: "to take in" ($han$ 含) and to "send out" ($san$ 散). Further, in the second line the perfume from a woman's boudoir pervades the whole atmosphere. And with the second couplet this transformation is intensified, as the focus shifts to a singing girl, with her slipping hairpins and glistening sweat—clearly a state of dissolution. But the neat parallel structure in the couplet nevertheless brings this physical dissolution under rhetorical control. While in the last two lines the image of setting sun does come back and the singing girl's view is directed out toward the passing carriages and horses, the activity indoors, already established, remains the dominant impression.

The language of this poem thus proves a point made earlier, that the strength of Palace Style poetic diction lies mostly in witty description of courtly activities, but it is ill-prepared to dealing with topics outside the court or the bedroom. The numerous "poems on objects" in Palace Style convention drive home this point. The topics treated in this genre are usually dainty objects of nature subject to manipulation, such as flowers, plants, or bedroom furnishings, such as mirrors and curtains. Although larger objects sometimes are described as well, they are often treated with the same diction and style. The uniform treatment accorded to these different objects in Palace Style convention is another illustration of its limitations. Consider the following two pieces by Xiao Gang:

| 詠初桃 | On Budding Peaches |
|---|---|
| 初桃麗新采 | Budding peaches are displaying their fresh beauty, |
| 照地吐其芳 | Their sprouting flowers are shining on the ground. |
| 枝間留紫燕 | Among branches linger purple swallows, |
| 葉里發輕香 | From leaves comes light fragrance. |
| 飛花入露井 | Flying flowers enter the open well, |
| 交榦拂華堂 | Twisting stems brush the colorful halls. |
| 若映窗前柳 | When they cast their shadows on willows in front of the window, |
| 懸疑紅粉妝[72] | They make me wonder if they are red makeup. |

Peach blossoms are a fitting subject for Palace Style poetic diction, because their daintiness and their strong connection with feminine beauty readily satisfy the aesthetic taste of this genre. Words like *li* 麗 (beautiful), *cai* 采 (pretty), *xiang* 香 (fragrance) are indeed clichés, but they do not seem to be out of place in this poem because of its subject matter. The same is true for the metaphor at the end of the poem: comparing a flower with a woman's face or makeup is too conventional to impress readers, but it does not sound far-fetched; on the contrary, it even looks "natural" within Palace Style convention. This is a very typical poem, and it is what one expects it to be.

But problems arise when the poet chooses to write about an object far removed from the boudoir:

| 詠雲 | On Clouds |
|---|---|
| 浮雲舒五色 | Floating clouds send out five colors, |
| 瑪瑙應霜天 | Agate mirrors the frosty sky. |
| 玉葉散秋影 | Jade leaves scatter autumn shadows, |
| 金風飄紫煙[74] | Gold wind[73] blows the purple mist. |

The main descriptive figures in this poem are ones often used to depict a courtly surrounding: *manao* 瑪瑙 (agate), *yuye* 玉葉 (jade leaves), *jinfeng* 金風 (gold wind), *ziyan* 紫煙 (purple mist) are quintessential Palace Style poetic diction. In these phrases the modifying words *yu* 玉 (jade), *jin* 金 (gold), and *zi* 紫 (purple) are all highly artificial and ornate noun-adjectives. They effectively transform the modified items, *ye* 葉(leaves), *feng* 風 (wind), and *yan* 煙(mist), from elements of nature into decorations of an all too familiar courtly world. The result of this transformation is that at the end of the poem the natural phenomenon and the topic of the poem—cloud—has completely disappeared and what is left is a highly artificial and ornate setting. This artificial feature is further foregrounded by the neat parallelism used throughout the quatrain. Here the conflict between the subject matter and the linguistic style is acutely apparent. We see that the power of Palace Style diction works mainly in one direction— that is, to transform the natural into the artificial.

Probably more than any other poetic genre, poetry on objects is about skilful display rather than expression of feelings or thought, because its goal is to describe external features. In this sense it trespasses into the realm of *fu* 賦 (rhyme-prose) and therefore constitutes a generic violation.[75] The assumption that poetry is essentially expressive dates back to the earliest stage of Chinese civilization.[76] In the Southern Dynasties era, but some two centuries earlier than Xiao Gang, this notion was further stressed by Lu Ji 陸機 (261–303) in his "*Fu* On Literature" ("Wenfu"文賦).[77] He states in memorable language that "poetry comes from feelings and is sensuously intricate; rhyme-prose gives the normative forms of objects and is clear and bright" (詩緣情而綺靡，賦體物而流亮).[78] To our present study, what is significant in this rephrasing of the ancient maxim of *shi yanzhi* (poetry expresses one's will) is that it defines poetry according to its generic *difference* from other genres, and particularly from *fu*. Whereas the former aims at conveying in colorful language what is deeply felt in the heart/mind, the main function of the latter is to portray the formal features of objects. The arbitrariness of this prescription is of course apparent, because since the late Han *fu* had become increasingly expressive, as the length of many works in this genre became shorter and their topics more personal.[79] Nevertheless as a generalization of the peculiar characteristics of *shi* (poetry) and *fu* (rhyme-prose) this view has been universally accepted.[80]

The poetry on objects in Palace Style convention defies this universally held opinion because it deliberately conflates the generic differences. It largely replaces the expressive function of poetry with the descriptive function of *fu*, and consequently in poetry on objects, especially those produced in Southern Dynasties courts, there remains little trace of personal feeling. Since ancient times description in *shi* has been a means of introducing the poet's personal response. This is the essential requirement in all three fundamental principles embodied in *The Book of Songs*, namely *fu* (賦, to describe), *bi* (比, to compare), and *xing* (興, to stimulate).[81] But in poetry on objects of the Palace Style convention, description has been separated from its deeper function as an introduction to something larger and more profound, and has become an independent, autotelic activity. What had been a means now becomes an end, and what had been merely a technique is now its own raison d'être.

It is probably for this reason that poetry on objects, especially that of the court poets, is never taken for serious literature. Although it was in vogue in Southern Dynasties period, it seldom receives serious consideration in later critical works,[82] because expressive function, as we have seen, has since the beginnings of the Chinese poetic tradition been the ultimate value, and therefore the ultimate standard of success, of poetry. To a traditional reader who upholds the Great Preface as the ultimate norm, the fastidious attention that Xiao Gang's poetry on objects lavishes on trivial objects is annoying enough. It becomes more irritating when it excludes from it expressive elements, such as personal response, that might have redeemed it.[83] Here is another example:

| 詠美人看畫 | ON A BEAUTIFUL WOMAN LOOKING AT A PAINTING | |
|---|---|---|
| 殿上圖神女 | A goddess is painted on the palace wall, | |
| 宮里出佳人 | A beautiful woman walks forth from the court. | |
| 可憐俱是畫 | Both are lovely and are pictures, | |
| 誰能辨偽眞 | Who can distinguish the real from the false? | 4 |
| 分明淨眉眼 | They clearly have elegant eyes and eyebrows, | |
| 一種細腰身 | Their slender waists are precisely the same. | |
| 所可持爲異 | The only difference between them is this: | |
| 長有好精神[84] | One of them always has a lively spirit. | 8 |

In Palace Style poetry a woman is usually treated as an object, despite the central place that she seems to "enjoy" in this poetry. The present poem illustrates this. The title of the poem efficiently changes a lively human being into a lifeless object by one word: *yong* 詠 (which literally means "to sing on, or about something"). This is so because this word is the first character in the compound *yongwu* 詠物 (on objects).[85] The choice of this word therefore indicates a citation of a specific genre, which in turn prepares the reader for a specific mode of reading. In other words the reader is alerted to read this poem as a poem on an object, and this object is none other than a beautiful woman looking at a picture of a goddess on the palace wall. As in his numerous other works, the description in this poem focuses on the delicate, erotic aspects of the woman and her world, but here the usually implicit gamelike nature of the poem is made explicit, for in line 4 the poet asks playfully, "Who can distinguish the real from the false?" The poet tells us this is a game and mischievously answers his own question at the end.

The whole poem plays upon the relation of illusion and reality, but it is only a play, a game, rather than a serious meditation on the philosophical meaning of that relationship. One critic has remarked that "the meaning implied in the concluding couplet is most pertinent to Xiao Gang's belief in the permanent value of art—that the beauty in the painting will live forever, while the real woman's existence is only ephemeral."[86] This interpretation of the text is not out of the question, but the playful tone of the poem seems to militate against such a serious reading. And similarly with many other poems on objects by Xiao Gang, they resist being read at a higher level. His language insistently directs our attention away from the allegorical. Even in this verse, where a thoughtful reading seems a possibility, it is undermined.

For instance, to interpret the last two lines as Xiao Gang's indirect statement of his belief in the permanence of art as opposed to the transience of humankind, a belief that had been stated by Cao Pi,[87] simply does not square with his descriptive language in lines 5 and 6. In these two lines words like *jing meiyan* 淨眉眼 (elegant eyes and eyebrows) and *xi yaoshen* 細腰身 (slender waists) simply defy a philosophical reading. Moreover, these words had *already* become too light-hearted and playful through repeated use in Palace Style poetry to carry any such serious meaning. We are forced by this poetic diction to read it like any other poem in which the same descriptions are adopted, as light-hearted amusements, rather than works of philosophical contemplation. An explication of this poem has to be made on this intertextual basis, for it is this intricate intertextual web that produces the meaning of the poem. In the case of Palace Style poetry the generic rules and expectations that determine meaning were already conventionalized by Xiao Gang's time. They are the semiotic system within which the individual poem works. They are the *langue*, whereas the poem is the *parole*; without the former the latter simply becomes incomprehensible. The last couplet should therefore be understood in the gamelike context of this poem. It is the poet's playful answer to the playful question that he posed to his readers in line 4.

The power of convention is also reflected in the expectations that it generates in the reader. The consistent denunciation of Palace Style poetry since Sui and Tang periods had created a powerful presumption that regards any poem in this genre as frivolous and decadent. This presumption is strengthened by the fact that because Xiao Gang and his followers seemed to have enjoyed defying the canonical tradition, there has been a circular development in the history of Palace Style poetry. The more it defies the canonical tradition, the more cogently it proves its agenda; and the more distinct its agenda, the more despised it is. Later generations' opinions of Palace Style poetry are to a great extent nourished and blinded by this circular development, as we tend to notice only those parts that have already been singled out and condemned by traditional criticism, for example, its artificiality, femininity, and eroticism. Thus, for more than a thousand years the study of Palace Style poetry has not advanced much beyond the criticism of Sui and Tang historians, whose denunciations are the ones most often cited by later critics. They have come to constitute the core of conventional wisdom on this issue.

A contemporary critic has commented on the "dissolution of the referent" and "the disappearance of *affect*" in modernist and post-modernist poetry in the West.[88] With some modifications these words come close to describing the changes that took place in the literature of the late Southern Dynasties period in China, because the loss of an ethical and allegorical referent and affective power is certainly the most striking feature in Palace Style poetry. The authors of *The History of Chinese Aesthetics* have pointed out that in the culture of the Liang there was a general tendency toward the artificial and the superficial.[89] The central intellectual activity among the literati of the preceding Wei and Jin periods had been the "pure talk" (*qingtan* 清談) in which scholars engaged in philosophical discussions about "being and nonbeing" (*youwu* 有無). During the Liang dynasty this activity had mostly disappeared. Watching the performance of singing girls and composing Palace Style poetry had become one of the principal intellectual activities of the court, which controlled the cultural life of the time. In "pure talk" a profound meaning is what is valued most, but in Palace Style poetry skilful description of the surface is the criterion for success.

This taste for the superficial is also reflected in the excessive attention devoted to the fastidious choice of diction and phrase. In his *Wenxin diaolong* Liu Xie says that since the Liu Song dynasty (420–79):

> Literary styles underwent some changes. [The thought of] Zhuangzi and Laozi receded and [the writings of] mountains and rivers flourished. [Writers] vied in weaving antithesis which might extend to hundreds of words, or in attempting to achieve the wondrous by a single line. In depicting [mountains and rivers] they tried to be exhaustive; and in literary phraseology they tried their best to achieve novelty. These are what the recent writers have been striving at.

> 體有因革，莊老告退，而山水方滋。儷采百字之偶，爭價一句之奇。情必極貌以寫物，辭必窮力而追新。此近世之所競也。[90]

This passage vividly describes the intense interest in linguistic artistry during Southern Dynasties era. In Chinese aesthetics language has usually been considered as a medium of expression. Therefore the more transparent it is, the better it is equipped to fulfill its function. Zhuangzi regards language as a fishing trap, which should be discarded as soon as the fish is caught.[91] Because of this notion of language the ideal in Chinese aesthetics has consistently been to evoke and produce an aftertaste, a lingering effect that goes beyond the linguistic materiality of a literary work. The presumption is that there must be a deeper meaning that cannot be confined to language because language constitutes only the surface of a literary work.[92] But in their pursuit of novelty and sophistication of poetic language, Xiao Gang and his followers deliberately ignored this deeper meaning and consequently dissolved the referent.[93]

A poetry without referent is a poetry of surface. In the classical Chinese poetic tradition, which valorizes above all the inexhaustibility of the poetic referent, this is a great offense. The harsh criticism directed at Palace Style poetry by Sui and Tang historians have proved this. But despite the denunciations, Palace Style poetry has demonstrated remarkable resilience. As a poetic genre it left a rich heritage that attracted many poets of later periods. It was particularly popular with the Late Tang poets Li He, Wen Tingyun, and Li Shangyin, who openly acknowledged their love of Palace Style poetry and injected a new life into it. To these poets and their works I now turn.

## Chapter 3

# Li He
## The Poetry of Beautiful Women and Ghastly Ghosts

A s has been stated previously, the Palace Style poetry of the Southern Dynasties enjoyed a revival in Late Tang thanks to the work of major poetic figures like Li He, Wen Tingyun, and Li Shangyin. These poets, seemingly obsessed with the culture of the Southern Dynasties court, wrote about it extensively. Unlike the historians of the Sui and Tang, however, they had little interest in its political and moral ways. Rather, what fascinated them were precisely those aspects of the culture that had been repeatedly condemned as decadent: its sensuality, its eroticism and its treatment of poetry as a sophisticated craft. Li He even tried to identify himself with Yu Jianwu 庾肩吾 (487–553?), a representative figure of the Southern Dynasties Palace Style poetry, as is seen in the following preface to one of his poems:

> During the Liang dynasty, Yu Jianwu used to write songs in Palace Style to match those of the Crown Prince [that is, Xiao Gang]. When the state was subverted, Jianwu fled to hide from the danger in Kuaiji. Later he was able to return home. I thought that he would have left some poems on this subject, but none of them has been found. So I wrote this "Song: Return from Kuaiji" to express his sadness for him.[1]

Yu Jianwu was Xiao Gang's literary mentor. Li He's poem aims to re-create the difficulty in which Yu found himself later on, when the country was collapsing and he had fallen from his high station. Li He sympathized, even empathized, with him, perhaps because the latter's unfortunate situation was reminiscent of his own. Yet he must also have been envious of the relationship that had once existed between Xiao Gang and Yu Jianwu, because by his own time such royal patronage of literature and the intimate, carefree atmosphere in which the Southern Dynasties court poets wrote their poetry was only a historical memory. Many poets of his own age were alienated from the establishment and had to struggle to make their voices heard. Therefore, the revival of Palace Style poetry in Late Tang occurred in a very different cultural milieu, and hence, the distinctions between Palace Style poetry of the Late Tang and its predecessor of the Southern Dynasties. As I indicated in Chapter 2, literary production during the Southern Dynasties, particularly the writing of poetry, was a form of public entertainment done mostly at the court, which controlled the cultural activities of the period. We see this in the following passage from *Nan shi*, or *The History of Southern Dynasties*:

> Since the situation in the central part of the country became chaotic and the Sima family moved [the capital] to the south [of Yangze River], literary writers have never been found lacking. Until the Liang dynasty this trend continued to grow in popularity. This was all because the monarchs of the time were well versed in culture and loved literature with passion. As a result, people with literary talent all concentrated [in court]. At that time whenever Emperor Wu graced his ministers with a visit, he would ask them to compose poems. Those who distinguished themselves in their writing would be rewarded with gold and silk. Therefore, scholars and officials all knew that they should be cultivating [their writing skills].[2]

The poetry written in such a setting was judged by a set of public rules. Whereas personal eccentricity and originality were considered aberrations, conformity was valorized. No wonder one finds such uniformity in Palace Style poetry of the Southern Dynasties period. In order to win "the gold and silk" the poet had to write to suit the emperor's taste. In Li Shangyin's biographical account of Li He, who lived in the Late Tang, one encounters a drastically different milieu:

[Li He] would often go out on a bony donkey with a young servant. On his back he would carry a tattered brocade bag, and whenever he got some [lines of poems] he would write them down and put them into the bag. In the evening, when he came back, his mother would ask the maids to take out the lines of poems he had written; when she saw how much he had written she would cry, "My son won't stop until he has spit his heart out!" Then she would light a candle and ask him to eat, but Changji [Li He] would take what he had written from the maids, prepare some ink and paper, complete them and put them into another bag.[3]

The poet in this instance was alone, away from the court, which no longer controlled the cultural life of the shattered nation.[4] The courtly decorum that had regulated the writing of poetry during the Southern Dynasties was a thing of the past, and the poet was left to develop his own personal style. The result was an increasingly private poetry and the flowering of different poetic styles.[5] Thus, it is not surprising that Li He, Wen Tingyun, and Li Shangyin each transformed Palace Style in his own way.

In what has become the definitive characterization of Li He's poetry, Du Mu 杜牧 (803–52), Li He's contemporary and himself a renowned poet, writes:

Clouds and mist gently intermingling cannot describe its manner; meandering waters cannot describe its feelings; the verdure of spring cannot describe its warmth; the clarity of autumn cannot describe its style; a mast in the wind, a horse in the battle-line cannot describe its courage; tile coffins and tripods with seal-characters cannot describe its antiquity; seasonal blossoms and lovely girls cannot describe its charms; deserted kingdoms and ruined palaces, thorny thickets and grave mounds cannot describe its resentment and sorrow; whales inhaling, turtles spurting, ox-ghosts and serpent-spirits cannot describe its extravagance and grotesqueness.

煙雲綿聯，不足為其態也；水之迢迢，不足為其情也；春之盎
盎，不足為其和也；秋之明潔，不足為其格也；風檣陣馬，不
足為其勇也；瓦棺篆鼎，不足為其古也；時花美女，不足為其
色也；荒國陊殿，梗莽邱壠，不足為其怨恨悲愁也；鯨呿鰲
擲，牛鬼蛇神，不足為其虛荒誕幻也。[6]

The variety of Li He's poetry is wonderfully evoked by Du Mu. It ranges over almost every aspect of the Chinese poetic repertoire—from social protest to personal lament, from descriptions of landscape to the depiction of the boudoir. In this chapter I will consider the two decadent aspects of Li He's poetry—namely, his adoption and transformation of the Palace Style poetry of the Southern Dynasties and his peculiar love of macabre subject and imagery, which earned him the nickname "demonic talent" (guicai 鬼才).

Du Mu clearly focuses on the unusual aspects of this rich body of work, stating that some of Li He's poetry "in searching for ways of description, depart far from the literary tradition. We cannot understand them."[7] This opinion was repeated almost verbatim by the author of Li He's official biography in Xin Tang shu 新唐書. He wrote that "his verse delights in the extraordinary and grotesque. Everything he wrote was startlingly outstanding, breaking with accepted literary tradition. No one could imitate his style at that time."[8] It is not surprising then that Li He is known to the general public mostly for his unconventional subject matter, such as demons and ghosts. It is the "ox ghosts and serpent spirits" (niugui sheshen 牛鬼蛇神) in his poetry that attract the critics' attention. Already in the Song dynasty he was labeled a "demonic talent" (guicai).[9] In a tradition that shied away from talking about supernatural creatures and phenomena,[10] this attribution would seem to demonstrate a certain uneasiness on the part of the critics. Indeed, this feeling of uneasiness had already been indicated in Du Mu's highly flattering characterization of Li He's poetry, because Du Mu describes Li He's poetry exclusively in negative terms. The best way to approach Li He's poetry, Du Mu seems to be suggesting, is to regard it as something we *cannot* know. This in turn implies that Li He's poetic works, at least those familiar to the general public, are highly unconventional, and that neither our conventional wisdom nor our wildest imagination can fully comprehend them.

Zhu Ziqing once remarked that "[Li] He's *yuefu* poetry comes from the Palace Style poetry of the Liang dynasty, and paves the path for

Wen Tingyun, Li Shangyin, and Li Qunyu 李群玉 (813–60). Encouraged by the emperor Taizong of Tang, Palace Style poetry flourished for a while, but it declined during the High Tang era. It was Li He who revived it."[11] A few pieces in Li He's oeuvre are modeled directly on the Palace Style poetry of the Southern Dynasties period, among them the following:

| 花遊曲 | EXCURSION AMONG FLOWERS: A SONG | |
|---|---|---|
| 春柳南陌態 | The air of spring willows by the southern path, | |
| 冷花寒露姿 | The look of cold blossoms with chilly dew. | |
| 今朝醉城外 | This morning, drunk outside the city walls, | |
| 拂鏡濃掃眉 | They wipe mirrors to thicken their eyebrows. | 4 |
| 煙濕愁車重 | Drizzling mist makes one worry the heavy carriages, | |
| 紅油覆畫衣 | Red oilcloth covers up the colorful dresses. | |
| 舞裙香不暖 | Their dancing skirts are perfumed but not warm, | |
| 酒色上來遲[12] | The color of wine slowly comes up to their faces. | 8 |

In his short preface to the poem Li He states that he wrote it in imitation of Xiao Gang's poetic style, to be performed by the singing girls (因採梁簡文詩調，賦花遊曲與妓彈唱). I have shown in detail in the first chapter that by the Sui and Tang dynasties the image of Palace Style poetry as represented by Xiao Gang and his followers was already fixed as the archetype of moral and artistic decadence—even the cause of social and political catastrophe. In explicitly emulating such poetry, Li He challenges the conventional views, such as those articulated by Wei Zheng and other Tang writers.[13] To Li He, Palace Style poetry is simply a poetic genre, devoid of political and social implications. Hence, like most of Xiao Gang's Palace Style poetry, Li He's piece is also lighthearted, dealing with the typical subject matter of this genre: an outing with singing girls. The flowers in the title are conventional metaphors for women. The word *qu* 曲 (song) in the title also identifies the piece with the *yuefu* genre, known for its relative fictionality because it is written in the voice of a persona.[14] The diction of the poem strongly echoes that of Palace Style convention: familiar to us by now are images of spring willows (*chunliu* 春柳), cold flowers (*lenghua* 冷花), colorful clothes (*huayi* 畫衣), dancing skirts (*wuqun* 舞裙), air (*tai* 態), and perfume (or perfumed, *xiang*

香). The activities described, such as getting drunk and putting on makeup, are also stock items in the repertoire. But in this all too familiar, imitative piece, there are also elements that differentiate it from a typical Palace Style poem. For example, instead of the erotically charged word *nuan* 暖 (warm), Li He uses the opposite, *leng* 冷 (cold) to describe the flowers in line 2, and he again suggests coldness in line 7, when he states emphatically that the fragrance from the girls' dancing skirts is "not warm" (*bunuan* 不暖).

Still, it is not for these features that Li He is remembered. Indeed, this type of imitative work is very rare in his oeuvre. More typically, he infuses his work with distinctive qualities, even if the motifs themselves are clichés. Thus, a woman putting on makeup is one of the most common subjects in Palace Style poetry, with the woman in question often turned into an object, as when a poet like Xiao Gang adopts the descriptive techniques of "poetry on objects." For a better appreciation of Li He's transformation of this convention, let us first look at a poem by Xiao Gang:

| 美人晨妝詩 | A Lovely Woman's Morning Toilette | |
|---|---|---|
| 北窗向朝鏡 | By the north window she faces the morning mirror, | |
| 錦帳復斜縈 | Twisted brocade curtains slant down by her side. | |
| 嬌羞不肯出 | Coy and blushing she is reluctant to come out, | |
| 猶言妝未成 | And says her makeup is not yet complete. | 4 |
| 散黛隨眉廣 | Kohl on her brows broadens with her eyes, | |
| 燕脂逐臉生 | Red rouge comes to life with her face. | |
| 試將持出眾 | I bet if you take her in front of the crowd, | |
| 定得可憐名¹⁵ | She will surely win the title of "The Adorable." | 8 |

Despite the woman's coy words and shy manner portrayed in lines 3–6, she is presented essentially as a precious toy. The almost rude intrusion by the poet in the last couplet indicates that the focus of the poem is actually not the woman, as its title suggests, but the poet, because the description of her manners in the first six lines only serves to advance the poet's hypothesis about this woman in the last two lines. It is he, the observer, who has the last word. The poem is skillfully structured to highlight the poet's position: the last couplet, which serves as the closure to and summary of the poem, is stated in his own voice.

Li He wrote a similar poem, but treated the subject matter differently:

| 美人梳頭歌 | A LOVELY WOMAN COMBING HER HAIR: A SONG | |
|---|---|---|
| 西施曉夢綃帳寒 | Xi Shi dreams at dawn, the silken curtains are cool, | |
| 香鬟墮髻半沉檀 | Half of her perfumed hair falls on the sandalwood pillow. | |
| 轆轤咿呀轉鳴玉 | The well windlass creaks—the turning of singing jade, | |
| 驚起芙蓉睡新足 | With a start it wakes up the newly slept lotus. | 4 |
| 雙鸞開鏡秋水光 | Twin simurghs open the mirror—two lights on an autumn water, | |
| 解鬟臨鏡立象床 | By the ivory bed she loosens her tresses in front of the mirror. | |
| 一編香絲雲撒地 | A skein of scented silk spreads on the floor like clouds, | |
| 玉釵落處無聲膩 | Jade hairpins fall down from her lustrous hair without a sound. | 8 |
| 纖手卻盤老鴉色 | Her delicate fingers pile up the color of old rook's plumage,[16] | |
| 翠滑寶釵簪不得 | Which is so sleek that the jeweled comb and hairpins cannot hold. | |
| 春風爛熳惱嬌慵 | The brilliant spring breeze vexes her lovely indolence, | |
| 十八鬟多無氣力 | Having tied eighteen knots or more her strength fails. | 12 |
| 妝成鬌鬢欹不斜 | Her toilette done, the beautiful hair sits firm without slipping, | |
| 雲裾數步踏雁沙 | In cloud skirt she dances to "A goose treading the sand." | |
| 背人不語向何處 | Silently she turns away—where is she going now? | |
| 下階自折櫻桃花[17] | Down the steps to pick herself some cherry blossoms. | 16 |

The general impression is that this woman is not portrayed as a precious, mechanical toy, or an object, but rather is a lively human being. The poet has replaced the static description of the woman's manners with the dynamic staging of her acts. The first couplet begins in the usual Palace Style manner: a beautiful woman is asleep in her bedroom. The images and diction too are from the Palace Style convention: Xi Shi is a conventional substitution for fair ladies; the silken curtains (*xiaozhang* 綃帳), the scented hair (*xianghuan* 香鬟), and sandalwood pillow (*chentan* 沉檀) are easily recognizable by readers familiar with Xiao Gang's work. The third couplet disrupts the static scene, however, with the creaking of the turning windlass and the startled awakening of the woman. *Yiya* 咿呀 (to creak or creaky), with its jarring sound and humble, colloquial origin, would be grotesquely misplaced in a Palace Style context; but it is really the word *jing* 驚 (to startle) that effectively differentiates Li He's poem from Xiao Gang's piece. It is precisely this kind of sudden movement that Xiao Gang's poem tries to avoid, since it tends to disrupt the ideal of delicate artistic balance and control. Suddenly, the woman is transformed from an inanimate object into a very lively person, an active agent.

Thus the rest of the poem portrays the woman's activity: she opens the mirror (line 5), loosens her hair (line 6), lets down her hair (lines 7 and 8), combs her hair (line 9), puts on her hairpin. Then she dances to an ancient tune (line 14) and finally goes down the steps to pluck some flowers. Except for lines 11 and 12, every couplet describes at least one act. The last line in particular is significant—no longer confined to her boudoir, as in the Palace Style convention, she is allowed out to perform a highly expressive act. The word "herself" (*zi* 自), combined with a transitive verb "to pluck" (*zhe* 折), gives her a much larger structural role than she ever enjoyed in Xiao Gang's poetry, where it is the observer poet who acts. In the present poem, the focus is on the woman's act and it is the poet who remains invisible.

All this is achieved mainly through the Palace Style convention itself, even as the poem *breaks with* that convention. For except a few terms (such as "to startle" *jing* 驚, "creaky" *yiya* 咿呀 and the characteristic "old" *lao* 老), nearly all the expressions in the poem come from the Palace Style repertoire. Besides Xi Shi, silken curtains, perfumed hair, and sandalwood pillow in the first couplet, words like "singing jade" (*mingyu* 鳴玉), "lotus blossom" (*furong* 芙蓉), "twin simurghs" (*shuangluan* 雙鸞), "autumn pool of light" (*qiushuiguang* 秋水光), "perfumed silk" (*xiangsi* 香絲)."jade haipin" (*yuchai* 玉釵), "delicate fingers" (*xianshou* 纖手), "jeweled comb" (*baochai* 寶釵), and "cloud skirt" (*yunju* 雲裾) are all standard descriptive tropes in Palace Style poetry. This common idiom demonstrates that Li He maintains a continuous relationship with it.

In pointing to the connection between Li He's work and the Palace Style poetry of Liang dynasty, Zhu Ziqing also observes that Li He "adopts an eccentric and obscure (*qipi* 奇僻) style to complement the superficiality of the Palace Style."[18] And with that style Li He transforms the old convention. "A Lovely Woman Combing Her Hair" is not the best example of this strategy, although it is hinted at by his use of unusual words like *yiya* (creaky) and *lao* (old). As has been shown, *yiya* creates a jarring effect in this context. As for *lao*, by the standard of poetic decorum it is a word to be avoided because what is "old" is diametrically opposed to the fresh female beauty that is the thematic center of the poem. In this aspect Li He resembles the English metaphysical poets, who, according to Samuel Johnson, aimed at "a kind of *discordia concors*; a combination of dissimilar images, or discovery of occult resemblance's in things apparently unlike. . . . The most heterogeneous ideas are yoked by violence together; nature and art are ransacked for illustrations, comparisons, and allusions."[19]

Remarkably, uneasiness about Li He's poetry in the Chinese tradition echoes what Johnson says of the English metaphysical poets. As early as Li He's own time, such voices were already heard. The Late Tang writer and poet Lu Guimeng 陸龜蒙 (?–881) once said, "I learned that those who hunt and fish excessively are called destroyers of nature. Nature cannot be destroyed, how can it be carved, cut, chiseled and exposed? If one lets a young life like a bud or ovum die of exposure, how could nature not punish him? Changji [Li He] died young. . . . He deserved it, he deserved it!"[20]

Lu Guimeng wrote these words after reading Li Shangyin's biographical sketch of Li He quoted at the beginning of this chapter. This anecdote not only reveals the poet's ailienation from society and his devotion to his art, it also suggests that for Li He composing poetry was already disconnected from spontaneous responses to external events and that it had become a somewhat mechanical activity to be repeated and programmed in a situation totally distinct from the poetic occasion that originally inspired the poet. For the poem—these lines pulled almost randomly from his bag—was obviously not written in one consistent act but in several disconnected ones.[21] It is not difficult to see the gap between this poetry, with its suggestion of disconnectedness and mechanicality, and the poetry dictated by the Great Preface to *The Book of Songs*, which emphasizes above all the naturalness and spontaneity of the creative process. Li He calls such poetic practice "painstaking composition" (*kuyin* 苦吟).[22] Let us now examine how he observed this poetic principle in his work.

The following is Li He's most obscure poem, the most illustrative of his effort to substitute the superficiality of the Palace Style convention with a baffling complexity:

| 惱公 | SELF-MOCKING | |
|---|---|---|
| 宋玉愁空斷 | Song Yu's heart has been broken in vain, | |
| 嬌嬈粉自紅 | Jiaorao's loveliness reddens itself. | |
| 歌聲春草露 | A song rings in dewy spring grass, | |
| 門掩杏花叢 | A gate is closed in apricot blossoms. | 4 |
| 注口櫻桃小 | Her rouged mouth is a little cherry, | |
| 添眉桂葉濃 | Her darkened eyebrows are lush cassia leaves. | |
| 曉奩妝秀靨 | Dawn at her vanity, she powders her pretty face, | |
| 夜帳減香筒 | Night inside curtains, incense fades from its tube. | 8 |
| 鈿鏡飛孤鵲 | A solitary magpie flies on the inlaid mirror, | |
| 江圖畫水葓 | Waterweed is painted on a riverscape screen. | |
| 陂陀梳碧鳳 | Up and down she combs her blue phoenix hair, | |
| 腰裊帶金蟲 | Along with it move the golden insect hairpins. | 12 |
| 杜若含清靄 | An iris is filled with transparent mist, | |
| 河浦聚紫茸 | A cattail is surrounded by purple shoots. | |
| 月分蛾黛破 | Her darked eyebrows are separate crescent moons, | |
| 花合靨朱融 | Her reddened cheeks are folded flowers. | 16 |
| 髮重疑盤霧 | Her heavy hair reminds one of coiling mist, | |
| 腰輕乍倚風 | Her slender waist leans on the wind. | |
| 密書題豆蔻 | She writes secret letters on cardamoms, | |
| 隱語笑芙蓉 | And laughs at the secret meaning of the word "lotus." | 20 |
| 莫鎖茱萸匣 | "Do not lock up the dogwood box, | |
| 休開翡翠籠 | Nor open the kingfisher-feather cage!" | |
| 弄珠驚漢燕 | Playing with pearls she frightens the Han swallows, | |
| 燒蜜引胡蜂 | Burning honey she allures the Hu bees. | 24 |
| 醉纈抛紅網 | She spreads out a dotted red net, | |
| 單羅掛綠蒙 | And hangs up a green gauze bird trap. | |
| 數錢教姹女 | She teaches her maid to count money, | |
| 買藥問巴賨 | And asks her page to buy medicine. | 28 |

| 勻臉安斜雁 | She balances her cheeks by putting on geese in flight, | |
|---|---|---|
| 移燈想夢熊 | And moves the lamp while contemplating dreams of bears.[23] | |
| 腸攢非束竹 | Her knotted intestines are not tied bamboo, | |
| 胲急是張弓 | Her tight belly is a taut bow. | 32 |
| 晚樹迷新蝶 | Evening trees entice new butterflies, | |
| 殘蜺憶斷虹 | Fading female rainbow longs for a vanished male. | |
| 古時填渤澥 | In ancient times a bird tried to fill up an ocean, | |
| 今日鑿崆峒 | Nowadays someone aims to cut a road through Mount Kongdong. | 36 |
| 繡杳褰長幔 | Embroidered ropes lift up long curtains, | |
| 羅裙結短封 | Silken skirt is tied at its short seam. | |
| 心搖如舞鶴 | Her heart flutters about like a dancing crane, | |
| 骨出似飛龍 | Her bones stand out like a flying dragon. | 40 |
| 井檻淋清漆 | Clear lacquer drops from the fence of the well, | |
| 門鋪綴白銅 | The door-knockers are molded in bronze. | |
| 隈花開兔徑 | A rabbit track opens along the hidden flowers, | |
| 向壁印狐蹤 | Fox traces are printed by the walls. | 44 |
| 玳瑁釘簾薄 | The tortoiseshell-studded blinds are thin, | |
| 琉璃疊扇烘 | The emerald folding-screens are warm. | |
| 象床緣素柏 | Ivory-bed has sides of white cypress, | |
| 瑤席卷香蔥 | Jade-mat rolls up fragrant water-shallot. | 48 |
| 細管吟朝幌 | At dawn she plays a fine flute by the curtains, | |
| 芳醪落夜楓 | At dusk maple leaves fall on scented wine-lees. | |
| 宜男生楚巷 | The Boy-producing grass grows in the lanes of Chu, | |
| 梔子發金墉 | Gardenias blossom along the golden walls. | 52 |
| 龜甲開屏澀 | Tortoiseshell screens are rough to open, | |
| 鵝毛滲墨濃 | Goose-feather brush is soaked with dark ink. | |
| 黃庭留衛瓘 | "The Yellow Courtyard" makes Wei Guan stay, | |
| 綠樹養韓憑 | The green trees feed the Han Ping birds. | 56 |
| 雞唱星懸柳 | Cocks crow, stars hang above the willows, | |
| 鴉啼露滴桐 | Crows cry, dew drops from the plane trees. | |
| 黃娥初出座 | The yellow beauty comes out to take her seat, | |
| 寵妹始相從 | And her little sisters follow in train. | 60 |
| 蠟淚垂蘭爐 | Waxen tears are falling down the vanishing orchid stamen, | |

| | |
|---|---|
| 秋蕪掃綺籠 | With an autumn-grass broom she sweeps the ornate lattice. |
| 吹笙翻舊引 | She plays an old tune on her windpipe, |
| 沽酒待新豐 | And waits for the wine from Xinfeng. 64 |
| 短佩愁塡粟 | Her sorrow is the grains engraved on her short pendants, |
| 長弦怨削菘 | The long-stringed zither moans under her slender fingers. |
| 曲池眠乳鴨 | In the crooked pond the ducklings are sleeping, |
| 小閣睡娃僮 | In the small pavilion the young maids are slumbering. 68 |
| 褥縫參雙線 | Her mattress is sewn with double thread, |
| 鉤縚辮五總 | And the hooked belts are woven of five braids. |
| 蜀煙飛重錦 | Mist from Shu flies over the fine brocade quilt, |
| 峽雨濺輕容 | Rain from the gorges sprinkles her silken robe. 72 |
| 拂鏡羞溫嶠 | She rubs the mirror, shy before Wen Jiao, |
| 燻衣避賈充 | And flees from Jia Chong in perfumed dress. |
| 魚生玉藕下 | Fish grow under jade lotus roots, |
| 人在石蓮中 | People reside within stone lotus. 76 |
| 含水灣蛾翠 | Mouth full of water, she knits her dark moth-brows, |
| 登樓渜馬鬃 | And ascends the tower to spray the horse's mane. |
| 使君居曲陌 | The governor lives in a winding street, |
| 園令住臨邛 | The Guardian of the Royal Tombs dwells in Linqiong. 80 |
| 桂火流蘇暖 | A cassia fire makes warm her curtains, |
| 金爐細炷通 | From the gold censer come wisps of smoke. |
| 春遲王子態 | The son of Wang shows his manners on this late spring day, |
| 鶯囀謝娘慵 | The indolent lady Xie sings in her oriole throat. 84 |
| 玉漏三星曙 | The jade waterclock ticks while the Three Stars tell dawn, |
| 銅街五馬逢 | In Bronze Camel Street she meets the five-horse carriage. |
| 犀株防膽怯 | Rhinoceros are capable of preventing fear, |
| 銀液鎮心忪 | Mercury fluid can calm the fluttering of heart. 88 |
| 跳脫看年命 | She uses a bracelet to predict her destiny, |
| 琵琶道吉凶 | And strums her *pi-pa* to tell good and ill fortune. |

| | |
|---|---|
| 王時應七夕 | "The auspicious time occurs on the Seventh Night, |
| 夫位在三宮 | And your lover has a post in the Triple Palaces." 92 |
| 無力塗雲母 | He has no strength to put powdered mica on his feet, |
| 多方帶藥翁 | So he has to bring with him prescriptions from a doctor. |
| 符因青鳥送 | The amulet is sent by the blue bird, |
| 囊用絳紗縫 | The bag is sewn with red silk. 96 |
| 漢苑尋官柳 | He passed the willows in the royal park, |
| 河橋閡禁鐘 | River bridges blocked the sound of curfew. |
| 月明中婦覺 | In the bright moonlight his wife wakes up, |
| 應笑畫堂空²⁴ | She should laugh to find the colorful room empty. 100 |

In many ways this is one of the most unusual and one of the most difficult poems in Chinese poetry, never selected by anthologists and rarely mentioned by critics. Written in the form of "extended regulated verse" *pailü* 排律, the poem consists entirely, except for the last two lines, of antithetical couplets. The technical complexity of the piece, combined with its playful title, indicates that it is a poetic exercise. It suggests an overwhelming concern with the technical feature of the poem, which is what the term *kuyin* has come to be associated with.[25] This challenges the traditional exegetical principle of *zhiren lunshi* 知人論世 (to explore the life and world of the author) and explains why several interpretations conducted in the light of this principle have proved unsatisfactory. For example, traditional poetic exegesis dictated by the notion of poetry established in the Great Preface stipulates that a poem should first be situated in a concrete historical context in order to establish its referentiality. A personal story from the life of the poet often provides such a context. This is probably why in Chinese literary studies compiling the authors' chronicles (*nianpun* 年譜) has proved to be an ever-popular enterprise and is often regarded as the cornerstone of any critical study of an author's work. The same holds for the interpretations of Li He's works, even though the eccentricity of Li He's poetic practice as recounted in Li Shangyin's biographical sketch has cast considerable doubt on such an approach. This is not to deny, though, some of Li He's works do have historical contexts, and that in studying them one must situate them historically.[26] But this approach is inadequate when it is applied to a work like "Self-Mocking," because its central concern is not merely to narrate a personal story or historical event but also to display the poet's masterful control of this difficult poetic form.

Not surprisingly, some critics have tried to naturalize this poem by making it into a narrative of a personal experience. The following is offered by the Qing scholar Wu Yanmu 吳炎牧:

[The poet] saw the color and heard the sound; a strong passion [for the woman] took possession of him. He dreamed of her beauty, as if she were right in front of him. He imagined her manners, and through a matchmaker communicated his love to her. They then set up a time for a tryst. When he got to her place, he entered by door, followed the path; then by wall and screen curtains he reached her bedside. In front of winecups they swore their oath and wrote of their love. They enjoyed the pleasure of love during the long night, but soon had to bid farewell to each other as dawn approached. The woman left her seat to see him off. Holding his hands she urged him to come for another meeting. Surprise, happiness, sadness, fear—all are described in great depth and subtlety. The beginning and the ending of the poem are nearly perfect. The readers tend to notice only its colorfulness and brilliance but to ignore its complex structure.

見色聞聲，遂切思慕；心懷彼美，彷彿儀容。揣摩情態，始因媒而通芳訊。繼定約而想佳期。當赴招時，由門而徑，由壁而簾屏，而及床席。對酒盟心，題詩鳴愛。方乘歡于永夜，又惜別于終宵。美人之出座相送，攜手叮嚀，再圖良會。驚喜悲恐，曲盡綢繆。篇中起結不爽絲黍。讀者但見其色之濃麗，而忽其法之婉密。[27]

This interpretation really smooths away many difficulties. Wu tries to turn this otherwise extremely twisted work into a coherent story with a beginning, middle, and end. Ye Congqi even attempts to determine the time of Li He's affair with the woman in the poem by connecting this verse to Li He's other pieces.[28] But such interpretations simply do not hold up—the text gives the reader a very different impression and in some places even contradicts these interpretations. Wu's complaint—that one tends to ignore the complex structure of the poem and notice only its colorful diction—is precisely the point, for the meaning production of the poem does emphasize the individual performance of certain metaphors, allusions, and images, instead of, and often at the expense of, the general structure of the poem. Wang Qi has suggested that since it is a playful exercise, we need not bother the several incomprehensible passages because the reading should strive for a general understanding of its meaning.[29] But he is wrong. Rather, the specifics of poetry constitute its meaning, and one can never reach a general understanding by ignoring its specifics.

The poem begins with two allusions that point to two different directions of the Chinese poetic tradition. Song Yu 宋玉 (fl. late third century B.C.) is one of the greatest poets of the *Chuci* genre. Three of his *fu* poems, "Shenü fu" 神女賦, "Gaotang fu" 高唐賦, and "Dengtuzi haose fu" 登徒子好色賦, are primary thematic and linguistic sources of Chinese amorous poetry.[30] Because in the second piece he is accused of being dissolute, it seems that Li He is alluding to this piece.[31] The implication seems to be that the hero is a talented, romantic poet like Song Yu. Jiaorao refers to the titular woman in an early *yuefu* poem "Dong Jiaorao" 董嬌嬈. Because she reappears so often in the works of later poets, she has become an epithet for fair women in general.[32] Ye Congqi and Frodsham take the reference to Song Yu as a self-reference on the part of the poet and the name Jiaorao as a substitute for the woman with whom the poet had been involved.[33] Since self-identification (*zikuang* 自況, that is, the identification of the poet with the person or object he is describing) is by Li He's time already a firmly established convention in Chinese poetry, this point could be accepted without much suspicion, at least at this point.

The antithesis in the first couplet (mainly through the two adverbs *kong* 空 "in vain" and *zi* 自 "itself") establishes two contrasting mental states: the helplessness of the man and the self-assurance of the woman. He is desperately, hopelessly in love with this beautiful woman, who does not seem to care about his sufferings. Thus the first couplet seems to establish a narrative framework by introducing the characters and their respective mental conditions. From the third line on, as the poet begins to describe the woman's environment, we step into a world of Palace Style poetry. The remarkable affinity with the Palace Style convention is revealed in the highly artificial, florid diction and the effort to confine the content to the world of the boudoir. But Li He also introduces elements that subvert this poetic world and its conventions, as we will see later.

The description in line 3 starts with an outdoor scene. The first image of the poem is auditory, the sound of song, which creates a mysterious impression because of its nonvisual quality. But even as this couplet begins the process of depiction, there is a reluctance to open this secluded world to the outside, for in line 4 we find that the gate is closed. Nevertheless, we manage to penetrate it, for line 5 brings us right into the woman's bedroom, where we find her in the midst of her toilette. Lines 7 and 8 hint at a long night of activity, since by early dawn the incense inside the curtain is still fading. From line 9 to line 18 the focus is entirely on the physical appearance of the woman and her highly decorated world—on the mirror, the screen, her hair, her eyebrows, her face, and her waist. Metaphor is the predominant figure of speech, as the woman is described as flowers (lines 13 and 14), and her eyebrows and cheeks are portrayed as crescent moons and folded blossoms (lines 15 and 16). Her hair is compared with mist (line 17), and her waist is portrayed as being so slender as to be moving with wind (line 18). In lines 19 and 20 the focus shifts from the physical features of the woman to the activity in her bedroom. The agent of the two acts, *shu* 書 (to write), and *xiao* 笑 (to laugh), is not clear. I take it as the woman, but that is not the only possibility.[34] Cardamom flower symbolizes love because its stamen has two parallel petals. The other name for lotus (*furong* 芙蓉) is *lian* 蓮, a homophone for *lian* 憐, which means "love." The use of image and pun in these two lines are evocative of the southern folk song tradition that had greatly influenced the works of Southern Dynasties court poets. Li He, we see, is aware of this poetic convention.

So far the description has been conducted from a third-person point of view; the perspective is distanced and the voice detached. But in lines 21 and 22 the text abruptly shifts to an imperative mode. The subject is omitted, but it seems to be the woman who is giving the orders: "Do not lock up the purple brocade box,/ Nor open the kingfisher-feather basket." After this abrupt interruption, the poem abruptly returns in lines 23 to 26 to a description of the woman's activities: she plays with pearls to entertain her guest, burns honey to attract bees, and hangs up dotted net to catch birds.[35] These are activities of the Palace Style convention, precisely what one expects of a courtesan or a singing girl. But in lines 27 and 28 the poet suddenly introduces into this highly ornate and refined world activities more suitable to a housewife in common household: she teaches her maid to handle money and tells her page what medicine to buy! The effect is jarring and Li He further accentuates this anticlimax by abandoning florid language for commonplace diction such as *shuqian* 數錢 (to count money), and *maiyao* 買藥 (to buy medicine).[36] The irony is unmistakable. By bringing into the world of Palace Style poetry elements that poets writing in the genre had taken pains to avoid, Li He undermines it.

In line 29 the poem shifts back to the florid Palace Style. Having given orders to her servants, the woman is then made to sit at her dresser powdering her face, and in the next line she moves her lamp and contemplates having baby boys. The matter of time is problematic in this couplet. In line 29 she is putting on (*an* 安) makeup, usually a morning activity, but the activity in line 30 clearly happens at night. Ye Congqi seems to have detected this inconsistency, since in his paraphrase line 29 describes the woman *removing* her makeup in preparation for going to bed.[37] The gap between the activities and time shifts described in lines 27–28 and 29–30 suggests this is not a coherent narrative sequence, and therefore casts into doubt the attempt to connect the poem to a particular event in the poet's life.[38] Abundant proofs in the poem show that the content, especially the narrative content, is not the most important factor and cannot guide our reading. Rather, it is the formal features of the poem that are consistently foregrounded, often at the expense of the content.[39]

The allusions in lines 35 and 36 illustrate the point. Line 35 refers to the story of Nüwa, the daughter of Yandi (Emperor Yan), a legendary ruler of China. According to the story, Nüwa was drowned in the ocean, and to avenge her death, she transformed herself into a Jingwei bird and every day carried stones in her beak to fill up the ocean.[40] Line 36 is an ambiguous reference, because Kongdong Mountain has several different stories attached to it, each with a different meaning.[41] Ye Congqi seems (I say "seems" because he does not make it clear in his annotation of this line) to take it to refer to the mountain near Linru, a town in Henan province. But Frodsham takes this as referring the story of Yugong (Master Simple in his translation) who set out to remove two mountains and finally succeeded with a god's help.[42] How is one to relate these explanations to the thematic structure of the poem?

Ye Conqi paraphrases these two lines as follows and carefully avoids tackling the possible implications of the second story: "Since ancient times sad ladies and deserted women can only throw themselves into the ocean with the attempt to fill it up like the Jingwei [bird], but nowadays they can overcome obstacles and seek their future."[43] Frodsham offers an entirely different interpretation of these two lines: "She is hopelessly in love with someone. . . . Her efforts to forget her love are as vain as those of the Jingwei bird that tried to fill in the Eastern Sea or Master Simple of North Mountain who set out to remove Mount T'ai-hang and Mount Wang-wu. Alternatively, the lines might well refer to Ho's [Li He's] efforts to gain her love, which though seemingly hopeless were finally crowned with success."[44] These explanations seem to contradict the narrative framework set up in the first couplet of the poem, because it is suggested there that it is the man who is hopelessly in love with the self-assured woman, not the other way around. That Frodsham offers explanations that give two completely different narrative contexts shows how difficult it is to naturalize this part of the text in the light of a personal story. What is more, these interpretations do not solve the difficulties involved, because they seem unable to answer such simple questions as "Why these allusions are used?" and "What their relations are to the preceding and following sections of the poem?" Ye Congqi probably realizes how abrupt this couplet is, but he tries to explain it away by arguing that "these two lines are the turning point of the poem. Up till now the poem has been describing [the woman's] morning toilette and play, until she goes to bed in sadness. From now on it begins to depict boudoir, curtains, partying, sojourn for the night, and departure."[45] First, this paraphrase is inaccurate (there is little "sadness" *chou* 愁 in the preceding section), but more important, it does not at all consider the significance of the allusions themselves. Why should the turning point, if there is one, of a boudoir poem be signified by two mythological stories of universal proportions? Is there any connection between this structural, syntactical change and these two morally charged legends? These questions apparently remain unanswered, because the link we are seeking is conspicuously lacking.

The contextual disjunction caused by this couplet not only discredits the attempt to view the text (at least this part of the text) as a coherent narrative sequence, but it also violates the formal unity that is essential in lyric poetry. It makes it impossible for the readers either to experience vicariously the events described in the text, which is typical of a narrative experience, or to identify with them, which is typical of a lyrical experience.⁴⁶ The disjunction does, however, foreground the couplet itself, as their obscurity demands the reader's attention, and this in turn greatly highlights their roles in the text. Contrary to Ye Congqi's smoothing away of this difficult section of the text, our reading finds it irksome and forces us to try to solve the difficulty and the puzzle. As a result, we know so much about the legends themselves that they tend to overwhelm the structural unity of the poem.

After this interruption, the poem resumes its description of the woman and her world. Lines 37 and 38 describe the bedroom furnishings and her clothes. The next two lines move inward and use two striking metaphors to portray her mental and physical being: her fluttering heart is compared to a dancing crane, and her bony body is envisaged as a flying dragon. Once more the woman as portrayed here contradicts her image in the second line where she is described as lovely and flourishing (*fenzihong* 粉自紅). Is this in fact the same woman? If so, and if this poem narrates a romantic affair of the poet, how can the heroine change so dramatically within such a short period, presumally one night?

In lines 41–42 the description moves outside and gives some hint of the secluded and somewhat mysterious place where the woman lives. Phrases like *tujing* 兔徑 (rabbit track) and *huzong* 狐蹤 (fox traces) in lines 43 and 44 indicate the difference between this woman and the archetype Jiaorao because in the *yuefu* poem where she first makes her appearance she is seen "by the east road of Luoyang town,/ Where peaches and plums grow by its sides."⁴⁷ The change from a public to a private location is not merely a change of narrative or descriptive locus. It also signifies an important modification of the earlier *yuefu* poetry, as had already occurred in the works of Southern Dynasties poets, and the increasing tendency toward a more private, personal poetry as opposed to the sociopolitical type of the classical tradition.⁴⁸

Characteristically this outdoor vision is not sustained very long, as the poem again moves inside the boudoir in line 45 to describe such luxurious furnishings as tortoiseshell blinds (line 45), emerald screens (line 46), an ivory bed (47), and a jade mat (line 48). Line 49 to line 56 describe a series of activities: singing, drinking, and writing (presumably of love letters). But interspersed in them are lines 51 and 52, which portray two symbolic plants. They not only interrupt the activities, but are again difficult to interpret, because their structural role is not at all clear. "The boy-producing grass" (*yinan* 宜男) is an auspicious plant thought to be able to increase the chance of giving birth to a male child. "Gardenias" (*zhizi* 栀子) are plants associated with love. As they are described as growing in two places separated by a long distance, we might follow Ye Congqi in taking this to mean that the lovers come from places far apart but are brought together by love.[49] But even this far-fetched interpretation[50] does not answer the question: Why does this couplet appears at this juncture? Is it related to the preceding and following parts of the poem, which depict the activities in the woman's bedroom? If it is meant to provide the information of the woman and her guest, which seems plausible, why does it come so late in the poem?

Further complicating matters are the two irreconcilable allusions in the next two lines. Wei Guan in line 55 was a famous calligrapher of the Jin dynasty.[51] "The Yellow Courtyard" is a Daoist classic. The relationship of the calligrapher and this document is unknown, but Wang Qi, Ye Congqi, and Frodsham all agree that Wei must have transcribed this classic work. Following Wang Qi, Ye Congqi takes this to be a metaphor for good calligraphy, but his paraphrase of this line does not make it clear who is compared with Wei Guan, the woman or her guest.[52] Frodsham takes the woman to be the one who is writing and therefore understands the comparison to be between her and Wei Guan.[53] Then there is the word *liu* 留 (to preserve, to detain). Ye Congqi and Frodsham think this refers to woman's plea for her guest to stay. The confusion is intensified in line 56, which alludes to some past tragic love story. Han Ping was a government official in the state of Song during the Warring States period. His lord, who had an eye on his beautiful wife, threw him into prison, where he died. His wife then committed suicide. The infuriated king had the two bodies buried separately, but in their separate tombs there grew two trees whose branches eventually become entangled in an embrace. In the branches of the trees two birds would come and sing. Han Ping birds, later named for Han Ping,[54] are "symbols of undying love," as Frodsham puts it.[55] But what has this beautiful, yet tragic love story to do with the present situation? Or more specifically, what is the relationship between the allusions in the two lines of the couplet? It is required both metrically and structurally that the antithetical items within the couplet parallel each other not only grammatically, but also semantically, so that they can set each other off or complement each other.[56] But can we understand the two lines better by relating "Yellow Courtyard" (*huangting* 黃庭) to "Green trees" (*lushu* 綠樹), or by comparing Wei Guan with Han Ping? The answer seems to be no, as the vast differences in meaning only add to our confusion, except for the strong visual impression evoked by the contrast between two colors (yellow and green). Ye Congqi and Frodsham offer no clarification. They merely retell the story and shun any explanation, especially the significance of the second line of this couplet.

Lines 57 and 58 seem relatively straightforward, but they also do not lend themselves to an interpretation that sees the poem in terms of a personal event. Since cockcrow (*jichang* 雞唱) is traditionally associated with dawn, and the cry of crow (*yati* 鴉啼) is usually a metaphor for dusk, the couplet indicates two different times of the day, not "late into the night," as Wang Qi and Ye Congqi would have it. Although the following section of the text does seem to be describing night activities, to incorporate two antithetical parts of the couplet into one simply because it lends itself to a particular interpretation (as Wang and Ye seem to be doing) is to distort the structure of the poem and to ignore its characteristic complexity. The problem, I believe, arises from the tension between the need for a narrative sequence and the formal requirements of parallelism.[57] In the context of a narrative framework the poem is certainly easier to comprehend if both lines describe one temporal point, but it would be a structural violation of parallelism to do so because *difference* is essential. Thus, *jichang* 雞唱 (cockcrow) has to be paralleled by *yati* 鴉啼 (crow cry), not only because they are of the same grammatical structure (both consist of a noun-adjective and a noun) and category (both are birds), but also because semantically they have different meanings. The structure of regulated verse itself therefore works to undercut the attempt to interpret the poem in a strictly narrative sense. And indeed in this poem the formal feature is consistently privileged at the expense of other factors, such as narrative content and sequence. Moreover, artistically speaking the antithesis and difference between the two lines should not then be explained away, for that would greatly diminish the charm of the poem. Hence, the contrast betweem the day scene and a night scene in this couplet is visually effective and would be lost if we read it simply as a description of night.

The next eight lines (59–66) describe another series of nighttime activities in the woman's boudoir. "The yellow beauty" (*huang'e* 黃娥), perhaps another name for the same woman, is the focus in this section. She emerges from inside acompanied by her maids (lines 59–60). The agent or the agents of the activities in the next six lines are not made clear. Instead of the "yellow beauty" herself as I translated, it might also be one or several of her maids, especially for the menial act of dusting the window lattice. As for the singing performances in lines 63–66, they could be done by either the woman or her maids.

The point of view of the poem moves out of the woman's boudoir in lines 67 and 68 to a description of a secluded outdoor world. The slumbering ducks in the pond and young maids in the small pavilion emphasize the lateness of the hour and the sense of quiet. But the poem returns inside immediately in lines 69 and 70, where the description shifts to the most private part of the boudoir—namely, the woman's mattress and her belts. One of the poem's erotic hints comes in the next couplet, since "Rain from the gorges" (*xiayu* 峽雨) is a standard trope for sexual pleasure.[58]

The allusions in lines 73 and 74 are another example of Li He's disguising a simple meaning beneath complicated references, so much so that the tenor tends to be replaced by the vehicle. Both of the stories are taken from *Shishuo xinyu* 世說新語, a collection of anecdotes of the intellectuals from the late Han to Jin periods.[59] Wen Jiao was a recent widower. He was asked by one of his relatives to find a spouse for the young daughter in the family. But he himself was interested in the girl; so when the time came to introduce the candidate to the family, he presented himself and gave a mirror to the girl as an engagement gift.[60] Jia Chong was a minister whose daughter fell in love with his handsome retainer, Han Shou. Jia Chong smelled perfume on Han Shou, and knowing that only his daughter had that particular kind of perfume, he discovered their liaison and married her to Han.[61] If the meaning of this couplet is simply that "the woman is shy before her guest," as Ye Congqi claims, Li He certainly takes a long detour to arrive at his destination. In conventional texts, allusions help to elaborate and expand the meaning, but this is not the case here. Rather, these two allusions obtain the status of independent stories or texts within the text. This status is enhanced by the fact that the acts denoted by the key verbs in these two lines, "shy" *xiu* 羞 and "flee" *bi* 避, are not used in the original sources. We must therefore look for a connection between them and the present context. We will find, as a result, that our understanding of the two allusions is superbly clear, but our understanding of their relationship to the main body of the text remains at least murky.

Lines 75 and 76 again use puns. *Yu* 魚(fish) is a homophone of *yu* 娛, which means "pleasure," and *ou* 藕 (lotus) is pronounced in the same way as *ou* 偶 (spouse). The erotic overtone is manifest because it can also mean "pleasure comes from [being together with one's] spouse, or copulation." Similarly *ren* 人 is a homophone for *ren* 仁, which in this context means "seed"; and *lian* 蓮, as has been explained earlier, has the same pronounciation as *lian* 憐, or "love" and as *lian* 連, or "connection." We thus have a complex meaning production, and the poet's sense of pleasure at playing with words.

Lines 77 and 78 are taken to be specific descriptions of the guest's departure (Frodsham), or the woman's attempt to detain him (Ye). Frodsham, quoting Suzuki, says, "It was the custom for singing girls to spray the mane of their lover's horse with water when he left."[62] Ye Congqi observes that "this admittedly most difficult couplet, when closely read together with the preceding and following couplets, clearly describes the woman's insistent plea to her guest not to leave."[63] While Ye avoids tackling this couplet verbatim by providing a general paraphrase, Frodsham as a translator cannot do so because he needs to make specific commitment in his rendering of it. Thus, based on the understanding that it describes the departure of the woman's guest, he translates this couplet as "She knits her blue eyebrows, mouth full of water,/From the terrace she sprays his horse's mane." This translation is a good example of sacrificing specific verbal meaning for the sake of a general understanding, because the first word of the second line *deng* 登 (to ascend) is deliberately mistranslated to avoid an insurmountable obstacle. "To ascend the tower to spray the horse's mane," which is the literal rendering of the second line 登樓灑馬鬃, seems absurd because common sense tells us that one does not keep a visitor's horse on the top level of the building. More importantly, a faithful rendering like this will ruin the comfortable interpretation that these two lines depict a parting ceremony that is more likely to take place outside the building. To avoid this, Frodsham translates *denglou* 登樓 ("to ascend the tower") into *From the terrace*, (my emphasis). To translate *lou* 樓 into "terrace" is a deliberate misrendering because *lou* is usually translated into "tower" or "building." Frodsham's translation also changes the verb *deng* 登 (to ascend) into a preposition "from," thereby reversing the direction of the movement described in this line.[64]

The allusions in the next two lines present a similar difficulty.[65] The governor refers to the one in an early *yuefu* poem "Mulberry Trees by the Road" 陌上桑.[66] He makes unwanted advances toward the beautiful heroine Luofu and is rejected by her. The Guardian of the Royal Tombs in Linqiong alludes to the story of the Han poet Sima Xiangru who, on his way to take up his post, enticed the lovely widow Zhuo Wenjun to elope with him.[67] The two stories seem irreconcilable because the governor and Sima Xiangru represent two extremes in romantic affairs: one is stupid and clumsy, the other talented and successful. What is the purpose of bringing them together? Which of them is compared to the guest? If the guest is compared to Sima Xiangru—if the poet were the guest then it would certainly be possible that he would compare himself to Sima Xiangru, because he actually did this in a number of occasions[68] —then what is the function of the governor? Ye Congqi takes them to mean the same thing, and his interpretation of these two lines is nearly meaningless: "Lines 79 and 80 describe the detaining of the guest. 'Winding street' was where Luofu picked mulberry leaves, and the governor was able to live there. Lingqiong was where Wenjun used to live, and Xiangru was able to stay there."[69]

Frodsham takes note of the apparent gap between the two allusions, but explains it away with an ingenious twist: "Presumably these two lines are spoken by the girl, who is comparing herself to the modest Lo-fu of the 'Mulberry Trees by the Road' and her lover (Li Ho?) to the romantic poet, Ssu-ma Hsiang-ju. The governor would then be a rejected admirer."[70] Frodsham also links these two lines with lines 85 and 86. After describing a warm, indolent bedroom atmosphere and the loving play of the woman (Lady Xie, which is the generic name for pretty woman at that time) and her guest (the son of the powerful Wang clan, which is a generic name for young man from aristocratic families)[71] in lines 81–84, the poet moves outdoors and refers for the second time to the "Mulberry Tress by the Road" in line 86, for in that poem the governor was also riding in a five-horse carriage. Frodsham takes these two lines to mean that the woman had received advances from another official but rejected him in favor of Li He. This is a rare instance where the urge for a narrative sequence seems to have brought about some solution to an otherwise impossible issue in the poem. But the change of perspectives is still baffling. If lines 78 and 79 describe a parting scene, as all commentators agree, then why does the focus of the poem move inside the boudoir in lines 81 to 84 before moving outside again in lines 85 and 86? Are there more than one partings in the poem? Might it be that the poet is not describing his own experience, but is imagining the activities of the others visiting a singing house?[72]

Lines 87 and 88 hint at the girl's mental state—frightened and anxious—which once more contradicts her representation at the beginning of the poem. In search of relief, she visits a fortuneteller (lines 89 and 90). Lines 91 and 92 seem to be the prediction of the fortuneteller. Then, from line 93 on, the descriptive perspective shifts, again somewhat abruptly, from the girl to the guest. It is said that putting powdered mica on one's feet can help a person avoid stumbling while walking on thorns. Unable to use such magical means, he is forced to rely on the prescriptions of ordinary doctors. The weak physical condition of the guest suggested by these two lines certainly provides some encouragement for commentators like Ye Congqi. He could identify him with the poet himself,[73] who died of an illness at the age of twenty-six. Lines 95 and 96 use two allusions. "Blue bird" (*qingniao* 青鳥) once served as a messanger from the Queen of the West 西王母 to Emperor Wu of Han.[74] It later became a common trope for messenger, particularly between lovers. The red silk bag in line 96 is supposed to be able to ward off misfortune. Together they seem to be suggesting a parting scene: the lovers agreed to find a messenger to keep them in communication, and the girl gave her lover a bag as a token.[75]

The last four lines are the most straightforward section of the entire poem. They seem to describe the departure of the guest and therefore the ending of a night-long adventure. As he walks under the palace willows and crosses the bridge, he imagines his wife[76] waking up in her empty but colorful room at midnight, and surprisingly, he imagines her laughing at finding herself alone. Both Wang Qi and Ye Congqi point out the strangeness of the word *xiao* 笑 (to laugh) in this context, since conventionally a poet would use the word *yuan* 怨 (to lament) to end a poem like this. But they both prefer to explain the use of the word as "endowing the poem with a subtle and deep meaning."[77] Besides being vague—what meaning are they talking about?—this reading is an attempt to use a conventional presumption to interpret a very unconventional text. It is hard to miss the irreverent, mocking attitude implied by the word *xiao* in this context, especially in a situation where one usually expects tears rather than laughter. But it is this mocking spirit, rather than the moral seriousness indicated by Wang Qi and Ye Congqi, that is consistent with the overall tendency of the poem, as is already suggested by its title.

The point of such a long, detailed, and sometimes tortured reading of this most intricate poem is that Li He has overhauled the Palace Style convention. In Palace Style poetry meaning is always on the surface and the text is always easy to penetrate. Li He's poem adopts the diction and the subject matter of this convention, but to opposite effects, with its hidden meaning and dense language. Like most of Palace Style poetry, "Self-Mocking" is also a display of poetic skill. But while in the works of Xiao Gang such a display tends to become monotonous and predictable after a few readings, Li He's poetry holds the reader's interest by first hinting at the poem's meaning and then frustrating the attempts to fathom it. My reading of "Self-Mocking" has shown how he first introduces the readers into a path, leads them for a while, and then suddenly leaves them without any signposts. At the poem's opening he leads us to believe that it is going to be a narrative of a love adventure. The mention of two highly evocative names, Song Yu and Jiaorao, in the first couplet offers the promise of a love story. But as the poem develops it becomes impossible to interpret some key passages in terms of a narrative framework, although such framework is never completely destroyed and is restored by the end. Consequently "Self-Mocking" has become a never fulfilled and never exhausted possibility. The destination is always in sight but at the same time forever receding. Each new reading brings with it new promises, but with them new problems as well. Line 33 of the poem, "Evening trees entice new butterflies" 晚樹迷新蝶, can serve as a metaphor for the relationship between this poem and its readers. Like misty trees in the dusk that allure the butterflies to them, the poem both entices its readers and leads them astray, for the Chinese word *mi* 迷 carries *simultaneously* two meanings, "to charm" and to "mislead."

Thus, an obscure work like "Self-Mocking" offers readers a unique experience, different from both Palace Style poetry and the works of High Tang poets like Wang Wei, where language is quickly penetrated and the main task is a full appreciation of the poetic state presented in the text.[78] In reading "Self-Mocking" trying to penetrate language *is* the main, if not the only, task. This is because whatever meaning is offered in one part of the text is quickly blocked and undermined in the next, and that language is deliberately foregrounded to defer and even substitute meaning. Opacity, allusiveness, involution of language and the ensuing difficulties are all intended to generate their own meaning.

It is tempting to speculate whether this rich, yet baffling poem is the necessary result of Li He's eccentric poetic practice as recounted by Li Shangyin.[79] What is clear is that a poem like this is not written as a spontaneous response to a historical event. On a large scale Li He's "Self-Mocking" makes a mockery of the orthodoxy of the Chinese poetic tradition, specifically, of the view that poetry must be a sincere, spontaneous expression of one's personal experience. It mocks the view that poetry must be written in the most simple and transparent medium, and finally it mocks the *zhiren lunshi* exegetical principle. This attitude is conveyed, as we have seen, by the deliberately dazzling and puzzling textual strategies. It is also suggested by the irreverent laughter in the last line of the poem, a laughter that has baffled nearly all its commentators. This poem is a playful reminder that poetry could be written for purely artistic purpose and as a verbal play. Consequently, it does not lend itself to traditional exegetical practice.

This tendency toward opacity and involution greatly reinforces the artificial nature of a work like this, and artificiality, we might recall, is a hallmark of decadence, a reflection of the desire for artistic control. This too links Li He with the Palace Style convention. Nevertheless, his densely allusive and intricately involved style in "Self-Mocking" represents a unique approach. Li He's poetry also displays a passion for figuration, especially kenning, since this substitute figure readily transforms the natural into the artificial. The following is one of his most famous poems:

| 夢天 | A DREAM OF HEAVEN |
|------|-------------------|
| 老兔寒蟾泣天色 | Old hare and cold toad weep off sky-color, |
| 雲樓半開壁斜白 | Cloud-towers are half-open, walls are slant and white. |
| 玉輪軋露濕團光 | Jade wheel creaks upon dew and dampens globe of light, |

鸞珮相逢桂香陌　Simurgh pedants meet on cassia-scented paths.　4
黃塵清水三山下　Yellow dust and clear water under the three
　　　　　　　　　　godly mountains,
更變千年如走馬　The change of a thousand years is like a horse
　　　　　　　　　　galloping by.
遙望齊州九點煙　I look from above—the Middle Kingdom is just
　　　　　　　　　　nine wisps of smoke,
一泓海水杯中瀉[80] And all the water of the ocean is merely
　　　　　　　　　　a spilt cup.　8

This entire poem is written in figurative language. The hare and toad are mythological animals living on the moon, hence are used as kenning for the moon. "Jade wheel" (*yulun* 玉輪) is another figure for the moon. "Simurgh pendants" (*luanpei* 鸞珮) are jewelry worn by women and therefore synecdoches for fairy girls on the moon. The most dramatic figuration occurs in the second part of the poem, where the invisible passage of time—thousands of years—is made visible by the figure of "horse galloping by" (*zouma* 走馬). The whole Chinese kingdom is transformed into "nine wisps of smoke" (*jiudianyan* 九點煙). And the vast ocean on earth is reduced into water in a "spilt cup" (*beizhongxie* 杯中瀉). The significance of this almost excessive use of figuration is a profound demonstration of the decadent poetic agenda to transform the natural into the artificial. The moon is no longer a planet, but a linguistic product that can be named differently by the poet via an artificial literary convention. Similarly, the fairy maidens on the moon are turned into descriptive tropes. The scale of the universe is reduced to the smallest degree to let the poet experience a moment of control and power. The poem ends with a greatly enlarged image of the poet facing a greatly dwarfed world as he looks down at the earth from above.

The striking nature of this poem is also reflected in the forced, far-fetched relations between tenors and vehicles of the metaphors. The color of the sky is envisaged by the poet as being "wept" out (*qi* 泣) by the hare on the moon. The usual gentle, soundless movement of moonlight on dews is portrayed as "creaking" (*ya* 軋), thereby giving it a jarring, almost unpleasant quality. Note too that the images in these two instances are synesthetic ones in that they confuse our experiences of different senses. They shatter and disorient the reading experience.[81]

It is certainly understandable that in the Chinese poetic tradition where the ultimate standard has always been "not a word said outright, yet the whole beauty revealed" (不著一字，盡得風流),[82] or "exhaustibility of language and inexhaustibility of meaning" (言有盡而意無窮), poetry like Li He's will be provocative. The language of his poetry is so dense and inpenetrable that it can never be untangled, let alone exhausted. The Ming dynasty poet and critic Li Dongyang 李東陽 (1447–1516) complains that "in the poetry of Li Changji [He] every word is intended to be passed to posterity, but it has been so elaborately carved that it has lost any trace of spontaneous and natural beauty."[83] To many critics the intense artfulness and obscurity of Li He's poetry are closely linked with his interest in macabre subjects like death and unseemly imagery like demons and ghosts—both are considered abnormal by the canonical tradition. A Song critic remarks that "in poetry the ideal should be subtle and natural, not broken and chiseled; . . . it should be plain and smooth, not eccentric and involved. The verses from the brocade bag of Li Changji [He] are not un-strange, but there are too many ox-demons and serpent-spirits in them. If they were used in the court they would frighten [people away]."[84] To a great extent this dark aspect accounts for the uneasiness caused by Li He's poetry. Even in those works where propriety and decorum are ultimate criteria, Li He tends to introduce upsetting diction or imagery. Thus, for example, in "A Lovely Woman Combing Her Hair" he uses the word "old" (*lao* 老) to describe the hair of a young woman and thereby challenges the convention.

Now let us look at a poem more typical of this characteristic in Li He's oeuvre:

| 感諷六首:其五 | SIX SATIRICAL POEMS: NO. 5 | |
|---|---|---|
| 曉菊泫寒露 | At dawn cold dew drips down chrysanthemums, | |
| 似悲團扇風 | The round-fan wind seems to be mourning. | |
| 秋涼經漢殿 | The chill of autumn creeps through the Han Palace, | |
| 班子泣衰紅 | Lady Ban weeps for her fading beauty. | 4 |
| 本無辭輦意 | She never intended to refuse to ride in royal carriage,[85] | |
| 豈見入空宮 | How could she expect to be sent to the empty palace? | |
| 腰裀珮珠斷 | The pearl belt on her waist is broken, | |
| 灰蝶生陰松[86] | Ash butterflies spring from gloomy pines. | 8 |

This poem deals with one of the stalest subjects in the Palace Style repertoire. Lady Ban, we may recall, was a famous concubine of Emperor Cheng of the Han dynasty (r. 32–7 B.C.). She was sent to reside in one of the "empty palaces" when she fell out of her lord's favor. She once wrote a well-known poem in which she compares herself to a round fan that is discarded with the coming of autumn.[87] Her story is a favorite with Southern Dynasties court poets, who had a fondness for portraying court ladies condemned to live in melancholy isolation after they were discarded by their patrons. "My Beloved" (有所思) by Xiao Gang discussed in chapter 2 represents the typical treatment of this topic by Palace Style poets in that it ends with the melancholy self-lament of Lady Ban in her ornate, yet empty and lonely, residential palace.

The first six lines of Li He's present poem conform to this convention both in diction and tone, but a radical change occurs in the last two lines. Whereas in Xiao Gang's poem Lady Ban is still alive, though she has lost most of her attraction, in Li He's poem not only has she been removed from her sumptuous environment but she has already died. Instead of closing in the empty, yet luxurious residential palace of court ladies, the poem ends in a graveyard. The setting is grisly, with its broken jewelry on an implied decomposed body in line 7 and the burned paper money in the shape of "ash butterflies" (*huidie* 灰蝶) fluttering around the gloomy pines. This couplet completely upsets the poetic decorum of the genre and changes an otherwise banal "palace lament" (*gongyuan* 宮怨) poem into a characteristic work of Li He.

In his use of such unconventional imagery to write about a conventional topic, Li He resembles English metaphysical poets, especially John Donne.[88] But unlike Donne, who uses macabre imagery to further a logical argument, Li He uses it for aesthetic effect. In this he shares much with Baudelaire, whose "notorious" title "Flowers of Evil" is self-explanatory in this matter.[89] Li He loves the unseemly imagery that disrupts the respected literary decorum, but he also insists that it be artistically appealing. The last line of "Six Satirical Poems: No. 5" works in that way. The flying paper money burned at the graveyard becomes butterflies, whose litheness and beauty to some extent bring the young Lady Ban back to life and thereby lightens the grim atmosphere somewhat. Although the beauty of this image is inevitably undermined or changed by its preceding modifier *hui* 灰 (ash or gray), and by *yinsong* 陰松 (gloomy pines, which are traditional symbols of graveyard and death in Chinese culture) around which the butterflies flutter, they do not completely cancel it out. The beauty remains.

This kind of "gloomy beauty"—an oxymoron like "flowers of evil"—fascinated Li He. Again, Dr. Johnson's phrase *discordia concors* is a very apt description for Li He's poetry. Here is another example:

感諷五首:其三　　FIVE SATIRICAL POEMS: No. 3

| | |
|---|---|
| 南山何其悲 | How sad is the Southern Mountain, |
| 鬼雨灑空草 | Ghostly rain falls on empty grass. |
| 長安夜半秋 | In Chang'an it is midnight in autumn, |
| 風前幾人老 | How many people have become old in this wind? 4 |
| 低迷黃昏徑 | Down there in the yellow twilight the paths are lost, |
| 裊裊青櫟道 | By the road chestnut-oaks are tossing gently. |
| 月午樹立影 | The moon moves to her height, reducing tree-shadows, |
| 一山惟白曉 | The entire mountain is immersed in a white dawn. 8 |
| 漆炬迎新人 | Lacquer torches welcome newcomers, |
| 幽壙螢擾擾[90] | Fireflies dance over these lonely tombs. |

The poem is set exclusively in a graveyard, Southern Mountain near Chang'an having been the site of many tombs. The "ghostly rain" (*guiyu* 鬼雨) spattering on the dead grass in the second line establishes a tone of apprehension. But this atmosphere is lightened somewhat in lines 5 and 6, where the diction, used elsewhere by the poet in very different settings, is removed from the graveyard. The word *mi* 迷 (to charm, to mislead) is used in "Self-Mocking" in a completely different context, to describe the seductive appeal of the courtesan's world: 晚樹迷新蝶 "Evening trees entice new butterflies." Therefore, when the same word is used in a very different setting, it brings with it other associations, associations that color our reading of the present usage. Thus, the word *mi* transforms the grim scene of the first two lines into a place with seductive power. And further, this transformation is reinforced in the next line by the highly poetic expression *niaoniao* 裊裊 (to toss gently), which is usually used to describe the beautiful, gentle movement or shape of trees.[91] In this way, an otherwise unseemly

107

setting is poeticized. This relief is only momentary, however, for in the last two lines Li He reintroduces his characteristic "demonic" elements. "Lacquer torches" (*qiju* 漆炬) are will-o'-the-wisps; the "newcomers" (*xinren* 新人) are the newly dead. The break of dawn in lines 7 and 8 is not a time of renewal, but rather a ceremony to welcome the newly dead, with the fireflies dancing about the vast, lonely graveyard.

Li He, who often uses poetic terms to portray death, is thus able to turn this dark obsession into an artistic presentation. The general impression produced by such poem, then, is not one of horror but of morbid pleasure. This is even more striking in "Su Xiaoxiao's Tomb" 蘇小小墓：

| | | |
|---|---|---|
| 幽蘭露 | Dews upon lonely orchids | |
| 如啼眼 | Are like tearful eyes. | |
| 無物結同心 | There is nothing to tie a same-heart knot, | |
| 煙花不堪剪 | Misty flowers cannot bear to be cut. | 4 |
| 草如茵 | Grass is like cushion, | |
| 松如蓋 | Pines are like awning, | |
| 風爲裳 | Wind is as skirt, | |
| 水爲珮 | Water is as jade pendants. | 8 |
| 油壁車 | In her oil-silk carriage | |
| 夕相待 | She is waiting at dusk. | |
| 冷翠燭 | Cold, kingfisher-green candles | |
| 勞光彩 | Are weary with shining. | 12 |
| 西陵下 | Under the Western Grave-Mound | |
| 風吹雨[92] | Wind is blowing the rain. | |

Su Xiaoxiao was a well known singing girl and concubine in the Southern Dynasties period.[93] Although the title of the poem promises another dark graveyard verse, that is not what one gets. Instead, the first thing one notices is the highly ornate nature of the language. Its florid style is not that associated with death, but sounds almost like Palace Style poetry. Words like *youlan* 幽蘭 (lonely orchids), *yanhua* 煙花 (misty flowers), *pei* 珮 (jade pedants), *cuizhu* 翠燭 (kingfisher-green candles) evoke strongly a well-known descriptive system[94]— that of the *Chuci* and Palace Style poetry. Li He's evocation of these terms puts him in the literary tradition of poets like Qu Yuan and Xiao Gang.[95]

We have already considered his relations to Xiao Gang and Palace Style poetry in the previous part of this chapter. Li He's relations with Qu Yuan and the *Chuci* shows a similar pattern of adoption and transformation. As he explicitly acknowledged his appreciation of Xiao Gang's work, so he expressed his admiration for the *Chuci* on several occasions.[96] Many of his works, with their wild imagination and colorful diction, reflect the strong influence of this genre. But Li He is never a passive imitator. He often uses an established convention to serve his own needs, which could be very different from the convention. We have seen some of his strategies in "Self-Mocking." In "Su Xiaoxiao's Tomb" he adopts some highly evocative diction and then cancels out its effects by setting it in a very different context. Thus, no one would expect the above-mentioned phrases to be used to describe a graveyard scene. There is, in other words, a disjunction between the phrases and the setting that they are expected to portray. This is precisely Li He's "talent," his hallmark style—to be able to turn an otherwise morbid scene into a setting for a romantic tryst and all the surrounding elements into the private, somewhat mysterious world of a singing girl.

Li He brings about this transformation with linguistic force. These two different worlds after all are not conventionally associated with each other (that is, there is no "natural" connection between them); the poet "yoked them together" (to use another phrase of Dr. Johnson's) by means of figurative language. "Dew upon the lonely orchids" is made to look like "tearful eyes" of the singing girl; wind and water are forced to resemble her clothes and jewelry, and the will-o'-the-wisp is replaced by boudoir candles. One critic has calculated that in Li He's poetry *ru* (如 to be like) and *si* (似 to resemble), the two simile tropes in Chinese, occur respectively eighty-nine and sixteen times.[97] In this poem alone, they are used five times. This frequent usuage signals an uneasiness on the part of the poet: because the structural unity of his poetic world is an artificial one (to say A is "like" B is also to acknowledge that A is not B), he must achieve it through the use of a forceful linguistic medium.

Some critics have pointed out the remarkable similarity between Li He and Keats.[98] Both are obsessed with death. Death in Li He's poetry is very different, however, from the "easeful death" in Keats' "Ode to a Nightingale."[99] Whereas "easeful death" provides Keats with spiritual balm and an escape from the tumult of daily life, for Li He death is mostly a morbid obsession that not only does not provide a refuge from the political and personal frustrations, but to the contrary, tends to enhance them. The haunting fear of human mortality has been a recurrent theme in Chinese poetry since Han dynasty. Its presence is particularly strong in some of the "Nineteen Ancient Poems" 古詩十九首, usually thought to have been composed during the Eastern Han period (25–220).[100] In the face of the transience of human life, the poets of these anonymous poems adopt an attitude of carpe diem which bears heavily upon poets of later periods,[101] so much so that it is difficult to think of a major Chinese poet who has not written a poem expressing such an attitude. Li He wrote many pieces in this convention, and some of them are not greatly different from similar works by other poets, such as "Dadiqu" 大堤曲. But those that best express his unique character tend to betray some discrepancies both in theme and in presentation. Here is an example:

秋來          THE COMING OF AUTUMN

| | |
|---|---|
| 桐風驚心壯士苦 | Wind in the plane-trees startles heart, the hero is bitter, |
| 衰燈絡緯啼寒素 | In the fading lamplight spinners cry out their cold thread. |
| 誰看青簡一編書 | Who will [bother to] read these slips of green bamboo, |
| 不遣花蟲粉空蠹 | And prevent flowery moths from reducing them into powders?    4 |
| 思牽今夜腸應直 | Such thoughts tonight surely make straight my intestines, |
| 雨冷香魂吊書客 | In cold rain fragrant ghost comes to condole with the poet. |
| 秋墳鬼唱鮑家詩 | On an autumn tomb a demon is chanting Bao Zhao's poems, |
| 恨血千年土中碧[102] | A thousand years in earth makes emerald that rancorous blood.    8 |

Autumn is a season traditionally associated with death and decline, and *beiqiu* 悲秋 (lamenting autumn) is a recurrent leitmotif in classical Chinese poetry.[103] In the works of other poets, this is usually expressed as a vague feeling of melancholy caused by the presence of desolation of the season—reminder of human mortality. But in most cases the impression the reader gets from these works is not that of overwhelming depression or pessimism. This is because the poet manages to avoid becoming morbidly entangled with the implications of autumn, and by extension, of death, by relating a very personal situation to a larger context that somewhat eases the poignancy of the present circumstance.[104] Chinese culture provides several options for such therapeutic solutions. The first one is history. The very fact that time treats all people equally and that great figures in history suffered decline and death too mitigates the agony for many poets.[105] The second is philosophy. The bitterness over death's inevitability can be lightened by the belief that humankind is a part of the universe and therefore that the decay suffered by a human being, however painful, is also part of the process by which the universe renews its life. This is inevitable and painful, but not without its grandeur.[106] The third option, which is often related without distinction to the second, is religion, particularly Buddhism. Death is regarded by Buddhism as insignificant because human life itself is an illusion. The poet who holds Buddhist beliefs is therefore able to treat autumn with a stoic detachment.[107]

Although Li He's "The Coming of Autumn" belongs to the "lamenting Autumn" genre, it also has features peculiar to Li He, especially Li He the "demonic talent." The poem opens in a very conventional manner, with the first two lines describing a bleak autumn night. *Shuaideng* 衰燈 (fading lamplight), *luowei* 絡緯 (spinner), *hansu* 寒素 (cold thread) are all images one expects in a "lamenting autumn" poem. But Li He's dark mood begins to show itself in the next couplet, as he abandons the classic Chinese beliefs that literary production is one of the chief means to obtain immortality. This is a Confucian dictum that makes life meaningful for the man of letters. Li He announces instead that the literary production of humankind will inevitably be reduced to powders by insects. Moreover, even as he describes this slow, macabre act of destruction his diction remains colorful, aesthetic. The destroyed books are slips of "green bamboo" (*qingjian* 青簡),[108] and the agent of destruction, the moths, are "flowery moths" (*huachong* 花蟲). The unseemly or even the ugly are treated as beautiful, again in line 6 where the ghost of the dead (*hun* 魂) is given the unexpected modifier "fragrant" (*xiang* 香). The grotesque combination of "fragrant ghost" (*xianghun* 香魂) defies covential meanings and works counter to the common meaning of the two words: "fragrant"

is usually connected with feminine atmosphere—sensual and intimate—while "ghost" evokes a world of darkness and terror. Semantically they could not be further apart, and in terms of senses they are
equally forced because usually ghost comes only to our sight, not our
smell. Li He's abundant use of catachresis like this serves wonderfully to "defamiliarize" or foreground the peculiar linguistic characteristics of many of his works. It indeed explains the strangeness and
uneasiness many have felt about his poetry. Consider the next line, in
which a demon is presented as *chang* 唱 (chanting or singing) by the
tomb the poetry of Bao Zhao 鮑照 (?–466), one of the greatest poets in
the Southern Dynasties period. The poem ends with an embittered
heart whose red blood has been transformed into a green emerald
during its thousand-year sojourn beneath the earth.

In commenting on a poem in *The Book of Songs*, Confucius said
that it was "expressive of pleasure without being unrestrained, and
of grief without being hurtfully excessive" (樂而不淫，哀而不傷).[109]
This remark was later turned into the poetic doctrine of "moderate
and mellow" (*wenrou dunhou* 溫柔敦厚),[110] the treatment of all subjects according to a golden mean. Avoid excess in the language and
structure of the poem, and maintain a healthy balanced mind. But in
the present piece the poet's bitterness is too intense to be tempered
(the blood of the dead poet is described as *henxue* 恨血, "embittered
or rancorous blood"), and the eccentric, sinister elements are impossible to naturalize in traditional terms. Pessimism, even nihilism,
pervade the poem. They effectively cancel out the "hero" (*zhuangshi*
壯士) in the first line. This, coupled with the deliberate destruction of
conventional poetic decorum, makes it one of the most striking pieces
in Li He's oeuvre.[111]

Li He descends even further into a disturbingly bitter and sinister
poetic world in the following verse, probably one of the darkest pieces
in Chinese poetry:

| 公無出門 | Do Not Go out of Your Gate, Sir! |
|---|---|
| 天迷迷 | Heaven is confused, |
| 地密密 | Earth is barred up. |
| 熊虺食人魂 | Nine-headed serpents are devouring people's souls, |
| 雪霜斷人骨 | Snow and frost are breaking people's bones. 4 |

| | |
|---|---|
| 嗾犬狺狺相索索 | Wild dogs are barking and howling listlessly at each other, |
| 舐掌偏宜佩蘭客 | Licking their paws, greedy particularly for the man with an orchid girdle. |
| 帝遣乘軒災自滅 | Once god sends a chariot to take you, misfortune will end itself, |
| 玉星點劍黃金軛 | The sword is adorned with stars of jade, the yoke with gold. 8 |
| 我雖跨馬不得還 | Even though I am on a horse, I cannot go home, |
| 歷陽湖泊大如山 | For the waves in Liyang loom large as mountains. |
| 毒虬相視振金環 | Poisonous, horned snakes are glaring, rattling their bronze rings, |
| 狻猊獓貐吐饞涎 | Lions and griffins are drooling from slavering jaws. 12 |
| 鮑焦一世披草眠 | For his whole life Bao Jiao slept under straw, |
| 顏回廿九鬢毛斑 | Yan Hui's hair turned white when he was just twenty-nine. |
| 顏回非血衰 | Yet Yan Hui's blood was not weak, |
| 鮑焦不違天 | Nor had Bao Jiao disobeyed Heaven. 16 |
| 天畏遭啣嚙 | Heaven was afraid that they would be devoured, |
| 所以致之然 | So it treated them thus. |
| 分明猶懼公不信 | This is clear, still I fear you would doubt it, sir, |
| 公看呵壁書問天[112] | But look at him raving wildly at the wall, as he wrote his "Questions to Heaven." 20 |

The landscape in the poem is indisputably sinister, even malevolent. Part of the poem (especially the first five lines) recalls the descriptions in "Zhaohun" 招魂 ("The Summons of the Soul") in *Chuci*, but the horrors in that poem are greatly discounted, because the poet is not claiming reality of his description; he is merely imagining a situation terrifying enough to cause the soul of the deceased to *return* to the kingdom of Chu.[113] Wang Yi says that "The Summons of the Soul" describes "the evils of an outside world, praises the beautiful things inside the Chu state, thereby indirectly criticizing King Huai so that he would wake up and allow [Qu Yuan's] soul to return."[114] In other words the terrifying description in "The Summons of the Soul" is a background to set in relief the pleasant life within the Chu state. Li He, however, reverses this order and brings the outside horror inside.

Moreover, he is trying to make us believe that he is describing reality. The poem opens with a matter-of-fact style, but a dark world intrudes after the first two lines, a world inhabited by sinister animals hunting for human flesh. Although the supernatural animal like "nine-headed serpents" (*souquan* 嗾犬) does raise questions about the credibility of the whole description, the image of "the man with an orchid girdle" (*peilanke* 佩蘭客, the stock metaphor for a virtuous, unappreciated gentleman like Qu Yuan)[115] and the reference to the other two models of Confucian morality (Yan Hui and Bao Jiao)[116] make it clear that the poem is intended to be read as an allegory for human society. This is further confirmed by lines 8 and 9, where the rare presence of the first person pronoun "I" (*wo* 我) introduces a concrete historical figure into the poem. This presence also establishes a connection between the "I" (presumably the poet, as the empirical subject and lyrical subject are usually identical in Chinese poetry)[117] and "the man with an orchid girdle," namely, Qu Yuan, the poet who wrote "Encountering Sorrow." The connection is suggested because the present poet is also "encountering sorrow" or trouble, for in line 8 he tells us he cannot go home, even though he has a horse. Like Qu Yuan's world, the society described in Li He's poem is one of moral perversity, where the virtuous are destroyed and the vicious thriving.

The first two lines present a visually dark scene; the third line describes terrifying animals engaged in the act of devouring human beings; line 4 introduces the grisly sound of human-hunting wild dogs, which in line 5 are seen as waiting greedily, and *particularly* (*pian* 偏) for an upright scholar like Qu Yuan. This description reaches its terrifying climax in lines 9 and 10, where "the poisonous, horned snakes are glaring" at us, rattling their teeth, and "Lions and griffins are drooling" in their lust for human flesh.[118] The perversity of this heinous world is illustrated by the absurd argument that the poet sardonically and bitterly introduces about the unwarranted misfortunes suffered by Yan Hui and Bao Jiao. Beneath the apparently feigned, cynical argument that their misfortune is actually a blessing in disguise (because they were killed by the gods to prevent them from being devoured by the horrific animals), there lies a disturbingly dark vision of the universe and the human world that reflects the poet's profound sense of insecurity and disillusionment. The lonely and nearly mad Qu Yuan shouting his unanswerable questions at the end of the poem can be viewed as an image of the poet himself.[119] For like Qu Yuan, who was persecuted for the reasons that he could not fathom, Li He was also stuck in an alienating, hostile environment, as he has already told us in lines 8 and 9.

Thus the title of the poem "Do Not Go Out of Your Gate, Sir!" is pertinent. For in a world like this the only way for the poet to survive is to lock himself up in his own world, in his metaphorical ivory tower[120]—namely, to retreat into his poetic craft. This explains why some of Li He's decadent poetry is viewed as a response to an increasingly antagonistic social reality. Unlike "Self-Mocking" and "A Beautiful Woman Combing Her Hair" which are difficult to allegorize, poems like "The Coming of Autumn" and especially the present piece lend themselves to an allegorical reading. Wang Qi takes the poem to be symbolic of the chaotic political and social situation of Li He's time.[121] Yao Wenxie regards it as Li He's protest against the unjust treatment that Han Yu, his patron, had received from his slanderers.[122]

Herein lies the crucial difference between the decadent poetry of the Late Tang and that of the Southern Dynasties periods. Palace Style poetry can be properly described as a kind of aestheticism, impersonal, and superficial. It is a clever verbal play devoid of deeper meaning. It does not try to conceal, because it has nothing to conceal. It cannot be social or political protest because its poets represent the status quo. But Li He was a frustrated intellectual, and it is possible, and to some critics even necessary, to adopt the traditional exegetical principle in interpreting his poetry, in particular, an allegorical reading. Moreover, his poetry, however unconventional, often hints at deeper meanings. This, together with the fact that many of his poems treat explicitly social and political themes, account for the very different reception accorded his decadent poetry from that accorded Palace Style poetry. While the latter was consistently condemned, the former was the object of both denunciation and praise. For the very fact that at least some of Li He's poetry has been described by critics as "the historical record of Tang Dynasty" (*Tang zhi chunqiu* 唐之春秋)[123] makes it possible to regard its grotesqueness, obscurity, opacity, and sensuality as not merely a marker of his poetic style, but also as a means to protect him from a world that constantly intrudes upon his integrity. In other words, on occasion the peculiar technical features of his decadent poetry were accepted because they are perceived not as the end (as they are in Palace Style poetry), but as the means to get to a deeper, more meaningful world.

There are two opposing views of Li He's poetry. One school (represented by Lu Guimeng) emphasizes only the "ox-ghost and serpent-spirit" elements in Li He's poetry. The other (represented by Yao Wenxie) wants to interpret his complete oeuvre in the light of his socially oriented works.[124] These different approaches to Li He's decadent poetry reflect its multiple layers of meaning, and it is precisely these multiple layers that distinguish Li He's works from the Palace Style convention and make it more acceptable to audiences of later periods. The Song critic Yan Yu, for instance, launched a most effective attack on Late Tang poetry. In *Canglang shihua* he warns the students of poetry not to study any works after the High Tang period, lest they risk having their minds filled with demons and ghosts of inferior poetry.[125] But elsewhere in the same book he also pays tribute to Li He and even considers the "grandeur and grotesqueness" (*guigui* 瑰詭) of his poetry to be indispensable.[126] To our present study his transformation of Palace Style poetry is particularly important because not only did it help to revive Palace Style poetry after a long period of condemnation, but it also greatly influenced the writings of Wen Tingyun and Li Shangyin, who are regarded as following closely in the footsteps of Li He.[127]

## Chapter 4

# Wen Tingyun
## The Poet Dandy

Wen Tingyun is one of the few Chinese poets who seems to have enjoyed flaunting his dandyism. In a short poem entitled "Rain on a Spring Day" 春日雨 he taunted those who attacked his poetry on moral grounds:

| | |
|---|---|
| 細雨濛濛入絳紗 | A misty drizzle enters the dark red gauze net, |
| 澧湖[1]寒食孟珠家 | On Cold Food Day by Lake Feng, Mengzhu's house, |
| 南朝漫自稱流品 | In Southern Dynasties social class was widely valued, |
| 宮體何曾爲杏花[2] | Who had ever taken Palace Style as Apricot Garden? |

The poet is at the home of a singing girl (Mengzhu 孟珠 is an emblematic name for singing girl or prostitute),[3] and is probably in bed with her, as suggested by the image of "dark red gauze net" (*jiangsha* 絳紗). He feels no shame or embarrassment at being in such an unseemly place. Quite the contrary, he justifies his behavior by saying that one's social class (*liupin* 流品) has no bearing on one's literary production and moral conduct.[4] Social class was highly cherished during the Southern Dynasties, the poet tells us, but nearly all noble and high-ranking personages of that period, from the emperor down, had composed Palace Style poems as he did. His own deplorable public career,[5] he seems to be arguing, had no connection to his loose lifestyle and his decadent poetry, even though people of his time may have

thought that it did. As far as he was concerned, therefore, there was
no need for him to apologize for his moral conduct and poetic works.

Although in his own time Wen Tingyun was widely admired and
although he along with Li Shangyin were considered the two masters
of the amorous "Wen-Li" 溫李 style,[6] his reputation in later periods
was based largely on the numerous amusing anecdotes about his
unconventional life preserved in various sources.[7] Liu Sihan 劉斯翰,
the editor of the only modern critical edition of Wen Tingyun's selected
poetry, *Wen Tingyun shicixuan* 溫庭筠詩詞選, opens his introduction
with the following remark:

Exceptionally ugly in looks, arrogant in manner, scandalous in
behavior, but with a marvelously quick poetic wit and absolutely
beautiful literary style: this is the general impression that Wen
Tingyun, the famous Late Tang poet, gave to the people of later
generations.[8]

But if his scandalous persona remained vivid during later periods,
his poetic works do not seem to have fared so well. As a poet Wen
Tingyun is remembered nowadays mostly as the author of the famous
couplet "Crow of cock, moon by the thatched inn,/ Tracks of people,
frost on the plank bridge" (雞聲茅店月，人跡板橋霜), and as one of
the first important *ci* 詞 (song lyric) writers of the ninth century.[9]
Among the once major poets of the Late Tang, Wen Tingyun suffers
most at the hands of later critics. Few any longer consider him as a
major poet. Liu Dajie, the author of the *Zhonguo wenxue fazhanshi*
(*Development of Chinese literature*), did not feel the need to offer even
a passing remark about his poetry. This judgment is also reflected in
A. C. Graham's *Poems of the Late T'ang*, which does not include a
single poem by Wen Tingyun. The reasons for this reversal of fortune
are complicated, but I hope in the present chapter to shed some light
on it.

The decadent poetry of Wen Tingyun shows both affinity with and
difference from the poets dealt with in previous chapters, Xiao Gang
and Li He. The Palace Style convention is carried on, but beneath the
florid rhetoric and erotic sensuality of Wen Tingyun's poetry there is
an acute historical sense, melancholy, and not infrequently anxiety.
This anxiety and historical sense are what differentiate Wen Tingyun's

decadent poetry from that of his predecessors and make it a peculiarly Late Tang phenomenon.

The Palace Style tendency in Wen Tingyun's poetry is apparent in many ways. In some poems he follows this mode very closely, as in the following piece:

| 湘宮人歌 | THE SONG OF A COURT LADY AT XIANG | |
|---|---|---|
| 池塘芳草[10]濕 | By the pond fragrant grass is damp, | |
| 夜半東風起 | At midnight east wind rises. | |
| 生綠畫羅屏 | Lively green is painted on silk screen, | |
| 金壺貯春水 | Spring water is stored in bronze kettle. | 4 |
| 黃粉楚宮人 | The court lady of Chu [has] a yellow makeup, | |
| 芳花玉刻鱗 | The fish carved on jade [looks like] fragrant flowers. | |
| 娟娟照棋燭 | The beautiful moon shines on chessboard and candles, | |
| 不語兩含顰[11] | Silently she knits her eyebrows. | 8 |

Poems like this show little of Wen Tingyun's own creativity and therefore are the least interesting in his oeuvre. The diction, structure, mannerism, and sentiment are all typical of Palace Style poetry of Xiao Gang and other Southern Dynasties court poets. In his more characteristic works, however, Wen Tingyun exploits Palace Style convention creatively to serve his own purpose. For example, he uses the textual strategies peculiar to Palace Style poetry to deallegorize and aestheticize poems that usually have strong moral associations. The most successful example of this is a poem called "Retired Scholar Guo Plays His Earthen Jars: A Song" 郭處士擊甌歌:

| 佶栗金虯石潭古 | The bronze dragon shudders in the ancient stone pond, | |
|---|---|---|
| 勺陂潋灩幽修語 | Flowing Shaopi Lake murmurs in subtle voice. | |
| 湘君寶馬上神雲 | The Goddess of Xiang River ascends to divine clouds on her brilliant steed, | |
| 碎佩叢鈴滿煙雨 | Pendants and bells clash, their sound fills the misty rain. | 4 |
| 吾聞三十六宮花 離離 | I have heard that by the thirty-six palaces bright flowers bloom, | |

| | |
|---|---|
| 軟風吹春星斗稀 | Soft wind blows in the spring, stars grow sparse. |
| 玉晨冷磬破昏夢 | In the jade morning cold chime breaks a fuzzy dream, |
| 天露未乾香著衣 | Dew still undried, incense remains on her clothes. 8 |
| 蘭釵委墜垂雲髮 | Lovely orchid hairpins dangle from her cloud hair, |
| 小響丁當逐回雪 | Light jingling sound follows the whirling snow. |
| 晴碧煙滋重疊山 | Mist in bright blue sky wraps the layered mountains, |
| 羅屏半掩桃花月 | Silk screen half-blocks the peach-blossom moon. 12 |
| 太平天子駐雲車 | The Son of Heaven in the age of peace halts his cloud-carriage, |
| 龍鑪勃鬱雙蟠拏 | Two coiled dragons on incense burner puff out dense smoke. |
| 宮中近臣抱扇立 | In the palace the intimates stand by, fans in their arms, |
| 侍女低鬟落翠花 | Jade flowers fall as the court girls lower their chignon. 16 |
| 亂珠觸續正跳蕩 | Pearls in disorder clash and jump about, |
| 傾頭不覺金烏斜 | She tilts her head, not knowing the Golden Crow has inclined. |
| 我亦為君長嘆息 | I too give out a long sigh for your sake, |
| 緘情遠寄愁無色 | I'd send my feelings in letter, but worry it would seem colorless. 20 |
| 莫霑香夢綠楊絲 | Do not get entangled in the fragrant dream of green willow silk, |
| 千里春風正無力[12] | Within a thousand miles the spring wind is blowing softly. |

Poetry on music is an important subgenre in Tang poetry. It usually involves a player and listener, a relationship that evokes the famous story of the ancient musician Boya 伯牙 and his friend Zhong Ziqi 鍾子期. According to the legend, the mutuality between them was such that when Zhong Ziqi died, Boya ceased playing because he believed that no one could understand his music anymore.[13] This story has become the *locus classicus* of one of the perennial themes in Chinese culture: the search for a friend who understands you, a *zhiyin* 知音 (literally, "one who understands your music.") During the Tang dynasty most poetry on music follows this thematic model. The poet uses the occasion of listening to a musical performance to express his feeling of identity with the musician, especially when both find themselves in a despondent state. The poet expresses his joy at finding a *zhiyin* in a largely alienating world. The discovery in turn makes his own woes more bearable. In Chinese culture the search for a *zhiyin* is also a metaphor for the intellectual's relationship with his state, which is often represented by its ruler or other high-ranking officials. Consequently, this topic sometimes has serious moral significance about an intellectual's sense of responsibility to his country and it critiques a social condition that often denies him a chance to serve.

Bai Juyi's "Pipa xing" 琵琶行 ("Song of Pipa") and Han Yu's "Ting Yingshi tanqin" 聽穎師彈琴 ("Listening to Master Ying Playing the Zither") are such poems.[14] Li He's "Li Ping konghouyin" 李憑箜篌引 ("Song: Listening to Li Ping Playing the Konghou") marks an important shift in the treatment of this topic because it completely dissociates the experience of listening to music from the story of Boya and Zhong Ziqi. Instead, the poet uses the experience to display his rich imagination and dazzling rhetorical skill.[15] Wen Tingyun follows Li He in aestheticizing this otherwise morally charged topic, but Wen Tingyun's "decadent" tendency is stronger: not only does he remove his poem from the tradition of searching for a *zhiyin*, but he turns it into an erotic verse in the Palace Style convention.[16]

The erotic elements are introduced early in the poem. The goddess of Xiang in line 3 is the object of erotic pursuit in two *Chuci* poems.[17] The phrase "misty rain" (*yanyu* 煙雨) in line 4 further indicates the sexually charged atmosphere because it evokes Song Yu's "Fu on Gaotang" where the King of Chu dreams that he had a sexual encounter with the goddess of Mount Wu.[18] Beginning in line 5 the poem moves indoors to describe the ornate living quarters of the unnamed court lady. Line 6 specifically sets the poem in spring time. Desire is stirred, as a "soft wind" (*ruanfeng* 軟風) blows. The bulk of the poem, from lines 7 to 18, further details this sumptuous, erotic world. Among the numerous familiar images and phrases such as *yuchen* 玉晨 (jade morning), *lanchai* 蘭釵 (orchid hairpins) and *yunfa* 雲髮 (cloud hair), "silk screen half-blocks the peach-blossom moon" 羅屏半掩桃花月 is particularly evocative of Xiao Gang's seductive poetry, with its typical strategy of half-concealing and half-revealing (an alluring female figure) and its examples of florid diction such as "silk screen" (*luoping* 羅屏) and "peach-blossom moon" (*taohuayue* 桃花月), a metaphor for a beautiful woman. This portion of the poem describes the royal visit with her and the entertainment that follows. The Son of Heaven rides on a "cloud-carriage" *yunche* 雲車 (line 13), an image that consolidates the connection between the present imperial visit to the singing girl or court lady and the Chu King's sexual liaison with the goddess of Mount Wu.

Then follows a section of four lines (lines 15–18) describing the entertaining women. The diction is the familiar Palace Style, terms such as *cuihua* 翠花 (jade flowers) and *jinwu* 金烏 (golden crow), both of which refer to the hairpins of the court women. Their performance is unrestrained and wild as their hair loosened by their quick movements, movements that are portrayed metonymically through the description of the pearls worn by the women: they are in "disorder" (*luan* 亂) and "jumping about" (*tiaodang* 跳蕩). Just as the performance is reaching its climax, however, the poet interrupts his fantasy in line 19 and turns his thoughts to an unnamed friend far away. This shift is somewhat abrupt. The connection between the erotic fantasy and the longing for this friend is not at all clear, unless this friend (*jun* 君) is a woman, in which case lines 19 and 20 express the desire for her and the amorous associations aroused by the music. But in line 21 the poet adopts an imperative voice *mo* 莫 ("do not") to urge his friend (and himself, too?) to abandon the erotic fantasy without providing any reason for doing so. The poem ends with an image of a softly blowing spring wind, which in all likelihood is meant to suggest the exhaustion and relaxation after an orgy.

Like the poetry of Xiao Gang, this poem seems to have created a world of sensual indulgence. The outside world is carefully kept at bay until the end of the poem, when the poet withdraws from his fantasy. However, in many other poems more typical of Wen Tingyun's age, the construction of such a world of pleasure is often accompanied by a threat of its potential destruction. The following is an example:

觀舞伎　　　WATCHING A DANCING GIRL

朔音悲嘒管　The northern frontier music mourns from the flute,
瑤蹋動芳塵　Her exquisite shoes stir fragrant dust.
總袖時增怨　Holding sleeves she adds more sadness to her air,
聽破復含嚬　She listens to the "Po" songs and knits her
　　　　　　eyebrows. [4]
凝腰倚風軟　Her slender waist leans on soft wind,

花題照錦春      Her flowery forehead radiates on brocade spring.
朱弦固凄緊      Red strings are after all grave and sad,
瓊樹亦迷人[19] Emerald trees are equally seductive.      8

Poems on dance or dancing girls are an important component of the Palace Style repertoire.[20] This poem by Wen Tingyun echoes this convention not only in its use of typical Palace Style diction, such as *yaota* 瑤蹋 (exquisite shoes), *fangchen* 芳塵 (fragrant dust), *tai* 態 (air), *hanpin* 含顰 (to knit eyebrows), *ningyao* 凝腰 (slender waist), *huati* 花題 (flowery forehead), *qiongshu* 瓊樹 (emerald trees), but also in its tripartite structure, which is the most enduring characteristic of court poetry. The first couplet presents the setting and general atmosphere. The middle two couplets, in parallelism, give the specific details of the dancing girl and her performance. The last couplet projects the poet's personal reaction to the girl and her performance. Yet in this all too familiar piece there are notes of uneasiness and potential disruption, notes that Wen Tingyun develops more fully in his other poems. The music being played to accompany her dance is the music of the northern frontier *shuo* 朔, and the songs she is singing are called *Po* 破, which literally means "to break" or "broken." As the editors note, during the Tang period music from the frontier was very popular in the capital.[21] During the High Tang period service on the frontier provided an opportunity for intellectuals to establish themselves in a public career. Its culture was also an indispensable source of inspiration for poets. In the hands of some High Tang poets, the frontier and its culture were exotic, romantic materials for expressing their confidence and outgoing spirit. They reflected the positive attitude of an optimistic age, in which the sacrifice and suffering on the frontier were rendered sublime, although not without their tragic elements.[22]

The irony in Wen Tingyun's poem is that by his time frontier and its culture, as represented here by its mournful music, had indeed "broken" into the heartland of the country. In the Late Tang they no longer merely represented something exotic, but rather signaled the disaster of civil war. The An Lushan rebellion (755–63 A.D.) that plagued the country for eight years and nearly brought down the Tang dynasty, drastically changed people's perception of life and the world, particularly of the frontier and its culture. In Wen Tingyun's poem the music of the frontier is transferred to a courtly setting and thus signals the intrusion of a coarse, hence incompatible element into a delicate, feminine environment. The juxtaposition of two widely different worlds in the first couplet creates a sense of discordance: "The northern-frontier music mourns from the flute,/ Her exquisite shoes stir fragrant dust." It thus disrupts the code of decorum—the hallmark of Palace Style convention. This will become clearer if we compare this poem with the following one by Xiao Gang:

| 夜聽妓 | LISTENING TO A SINGING GIRL AT NIGHT |
|---|---|
| 合歡蠲忿葉 | The paired pleasure trees and their anger-relieving leaves, |
| 萱草忘憂條 | Day lilies and their sorrow-forgetting branches. |
| 何如明月夜 | How could they compare with a bright moonlit night |
| 流風拂舞腰 | When flowing breezes waft her dancing waist! 4 |
| 朱唇隨吹盡 | Her red lips follow flute to the finish, |
| 玉釧逐弦搖 | Jade bracelets move with the string. |
| 留賓惜殘弄 | She urges the guests to remain for the rest of her songs, |
| 負態動餘嬌[23] | Her manners display her bounteous charms. 8 |

Xiao Gang's poem deals with a similar topic, but without the jarring note in Wen Tingyun's poem. Beneath the richly sensual surface of Wen Tingyun's poem there lurks a deep anxiety. Sadness and seductiveness increase *simultaneously* in the last couplet of his poem, causing a tension between the two poles of this discordant world. This is no longer the self-assured courtly environment of the Southern Dynasties Palace Style poetry.

Consequently in Wen Tingyun's poetry the desire for an ivory tower is especially strong, as is reflected in the following poem:

| 偶遊 | A CHANCE EXCURSION |
|---|---|
| 曲巷斜臨一水間 | Meandering lane stands by a river, |
| 小門終日不開關 | Small gate does not open throughout the day. |
| 紅珠斗帳櫻桃熟 | Red pearls, small dome net, cherries are ripe, |
| 金尾屏風孔雀閑 | Golden-tailed peacocks are at ease on the screen. 4 |
| 雲髻幾迷芳草蝶 | Her cloud hair nearly deceives the butterflies in fragrant plants, |

額黃無限夕陽山　The yellow makeup on her forehead is limitless
　　　　　　　　mountain in sunset.
與君便是鴛鴦侶　You and I, my lord, are the paired
　　　　　　　　mandarin ducks,
休向人間覓往還[24] Do not seek to return to the human world.　8

An artificial verbal construction is used here to shut out the world and its unpleasant intrusions. The first couplet indicates the location of the lovers' rendezvous. Like Li He's "Self-Mocking," the poem is set in a small, isolated, and delicate environment—meandering lane (*quxiang* 曲巷), small gate (*xiaomen* 小門). But it can shut out the hurly-burly of the outside: the gate refuses to open throughout the day; it is self-sufficient. The verbal phrase *bukaiguan* 不開關 (does not open the door latch) is emphatic; this is not a static state, as a passive adjective might have made it, but an emotionally charged act. The middle two couplets, which describe the woman's boudoir, demonstrate the characteristics of Wen Tingyun's poetry par excellence. The highly sensual, ornate diction and images in lines 3 and 4, such as red pearls (*hongzhu* 紅珠), ripe cherries (*yingtaoshu* 櫻桃熟), golden peacock screens (*jinwei pingfeng* 金尾屏風), and the woman's elaborate makeup that defies the work of nature in lines 5 and 6—all these constitute a world of sensual indulgence.

The artificial triumphs over the natural, for the natural world is to a great extent subsumed by the woman's elaborately artificial bedroom, as many of its features, such as the cherries, the peacocks, the fragrant plants, the butterflies, and even the setting sun, are refigured on the woman's body, in her makeup, and in her bedroom furnishings. Lines 5 and 6 play a conventional game, as the natural and the artificial are deliberately confused, but the poet makes it clear that it is the natural that succumbs to the charm of the artificial, not vice versa. Thus, butterfly flies *into* the woman's boudoir, mistaking her hair for fragrant plants. As if to further consolidate this victory, the poem ends with the woman's supplication to her lover not to break their union by returning to the human world.

The structure of regulated verse, in which the present poem is written, poses a particular challenge for the poet dealing with the theme of escape. The rigorous requirements of antithesis and parallelism in the middle two couplets always have the tendency to close off, because the parallel items within a couplet must be chosen from the same category. A word or phrase is selected in relation to the corresponding word or phrase in the other line of the couplet. Therefore, "red pearls" at the beginning of line 3 requires "golden tail" at the beginning of line 4. Not only do they have to be in the same adjective-noun structure, but they must also belong to the same category: red and golden belong to the category of color, while pearl and tail are both objects of the natural world. This is advantageous for our present poet because it tends to reinforce the self-sufficiency of the world described in the poem, which is precisely the theme of this verse.

Wen Tingyun uses this structure to his own ends. But the last two lines present a challenge to him, for after the mutual dependence in the middle two couplets, the last two lines do not and should not have a structural dependence upon the previous part of the poem. The tripartite structure of regulated verse usually prescribes that the first couplet gives the setting, the middle two couplets describe and expand it, and the last couplet brings in the response of the poet or, by extension, of the audience. How is he to maintain the self-enclosure so effectively constructed in the previous part of the poem with this somewhat loose couplet? Wen Tingyun solves this problem by making these two lines into an apostrophe that prays for the continuity of the lovers' indulgence. But this solution is a very precarious one, because the woman's prayer also reveals the need for such prayer, hence anxiety over the insecurity of their situation.

Wen Tingyun's poetry, like Palace Style poetry, is deeply concerned with transforming the natural into the artificial. But the awareness of the potential threat to such a poetic agenda gives Wen Tingyun's work an edge of doubt or uncertainty, which sometimes manifests itself as anxiety, as in "The Chance Meeting." At other times it takes the form of irony, as in the next poem:

| 和友人谿居別業 | A Country Villa by the Stream: In Reply to a Friend |
|---|---|
| 積潤初銷碧草新 | Accumulated dew just dissolves, emerald grass is fresh, |
| 鳳陽晴日帶雕輪 | The phoenixlike bright day brings the carved wheel. |
| 絲[26]飄弱柳平橋晚 | Fine threads float on tender willows: evening by the level bridge, |

| | |
|---|---|
| 雪點寒梅小苑春 | Snow dots on cold plums: spring in the small courtyard.     4 |
| 屏上樓臺陳後主 | On the screen is Chen Houzhu in his towery palaces, |
| 鏡中金翠李夫人 | In the mirror is Lady Li in her golden jewelry. |
| 花房透露紅珠落 | Dews penetrate the corolla, red pearls fall, |
| 峽蝶雙雙[27]護粉塵[28] | Paired butterflies protect the powdery dust.     8 |

The title of this regulated verse announces an eremitic poem: "country villa by the stream" 溪居別業 signals a locus traditionally associated with poetry of seclusion.[29] By invoking this well-established poetic convention, Wen Tingyun would seem to be making a commitment to follow its generic rules and expectations. But we soon discover that this is not the case at all. Having given a powerful signal about the nature of the poem in the title, the poem quickly moves in a completely unexpected direction.

The first couplet plunges us into the world of Palace Style poetry, which, with its sophistication and ornamentation, is diametrically opposed to the simple world of eremitic poetry. The grass is "emerald" (*bi* 碧), and even the sun has to be "carved" and made into an artifact, "carved wheel" (*diaolun* 雕輪). The middle two couplets provide further details of this "country villa" turned into a courtly environment. This may be a cozy, feminine world, but as the poet reminds us, potential disaster looms nearby. For in the third couplet the poet tells us that his friend's "country villa by the stream" is furnished by screens and mirrors that have on them the pictures of Chen Houzhu and Lady Li, historical allusions reinforcing the poem's connection with the Palace Style convention. We might recall here that Chen Houzhu was a notoriously corrupt ruler *and* poet whose depravity is commonly blamed for the fall of Chen, which is the last dynasty of the Southern Dynasties period. Lady Li is a woman at the Han court who won the favor of Emperor Wu with her dancing skills.[30] Of the two allusions, the first produces an ominous effect, in suggesting that this sumptuous, artificial safe haven resembles the palaces of the Chen Houzhu, that were overrun by the invading Sui troops. But this is by no means all that is suggested: Is Wen Tingyun hinting a connection between Chen Houzhu, this historical figure of artistic taste and moderate poetic skill and himself or his friend? Otherwise why introduce such a figure, since normally a poet builds a world of seclusion to escape from the life of court and society. But Wen Tingyun reverses the situation: by introducing the courtly life into this eremitic poem, he signals his desire to transform the eremitic tradition with the Palace Style convention, while *at the same time* reminding us of the extreme vulnerability of this agenda.

The last two lines of the poem reify this sense of vulnerability. The "corolla" (*huafang* 花房) is being invaded: the cold dews are "penetrating" (*tou* 透), and as a result of this invasion, the "red pearls" (*hongzhu* 紅珠) are "falling" (*luo* 落). The line is rich in sexual overtones, intimated at by corolla and the penetrating dew. Significantly, sexual consummation is accompanied by a deterioration of this delicate ivory tower, for the "red pearls" are "falling." This is probably why the "paired butterflies" (*jiadie shuangshuang* 蛱蝶雙雙) try desperately to "protect" (*hu* 護) these delicate beauties, which have already been reduced to "powdery dust" (*fenchen* 粉塵).

Compared with other Late Tang poets (such as Du Mu and Li Shangyin), Wen Tingyun is relatively detached from the political and social issues of his time. The aesthetic tendency in his poetry not only distances the political and social disasters of the past, but also makes their representation decadently aloof. Like Xiao Gang's deallegorization of the traditional allegorical and moral themes of the *yuefu* convention, Wen Tingyun used these events of enormous consequences as artistic materials. Uninterested in the political and social implications of historical events, he is rather fascinated by the pomp and sensuality of the events themselves. Thus he has written numerous poems on the Southern Dynasties and Sui rulers, and on the tragic, disastrous affair between Emperor Xuanzong of Tang 唐玄宗 (r. 712–56) and his "precious concubine," Yang Guifei 楊貴妃. Conventional wisdom has it that the An Lushan rebellion and the ensuing decline of the Tang dynasty were brought about largely by the corruption in Xuanzong's court. This corruption was caused in part by Xuanzong's doting affection for Yang Guifei, who by Late Tang had become the most notorious *femme fatale* in Chinese history.

Many poets had already written about this event. The most well known example is Bai Juyi's "Changhenge" 長恨歌 ("Song of Everlasting Sorrow"), which seems to have inaugurated the romantic treatment of this otherwise disastrous story. But Bai Juyi did make a gesture toward political criticism, in showing that rulers who indulged in their sensual pleasures suffered dire consequences.[31] Wen Tingyun, in his

numerous poems on this theme, rarely mentions the social aftermath
of this event and offers no political and moral criticism.[32] In Chinese
tradition it is, of course, one of the chief functions of poetry, particularly when the subject is one of national interest.

Consider the following short poem in the form of a sacrilegious
humor and mockery, aimed both at Xuanzong and his critics:

龍尾驛婦人圖　THE PICTURE OF A WOMAN AT DRAGON-TAIL INN

慢笑開元有倖臣　Do not jeer that there were vile ministers during
　　　　　　　　　Kaiyuan
直教天子到蒙塵　Who made the Son of Heaven meet shameful dust.
今來看畫猶如此　Even today looking at her picture is like this,
何況親逢絕世人[33]　Not to mention meeting in person this beauty of
　　　　　　　　　beauties.

Kaiyuan is the name of Emperor Xuanzong's first reign. The poet
is looking at a picture of Yang Guifei in one of the inns in the capital
area. So overwhelmed is he by the artistic re-creation of this beautiful *femme fatale* that he thinks he understands why Xuanzong let the
state "topple" for her (*femme fatale* in Chinese is *qingchen meiren* 傾
城美人, the beautiful woman who topples the city, or the kingdom).[34]
The poet speculates that a woman so charming in painting must have
been irresistible in the flesh. This is the amoral dandy speaking. Surely,
the morally earnest Confucian readers must have been outraged by
the humor and sarcasm.

This was a terse poem, however, constrained by its brevity. Wen
Tingyun's appetite for sensual description is released in full in the
longer poem:

過華清宮　　　PASSING THE HUAQING PALACE:
二十二韻　　　TWENTY-TWO RHYMES

憶昔開元日　I remember during the Kaiyuan period in the past,
承平事勝游　In a time of peace they enjoyed grand tours.
貴妃專寵幸　The Precious Concubine enjoyed the sole favor of
　　　　　　　the Son of Heaven,
天子富春秋　Who was then in his prime.　　　　　　　　4
月白霓裳殿　Bright moon shines on the Rainbow Skirt Palace,
風乾羯鼓樓　Dry wind blows on the Jie Drum Mansions.

| 斗雞花蔽膝 | Cockfight boys wear aprons of flowery patterns, | |
|---|---|---|
| 騎馬玉搔頭 | Horse riders all have jade scratchers. | 8 |
| 繡轂千門仗 | Palace girls from ten hundred gates sit in decorated carriages, | |
| 金鞍萬戶侯 | Lords of ten thousand households ride on gold saddles. | |
| 薄雲攲³⁵雀扇 | Thin clouds lean on swallow fans, | |
| 輕雪犯貂裘 | Light snow encroaches on marten coats. | 12 |
| 過客聞韶濩 | Passing travelers hear banquet music, | |
| 居人識冕旒 | Residents recognize the imperial banners. | |
| 氣和春不覺 | In the harmonious atmosphere spring comes unnoticed, | |
| 煙暖霽難收 | Warm mist does not melt as the day clears. | 16 |
| 澀浪和瓊甃 | Ripples move with the jade tiles of a pool, | |
| 晴陽上彩斿 | Bright sun ascends on the colorful banner-pendants. | |
| 卷衣輕鬢懶 | She rolls up her robe, hair falling from her forehead indolently, | |
| 窺鏡澹蛾羞 | She looks secretly into mirror, pale moth-eyebrows shy. | 20 |
| 屏掩芙蓉帳 | Screens block the hibiscus net, | |
| 簾褰玳瑁鉤 | Curtains are held up by the tortoise-shell hooks. | |
| 重瞳分渭曲 | Her double pupils divide the place of Weiqu, | |
| 纖手指神州 | Slender fingers point at the nation's capital. | 24 |
| 御案迷萱草 | Imperial tables entice the worry-forgetting grass, | |
| 天袍妒石榴 | Heavenly robes make the pomegranates jealous. | |
| 深岩藏浴鳳 | High rocks hide the bathing phoenix, | |
| 鮮隰媚潛虯 | The lovely bank charms the lurking dragon. | 28 |
| 不料邯鄲蝨 | Unexpectedly that flea of Handan | |
| 俄成即墨牛 | All of a sudden turns himself into a wild bull of Jimo. | |
| 劍鋒揮太皥 | [Like] Tai Hao the ancient father he waves his sword, | |
| 旗焰拂蚩尤 | Chi You and his troops sweep by with banners and flames. | 32 |
| 內嬖陪行在 | The royal concubine goes along with the retreating retinue, | |
| 孤臣預坐籌 | While a minister makes his secret plan alone. | |
| 瑤簪遺翡翠 | Jade hairpins drop from kingfisher feathers, | |

| | | |
|---|---|---|
| 霜仗駐驊騮 | Frosty spears stop the imperial carriages. | 36 |
| 艷笑雙飛斷 | Lovely smiles are broken in a paired flight, | |
| 香魂一哭休 | The fragrant soul ended in a cry. | |
| 早梅悲蜀道 | Early plums sorrow over the road of Shu, | |
| 高樹隔昭丘 | Tall trees block the hills at Zhaoyang. | 40 |
| 朱閣重霄近 | Red palaces approach the clouds in sky, | |
| 蒼崖萬古愁 | Green cliffs are filled with eternal sorrow. | |
| 至今湯殿水 | Till today the water from the palace springs | |
| 嗚咽縣前流[36] | Mournfully flows through the district. | 44 |

This poem illustrates Wen Tingyun's typical decadent treatment of historical events as merely poetic material, devoid of the moral and instructional values considered essential in the Confucian tradition. Except for the first four lines which serve as a historical introduction, I have translated the rest of the poem in the present tense because it clearly aims to conjure up with some immediacy the grandeur and the drama of a past era. It lends a sense of participation, instead of distancing that a past tense rendering would force on it. The poem quickly sets about detailing the extravagant lifestyle of Emperor Xuanzong and Yang Guifei. Lines 5 and 6 depict the night-long party in the imperial court. "Rainbow Skirt" (nishang霓裳) refers to a tune called "The Tune of Rainbow Skirt and Dancing Robe" 霓裳舞衣曲. It originally came from the frontier region but was later revised by Xuanzong himself. It is said that Yang Guifei was particularly gifted at dancing to it.[37] The Jie Drum (jiegu 羯鼓) is another "barbarian" musical instrument of which Xuanzong was fond.[38] As in "Watching a Dancing Girl" discussed earlier, the allusion to these two examples of frontier culture highlights the scandal of this couple's life. But it also carries with it an irony, for it was precisely the rebellion from a barbarian region that ended Yang Guifei's life and pushed the Tang dynasty into irrevocable decline.

But the chief concern of the poem is to re-create the activities at Xuanzong's court. Besides the night-long dancing party, the pleasure-seeking is described in many ways: in cockfightings (line 5), in outings (line 6), and in the luxurious clothing and ornaments worn by the people connected to the court (lines 6–12). Then in line 15 the poem moves inside to describe Xuanzong and his concubine. Nature becomes insignificant in the atmosphere (qi 氣) of this court—the couple do not even sense the coming of spring (chunbujue 春不覺). Line 16 further emphasizes the point as the warm mist (*yannuan* 煙暖) curling around the court remains unmovable even as a clear day approaches (*jinanshou* 霽難收). Line 17 introduces the erotic aspect of the royal couple's life: bathing in a hot spring pool. Lines 19 and 20 describe Yang Guifei's famous indolence after her bath.[39] Lines 21 and 22 once more play the game of half-concealing and half-revealing so often found in Palace Style poetry. Our view of the innermost part of the bedroom, the net, is blocked by the screens, but somehow we are still able to see it, and by extension, the people inside it, because the curtains are held up by ornate hooks. Lines 25 and 26 present another victory of artifice over nature: the rare plant that can make people forget their worries (*xuancao* 萱草) is enticed (*mi* 迷) by one of the most commomplace items in court, the imperial table, and pomegranates are shamed (*du* 妒) by the robes worn by the royal couple (*tianpao* 天袍).

Lines 27 and 28 are ambiguous, because the referents are not clear. Who is the "bathing phoenix?" Who is the "lurking dragon"? The previous lines have depicted Xuanzong and Yang Guifei, so we assume they are Yang Guifei and Xuanzong respectively.[40] But are they? This interpretation has its problems. Line 28, for example, derives from the first line of Xie Lingyun's poem "Deng chishanglou" 登池上樓 ("Ascending the Tower by the Pond"): 潛虯媚幽姿 ("The hidden gesture of lurking dragon is beautiful").[41] As various commentators have remarked, for Xie Lingyun the "lurking dragon" symbolizes a longing for a reclusive life and a protected moral integrity that he himself had regrettably not achieved.[42] This meaning is irrelevant in the context of Wen Tingyun's poem, for surely Xuanzong, indulging with his concubine and thereby neglecting his state responsibilities, was not agonizing over his integrity. Gu Sili, the Qing editor of Wen Tingyun's poetry, thinks the "lurking dragon" refers to An Lushan[43] and that these two lines imply a criticism of the royal couple (*yinhan fengci* 隱含諷刺). Whatever the case, the images work well in the poem because they produce a picture with strong erotic overtones.

Beginning in line 29 the poem turns to An Lushan rebellion and its disastrous consequences, not for the nation, however, but for the royal couple. This section is much shorter: only twelve lines, compared with twenty-six lines devoted to the pomp of the court. But even here Wen Tingyun targets the sensual and the dramatic. Tai Hao 太皞 in line 31 is another name for Fu Xi 伏犧, one of the legendary fathers of China.

It was he who created the eight diagrams and thereby gave language to the Chinese people. If Wen Tingyun compared An Lushan to Fu Xi merely to give "an elegant description of An's troops moving west on the capital,"[44] as Rouzer claims, then he has committed an act of blasphemy; for to compare a much hated villain like An Lushan with the founder of the Chinese race is an outrage. More likely, it indicates Wen Tingyun's apolitical, amoral, and purely aesthetic attitude: he is interested only in artistic effect, to the exclusion of any moral implications.

Line 32 alludes to the ancient legend concerning the battle between Huangdi黃帝, another legendary ruler of China, and his minister Chi You蚩尤, who rebelled against him. What follows is one of the numerous colorful descriptions of their battle found in ancient documents:

Before Huangdi took power, there were eighty-one Chi You brothers. They all had animal bodies, but could speak human language; they had bronze heads, iron foreheads; they ate sand and stone. They made various weapons like spears, knives, and bows. They slaughtered people for no reason and were completely wicked. The people of the land wanted Huangdi to be the Son of Heaven. Since Huandi was a virtuous ruler, he could not defeat Chi You and his brothers. Heaven then sent down the Dark Lady who taught Huangdi magic military strategies. By these he was able to bring them under control, and made the country peaceful.[45]

In alluding to this story Wen Tingyun evokes the drama and its legendary details. From the moral point of view the comparison of the battle between the imperial army and the rebelling troops with the battle between Huangdi and Chi You reverses the situation of the previous line. But again, Wen Tingyun's concern is dramatic effect, not the moral or political correctness of his comparison. How else to explain the extreme liberty he has taken in his use of allusions?

In depicting the fate of Xuanzong and Yang Guifei, Wen Tingyun highlights two dramatic occurrences: the execution of Yang Guifei (lines 37–38) and Xuanzong's desire to remove her body for reburial (lines 39–40). The "fragrant soul" in line 38, we may recall, comes from Li He's "The Coming of Autumn." But while the latter poem uses it to refer to the ghost of the dead, Wen Tingyun has used it as a metaphor for Yang Guifei at the moment of her death. Zhaoyang Hill is the place where the Emperor Taizong of Tang buried his consort Lady Sun. The mention of this burial place hints at Xuanzong's desire to bury Yang Guifei there, but unsuccessfully, for it is "blocked by tall trees."

According to the *Jiu Tang shu*, after the rebellion was crushed, Xuanzong ordered Yang Guifei's body recovered from the place it had been hastily buried. The body, however, was already decomposed; only the fragrant sachets remained unchanged. Overwhelmed with grief, Xuanzong had her picture painted and hung in court,[46] a sentimental episode that moves the poem in a different direction—from dramatic description to the final ironic, if sympathetic, four lines of the poem. The presence of the poet is felt once again: having relished the theatricality of this pompous yet tragic story from afar (from line 3 to line 40), he moves closer to give the poem a very conventional ending: that while the past glory has disappeared, nature, which has served as the stage of this drama, remains the same. The water of the hot spring that used to wash the jadelike skin of Yang Guifei now flows through the field of the district. A mournful murmur, projected by the poet through a pathetic fallacy, is all that it can offer of its sympathy, if it has any at all.

As has been observed earlier, Southern Dynasties is another period that fascinates Wen Tingyun. If Xuanzong was too close to Wen Tingyun's own time to be criticized overtly, Southern Dynasties had already established itself as the archetype of corruption and was rountinely condemned by Sui and Tang historians. For Wen Tingyun's decadent aesthetic, however, it is above criticism, as we see in the following piece:

| 雞鳴埭歌 | "A SONG OF COCKCROW DIKE" |
|---|---|
| 南朝天子射雉時 | When during the Southern Dynasties the Son of Heaven goes for pheasant hunting, |
| 銀河耿耿星參差 | The Milky Way is bright, and stars scatter around. |
| 銅壺漏斷夢初覺 | Bronze waterclock stops, they first wake up from their dreams, |
| 寶馬塵高人未知 | Bejeweled horses stir up dust, all to the ignorance of others. 4 |
| 魚躍蓮東蕩宮沼 | Fish leap east of the lotus, disturbing the Xuanwu Pond, |

| | |
|---|---|
| 濛濛御柳懸棲鳥 | Nesting birds hang on the misty royal willows. |
| 紅妝萬戶鏡中春 | Crimson faces by myriad windows: Spring in mirrors, |
| 碧樹一聲天下曉 | From emerald trees a sound announces the dawning of day. 8 |
| | |
| 磐踞勢窮三百年 | For three hundred years they occupied this place, then their power declined, |
| 朱方殺氣成愁煙 | On this dark red land killing air turns into sorrowful smoke.⁴⁷ |
| 慧星拂地浪連海 | Comet brooms sweep the earth, one ocean wave after another, |
| 戰鼓渡江塵漲天 | Battle drums cross the river, the sky is filled with dust. 12 |
| | |
| 繡龍畫雉塡宮井 | Embroidered dragon and painted pheasants throw themselves into the palace well, |
| 野火風驅燒九鼎 | Wind drives the wildfire to burn the Nine Tripods. |
| 殿巢江燕砌生蒿 | The Palaces are nesting places for river swallows, weeds grow from their steps, |
| 十二金人霜炯炯 | Twelve bronze guardians glitter in the frost. 16 |
| | |
| 芊綿平綠台城基 | Lush and level green fields stretch to the old palace base, |
| 暖色春空⁴⁸荒古陂 | The warm color of empty Spring hangs on the ancient slope. |
| 寧知玉樹後庭曲 | Who could have known that the tune of "jade-trees and rear-court flowers" |
| 留待野棠如雪枝⁴⁹ | Would wait to turn into wild crabapple trees, with their snowy boughs? 20 |

These are the activities in the courts of Emperor Wu of Qi Dynasty 齊武帝 (r. 483–93) and Chen Houzhu 陳後主. The latter, as we already know, was the most notoriously corrupt ruler of the Southern Dynasties period. Wen Tingyun worte the poem in *yuefu*, a form of which he was especially fond,⁵⁰ and for understandable reason. *Yuefu* is liberating in ways other genres are not. The dictum that "poetry expresses one's will" demands historicity and requires that the poet write from personal experience. Fictionality is viewed as a sign of insincerity,

135

thus of bad poetry, because it misleads readers in their attempt to grasp the will of the poet. This notion of poetry seriously limits the scope of the poet's imagination, particularly for one who writes not about his own experience, but about something removed from his life. For such a one fictionality offers liberation from a narrow historical framework and the opportunity for his imagination to roam, even to re-create history.

The generic characteristics of *yuefu* poetry provide an ideal compromise. Because it is taken for granted that the *yuefu* poets are not speaking in their own voices, but in the voices of the other,[51] a certain amount of fictionality is acceptable. The poet is allowed to write from his imagination, other than from his experience, as long as it is kept under control. This usually means that it can be incorporated into a historical context through an allegorical reading.[52] The "Cockcrow Dike" and many other *yuefu* poems of Wen Tingyun meet that criterion. Like the *yuefu* poems in Palace Style convention, they often thwart our attempts to allegorize them, but unlike the *yuefu* poems in Palace Style convention, these poems by Wen Tingyun deal with historical topics. The generic features of *yuefu* free him to write his own version of history.

"Cockcrow Dike" uses the same textual strategy found in "Passing Huaqing Spring: Twenty-Two Rhymes," although the latter was written in "extended regulated verse." The present poem focuses largely on the sensuality and drama of life at court. It is written in the unit of four-line stanzas, with each stanza using a same rhyme and dealing with a specific aspect of the general topic. The first stanza describes an early outing. "The Son of Heaven" in the first line refers to Emperor Wu, who according to *Nan shi* would go out with his courtiers and court ladies very early in the morning. The cocks would start crowing just as they arrived at the northern dike of Xuanwu Pond, hence the name "Cockcrow Dike."[53] The focus of this stanza is not on any specific people or activities, but on the overall setting: under the beautiful starry sky the emperor's retinue makes its imperial start.

Stanza 2 opens the scene up, as the dawn approaches. This sensual, yet delicate, environment is suggested by carefully chosen images such as the leaping fish (*yuyue* 魚躍), misty royal willows (*mengmeng yuliu* 濛濛御柳), hanging nesting birds (*xuanqiniao* 懸棲鳥), and women with rich makeup (*hongzhuang* 紅妝) gazing at themselves (who are compared with spring) in mirrors; even the cockcrow announcing the dawn is described as coming from the emerald trees (*bishu* 碧樹) of the palaces.

But in stanza 3 this delicate world is suddenly turned into a battle-field. The drama is spectacular. There is little information to explain the vague phrase "killing air" (*shaqi* 殺氣) in line 10. On the contrary, the description in lines 11 and 12 conjures up magnificence and gran-deur: the long comet-tails from the sky, the huge waves, the racing battle boats cheered by the accompanying drum music. Then the next stanza recounts a hilarious story about Chen Houzhu. In his official biography in *Nan shi* it is recorded that when the invading troops entered the city, the emperor, together with his two favorite concu-bines, hid themselves in a well in the palace. When the soldiers were about to throw stones into the well, his majesty finally answered their calls and the three were pulled out by a rope.[54] "Embroidered dragon" and "painted pheasants" are patterns on the clothes worn by the emperor and his consorts, respectively. Instead of referring to them directly by names or titles, the poet uses synecdochical tropes to enhance the visual quality and dramatic effect of this line. The "Nine Tripods" in line 14 is a symbol of the whole nation. Thus the emperor's ludicrous act of hiding is juxtaposed with the tragic destruction of the nation. The second couplet of this stanza (lines 15 and 16) brings us for the first time to the poet's position: the palaces have decayed, nature has silently, gradually regained its control over this place where human arrogance and corruption once reigned. In these two lines Wen Tingyun is indirectly alluding to two Mid Tang poets, Liu Yuxi劉禹錫 (772–842) and Li He. Line 15 is a rewriting of Liu Yuxi's famous qua-train poem on the loss of Southern Dynasties vainglory:

烏衣巷 — DARK CLOTHES LANE

朱雀橋邊野草花 By the Red Sparrow Bridge wild flowers and grass grow,
烏衣巷口夕陽斜 Above Dark Clothes Lane the sun is setting,
舊時王謝堂前燕 The swallows that used to nest under the roofs of aristocrats
飛入尋常百姓家[55] Now are flying into the households of common people.

Whereas in Wen Tingyun's poem nature replaces the old pomp, in this poem the old vainglory degrades into the commonplace. But using the same image of the swallow suggests a connection between the two pieces, and both share a mood of melancholy and irony. As for the "bronze guardians" (*jinren* 金人) in line 16, it alludes to Li He's "Jintong xianren ci Han ge" 金銅仙人辭漢歌 ("A farewell song of the bronze immortal leaving Han").[56] Li He expresses the sadness of the bronze figure brought about by the change of its fate: it was originally made by the decree of Emperor Wu of Han, but now it is being moved to the court of Emperor Ming of Wei 魏明帝 (r. 227–39). The twelve bronze gardians in Wen Tingyun's poem have undergone a similar experience. The last stanza of "Cockcrow Dike" reinforces this process of human and cultural change and decay even as nature is resuscitated: the palace buildings are leveled by the lush green fields, and the "Jade-tree and Rear-court Song" that Chen Houzhu and his consorts used to play at court[57] is now replaced by the wild crabtrees with snowy branches.

This focus on the sensuality and drama of historical event, then, is most characteristic of Wen Tingyun's poetry on history. However, I think it is an exaggeration to claim, as one critic did, that "Wen does not lament the loss of the past; he makes it up out of his imagination."[58] In fact, his artistic re-creation of history, done so well in this and other poems, does not mean that Wen Tingyun lacks a keen historical sense. Rather, his historical sense is often presented as an awareness of a past glory irrevocably lost, and as a realization of the belatedness of his age. To demonstrate this let us look at the following poem:

| 題翠微寺 二十二韻 | TWENTY-TWO RHYMES ON CUIWEI TEMPLE |
|---|---|
| 邠土初成邑 | When the land of Bin first became a district, |
| 虞賓竟讓王 | The ancient sage kings voluntarily gave up their thrones. |
| 乾符初得位 | When Taizong first received the imperial seal, |
| 天弩夜收鋩 | By night the Bow Star in heaven withdrew its sharp edge. |
| 偃息齊三代 | The world was peaceful as the times of Xia, Shang, and Zhou, |
| 優游念四方 | Conscientiously he tended the land in four directions. |

4

138

| | |
|---|---|
| 萬靈扶正寢 | People all over the country gave support to their Lord,[59] |
| 千嶂抱重崗 | Myriad mountains embraced multiple layers of hills. |
| 幽石歸階陛 | Seclusive stones returned to be ascending steps, |
| 喬柯入棟梁 | Tall trees entered to be palace columns. |
| 火雲如沃雪 | Burning clouds were like bright snow, |
| 湯殿似含霜 | Hot Spring Palace seemed wrapped with frost. |
| 澗籟添僛曲 | Sound from valleys added its godly tune,[60] |
| 巖花借御香 | Flowers on rocks borrowed from imperial fragrance. |
| 野麋陪獸舞 | Wild deer danced in company with beasts, |
| 林鳥逐鵷行 | Forest birds followed phoenixes in their flight. |
| 鏡寫三秦色 | Mirrors portrayed the colors of Sanqin area, |
| 窗搖八水光 | Windows shook the light of Eight Rivers. |
| 問雲徵楚女 | Asking clouds to seek the girls of Chu, |
| 疑粉試何郎 | [Offering hot soup to] test if He Yan's face was powdered.[61] |
| 蘭芷承雕輦 | Carved wheels rolled on orchid grass, |
| 杉蘿入畫堂 | Vines and firs came into the colorful hall. |
| 受朝松露曉 | The Son of Heaven received his ministers in pine-dewed morning, |
| 頒朔桂煙涼 | And distributed the coming year calendar in laurel-mist chill. |
| 嵐濕金鋪外 | Beyond the gold door knockers the mountain wind was damp, |
| 溪鳴錦幄旁 | Streams murmured by the brocade canopy. |
| 倚絲憂漢祖 | [Lady Qi] played the string music by the sorrowing emperor, |
| 持璧告秦皇 | [The envoy] held the jade seal to tell his majesty's death. |
| 短景催風馭 | Brief sunlight hastened the wind chariot, |
| 長星屬羽觴 | By the long stars they toasted with bird-shaped cups. |
| 儲君猶問豎 | The crown prince was still asking questions to serving boys, |
| 元老已登床 | But the old minister was already by his majesty's bed. |

| | | |
|---|---|---|
| 鶴蓋驅平樂 | The crane chariot marched to Pingle palace, | |
| 雞人下建章 | The cock people went down to Jianzhang. | |
| 龍髯悲滿眼 | The dragon whiskers filled people's eyes with grief, | |
| 螭首淚沾裳 | And the dragon head made their clothes wet with tears. | 36 |
| 疊鼓嚴靈仗 | The light drum music accompanied the solemn procession, | |
| 吹笙送夕陽 | The whistle of pipes saw off the setting sun. | |
| 斷泉辭劍佩 | Broken spring bade farewell to sword pendants, | |
| 昏日伴旂常 | Darkening day attended the dragon banners. | 40 |
| 遺廟青蓮在 | The old temples and green lotus still exist, | |
| 頹垣碧草芳 | Their walls have decayed, emerald plants are lush. | |
| 無因奏韶濩 | For no reason someone is playing an ancient tune, | |
| 流涕對幽篁[62] | Tears streaming down, I face the solitary bamboos. | 44 |

Cuiwei Temple is where Emperor Taizong of Tang dynasty died.
Taizong is one of the most respected political rulers in Chinese history.
His two-decade reign is said to have laid the foundation for the glory
of the Tang dynasty. Wen Tingyun's poem falls into the category of
the *huaigu* 懷古 or "recalling the antiquity" convention that was particularly popular during the Mid and Late Tang era. It describes a
visit to an ancient site and the stream of thoughts evoked by this
occasion. This piece too betrays a fascination with the sensual details
and pomp of the past. But what distinguishes this from his other poems
is the seriousness of the topic: not the corrupt Southern Dynasties or
the love affair between Xuanzong and Yang Guifei, but rather the
historical figure considered to be the paragon of Confucian statesmanship. But even so, Wen Tingyun's Palace Style mentality intrudes,
with the result that Taizong's political achievement is praised in the
vocabulary of such convention.

The first section (lines 1–6) provides some background about Taizong's reign. Wen Tingyun compares him with enlightened rulers of
ancient times and tells us that when his majesty came to power, the
country was at peace. The long descriptive section from line 14 to line
26 is filled with the ornate, artificial diction typical of Palace Style
poetry. The emperor's chariots have "carved wheels" (*diaonian* 雕輦,
line 21); the palace halls, which bid the plants to "enter," are described

with the cliché "colorful halls" (*huatang* 畫堂, line 22). The solemn state activities conducted by the emperor (lines 23–24) are figured by artificial conceits like "pine-dewed morning" (*songluxiao* 松露曉) and "laurel-mist chill" (*guiyanliang* 桂煙涼), meaning simply that Taizong worked from early morning till dusk.

Another example of this tendency toward the Palace Style is the introduction of an erotic element that seems irrelevant to the topic of the poem. Line 19 "Asking clouds to seek the girls of Chu" (問雲徵楚女) apparently alludes to the sexual encounter between King Xiang of Chu and the goddess of Mount Wu described in Song Yu's "Gaotang fu." Line 20 refers to the story of a handsome gentleman called He Yan 何晏 (?–249). Suspicious that He Yan might have used makeup, Emperor Ming of Wei 魏明帝 (r. 227–39) gave him a bowl of hot soup in a sultry summer day, only to find that his face was even more brilliant.[63] The significance of these two allusions is not at all clear here. Had this couplet occurred in a poem on a less serious topic, it would have been well taken, but in this context it simply does not justify its presence, unless it is meant for a specific purpose that escapes us.

This poem demonstrates Wen Tingyun's keen awareness of the decadence of his own age. It enacts the evolution of the phrase *tuifei* from its first literal use in describing the physical breakdown of nature to its later metaphorical reference to spiritual and moral decline. The poem recounts the glories of the past with great nostalgia, not simply from the beginning of Tang dynasty, but from the beginning of Chinese civilization, when the sage kings passed the throne to their successors, not according to the principles of blood relationship, but according to the merit of the people chosen (lines 1–2). While that age was long past, while the later practice of handing down the kingship to one's own son represented decline, society still had many positive qualities, which are embodied in the peaceful and colorful life of Taizong's reign (lines 3–26). The sometimes nearly Edenic description of the world at peace, for instance, "Wild deer danced in accompany with beasts,/ Forest birds followed phoenixes in their flight" (野麋陪獸舞，林鳥逐鸞行), is utopian. It reveals a passionate longing for that past glory.

The description of Taizong's passing away occupies fourteen lines (lines 27–40) in this forty-two line poem. In lines 27 and 28 the poet portrays this event using two allusions that did not come across in my translation. Specifically, Taizong is compared with two monarchs.

Hanzu 漢祖 refers to Han Gaozu 漢高祖 Liu Bang 劉邦 (256–195 B.C.); Qinhuang 秦皇 refers to Qin Shihuang 秦始皇 (259–210 B.C.); both are founding emperors of the Han and Qin dynasties. Apparently they are used as substitutes for Tang Taizong, who is the focus of this poem. But the choice of Qin Shihuang seems to have resulted from the metrical requirement, since *huang* 皇 contains the rhyming vowel of this regulated verse. Yet again Wen Tingyun displays his disregard for the political implications of his allusion. Qin Shihuang and Tang Taizong, that is, are usually regarded as two completely different types of monarchs: the former as a cruel tyrant, the latter an enlightened ruler. Once more aesthetic presentation, rather than the political and historical significance, is the driving force in treating this otherwise very solemn topic.

The lengthy depiction of Taizong's death and funeral ceremonies not only reveals Wen Tingyun's usual fascination with dramatic details, but also conveys a sense of loss, the poet's obsession with the process of decline. His feelings of sadness are mostly submerged in the vivid description of the process itself, but occasionally they surface, as in lines 35 and 36, which describe the people's genuine grief at Taizong's death. This sadness erupts in the last four lines of the poem, as the poet weeps over the remains of a lost glory, marked by collapsed buildings. Interestingly, the word Wen Tingyun uses to describe this broken condition is *tui* 頹, which, as has been explained in detail in the Introduction and chapter 1, is the first and the main component of the compound *tuifei* 頹廢, the Chinese equivalent of "decadence." For Wen Tingyun these broken walls of Cuiwei Temple not only recall the buildings of the past; they are also signs of moral, political, and literary decadence in his own time. This historical awareness brings about a rare emotional display in Wen Tingyun's poetry, for the poet allows himself to weep: "Tears streaming down, I face the solitary bamboos" 流涕對幽篁.

At other times Wen Tingyun's sense of history is presented as sarcastic and mocking, as in the following:

春江花月夜詞　The Night of Spring River and Flowery Moon

玉樹歌闌海雲黑　The "Jade Trees" tune ended, the ocean clouds
　　　　　　　　　became dark,
花庭忽作青蕪國　The flowery courtyards suddenly turned into
　　　　　　　　　a land of green weeds.

| | |
|---|---|
| 秦淮有水水無情 | Water is still flowing in Qinhuai River, but it has no feelings, |
| 還向金陵漾春色 | It still ripples off spring color to the old capital Jinling. |

4

| | |
|---|---|
| 楊家二世安九重 | The second of the Yang clan rested under the heaven, |
| 不御華芝嫌六龍 | He discards the grand carriages, grows tired of the dragon team. |
| 百幅錦帆風力滿 | Hundreds of brocade sails [speed], the wind is full in power, |
| 連天展盡金芙蓉 | And golden lotus stretch to the end of sky. |

8

| | |
|---|---|
| 珠翠丁星復明滅 | Starry pearls and emeralds glitter now and then, |
| 龍頭劈浪哀笳發 | Dragon-heads cut into waves, whistles give out sad tunes. |
| 千里涵空照[64]水魂 | For thousands of miles the sky is mirrored in the river, reflecting water spirits, |
| 萬枝破鼻團[65]香雪 | Tens of thousands flowers are budding forth in fragrant snow. |

12

| | |
|---|---|
| 漏轉霞高滄海西 | As the waterclock clicks, colorful clouds ascend west of the vast sea, |
| 玻璃[66]枕上聞天雞 | From the glass pillow he hears the crow of heavenly cocks. |
| 蠻弦代雁[67]曲如語 | Songs from all over the country murmur on, |
| 一醉昏昏天下迷 | In his dead drunkenness the world goes astray. |

16

| | |
|---|---|
| 四方傾動煙塵起 | All of a sudden smoke and dust burst out in four directions, |
| 猶在濃香夢魂里 | While he is still in a dream of thick fragrance. |
| 後主荒宮有曉鶯 | By the deserted palaces of Chen Houzhu there are morning orioles, |
| 飛來只隔西江水[68] | Which need only cross a Western River to fly over here. |

20

"The Night of Spring River and Flowery Moon" is a tune first created by Chen Houzhu. Although its lyrics did not survive, we know from history books that it was a tune perfomed in his court.[69] The second of the Yang clan refers to the second emperor of Sui, Emperor Yang 隋煬帝 (r. 605–18), another infamous ruler of another short-lived dynasty. He composed two poems to this tune, both of which are still extant. Since it illustrates the unique character of Wen Tingyun's verse, we will look at one of them:

| | |
|---|---|
| 春江花月夜 | THE NIGHT OF SPRING RIVER AND |
| 二首：其一 | FLOWERY MOON: TWO POEMS. No 1 |
| 暮江平不動 | The dusk river is level without movement, |
| 春花滿正開 | The spring flowers are just now blooming in full. |
| 流波將月去 | The waves move away with the moon, |
| 潮水帶星來[70] | The tides bring the stars down. |

This poem was written in two parallel couplets. The last two lines display a particular poetic wit that plays on visual illusions: the moon seems to be taken away by the waves, and the stars seem to be brought down by the increasing tides. How carefully the movement in this couplet is constructed: the waves move up into the sky, while stars come down to earth. This piece demonstrates Emperor Yang's expert training in Palace Style Poetry, but it is also striving for total neglect of the historical origins of this tune. The Early Tang poet Zhang Ruoxu 張若虛 (fl. early eighth century) wrote another poem for this tune.[71] Although his piece demonstrates a philosophical contemplation and universal spirit that are absent in Emperor Yang's poem, like the other poem it too is not interested in the tune's historical associations.

In his poem, however, Wen Tingyun does evoke these historical associations. Thus we see them to a great extent as a Late Tang creation, essential to an understanding of this and many other poems of the period. The first four lines of Wen Tingyun's piece portray the rapid end of the Chen dynasty. "Jade Trees" is the short title of "The Tune of Jade Trees and Rear Court Flowers," another song by the Chen Houzhu. Its connection with the collapse of Chen is established at the very beginning of the poem: dark clouds arise as soon as the song is finished, and the palace courtyards are suddenly reduced to weeds. The second stanza introduces Emperor Yang. Blind to the lessons of Chen Houzhu, he indulges in an even more extravagant life, refusing to travel by the traditional imperial vehicle: "He discards the grand carriages, grows tired of the dragon team" (不御華芝嫌六龍).

Lines 7 to 16 describe his grand tour along the Grand Canal, which he ordered built for his own pleasures. In this seemingly objective description of the trip, Wen Tingyun has projected his own response to it, a rarity in his poetry. He describes the music played on the emperor's boat in line 10 as "sorrowful" (*ai* 哀) —sorrowful to Wen Tingyun because he knew that like the music in the court of Chen, it had brought down an entire country. Here the poet poses as an observer, reflecting upon that aesthetically attractive but politically disastrous episode in history. For a moment he seems to be affirming the traditional link between the loss of the nation and the corrupt lifestyles of these two rulers,[72] lifestyles that he portrays with full relish in his other poems. But he only hints his judgment with such subtle words like *ai* (sorrowful) in line 10 and *mi* 迷 "to get lost" in line 16. By the last stanza, however, even this trace of subjectivity is completely erased. We are left with a situation of intense irony: the deserted palaces of Chen—reminders of an earlier tragedy—are located right across the river. But Emperor Yang paid them no heed.

Despite the historical sense and sense of irony in the poem, however, Wen Tingyun remains fascinated with the sensuality of the Southern Dynasties court life. They are often mixed together in a very subtle manner, as our discussion of the previous poems has demonstrated. This complex mentality is most typical of Wen Tingyun's age. I quoted Liu Yuxi's "Dark Clothes Lane" earlier. To further demonstrate the point we need only look at Du Mu's "Mooring on Qinhuai River" 泊秦淮 :

煙籠寒水月籠沙　Mist wraps the cold water, moonlight wraps the sand,
夜泊秦淮近酒家　At night I moor near a wineshop on Qinhuai River.
商女不知亡國恨　The singing girl does not know the pain of nation
　　　　　　　　 lost,
隔江猶唱後庭花[73] Across the river she is still singing "Rear court
　　　　　　　　 Flowers."

Southern Dynasties, represented here by the "Rear court Flowers" tune first composed by Chen Houzhu, is by Late Tang a metaphor for fallen states. It is impossible to write about it and *not* evoke all its painful, yet sensual, aesthetic associations. However, Du Mu draws parallel, not between two past periods, but between a past period and his own age. Consequently the deep pain (*hen* 恨) in his poem signals his own personal involvement, an involvement conspicuous for its absence in most of Wen Tingyun's poetry. Except in "Twenty-Two Rhymes on Cuiwei Temple," where he pours out his emotions, more typically in writing about historical events Wen Tingyun prefers to be an aloof onlooker, rather than a passionate participant. Even when he verges on casting judgment on historical events, as in some parts of "The Night of Spring River and Flowery Moon," he quickly returns to his detached, mocking attitude. The morning orioles flying across the river from the deserted palaces of Chen Houzhu are vivid embodiment of this mockery.

The historicity of poems such as this lies not only in the fact that they are poems *about* history, but also in the fact that there is a zeitgeist peculiar to Late Tang—a feeling of loss, a sense of irony, a vague melancholy resulting from historical associations. The pervasive melancholy of Late Tang is tinged with an awareness of something irrevocably lost, be it the sensual life and drama in Southern Dynasties and Xuanzong's courts or the glory and vainglory of a past era. In this sense only the melancholy of late Tang may be defined as decadent, because it is caused by a historical sense. It is this historical sense that differentiates late Tang decadent poetry from the poetry of earlier periods, such as "Nineteen Ancient Poems," the poetry of Cao Zhi, Ruan Ji, and Southern Dynasties poets like Bao Zhao and Yu Xin. For these poets, melancholy stems from a keen sense of the transience of human life or from their personal frustrations.

Sometimes this melancholy is not connected to any specific historical moment, as it is in "The Night of Spring River and Flowery Night" and many other pieces about Southern Dynasties or the love affair between Xuanzong and Yang Guifei. The following piece illustrates this:

| 清涼寺 | THE LIMPIDLY COOL TEMPLE |
|---|---|
| 黃花紅樹謝芳蹊 | By the fragrant path yellow flowers and red tree leaves fall, |
| 宮殿參差黛嶬西 | Palaces are scattered around by the west of darkening hills. |
| 詩閣曉窗藏雪嶺 | Poetry pavilion and enlightening window gather the snowy peaks, |
| 畫堂秋水接藍溪 | Colorful hall and autumn waters connect with Blue Stream. [4] |

松飄晚吹摵金鐸　The scent of pine floats with evening wind,
　　　　　　　　　　　bronze bells are being drummed,
竹陰寒苔上石梯　Under bamboo shadow cold moss ascends the
　　　　　　　　　　　stone steps.
妙跡奇名竟何在　Where on earth are those wonderful deeds and
　　　　　　　　　　　outstanding names?
下方煙暝草萋萋[74]　Down there lush grass is seen amid the
　　　　　　　　　　　blurry mist.　　　　　　　　　　　　　　8

This lucid, colorful regulated verse brings us into a beautiful, yet belated world of nature in all its grandeur, whereas human presence is suggested only by the scattered, but equally elegant temples and their music. Even in this brilliant description of a largely natural world Palace Style clichés still abound, such as *fangxi* 芳蹊 (fragrant path), *huatang* 畫堂 (colorful hall), and *jinduo* 金鐸 (bronze bells). But what truly distinguishes this poem from Palace Style poetry is the sense of loss and the resultant melancholy found in the last two lines. Amid this spectacular autumn scene the poet's thought is directed to something that is absent: *miaoji* 妙跡 (wonderful deeds) and *qiming* 奇名 (outstanding names). The poet's question about their whereabouts, underscored by the emphatic word *jing* 竟 (on earth) in *jinghezai* 竟何在 ("where on earth are [they]?"), surely suggests a feeling of loss. The blurry mist (*yanming* 煙暝) and lush grass (*caoqiqi* 草萋萋), presented in the last line to evade answering such a highly emotional question, greatly enhance this sense of loss. With their physical extendedness, vagueness, and lushness, they are objective correlatives of the poet's mood.

Having read the poetry of Wen Tingyun, we may speculate about why his fame as a poet of *shi* declined in later periods. He is greatly indebted to Xiao Gang and Palace Style convention, but his transformation of this genre is not as thorough as that accomplished by Li He. Wen Tingyun's best poems—those that do demonstrate his personal style—are the ones that use the textual strategy of Palace Style convention inventively to aestheticize topics that usually carry heavy political and moral undertones in the Chinese tradition. This is particularly true with regard to his treatment of history. But it is precisely this decadent treatment of history and other serious subjects that is most offensive to canonical taste. The traditional reader who cherishes the social and political function of poetry will naturally look askance at the juxtaposition of An Lushan with Fu Xi or of Tang Taizong with Qin Shihuang merely for the sake of aesthetic effect. Thus what Wen Tingyun does best will be most despised by such readers— thus his marginal position in the history of Chinese poetry.

Furthermore, this is not the only bias in the Chinese poetic tradition that militates against Wen Tingyun's poetic agenda. When Confucius laments the passage of time it is deeply felt.[75] *Huaigu* ("recalling the antiquity") poetry requires that the poet combine the contemplation of history with the contemplation of his own personal life. History is not simply a material to be molded, but it is a source of education with which to enrich one's self-understanding. Thus when Du Fu writes about Song Yu or Zhuge Liang, he sees himself in these historical figures,[76] achieves an understanding of himself and his life that is otherwise not possible. But, as I have shown, except in the rare case Wen Tingyun usually assumes a stance of aloofness. If history is a drama, he is the most detached member of the audience. This lack of political and moral empathy only further substantiates the impression produced by his poetry, especially the pieces in the Palace Style, that he is a poetic dandy who, like his predecessors in the Southern Dynasties courts, is unconcerned with the fate of his country. Indeed, Wen Tingyun's mocking nonchalance may cause more offense, because while the Southern Dynasties court poets had no precedents to warn them of their behavior, Wen Tingyun had plenty. He deliberately chose the career of an aesthete, and as the quatrain cited at the beginning of this chapter shows, he was willing to pay for his belief, which may well be formulated as art for art's sake. The decline in popularity that his poetry suffered in later ages proves that he did.[77]

## Chapter 5

# Li Shangyin

## Negotiation with Tradition

One hundred years after Li Shangyin's death, about the middle of the ninth century, the historian Liu Xu 劉昫 and his colleagues compiled *Tang shu* 唐書 (*The history of Tang dynasty*, now known as *Jiu Tang shu* 舊唐書). They noted that like Wen Tingyun, Li Shangyin was arrogant about his literary talents (*chicai guiji* 持才詭激) and was also spurned by his superiors for his low moral character. At the same time they also juxtaposed Li Shangyin's poetry with that of Wen Tingyun, and concluded that in terms of "limpid elegance" (*qingli* 清麗) Wen Tingyun surpassed Li Shangyin.[1] This judgment is also reflected in the naming of the so-called Wen-Li style, which is characterized as "frivolously amorous and ornate poetry" (*ceci yanqu* 側詞艷曲),[2] and in the number of their poems collected in the Late Tang anthology *Caidiaoji* 才調集: sixty-one by Wen Tingyun, forty by Li Shangyin.[3] This number becomes more significant in light of the complete oeuvre of each poet: Wen Tingyun wrote about 340 poems, compared with more than 600 pieces by Li Shangyin.

Since the Song dynasty (960–1279), however, Li Shangyin's status as a poet has been steadily growing, while Wen Tingyun's has declined.[4] Wang Anshi 王安石 (1021–86), the renowned Song statesman and writer, even went so far as to claim that of all poets of the Tang dynasty Li Shangyin comes closest to Du Fu.[5] A Ming dynasty (1368–1644) scholar who praised Li Shangyin's poetry as being "charming with graceful feelings" (麗色閑情) viewed Wen Tingyun's work as "having diction without feelings" (有詞無情), echoing Yan Yu's accusation that Palace Style poetry was superficial.[6] The Qing critic Xue Xue 薛雪 once complained about the unfair juxtaposition of Li Shangyin and Wen Tingyun on the grounds that Du Fu and Li Shangyin were the only Tang poets worthy of loud praises.[7] To compare Li Shangyin with Du Fu is not only to elevate Li Shangyin's poetry, but also to attempt to clear him of the accusations against his moral character, since Du Fu is considered as a paragon of both. Over time, then, the fortunes of these two Late Tang poets went in opposite directions: whereas Li Shangyin stands enshrined as a major poet in Chinese literary history, few would lay claim to that stature for Wen Tingyun.

This chapter is not, however, about Li Shangyin's evolution from a decadent poet of "frivolously amorous and ornate poetry" (*ceci yanqu*) to a canonically acclaimed figure.[8] Instead, I seek to identify those qualities of his poetry that made such an evolution possible. Li Shangyin's poetry covers a broad range of subjects. There are indeed political and social poems, strongly influenced by Du Fu, as Wang Anshi suggested.[9] But there are also "frivolously amorous and ornate poems," or poems in the decadent line. It is the latter with which this chapter is concerned.

A Song dynasty critic once remarked that in its "ornate amorous-ness" (*yeyan* 冶艷) Li Shangyin's poetry resembles that of Yu Xin 庾信 (513–81) and Xu Ling, two representatives of Southern Dynasties Palace Style.[10] Like Li He and Wen Tinyun, Li Shangyin never tried to hide his love of Palace Style poetry, which he makes clear in a poem entitled "In Imitation of Xu Ling's Style: To a Court Maid in Charge of Changing Clothes" 效徐陵體贈更衣:

| | |
|---|---|
| 密帳眞珠絡 | Dense curtains and pearl nets, |
| 溫幃翡翠裝 | Warm drapes and kingfisher-feather clothes. |
| 楚腰知便寵 | Her Chu waist knows how to obtain favor, |
| 宮眉正鬥強 | Her palace brows struggle to show strength. 4 |
| 結帶懸梔子 | Gardenia seeds hang from her knotted sash, |
| 繡領刺鴛鴦 | Mandarin ducks are woven on her embroidered collar. |
| 輕寒衣省夜 | At a crispy night in the clothing room |
| 金斗熨沉香[11] | She smoothes the "sinking incense" with a bronze iron. 8 |

The trademark eroticism of Palace Style poetry is indicated even by the title of the poem, for the court maid referred to as *gengyi* 更衣 (changing clothes) is tasked with helping aristocrats change their clothing, often in their bedrooms. This expression alludes to a story about Zifu 子夫, who seduced the Emperor Wu of Han into taking her as a concubine as she helped him change his clothes at night.[12] The first couplet describes a familiar setting for court poetry: the bedroom; its private, affluent qualities are suggested by the use of typical Palace Style diction like "dense curtains" (*mizhang* 密帳), "pearls" (*zhenzhu* 眞珠), and "kingfisher-feather clothes" (*feicuizhuang* 翡翠裝). It is worth repeating that the word *mi* (密, dense) also means "intimate" and that when combined with its parallel counterpart in the second line, *wen* 溫 (warm), it suggests the erotic.

The second couplet moves away from this context to the direct portrayal of the court maid's manner. "Chu waist" refers to the story of a Chu king who starved his court ladies to make their waists slender,[13] but it later became a metaphor for an attractive woman, as it is used in this poem. The combination of the waist and brow movements of the court woman trying to attract the attention of her patron creates a humorous scene. The third couplet describes her clothes; the mandarin duck embroidery on her collar is also erotically suggestive, while gardenia seeds, as we have seen in Li He's "Self-Mocking," symbolizes love. The last two lines present the maid at work. Note how an otherwise commonplace job is rendered artificial and refined by a phrase like "bronze iron" *jindou* 金斗, and by the use of a metonymical figure of speech, "sinking incense" (*chenxiang* 沉香) for the scented robes.

Li Shangyin wrote another piece in similar style, but he connected it with Li He and called it "In Imitation of Changji [Li He]" ("Xiao Changji" 效長吉). It deserves to be examined because it illustrates the continuity of Palace Style poetry from Southern Dynasties to Late Tang and the poet's full awareness of it:

長長漢殿眉　The long eyebrows of Han palace,
窄窄楚宮衣　And the slender robe of Chu court.
鏡好鸞空舞　In vain the phoenix dances in the wonderful mirror,
簾疏燕誤飛　By mistake a swallow flies in through the sparse
　　　　　　　curtains.　　　　　4

君王不可問　　She had no way to inquire about her lord,
昨夜約黃歸[14]　Last night she returned with her light yellow
　　　　　　　　temples.

The poem reminds the reader more of Xiao Gang than of Li He, and it shows that by Li Shangyin's time, Li He was considered an important figure in the Palace Style convention. The first couplet uses synechdochical tropes to describe a court lady, as her long eyebrows and slender robes are used to represent the lady herself. The second line alludes to a poem by Yu Jianwu,[15] who we may recall was Xiao Gang's literary instructor, and that Li He had written a sympathetic poem about him. The second couplet portrays the court lady's manner: she is compared to a phoenix, and her putting on makeup is compared to the dancing of the bird. Her loneliness is suggested by the word "in vain" (*kong* 空), by its parallel word in the next line "by mistake" (*wu* 誤), and is further stressed by the ironic intrusion of a swallow through the sparse curtains (*lianshu* 簾疏), which have been put up to invite her lord, not the swallow, to come in. The last couplet describes, as most Palace Style poems do, the abandoned state of the woman. It adopts an image that has been used by Xiao Gang in his "On a Beautiful Woman:" the "light yellow temples" (*yuehuang* 約黃), thereby solidifying the reader's impression that this is a typical Palace Style poem.

These are Li Shangyin's lesser-known poems. Like others in the Palace Style convention, they are essentially poems of surface, lacking the kind of elusive meaning and lingering tone for which Li Shangyin is famous. Indeed, for those familiar with only the better known pieces in his oeuvre, such as his tantalizingly ambiguous and sometimes obscure "untitled" (*wuti* 無題) poems, it might be difficult to believe that they were written by him at all. They contradict the conventional view of his poetry.[16] Such readers may be disappointed at the aloof dandy suggested by them, not so different from Wen Tingyun.

His well-known works, by contrast, display a deep personal involvement; despite overwhelming odds, he or the hero of his poems typically cherishes an unyielding faith in love, as is suggested in the couplet "The spring silkworm will not die till all its silk is spilled out,/ The tears [of the candle] will dry up only after the candle is turned to ashes" (春蠶到死絲方盡，蠟炬成灰淚始干).[17] The reader is engaged by the sense of romantic frustration and determined steadfastness, and the continuing popularity of Li Shangyin's poetry since the Song depends to a great extent on his ability to convey these two qualities in poems that are usually considered "amorous and ornate." But these qualities are not foregrounded for their own sake as is often the case in Palace Style poetry. Instead, they are used to enhance the sensuality and textuality of the poems and thereby captivate the reader, which in turn underscores the message of the poem. The following is an example:

| 無題 | UNTITLED |
|---|---|
| 昨夜星辰昨夜風 | Last night's stars and last night's wind, |
| 畫樓西畔桂堂東 | The west side of colorful house and east of cassia hall. |
| 身無綵鳳雙飛翼 | Our bodies do not have wings to fly in pair like phoenixes, |
| 心有靈犀一點通 | Our hearts are connected together by a magic horn.[18] |
| 隔座送鉤春酒暖 | From separate seats the hook is passed, the spring wine is warm, |
| 分曹射覆蠟燈紅 | In divided teams we guess at riddles, the candle light is red.[19] |
| 嗟余聽鼓應官去 | Alas, I must leave for official duty as the drum sounds, |
| 走馬蘭台類轉蓬[20] | I ride my horse to the Orchid Terrace, like an uprooted weed. |

Like Li He and Wen Tingyun, Li Shangyin is also interested in building an enclosure, a kind of ivory tower to which he can retreat from the outside world. This inward turn during the Late Tang period is regarded by some cultural historians as the spirit of time. A contemporary Chinese critic says that during the Late Tang:

The aesthetic taste and artistic leitmotifs have become completely different from those of High Tang. From Mid Tang on they have become preoccupied with the pursuit of subtle sensual pleasures and emotions. . . . The spirit of the time was no longer to be found on horseback [i.e., battlefield] and in society, but in the bedroom and people's minds. . . . The theme of art is no longer to conquer the world, but to withdraw from the world."[21]

If this remark is intended to characterize the overall Late Tang culture, it is apparently a simplification. One can easily refute such a generalization by citing the socially oriented works of Li He and Li Shangyin. But as a characterization of the *one* aspect of the Late Tang culture that is our concern here, it nevertheless is a useful observation.

The present poem demonstrates nicely the tension between the poet's personal world and the outside world. It begins with a reminiscence of a social occasion at which the poet and his lover had once met. Two Palace Style images occur in the second line, namely, "colorful house" (*hualou* 畫樓) and "cassia hall" (*guitang* 桂堂). Readers familiar with the courtly convention therefore come away with certain expectations.

The second couplet indicates the insurmountable obstacle posed by the external world: physically there is no way for the lovers to unite; unlike the phoenixes, they do not have wings to "fly in pair." Consequently their only alternative is to withdraw into their inner hearts where they take refuge in an intuitive, somewhat mysterious, union. In the third couplet, the physical, external separation of the lovers is reinforced by two games in which they are divided into two teams. The initial words in both lines (*ge* 隔 and *fen* 分) are strong verbs with the same meaning: to divide or to separate, and their prominent placement in the couplet emphasizes the helpless situation of the lovers.

Their frustration is only intensified by the end of the poem, when the exterior/body completely triumphs over the interior/heart in a somewhat violent manner: like weed uprooted by a strong wind, the poet is called away from his lover by his outside duties or commitments, duties or commitments that in a larger sense may represent the indifferent and capricious external forces that are beyond the poet's control.

Several elements in the poem distinguish it from Palace Style poetry, despite the courtly environment of the first couplet and the common theme of separation. First, the poem is not a detatched description of a courtly entertainment. It is about a thwarted love affair in which the poet plays a direct part. The unusual presence of the first person pronoun *yu* 余 in line 7 not only underscores the pathos of the poem, but it also makes it explicitly personal. Second, at the end of the poem the poet adopts an image that belongs to a convention diametrically opposed to Palace Style poetry: the uprooted weed—one of the most beloved metaphors in the poetry of Jian'an period, notably the poetry of Cao Cao 曹操 (155–220) and Cao Zhi.[22] For them, it symbolizes a disoriented human being in a disorderly world. Since Jian'an litera-ture had been canonized as early as the sixth century in Liu Xie's *Wenxin diaolong* for its profoundly personal involvement with social reality,[23] by invoking the poetry of that era, Li Shangyin links his poem to the canonical tradition, which in turn opens the door to an allegorical reading.

And indeed many critics did interpret Li Shangyin's amorous poetry in terms of allegory. This poem is viewed by some as "using an ornately amorous style to represent [the poet's] feeling of frustration [about his official career]."[24] I have noted in chapter 2 that since Qu Yuan, especially since the Han dynasty when an allegorical reading of Qu Yuan's work was firmly established, it had become a convention to treat poetry on amorous topics as representing some larger moral and political themes. But as I have also showed, some works (particu-larly Palace Style poetry) resist such treatment. In the case of Li Shangyin some critics are over eager to apply an allegorical reading to all his works, even to those that betray obvious Palace Style tenden-cies. For instance, "In Imitation of Xu Ling's Style: To a Court Maid in Charge of Changing Clothes" is interpreted by the Qing scholar Yao Peiqian 姚培謙 as "a failed attempt to win the favor [of his superior]."[25]

In fact, the most widely read poems by Li Shangyin are those that lend themselves to allegorical readings. They meet the canonical de-mands that a literary work embody meanings beyond the linguistic medium, preferably meanings that express the poet's feelings or thoughts. The following piece is another example:

無題二首：其一    TWO UNTITLED POEMS: NO. 1

| | |
|---|---|
| 鳳尾香羅薄幾重 | How many thin folds are the phoenix tail like, scented silk? |
| 碧文圓頂夜深縫 | Under round emerald patterned net she is sewing late at night. |
| 扇裁月魄羞難掩 | The moon-shaped fan can hardly hide her shy face, |
| 車走雷聲語未通 | In the rumbling sound of carriage no word is passed.    4 |
| 曾是寂寥金燼暗 | Once she was lonely, the bronze censer grew dim, |
| 斷無消息石榴紅 | Absolutely no news is heard amid the red pomegranate trees. |

155

斑騅只繫垂楊岸　The spotted horse is tied only by the
　　　　　　　　willowy bank,
何處西南待好風[26] Where could I wait for the auspicious
　　　　　　　　southwest wind?　　　　　　　　8

Li Shangyin is particularly famous for his "untitled" (*wuti* 無題)
poems. Paradoxically, the very absence of a title only serves to generate
numerous titles in the reading process: the tantalizing nature of much
of Li Shangyin's poetry is thus apparent from the very outset. The
reader is in suspense and desires a solution. The first couplet presents
a familiar scene: a woman's elegant bedroom. The ornate images of
"phoenix tail" (*fengwei* 鳳尾), "scented silk" (*xiangluo* 香羅), and "emerald patterned" (*biwen* 碧文) cannot but remind us of Palace Style
poetry. This is confirmed by the lady's occupation, idling away an otherwise unbearably lonely life with an activity charged with longing to
be reunited with her lover or spouse: she is making an elaborate silk
wedding net[27] that could be shared by *both* of them. The next couplet
seems to describe her memory of a chance encounter between the
lovers. Li Shangyin chooses a quintessential Palace Style image: the
moon-shaped fan first used by the courtesan Lady Ban and later repeatedly used by other court poets during the Southern Dynasties
period. But Li Shangyin has twisted the image. In the poems by Lady
Ban and others, the round fan is merely a metaphor for a court woman
who has been discarded by her lord (just as a fan is laid aside when
autumn comes), but in Li Shangyin's poem it actually *is* a fan with a
physical function to perform: it is a part of the failed attempt by the
woman to hide her shyness from her lover.

Still, the metaphorical significance of the image remains, because
it also indicates the status of the lady—like Lady Ban, a deserted
court women. This is reinforced in line 4 by an allusion to Sima
Xiangru's "Changmen fu" 長門賦, which describes the life of Empress
Chen who was put away at Changmen Palace by emperor Wu of the
Han dynasty.[28] The allusion suggests the woman's agitated mental
state: the rumbling sound of the carriage is directly compared with
thunder and indirectly compared with the woman's heartbeat. Like
Empress Chen, who whiled away her days waiting for a visit from the
Emperor and was excited but also frightened by the sound of the car-
riage for fear of disappointment, our heroine is so overwhelmed by

the occasion that she cannot even bring herself to make her heart known to her lover.

The third couplet directs our attention away from the moment of encounter to the woman's despondency after that brief meeting. Her mental condition is both related directly by the adjective "lonely" (*jiliao* 寂寥), and indicated indirectly by the image of "bronze censer grew dim" (*jinjinan* 金燼暗), which suggests a sleepless night. The first word in line 6 is the abrupt and violent *duan* 斷 (absolutely), which when used as a verb also means to break up something physically. The heroine's broken state is further highlighted by the blossoming pomegranate trees: nature resuscitates itself organically. But for her resuscitation is possible only in her mind, and the discrepancy between her mental and physical states is the source of much of her unhappiness. Thus, seeing in her imagination the horses at the willowy bank where the lovers bid each other farewell, she asks herself "How could I become the southwest wind and enter the heart of my lover?"

The last line of the poem alludes to a poem by Cao Zhi, in which the speaker is also female. She laments her separation from her lord, and wishes she could be the southwest wind so that she could bridge the separation and enter her lord's heart (願爲西南風，長逝入君懷).[29] This piece, particularly these two lines, have been interpreted, as have many of his *yuefu* poems, as his wish to serve his lord.[30] Li Shangyin's invocation of the *yuefu* convention at the end of this poem directs his readers toward the type of reading usually employed for works within this genre—allegorization. To consolidate this move, Li Shangyin makes a corresponding change in his use of diction in the last line: in contrast to the florid, elegant, elusive words and phrases in the main body of the poem, the last line is written in straightforward, colloquial speech of the type one expects in *yuefu* poetry.

This textual strategy transforms an otherwise "ornately amorous poem" in Palace Style convention into a work of allegorical dimension, thereby allowing later critics to incorporate it and many others like it into the canonical tradition. The following commentary on this poem is by the Qing critic Lu Kunzeng 陸崑曾:

Li Shangyin's biography [in *Tang shu*] says that "when Linghu Tao was the prime minister Shangyin tried several times to make his feelings known, but Linghu Tao would not listen to him." It seems that these two poems were written for Linghu Tao. Since it is not convenient to state directly, [Li Shangyin] wrote it in the disguise of a poem about relations between man and woman. This is what is remained of "Feng" [the "airs" in *The Book of Songs*] and "Sao" ["Li Sao"].

按本傳："令狐綯作相，商隱屢啓陳情，綯不之省。" 二詩疑為綯發。因不便明言，而托為男女之詞，此風騷遺意也。[31]

As *The Book of Songs* and Qu Yuan's poetry are supreme examples of the canonical tradition, Lu Kunzen's claim that Li Shangyin's poem originates with them is the highest compliment. Li Shangyin, it seems, was a master at manipulating audience response; his amorous poetry is accepted without suffering the criticism leveled at Palace Style poetry earlier on.[32]

Both Li He and Li Shangyin sought to change Palace Style poetry. But as we saw in chapter 3, Li He tried to rectify its superficiality with eccentricity and grotesqueness, but that in turn caused another reaction. By contrast, Li Shangyin's strategy was to introduce canonical elements into his poetry, in particular, into his ornately amorous pieces. He employed other techniques as well; readers found the highly elusive nature of his poetic language very engaging, for example.

I noted in chapter 2 that Palace Style poetry was so despised in part because its language remains stubbornly superficial. It is a style without any of the "deeper significance" (*xingji* 興寄, to use Chen Zi'ang's phrase) that has always been a hallmark of great poetry in the Chinese tradition. This canonical notion of poetry is based on the principle of *xing* 興 (to arouse or evoke) in *The Book of Songs* and the Daoist concept of linguistic medium as a steppingstone to a meaning that transcends its carrier. Li Shangyin was certainly aware of this. Many critics have interpreted the obscurity of his style as his attempt to conceal his private life, but it is also possible that such a style comes from a desire to resuscitate a much condemned literary genre—namely, Palace Style poetry. From the literary point of view an effective way to achieve this goal is to endow such writing with multiple meanings, particularly meanings along the canonical line. In this way Li Shangyin could keep what he valued most in Palace Style poetry—its sensuality and ornateness—and at the same time disarm the critics with its ambiguity. Let us take a look at the first of his "Yan Terrace: Four Poems" ("Yantai sishou" 燕臺四首):

| 春 | SPRING |
|---|---|
| 風光冉冉東西陌 | Wind and light slowly move along cross-paths, |
| 幾日嬌魂尋不得 | In vain I have sought her tender soul for several days. |
| 蜜房羽客類芳心 | The winged traveler in honeycombs resembles her fragrant heart, |
| 冶葉倡條徧相識 | And knows all charming leaves and wanton branches. 4 |
| 暖靄輝遲桃樹西 | West of peach trees the haze is warm and light is late, |
| 高鬟立共桃鬟齊 | Her tall hairknot is as high as the knots of peaches. |
| 雄龍雌鳳杳何許 | How far is the male dragon separated from the female phoenix? |
| 絮亂絲繁天亦迷 | Among chaotic catkins and entangled gossamers even the heaven is lost. 8 |
| 醉起微陽若初曙 | I wake up in intoxication, the dim gleam looks like sunrise, |
| 映簾夢斷聞殘語 | Through the sunlit curtain incomplete words are heard in a broken dream. |
| 愁將鐵網罥珊瑚 | In sadness I enmesh corals with an iron net, |
| 海闊天翻迷處所 | The ocean is vast, the heaven is upset: the place is lost. 12 |
| 衣帶無情有寬窄 | The girdle has no feelings but has a way to loosen and tighten, |
| 春煙自碧秋霜白 | Spring mist is naturally green and autumn frost white. |
| 硯丹擘石天不知 | I grind vermilion, break stones, but heaven does not know, |
| 願得天牢鎖冤魄 | How I wish to have a heavenly jail to lock up the wronged soul. 16 |

夾羅委篋單綃起　She puts away her lined robe and takes up a thin
　　　　　　　　　silken dress,
香肌冷踏踏珮　　　Her fragrant flesh coolly sets off tinkling
　　　　　　　　　pendants.
今日東風自不勝　　Today the east wind can bear it no longer,
化作幽光入西海³³　It changes into a subtle light and enters into the
　　　　　　　　　western sea.　　　　　　　　　　　　　　20

As Zhang Caitian notes, this poem shows the strong influence of Li
He,³⁴ written as it is in the ancient song style for which Li He was
particularly famous. It consists of five four-line stanzas that are relatively independent of one another, as their different rhymes indicate.
This is one of Li Shangyin's most obscure poems. Its obscurity seems
to come, I think, from the lack of a consistency between individual
stanzas and the frequent shifts of perspectives. The first line of the
poem gives the time, and as James Liu observes, it is set in a sensu-
ally provocative season—namely, spring.³⁵ The location is a secluded
one, as is suggested by the word *mo* 陌, which originally means paths
in the field. The sense of disorientation is present at the outset, because these small paths lead in different directions (literally to "east
and west"). No wonder, then, that one should fail to find the person
one is looking for. The expression "tender soul" (*jiaohun* 嬌魂) usually
refers to a woman, and we are told that she is the object of a failed
search. Uncertainty is manifested already in the relatively straightforward second line: Who is the subject of the search? In my translation
I have followed Liu Xuekai and Yu Shucheng, but there are critics
who consider the subject to be the "tender soul."³⁶

This ambiguity becomes even more striking in the next two lines.
The "winged traveler" (*yuke* 羽客) is a metaphor for bee, which pays
a visit to someone among the honeycombs (*mifang* 蜜房). The eroticism of the image is apparent, particularly with the stock wordplay in
*mi* 蜜, which as we know, is a homophone for *mi* 密, or "intimate."
But who is this "winged traveler"? If it refers to the "I," as I think it
does, how is it connected to the second part of the line? The bee usually goes to gather honey in the "heart of flower" *huaxin* 花心 (which
I believe has been deliberately written as "fragrant heart" *fangxin* 芳
心 to cause ambiguity, because *fangxin* can be read as a metaphor for
young woman), in what way does the former ("winged guest") resemble
(*lei* 類) the latter ("fragrant heart")? In the next line "charming leaves"

(*yeye* 冶葉) and "wanton branches" (*changtiao* 倡條) are usually meta-phors for singing girls.[37] This line provides some valuable information for our understanding of the first stanza, because it indicates that like the bee, which has seen all sorts of flowers, the "I" has had expe-riences with women of all kinds. But his love is lost in this highly seductive but elusive world.[38]

The second stanza seems to describe what the "I" imagines about his lover. The hazy atmosphere is presented as the background for this imagination, while the sun sets west of the peach trees (line 5). He imagines the beauty of her hair, which competes with the beauty of nature (line 6). The "male dragon" and "female phoenix" in line 7 are said to be far apart from each other, thus giving the first specific information about the whereabouts of the two lovers. But their sepa-ration is given a cosmic setting in the next line, because even heaven is getting lost in this confusing world. Adding to this sense of loss is the feeling of melancholy evoked by the images of catkins and gossamer, which as James Liu explains, often "suggest groundless, nameless, feelings of melancholy and ennui."[39]

The uncertainty of perspective is even more keenly felt in the third stanza, and although I translated it according to the perspective of the "I," I am not at all certain that this is the case. The problem lies in the disconnection between lines 9 and 10. If it is the "I" who wakes up drunk at sunset, who is the person who hears the "incomplete words?" The image of "sunlit curtain" (*yinglian* 映簾) indicates that this person is outside the room where the "I" just wakes up, because the sound is presented as coming through it, but how can the "I" say that he knows the other person is listening to his dreamy words?[40] This is logically incomprehensible, yet sometimes we do not expect or demand logic in poetry, especially in Li Shangyin's poetry. In many cases, however, the illogical parts in his poetry nevertheless produce a general, although vague, effect, which is helpful to our understanding of the whole piece.[41] This is clearly not the case here. This difficulty directly affects our reading of the next two lines in this stanza, because we must decide whether it is the "I" who wishes to trap corals ( which are the symbols of his love?) with iron nets, or it is the other person. The first choice makes more sense, judging from the structure of the poem, especially since in my interpretation this stanza is read from the perspective of the "I."

But such a willful interpretation is immediately denied by the poet, as he tells us that in this confused and confusing world one inevitably gets disoriented. In line 12 the word *mi* 迷 appears for the second time in the poem. We may recall that this is the word that Li He uses in his "Self-Mocking" to describe the disoriented movement of butterflies in evening trees. I have explained in that context that *mi* can simultaneously mean to charm and to misguide. The significance of this word in the present poem seems to be the same: the seductiveness of the text causes the reader to get lost, precisely as the person or persons in the poem are lost in their sensual yet bewildering world.

Stanza 4 focuses on the indifference of the universe to the suffering of the lovers. It moves from the microcosmic to the macrocosmic, from the girdle on the human body to the temporal seasons that guide human life: they move according to their own laws, unconcerned with what their movements might mean to humankind. This nearly callous attitude is accentuated by the use of antithesis in line 13—the girdle *does not have* feelings, yet it *does have* a way to loosen and tighten—and by the word "naturally" (*zi* 自) in line 14, which implies that while the changing of seasons might look indifferent to human feelings, it is nevertheless a perfectly natural phenomenon. It is under such circumstance that the desperate acts of the "I" in the next two lines are bound to yield no results: heaven remains unaware of his passionate gestures of love, and the impossibility of his wish to get a heavenly trap to hold the wronged soul is revealed in the very way that he expresses it: in a subjunctive mood (*yuan* 願), which implies that this is only wishful thinking.

The perspective of the poem shifts again in the last stanza, this time to the woman. The echoes of Palace Style poetry are particularly loud in lines 17 and 18, as the setting is moved inward again, this time to her bedroom, with a series of stock tropes from the Palace Style convention: the images of thin clothes (*danxiao* 單綃), fragrant flesh (*xiangji* 香肌), and tinkling pendants (*zhengzhengpei* 琤琤珮). In the last two lines the poem reverses its treatment of nature and turns nature into one that sympathizes with human suffering. Even the east wind is unable to bear the situation any longer; it turns itself into a subtle light and goes into the western sea. But this treatment of nature accommodates the need of the poetic structure, rather than signaling a change of attitude, because the next poem in the series is about summer, so the last couplet serves as a transition from spring to summer.[42]

The language of the poem is not very involved but nor is it straightforward. It does not contain many allusions, as in Li Shangyin's other difficult poems. And treated separately, the images and descriptions all make perfect sense, but try to bring them together in a coherent reading and they become baffling. The gaps and disconnections in the text suggest a deliberate effort to thwart a thorough understanding. The ambiguity caused by such textual strategy makes it all the more likely that critics will read the poem allegorically. Thus Zhang Caitian comments that this poem shows "how good the poet is at concealing his emotions and thoughts." He continues with confidence that "in [Li Shangyin's] collected works all those that deal with national affairs and personal experiences are written in such obscure language. It would be a great mistake to regard this as an amorous poem."[43] Du Tingzhu 杜庭珠 notes that this poem "has a profound significance. Its method is similar to that of 'Li Sao' where [Qu Yuan] uses beautiful women and matchmakers to express his feelings and thoughts."[44] The remarkable thing is that nearly all commentators feel it is highly *unlikely* that an obscure poem like this by Li Shangyin *would not* point to some deeper or larger meaning. Even those who regard this as an amorous poem concede that it has an allegorical significance.[45]

Thus, we see that this poem shares many stylistic features (especially in diction) with Palace Style convention and that later critics acknowledged the presence of amorous elements in it, though they considered these to be only surface meaning. All this is indicative of the continuity between Li Shangyin's poetry and Palace Style convention. But the reluctance of later critics to treat it as a Palace Style poem points to Li Shangyin's success in transforming the genre. Their allegorical readings demonstrate that this "ornately amorous poem" could be accepted by the canonical tradition. Let us now look at another example of such transformation:

| 獨居有懷 | FEELINGS ON SOLITARY LIVING |
|---|---|
| 麝重愁風逼 | The scent of musk is heavy, a sorrowful wind presses, |
| 羅疏畏月侵 | In the sparse gauze net she fears the moon's encroachment. |
| 怨魂迷恐斷 | A wronged soul is lost, fearing being broken, |
| 嬌喘細疑沉 | Delicate panting is weakening, as if sinking. 4 |
| 數急芙蓉帶 | Several times she fastens her lotus belt, |
| 頻抽翡翠簪 | And frequently takes out her emerald hairpin. |

| | | |
|---|---|---|
| 柔情終不遠 | Tender feelings are not far after all, | |
| 遙妒已先深 | Distant jealousy is deep already. | 8 |
| 浦冷鴛鴦去 | The river's edge is cold, mandarin ducks have left, | |
| 園空蛺蝶尋 | The garden is empty, butterflies are searching. | |
| 臘花長遞淚 | Tears flow down from candle flowers, | |
| 箏柱鎮移心 | Zither fret constantly stirs heart. | 12 |
| 覓使嵩雲暮 | She seeks for a messenger, clouds in Mount Song are darkening, | |
| 回頭瀰岸陰 | And looks back, the bank of Ba River is overcast. | |
| 只聞涼葉院 | She can only hear in the yard of chilly leaves | |
| 露井近寒砧[46] | The freezing sound of clothes beating by dewy wells. | 16 |

The title immediately evokes the poetry of seclusion: it is a generic marker that places the poem in a canonical context. The image of a solitary gentleman writing a poem that expresses his feelings and thoughts (*huai* 懷) conjures up the canonical figures like Tao Yuanming and Wang Wei.[47] But the poem opens on a different note—the first two lines suggest a typical Palace Style environment. Although the person who "lives in solitude" is not specified, words like "heavy scent of musk" (*shezhong* 麝重) and "sparse gauze net" (*luoshu* 羅疏) show that it is not the poet himself, as one might expect to be the case in the poetry of Tao Yuanming or Wang Wei. Because these terms point to a feminine world, we are forced at the outset to adjust our mode of reading. The voice of the poem is not the intimate voice of the poet expressing his own feelings and thoughts, but rather is the voice of a detached observer commenting on the feelings and thoughts of someone else. This change immediately shifts the direction of the poem, since to describe a woman's world from the removed third-person point of view is much closer to Palace Style convention.

Lines 3 and 4 are ambiguous. A "wronged soul" seems to allude to Song Yu's "The Summon of Soul," which, according to Wang Yi, was written to summon the soul of the unjustly persecuted Qu Yuan.[48] The word *mi* 迷 might be taken as an adjectival verb describing the lost condition of the wronged soul, which evokes the description of Qu Yuan's soul in Song Yu's poem. The subject of "fearing being broken" (*kongduan* 恐斷) in line 3 might be the wronged soul as it is in my translation. But it could also be the implied poet who, like Song Yu, is saying that he fears that the wronged soul could suffer destruction. This is a plausible interpretation, but confusion arises in line 4. "Delicate panting" (*jiaochuan* 嬌喘) carries erotic overtones as it is suggestive of the woman's panting in the act of lovemaking. In that case, does the word "sinking" (*chen* 沉) indicate postcoital relaxation or exhaustion? This must be how the Qing scholar Ji Yun 紀昀 reads it, because he charges that the couplet to be "particularly obscene,"[49] although he does not specify the reason for this accusation. But most commentators prefer to treat the couplet allegorically. Liu and Yu, for example, take it to mean that "[she] laments separation; her soul is haunted and lost. [Her] delicate breath is so weak that it looks she is sinking [that is, passing away]."[50] Thus an otherwise erotic description is made to represent a positive moral quality instead, for the woman's pining is interpreted as the result of her undying loyalty to her lover or lord, which in turn can be explained as Li Shangyin's longing to win the understanding of his patron— namely, Linghu Tao.[51] But the point is that these two interpretative possibilities exist simultaneously in the text. On the literal level the description conveys an erotic sense, but on the metaphorical level the allusion to Qu Yuan in line 3 provides the basis for an allegorical reading, because it was Qu Yuan who began the convention of using a beautiful woman to symbolize a steadfast gentleman.

Lines 5 and 6 allude to the works of two Southern Dynasties court poets: the image of "lotus belt" (*furongdai* 芙蓉帶) comes from a poem by Xiao Yi, Xiao Gang's brother.[52] "Emerald hairpin" (*feicuizan* 翡翠簪) refers to a poem by Fei Chang 費昶.[53] In both cases the source poems are typical Palace Style works. But as used in Li Shangyin's poem, these two images take on new meaning, because the woman is not an indolent woman or singing girl in a typical courtly environment, but rather is a woman who resides in a besieged world. Already in the first couplet we are told that her world has been mercilessly invaded. The sorrowful wind is pressing, and even the moonlight is a forceful intrusion (*bi* 逼). This change of setting is important because it allows one to interpret the sensual, ornate Palace Style clichés in Li Shangyin's poem on another level. Because Qu Yuan was invoked in a previous line, we can now interpret "lotus belt" and "emerald hairpin" in a way consistent with his poetry. Consequently, like the beautiful flowers worn by Qu Yuan, these originally superficial ornaments can be understood as symbols of the heroine's moral steadfastness, just as the ambiguously erotic description in line 4 can be taken to represent the same quality. She constantly refastens her belt because she is pining away for her love; she frequently takes out her hairpins because she has been losing her hair.

The language of the poem changes abruptly in lines 7 and 8. Hitherto it has been describing the heroine and her world in florid diction, and the voice has been consistently that of a detached observer. In these two lines, however, the poem suddenly becomes declarative and the language straightforward. The voice of these two lines is also ambiguous: Is it the heroine who is speaking, or is it the poet speaking for her? This ambiguity makes it more tempting to understand the poem allegorically, because such a reading presumes that a work has different levels of meaning.[54] Ye Congqi takes this couplet to mean that "[the heroine] herself is steadfast, but jealous people on the other side fear their union,"[55] thus interpreting it as a statement by the woman.

The poem reverts to its descriptive mode in line 9 and carries it until line 12. Mandarin ducks and butterflies are stock images in the Palace Style repertoire, but here they are placed in settings not usually associated with them: mandarin ducks are not to be found in a cold river, nor butterflies in an empty garden. But this vivid juxtaposition serves to conjure up a frustrated, nearly destroyed love, for we cannot help but think what might have been the case had the mandarin ducks been in a warm pond or the butterflies in a garden full of flowers. Then, having depicted a desolate external world, the poem moves indoors again to present the lonely heroine playing a zither by candlelight. Mount Song in line 13 refers to where her lover is staying, while Ba River in line 14 is a river in the capital Chang'an. The woman's frustration is suggested by the last word in each line of this couplet: darkening clouds (*mu* 暮) make it hard for her to find a messenger at her end, while at the other end the overcast (*yin* 陰) capital makes it equally difficult to reach her lover. Line 14 alludes to a poem by the Jian'an poet Wang Can 王粲.[56] This allusion to a canonical poet by the end of the poem is significant because it again connects the poem with the canonical tradition. But unfortunately the grand pathos evoked in Wang Can's poem proves to be too sublime for a poem like this, for in the next two lines it immediately withdraws from the vast

166

scene into the chilly inner courtyard. The poem ends with one of the most hackneyed images in Chinese poetry: a lonely woman hearing the sound of clothes beating late in a chilly autumn night.[57]

The shifting back and forth between the canonical tradition and Palace Style poetry blurs the line that separates them. While it is clear that this poem was written in a predominantly Palace Style mode, nearly all commentators have chosen to place it within the canonical tradition. Zhang Caitian notes that "its language is elegant, its feelings are deep. It seems to refer to Linghu Tao."[58] Ye Congqi claims that it "uses an amorous poem as a mask to express a disconsolate feeling."[59] In short, they all prefer to read it in keeping with its title, as a poem of intense personal engagement. This is a critical difference between Li Shangyin's "frivolously ornate and amorous poetry" (ceci yanqu ) and Palace Style poetry or, for that matter, the ceci yanqu of Li He and Wen Tingyun. In the eyes of various commentators it is this personal involvement expressed in elusive language that "redeems" Li Shangyin's poems, because this is precisely what is demanded by the principle that "poetry is the expression of one's will." In this sense Li Shangyin's amorous poetry marks a reconciliation with the canonical tradition. But as the word "reconciliation" implies, it is a process in which both sides gain. Li Shangyin's effort to reconcile with the canon also marks a resuscitation of Palace Style convention, although this was done behind an artful mask.

In some cases this resuscitation is so thorough that we even tend to forget that some of the most widely read poems of Li Shangyin are often those that belong to the Palace Style convention. "Patterned Zither" ("Jinse" 錦瑟) demonstrates the point:

| | |
|---|---|
| 錦瑟無端五十弦 | For no reason the patterned zither has fifty strings, |
| 一弦一柱思華年 | Each string, each fret calls back those youthful years. |
| 莊生曉夢迷蝴蝶 | Zhuangzi dreamed at dawn he was lost in a butterfly, |
| 望帝春心託杜鵑 | Wang Di's spring heart was given to a nightjar. |
| 滄海月明珠有淚 | Bright moon on the vast sea, pearls have tears, |
| 藍田日暖玉生煙 | Warm sun on Blue Field Mountain, jade sends out mist. |

4

此情可待成追憶　How could this feeling wait to be remembered?
只是當時已惘然[60]　Even by then it has already been lost in a trance.　8

This is one of the most difficult, as well as one of the most beautiful, poems in the Chinese poetic tradition.[61] It would be pointless to rehearse the numerous, often widely different interpretations of this poem.[62] The difficulty is that it is nearly impossible to assign a meaningful structure to the poem's beautiful, sensual images and allusions. Line 3 alludes to the passage in *Zhuangzi* where Zhuangzi says that he dreamed he had become a butterfly, but when he woke up he was not certain whether it was he who had become a butterfly or vice versa.[63] Line 4 refers to a king of Shu who once seduced the wife of one of his ministers while the minister was away on a government mission. Out of great remorse, he abdicated his crown in favor of this minister, and when he died his spirit became a nightjar.[64] How is one to connect these two stories? Structurally speaking, they should be related because they appear in a parallel couplet, and technically the parallel items in the couplet should help to explain one another.

But Zhuangzi's story has strong philosophical overtones. It seems to convey the quintessential Daoist idea that life is relative and uncertain, because as one changes one's perspective, one gets a very different view of life. And so it was that Zhuangzi himself was at a loss to fathom the meaning of his dream while awake. The story of Wang Di is both amorous and moral, but does it hint at the poet's personal experience? Again, what is the connection between these two allusions? Perhaps the philosophical implication of the first line in the couplet can explain the structural relationship between the two allusions: from one perspective they are unrelated, but from another it really does not make a difference—just as it makes no difference whether it was Zhuangzi who dreamed he became a butterfly or vice versa. In other words, the etiological concerns are rendered irrelevant by the ontological qualities of the images in the poem.

This is why, despite all the puzzle, the beauty, the sensuality of the images, and the elegant, graceful sense of loss conveyed by the poem all come through vividly. The image of the butterfly in line 3, for example, takes on independent meaning and function outside its original source. The same is true for the image of nightjar: together with the images in the next couplet, such as sea, moon, pearls covered by tears, Blue Field Mountain, warm sun, jade in mist, and the haunting music, they form a vividly beautiful, charming, yet elusive poetic world. Intellectually one might not be able to articulate exactly what it means, but one also cannot help but be struck by it. This is the intense moment of an aesthetic experience that Keats once discussed: in this moment "the sense of beauty overcomes every consideration."[65]

Some critics have suggested that intellectual understanding is of no importance whatsoever in approaching a Li Shangyin poem like this one. Liang Qichao 梁啓超 once said that although he did not understand at all what the poem meant, he could not help loving it, could not help being fascinated by its beauty.[66] Burton Watson made a similar remark in his *Chinese Lyricism: Shih Poetry from the Second to the Twelfth Century.* He says that in reading the untitled poems of Li Shangyin, "as in the case of Li Ho's obscurer poems, the reader can perhaps best approach them by setting aside the question of precise meaning and noting instead the richness and beauty of their imagery and the striking skill with which they are put together."[67]

There is some truth in such remarks, but it seems nevertheless that the role of intellectual understanding cannot be completely discounted in reading such poems. Yes, there are images that appeal directly to our senses, but part of the poem is also written in propositional language meant to be grasped by intellect.[68] More importantly, it is this part of the poem that provides the tantalizingly elusive hints about the poet's personal experience. We are told in line 2 that the music of zither reminds him of his "youthful years." He tells us in the last couplet that his sense of loss was with him even during those youthful years. When exactly were these youthful years, we want to know, and what are the events that aroused the feeling of melancholy? When we in fact try to relate these questions to the imagery in the poem, they turn the intellectual effort itself into an aesthetic experience.

In this sense Burton Watson's comparison of the untitled poems of Li Shangyin with the "obscurer poems" of Li He is inappropriate. The opaque language in Li He's "Self-Mocking" aims to block meaning, while the semitransparent diction in "Patterned Zither" is designed to entice, although in both cases meaning is indefinitely deferred. "Self-Mocking" leaves the reader frustrated and exhausted, but "Patterned Zither" keeps the reader enthralled because it seems to offer the possibility of complete understanding. Li He's "Self-Mocking" is a labyrinth in which the way out is deliberately cut off, but Li Shangyin's

"Patterned Zither" seems to provide the readers with a faint path in the woods. We are lured into believing that there must be something in the poem that can serve as a key to unlock the poem. Yet the ongoing, unresolved debate about "Patterned Zither" proves that what Li Shangyin offers is only a possibility. The Qing scholar Feng Hao 馮浩 suggested that line 6 "Warm sun on Blue Field Mountain, jade sends out mist " 藍田日暖玉生煙 comes from a remark by the Tang critic and poet Sikong Tu 司空圖 (837–908), which goes:

Dai Shulun 戴叔倫 (732–89) said that the scene of poetry is like the warm sun over the Blue Field Mountain and jade sending out mist: one can watch it from a distance, but one can never put it in front of one's eyes.

戴容州叔倫謂詩家之景，如藍田日暖，良玉生煙，可望而不可置於眉睫之前也。[69]

Herein is the best explanation of "Patterned Zither," because it conveys vividly the tantalizing beauty of the poem. Its continuing popularity since Song dynasty to the present time should not surprise us, since in addition to its beautiful language, it combines "a meaning beyond words" (*yanwai zhiyi* 言外之意) with the personal engagement of the poet—the two pivotal elements in the canonical notion of poetry.

Yet who might have noticed that generically speaking this poem is actually a "poem on object"? We might recall that "poetry on objects" is an important subgenre of Palace Style poetry, and that like most of Palace Style poetry, it tends to be superficial and impersonal. But this poem is anything but that.[70] In fact, the only indication in the poem of its generic origin is the title. But in the poem itself, the poet proceeded along a very different path: except for the title and the first line, the poem hardly mentions the zither, though one would have expected a poem on object to do so. Instead, the musical instrument functions merely as a *xing* 興, or an evocative image that leads to something larger, which in this poem is an epiphany on the part of the poet. How thoroughly Li Shangyin has transformed this poetic genre; the fact that only a very few readers have approached "Patterned Zither" as a poem on object also demonstrates the significant change Li Shangyin brought about in people's perception of this genre.[71]

The Song critic Huang Jian 黃鑒 once charged that Li Shangyin's poetry was "too bookish in style. He loves to accumulate literary items and put them side by side, the way a sea otter loves to worship the fish it has caught" (義山爲文多簡閱書冊，左右鱗次，號獺祭魚).[72] The metaphor in this accusation is both striking and pertinent. Li Shangyin's passion for his craft, particularly the love of allusion that this criticism singles out, is said to have reached the point of narcissism. Like the sea otter that loves to display and *worship* (*ji* 祭) its fish, so Li Shangyin *worships* his poetry. His poems are trophies, and he is his own most loyal audience. Li Shangyin shares Li He's notion of poetry as a "painstaking work" (*kuyin* 苦吟),[73] and composed a few poems that echo strongly Li He's obscure, opaque works. These poems stand in sharp contrast to "Patterned Zither" and other untitled poems, which, as we have seen, show a marked bent to reconcile with the canon in their treatment of Palace Style topics. Some of them are rarely mentioned by later critics and therefore are not known to the general public. But since it must be these poems that provoked the above accusation, let us look at one piece in this group:

| 擬意 | IN IMITATION OF A THOUGHT | |
|---|---|---|
| 悵望逢張女 | He longs to meet with the girl of Zhang, | |
| 遲迴送阿侯 | Reluctantly he sees off A Hou. | |
| 空看小垂手 | In vain he watches the "Small Hands Down" dance, | |
| 忍問大刀頭 | How can he bear to ask for a "Big Knife Ring" song? | 4 |
| 妙選茱萸帳 | This beauty is selected from a dogwood net, | |
| 平居翡翠樓 | She lives usually in an emerald house. | |
| 雲衣[74]不取暖 | Cloud dresses do not provide warmth, | |
| 月扇未遮羞 | Moon fan does not cover her shyness. | 8 |
| 上掌眞何有 | What is the point of being able to dance on a man's palm? | |
| 傾城豈自由 | Who says that a town toppler is free? | |
| 楚妃交薦枕 | Courtesans of Chu compete to serve on pillows, | |
| 漢后共藏鬮 | Empresses of Han together play hiding hooks. | 12 |
| 夫向羊車覓 | She seeks a husband in a goat carriage, | |
| 男從鳳穴求 | And searches for a man in a phoenix-nest. | |
| 書成祓禊帖 | She practices calligraphy after the "Orchid Pavilion Preface," | |

| | | |
|---|---|---|
| 唱殺畔牢愁 | And sings a song called "Sorrows in Separation." | 16 |
| 夜杵鳴江練 | At night clothes beating is heard from the riverside, | |
| 春刀解石⁷⁵榴 | In spring scissors cut out pomegranate skirts. | |
| 象床穿幰網 | Ivory bed is surrounded by gauze curtains, | |
| 犀帖釘窗油 | Rhino drapes are attached to the painted windows. | 20 |
| 仁壽遺明鏡 | Bright mirrors are from the "Virtue-Longevity Hall," | |
| 陳倉拂綵球 | Colorful balls are from Chen Cang. | |
| 眞防舞如意 | Sincerely she protects herself from "Scratcher Dance," | |
| 佯蓋臥箜篌 | In pretense she covers the reclining harp. | 24 |
| 濯錦桃花水 | She washes her silken dress by peach flower pond, | |
| 濺裙杜若洲 | And splashes her skirt at scented-grass isle. | |
| 魚兒懸寶劍 | Precious sword hangs from fish [handle], | |
| 燕子合金甌 | Gold cup is encircled by a swallow [pattern]. | 28 |
| 銀箭催搖落 | Silver waterclock hastens the falling leaves, | |
| 華筵慘去留 | Heartbreaking separation takes place at the grand party. | |
| 幾時銷薄怒 | When will her angrily proud air dissipate? | |
| 從此抱離憂 | From now on sadness of departure will linger in heart. | 32 |
| 帆落啼猿峽 | The sail is let down in gorges filled with crying monkeys, | |
| 樽開畫鷁舟 | Wine glasses are passing around in boat painted with colorful birds. | |
| 急弦腸對斷 | Strings are hastening, hearts are broken, | |
| 剪蠟淚爭流 | Candles are being trimmed, tears streaming down. | 36 |
| 璧馬誰能帶 | Who can wear the jade horse? | |
| 金蟲不復收 | Gold, insect-shaped hairpins are no longer collected. | |
| 銀河撲醉眼 | The Milky Way fills her intoxicated eyes, | |
| 珠串咽歌喉 | Her pearl sounding throat is choked. | 40 |
| 去夢隨川後 | In dream she leaves with the river god Chuan Hou, | |
| 來風貯石郵 | And waits for the coming of Shi You wind. | |
| 蘭叢銜露重 | The orchid bush is covered by heavy dews, | |

| 榆莢點星稠 | Elm leaves are scattered around [like] dense stars. | 44 |
| 解佩無遺跡 | No traces remain where the two fairies took out their pendants, | |
| 凌波有舊游 | But in the waves there are the marks of their former trip. | |
| 曾來十九首 | In the past people wrote "Nineteen Ancient Poems," | |
| 私讖詠牽牛[76] | Silently she chants the one about the cow herd. | 48 |

In many ways this poem resembles Li He's "Self-Mocking." Although shorter, it was written in the form of extended parallelism, and is about an encounter with a singing girl. Like "Self-Mocking," the playful title of this poem "In Imitation of a Thought" is meant to disarm possible criticism on moral or political grounds, since the poet tells his readers that this poem is merely a poetic exercise. Yet this title also has a serious function to perform; it distances the poet from the experiences described in the poem and thereby warns the reader against interpreting it in the light of his life. The poem, the poet tells us, is only an *imitation* of someone else's thought, not the *expression* of his own, as is demanded by the Great Preface to *The Book of Songs*. Thus, the poet makes clear that the work should not be read as a poem in the canonical tradition[77] but instead should be read as a literary exercise and display of poetic skill in Palace Style convention. The content of the poem, though about "thought" (*yi* 意), is turned around by the word "imitation" (*ni* 擬). The poem shifts from a concern for expressing inner feelings and thoughts to a portrayal of external features and behaviors.

The first two lines provide the background. "The girl of Zhang" and "A Hou" are common names for a singing girl and in this context actually refer to the same person.[78] The identity of the person is not clear. In translating this part of the poem I have adopted the third-person pronoun because a first-person pronoun "I" would imply an intimacy that has been eschewed by the poet already in the title. More importantly, it seems to me that this poem was written in the voice of an aloof observer and commentator, as will become clearer as we proceed with our discussion.

The first two lines mention a brief meeting and separation between "he" and the singing girl. Lines 3 and 4 seem to describe the despondent

mental state of the man after the separation: lovely dances are no
longer interesting to him; love songs only make him more miserable,
because the title of one song has the word for a ring on a knife's handle,
*dadaotou* (大刀頭), which is a traditional symbol of union.[79] From
line 4 the poem's perspective turns away from the man to focus on
the singing girl. Lines 4 to 10 describe her sumptuous living quarters
and her loneliness in it. Note the typical Palace Style images: such as
"dogwood net" (*zhuyuzhang* 茱萸帳), "emerald house" (*feicuilou* 翡
翠樓).[80] Note also the typical Palace Style erotic hints, for we are led
to view the woman's bedroom: she is thinly dressed (line 7) and not
adequately screened (line 8). Line 9 is an allusion to Zhao Feiyan趙飛
燕, the consort of Emperor Cheng of the Han dynasty, and the Southern Dynasties dancer Zhang Jingwan 張淨琬; both are said to have
such slender bodies that they could dance on men's palms.[81] The "town
toppler" in line 10 is a cliché for a stunning beauty.[82]

The next few lines, from 11 to 18, describe several activities in this
woman's world. The sexual overtones are made explicit in line 11,
with the direct allusion to Song Yu's "Fu on Gaotang," which recounts
a sexual encounter between the king of Chu and the goddess of Mount
Wu. Sex and trivial games (line 12) are two activities in her world,
which probably explains her discontent: she starts to search for new
love (lines 13–14). "Goat carriage" refers to the story of Wei Jie 衛玠
(286–312) of the Jin dynasty. It is said that he was a very handsome
man and that while still a boy he went for a ride in town in a goat
carriage. The people on the street thought he was made of jade and
the whole town rushed to see him.[83] "Phoenix nest" is a metaphor for
the place where talented writers meet; it was originally used to describe
some famous writers of the Southern Dynasties period.[84] Lines 15
and 16 allude to two famous literati. "Orchid Pavilion Preface" is a
beautiful piece of writing by the great calligrapher Wang Xizhi 王羲
之 (303–61). "Sorrows in Separation" was written by the Han scholar
Yang Xiong. The allusions to these handsome, talented, renowned
historic figures are probably meant to show off the highbrow taste of
this singing girl, but they also disclose the dullness and vulgarity of
her own world. The clothes beating in autumn and clothes cutting in
spring (lines 17–18) are two additional routine activities that further
highlight her loneliness and desire.

The next four lines (19–22) constitute another brief descriptive
section that provides more information about her bedroom. "Ivory

bed" (*xiangchuang* 象床), "gauze curtains" (*xianwang* 幰網), "rhino drapes" (*xitie* 犀帖), "painted windows" (*chuangyou* 窗油): all these are familiar images by now. "Virtue-Longevity Hall" is at Luoyang, the eastern capital. It is said that there was a huge bright mirror in it. Chen Cang is the name of a place, known, it seems, for its colorful balls. The function of these two place names is to accentuate the valuables, thereby foregrounding the ornateness and elegance of the woman's world and, by extension, of the verse.

The poem shifts its perspective again in line 23, as it moves back to describe some activities in the girl's life. The "Scratcher Dance" refers to an erotic anecdote of someone named Sun He孫和. It is said that he liked a certain woman very much and often held her on his lap. Once Sun He danced with his scratcher under the moon and mistakenly hit the woman's face.[85] Together with the next line this couplet seems to hint at an act of sexual seduction by the woman: we do not know how she protects herself from possible injury, but we do know that she is lying on the harp, and the poet tells us that she is doing so not to cover the instrument, as she pretends.[86] The activities described in lines 25 and 26 are annual rituals that are supposed to help people avoid unlucky events. The images in these two lines echo the writings of Tao Yuanming and Qu Yuan. "Peach Flower Pond" (*taohuashui* 桃花水) evokes Tao Yuanming's "Peach Flower Spring" 桃花源記, which describes a fisherman's accidental discovery of a Daoist paradise.[87] "Scented-grass isle" (*duruozhou* 杜若洲) is a direct reference to a line in one of "Nine Songs" 九歌 attributed to Qu Yuan: "I plucked scented grass at the fragrant isle" 采芳洲兮杜若.[88] The texts alluded to have a serious philosophical and moral significance that is not actualized in this context. In this poem, the diametrically opposite context obviates any such meaning. These images are meant to be read only for their superficial value, as beautiful decorations of the girl's world, like any other decorative items in the poem. Whereas on other occasions Li Shangyin uses canonical convention to transform works written in Palace Style, in this instance the transformation goes the other way— it is the canonical works that are made to adapt to the needs of decadent poetry.

Lines 27 to 36 describe the lovers' parting. The sword with the fish-shaped handle indicates that the man is a government official. The swallow in line 28 seems to refer to the pattern on the cup.[89] The ticking of the waterclock is a cruel reminder the lovers' imminent separation (lines 29–30). Lines 31–32 seem to be the poet's comment on their feelings at that moment; the phrase *bonu* 薄怒 (angrily proud air) was first used by Song Yu to describe his recollection of the coy and seductive manner of the goddess in his "Shennü fu."[90] The man boards his colorful boat in the midst of sorrowful monkey cries, hastening music and tears (lines 33–36).

The last section of the poem (lines 37–48) focuses on the girl after she is separated from her lover. Her despondency makes her neglect her makeup (lines 37–38), and she is unable to continue with her performance (lines 39–40). Lines 41–42 use two allusions. The river god Chuan Hou 川後 appears in Cao Zhi's "Luoshen fu" 洛神賦, which, as Cao Zhi himself says in the preface, is modeled after Song Yu's "Gaotang fu" in describing a meeting in a trance between the poet and the goddess of Luo River.[91] "Shi You wind" alludes to a *yuefu* poem[92] based on the following story: it is said that a woman from a Shi family married a man called You Lang (hence her name Shi You). Her husband once went on a business trip and never returned. On her deathbed the woman said that she would become a gale to prevent all businessmen from leaving their wives.[93] The last four lines consist entirely of literary allusions. Line 45 refers to the story of Zheng Jiaofu 鄭交甫 and two fairy maidens he met by Han River. The two maidens took off their pendants and gave them to Jiaofu, who had no idea that they were fairy creatures. But almost immediately after that, the fairies took off with their gifts, leaving behind a bewildered and saddened Jiaofu.[94] Many earlier poets, such as Cao Zhi and Ruan Ji 阮籍 (210–63), had written on this subject.[95] Line 46 again alludes to Cao Zhi's "Luoshen fu."[96] All these allusions deal with separation, and the stories of Zheng Jiaofu and the goddess of Luo River particularly evoke a feeling of loss. The final two lines, as the poet makes clear, allude to "Nineteen Ancient Poems," which have always been revered as classics.[97] The specific poem in question is the tenth of the series.[98] It treats the legendary love story of the weaving girl and the cowherd who were separated by the Milky Way and allowed to meet only once a year. The dense allusions in this part of the text do not present any obstacles in reading because they are archetypes in this genre and have become part and parcel of convention. All are explicitly related to the theme of frustrated love, a theme this poem clearly shares.

But what is the effect of ending an "ornately amorous poem" with a direct invocation of a canonical text? Does it change our mode of reading as normally such an invocation would? The answer seems to be no, for although it attempts to connect this poem to the canonical tradition, it fails to convince the reader because the overall tendency of the poem is slanted too much in one direction to be shifted merely by a reference to the canon. In the meantime, however, the canonical text does not seem to be inappropriate because, as mentioned in the previous paragraph; it has the same subject matter as the present poem, and it is the content, not the manner of its treatment, that is invoked. This is another example how a canonical work can be made to serve in a different, shall we say, decadent context.

Compared with Li He's "Self-Mocking," this poem is less opaque. Its obscurity comes mainly from the frequent shift in perspective, as in many other difficult poems by Li Shangyin. The numerous allusions do slow down the reading, but generally speaking they belong to the same thematic structure. Thus it is different both from Li He's "Self-Mocking," which remains largely impenetrable on a textual level, and from Li Shangyin's untitled poems whose meaning is tantalizingly elusive. This is one of the few poems in Li Shangyin's oeuvre that does not lend itself to an allegorical reading. As Ji Yun says, "This is an amorous poem (*yanci*艷詞) and does not have any allegorical meaning."[99] Another Qing critic Feng Hao 馮浩 says that "this is definitely a poem in amorous style (*yanti* 艷體)" and accuses it of being "deeply offensive to [the principle of] loyalty and moral seriousness" (zhongshang zhonghou 重傷忠厚).[100] There is some justice in Feng Hao's accusation. Except the structural complexity and allusive density, "In Imitation of a Thought" is essentially a Palace Style poem— that is, a lighthearted, erotic wordplay.

But more often the line between the decadent and the canonical in Li Shangyin's poetry is not clean-cut, for even though the general tendency is to lean more in one direction, there are often other elements in the poem to balance it, which leads to different readings. The following piece is about an extremely unusual subject, but our discussion will show how some critics try to make it acceptable by "naturalizing" it:

藥轉      REFINING ELIXIR

鬱金堂北畫樓東    North of tulip hall, east of colorful house,
換骨神方上藥通    The magic prescription for changing bone and supreme medicine for release.

| | |
|---|---|
| 露氣暗連靑桂苑 | Dewy air is secretly connected with green cassia court, |
| 風聲偏獵紫蘭叢 | Wind's sound particularly blows through purple orchid bush. 4 |
| 長籌未必輸孫皓 | The privy stick will not necessarily lose to Sun Hao, |
| 香棗何勞問石崇 | To eat fragrant jujubes what is the need of asking Shi Chong? |
| 憶事懷人兼得句 | Remembering past events and longing for someone I got this verse, |
| 翠衾歸臥繡簾中[101] | While returning to silken quilt in embroidered net. 8 |

Critics disagree about the meaning of the title of this regulated verse. Liu and Yu, citing earlier commentators, take it to mean the process of refining elixir, which, in popular Daoist thought and practice, is one of the main methods of achieving immortality.[102] But Ye Congqi regards it as referring to a kind of constipation-relieving medicine and says that this poem is "a playful piece about the pleasant feeling that the poet felt after defecation."[103] The poem opens with highly ornate, Palace Style language. The first line in particular reminds the reader of another line from an untitled poem discussed earlier: 畫樓西畔桂堂東 (west side of colorful house and east of cassia hall). That poem describes a brief meeting of two lovers in a courtly setting, and thus the important position that this line has in the present poem creates great expectations in the reader and also sets the tone for the entire poem. The echoes of the Daoist search for immortality in the second line are especially loud, with the expressions like "changing bone" (huangu 換骨) and "magic prescription" (shenfang 神方). The first term refers to the account of Emperor Wu's meeting with the Queen of the West 西王母, who once told him that if he held fast to spirit, balanced his breath, and swallowed a fluid, he would be able to change his bone in nine years.[104] The "supreme medicine" (shangyao 上藥) is from the Daoist document The Classic of Life Nourishment 養生經 and is said to give one immortality.[105]

So far the language of the poem clearly lends itself to the first of the two interpretations of the title noted at the beginning of our discussion, that it refers to the Daoist search for an immortal life. The second couplet continues the elegant description: the "dewy air" (luqi 露氣),

"cassia court" (*guiyuan* 桂苑), and "purple orchid bush" (*zilancong* 紫蘭叢) ring a bell in a reader familiar with *Chuci* and Palace Style poetry. The simultaneous evocation of these two genres is important, because both affect the subsequent reading of the poem, as we shall see later. In line 3 we are told that "dewy air is *secretly* connected with green cassia court" 露氣暗連青桂苑. This hint at something secret, obscure, uncertain—in short, something beyond the textual level—is one of Li Shangyin's trademarks. It serves to disarm possible attacks by moralists and at the same time to enthrall his interested readers. Moralists are informed that the text points to a deeper meaning, and interested readers are led to find out what the secret is about.

The third couplet uses two historical allusions, and to our surprise, both are related to events happened in the privy. Line 5 refers to the story about a man named Sun Hao 孫皓 (243–84). It is said that he was a very irreverent person, who once found a gold figure of the Buddha in the back garden of Nanjing and placed it in his privy as the holder for privy stick. On the day when he was supposed to wash the stauette of Buddha, he urinated on its head. Soon his penis became swollen and unbearably painful. Hearing his loud screams, one of his pious maids told him: "Buddha is the greatest god, and you, my lord, insulted it. Why don't you pray now?" Sun Hao immediately knelt down and let himself be converted. After sincere repentance, his pain gradually went away.[106] Line 6 alludes to the rich aristocrat Shi Chong 石崇 (249–300). He once ordered his maids to put brocade and painted boxes filled with fragrant jujubes in his privy to ward off the stench. An army general came and took the jujubes from the boxes and ate them, which provoked laughter from the maids.[107]

This sudden shift from a heavenly Daoist environment to the privy is puzzling, to say the least. It also creates a huge gap between this couplet and the previous four lines. But as if this change were still not enough, the poem shifts again in the last couplet. The simple, straightforward language in the seventh line 憶事懷人兼得句 ("remembering past events and longing for someone I got this verse") not only contrasts starkly with the rest of this ornate and allusive poem, but it also seems to reveal the poet's motivation in writing the poem: "remembering past and longing for friend," which strongly evokes the canonical concept of poetry as an individual's response to a historical experience. Hence it registers the poet's attempt to give an acceptable raison d'être to an otherwise extremely controversial work. But even if this is the motivation of the poem, the question still remains—What past and which friend are meant here, and in what way are they relevant to the present context? The last line of the poem reverts to the Palace Style mode that opens the poem, as the poet returns to the sumptuous bedroom of an unnamed woman.

Aside from the despair voiced by some critics,[108] there are three interpretations of this poem. The first takes it to be a poem about abortion; the second regards it as a poem about going to the toilet; and the third prefers to read it as an allegory of the poet's disdain for the vulgar and corrupt world and his search for someone noble to serve. I will offer an example of each of these interpretations.

Among those who take it to be a poem about abortion are Qing scholars Feng Hao, Zhang Caitian, and Liu and Yu, who give the following summary of this view:

> The person in the poem must be a maid of an aristocratic family. The "tulip hall" and "colorful house" in the first line obviously indicate that the setting is in a household, rather than in a monastery. The middle two couplets are incomprehensible. The "green cassia court" and "purple orchid bush" in the second couplet refer to the place where the abortion takes place; "dewy air is secretly connected with" and "wind particularly blows through" suggest that the abortion is carried out secretly on a dewy and windy night so as to prevent possible leaking [of this news]. In the third couplet the allusions to Sun Hao's privy stick and Shi Chong's fragrant jujubes are both related to the privy: this is secretly writing about abortion. "Not necessarily lose to" and "what is the need of asking" illustrate the wealth and status of the household. The last couplet writes about the return [of the maid] to the bedroom after the abortion and [her] exhausted condition. What is remembered and longed for is not the master of this wealthy household. We may infer from "return to the silken quilt" that the middle couplets are about abortion.[109]

This interpretation takes the maid to be the subject of line 7, thus making her the persona and author of this poem. Although such a possibility is not excluded by the text, it is unlikely this is the case, because this is not a *yuefu* poem. Furthermore the generic expectations generated by the regulated verse in which this poem was written militate against fictional treatment of the topic. The second interpretation avoids this difficulty because it regards the last two lines of the poem as sharing one subject. As my translation indicates, it is the poet who wrote this poem in remembering past and friend, and then returned to the bedroom, which, we may guess, belongs to the woman he was visiting. Among those who hold this views are Qing scholars He Zhuo 何焯, Cheng Mengxing, and Ye Congqi. The following is Ye Congqi's interpretation:

> The first line indicates the location of the privy. . . . The second line discloses the topic and uses "changing bone" to compare the feeling of relief after defecation. . . . The third line describes the cold air felt in the privy, and the fourth line depicts the sound of wind. These two lines adopt an ethereal style to set off the scene when he enters the privy. Because the privy is located at the corner of the house, so the words like "secretly" and "on the side" [*pian* 偏, "particularly" in my translation] are used. Lines 5 and 6 aim to further emphasize the pleasant feeling after the defecation; the meaning of "not necessarily lose to" and "what is the need of asking" is obvious: to put it simply, it means that the pleasant feeling is such that who can say it is not like the elegance of Sun Hao, and what is the need to be so luxurious as Shi Chong? The last two lines speak of the return after defecation; since he felt comfortable and relieved, he thought of his friends and wrote a poem.[110]

Ye Congqi is so confident in his interpretation of this poem that he even claims that "throughout the poem the meaning is clear and obvious and there is nothing difficult and obscure about it."[111] But there are problems with his interpretation. For instance, his explanation of the two allusions in lines 5 and 6 are particularly unsatisfactory. The stories that happened *in* the toilets were hilarious and irreverent to say the least. It seems strange to use them to convey a pleasant feeling, albeit a feeling resulting from defecation.

These two interpretations share one crucial point, however; both regard the poem as a playful piece, devoid of any serious meaning and suggestions required by the canonical notion of poetry. This explains the outrage of these critics. Zhang Caitian finds the poem to be "extremely frivolous."[112] Feng Hao condemns it as "an example of how far a desecration of language and literature could be carried out."[113]

While these critics remain guarded in their interpretations of line 7, there are critics who prefer to take it with all seriousness and awe. A contemporary critic regards this poem to be a political satire against the corruption of aristocracy.[114] The following comment by the Qing critic Lu Kunzeng offers a more elaborate, allegorical reading:

> In the collected poetry of Li Shangyin, [this poem] belongs to the category of "untitled poems." This is shown by that line "remembering past and longing for friend." Throughout the poem the person's high status is emphasized. His living place is tulip hall and colorful house, which clearly indicates that he is not of an ordinary kind. What he takes are "magic prescriptions" and "supreme medicines," which tell us that his is not an ordinary body. Moreover, the intertwined green cassias and purple orchids make wind and dew filled with fragrance. How could the ordinary world have the privilege of sharing this? There is someone who considers Sun Hao's privy stick and Shi Chong's fragrant jujubes to be vulgar and not worthy of mention. This is someone that I hope to meet with day and night. [I] alone lie in the silken quilt, having no means to see him. How could I help but chant about it in poem?[115]

This reading reminds us of Wang Yi's reading of Qu Yuan's works, as it turns the poem into a moral allegory of a Confucian gentleman's search for a worthy lord to serve. The luxurious environment, the Daoist medicine, the elegant plants are all taken as markers of a noble character. What is significant is that this reading, or the possibility of this reading, is provided by Li Shangyin's poem itself, as Lu Kuzeng tells us. Given the indication of such potential in line 7, Lu Kunzeng grasps it as a guiding principle and uses it to incorporate all elements in the poem, including those elements that clearly resist such treatment. For instance, the two allusions to the privy would be absurd in a poem about a gentleman's search for a worthy lord, because the irreverent, hilarious stories that these allusions tell are in total conflict with such serious intent. Would it not be more likely for the poet to avoid mentioning the unmentionable privy if he were writing a poem of a highly solemn nature? But the fact that someone should have ventured to do a far-fetched reading like this is indicative of certain expectations that Li Shangyin's poetry has raised in the minds of at least some readers.

Like Li He and Wen Tingyun, Li Shangyin also wrote many poems about Southern Dynasties. Some of these poems demonstrate a similar interest in the sensuality and pomp of life in the Southern Dynasties court, as with the following piece:

| 陳後宮 | THE INNER COURT OF CHEN |
|---|---|
| 茂苑城如畫 | The garden city looks like a painting, |
| 閶門瓦欲流 | On its front gates shining tiles are about to flow. |
| 還依水光殿 | Still by the side of Water-Light Palace, |
| 更起月華樓 | They again built another Moon-Brilliance Pavilion. 4 |
| 侵夜鸞開鏡 | As night comes she opens the phoenix mirror, |
| 迎冬雉獻裘 | In winter he is presented a bird-head coat. |
| 從臣皆半醉 | His accompanying ministers are all half-drunk, |
| 天子正無愁[116] | And His Majesty is thoroughly without worry. 8 |

The poem is set in the court of Chen Houzhu, which immediately evokes the notoriously corrupt life recorded in historical books like *Nan shi* and *Sui shu*. The first four lines describe the grand buildings in and around the court. Phrases such as "like painting" (*ruhua* 如畫) and "about to flow" (*yuliu* 欲流) stress the sensual qualities, both visual and tactile, of the buildings. The two adverbs in lines 3 and 4, "still" (*hai* 還) and "again" (*geng* 更) suggest the extravagance of court life in the Chen dynasty. They also imply a moral judgment: to suggest that such construction is unnecessary is tantamount to a reprimand. To open a phoenix mirror (line 5) is a conventional metaphor for woman making her toilette. Common sense tells us that this usually occurs in the morning, but line 5 places this activity in the evening, which may suggest the abnormal nature of life at court. Line 6 alludes to an anecdote about Emperor Wu of the Jin dynasty 晉武帝 (236–90). It is said that one winter the imperial doctor presented a bird-head coat to the emperor, who then ordered it burned because he thought such outlandish clothes were not tolerated by the Confucian rites.[117] But in the present poem Chen Houzhu has no qualms about accepting such clothes, thereby showing his indifference to the rites, which are the guiding principles in Confucius's theory of government.

The last couplet further emphasizes the moral indifference and irresponsibility of Chen Houzhu: surrounded by his drunken ministers, the last emperor of Chen remains unconcerned. The phrase "without worry" (*wuchou* 無愁) carries strong satirical force because the fate of the Chen dynasty proves that Chen Houzhu actually had plenty to worry about. The irony and satire of the poem come from the reader's awareness of the great gap between the way Chen Houzhu and his people actually acted and the way they should have acted. In other words, instead of explicitly criticizing the corruption in the Chen court,[118] the poet relies on his reader's historical knowledge to get his message across.[119]

In Li Shangyin's poems on history the pompous drama that fascinated Wen Tingyun is greatly reduced, although it is still important. Li Shangyin did not use extended parallel verse to write about historical topics. He was interested not in the details of historical events that the form of extended parallelism can help to enumerate and display; rather, he was mostly interested in using historical events to create a mood that is peculiar to Late Tang. Generally speaking, Li Shangyin's poems on history are rather short and are either in the form of quatrain or in the form of regulated verse. The concise structure of these two forms limits the space for description and also challenges the poet to convey his message in a most efficient manner. Let us look at the following quatrain:

南朝                        SOUTHERN DYNASTIES

地險悠悠天險長    Earthly protection is vast, heavenly protection is
                             long.
金陵王氣應瑤光    The kingly air of Jinling corresponds to the light of
                             Dipper Stars.
休誇此地分天下    Do not boast that with this place one could assign
                             the entire nation,
只得徐妃半面妝[120] For they only got half of Lady Xu's powdered face.

The first two lines describe the geographical advantage of Jinling as the capital. The next couplet derides Southern Dynasties rulers for their lack of ambition to reunite the country with this geographical advantage. The crux of the meaning of the poem is in the last line. It is said that Lady Xu, who was the consort of Emperor Yuan of the Liang dynasty 梁元帝 (r. 555), had a very plain face. The emperor came to her bedroom only once every two or three years, and when he came, Lady Xu, knowing that his majesty was blind in one eye, would powder half of her face while waiting for him. Enraged, the emperor would leave immediately.[121] Some critics have complained that to compare the country with the face of a court woman is too frivolous and irreverent.[122] In fact, the comparison is apt, because this is precisely how Southern Dynasties is perceived by later generations: amorous and farcical. This metaphor also implies the presence of an amused, satirical observer, such as one finds in Wen Tingyun's poetry on history. This is probably why Ji Yun lables the poem "frivolous and ignoble."[123]

But such a lack of personal engagement is not typical of Li Shangyin's poetry. His more memorable or characteristic poems on history reveal an emotional involvement with the historical events described. The following poem on the subject of Emperor Xuanzong of Tang and his consort Yang Guifei is a good illustration of this:

| 馬嵬二首:其二 | Two Poems on Mawei Slope: No. 2 |
|---|---|
| 海外徒聞更九州 | What is the point of learning that another realm exists beyond ocean? |
| 他生未卜此生休 | While the other life is unpredictable this life will surely be over. |
| 空聞虎旅傳宵柝 | In vain did he hear the tiger nightwatchers beat their bells, |
| 無復雞人報曉籌 | No more would he find cock guards to announce the approach of dawn. |
| 此日六軍同駐馬 | On this day the six armies simultaneously refused to move, |
| 當時七夕笑牽牛 | At that time on the seventh day they had smiled at Cowherd Star. |
| 如何四紀爲天子 | Why is it that being a monarch for four dozen years |
| 不及盧家有莫愁[124] | Cannot compare with the [carefree] life of Mochou? |

Many commentators take this poem to be a satire about Emperor Xuanzong, who was foolish enough to let Yang Guifei, the archetypal *femme fatale*, "topple" the country.[125] This is confirmed by the title of the poem: Mawei Slope is where Yang Guifei was buried after her execution, and the events recounted in the poem are all related to this famous couple. But there is a deeper meaning to the poem. It is not simply a dramatic re-creation of a historical event, as many of Wen Tingyun's works are. It is the poet's reflection on that event. Li Shangyin is not simply repeating the stale theme of the danger of a *femme fatale*. Rather, the tragic story of Emperor Xuanzong and Yang Guifei leads him to reflect on the meaning of human life as a whole. His pessimistic conclusion accounts for the melancholy tone of not only this poem, but also of his many others.

The poem opens on a very general note, even though the first line might refer to the story of Emperor Xuanzong's search for the spirit of the deceased Yang Guifei with the help of a Daoist priest.[126] Thus, I do not think, as James Liu does, that the voice of the first couplet is that of Emperor Xuanzong. I believe it is the voice of the poet, meditating on the vanity of the pursuit of immortality. We cannot predict what happens after life, and the only thing of which we are certain is that this life will come to an end. The first couplet sets the tone for the entire poem. The melancholy, even hopelessness, experienced by the poet is conveyed by the word *tu* 徒, which can be translated as "vainly" or "what is the point?" This sense of the futility of human effort is carried on by the first word of the next two lines: *kong* 空 (in vain, empty or emptiness) and *wu* 無 (no, nothing, or nothingness). These two words strongly evoke the Daoist and Buddhist notion of nothingness, which regards human life as being in endless and illusory flux. Thus, the pointless activities described in these two lines are negated from the very beginning: the guards' announcement of the arrival of night and day are pointless on the personal level, since after the An Lushan rebellion the emperor was living a life in death. They are even more pointless in the universal framework that the poet set up in the previous part of the poem. The third couplet contains the only dramatic details. It compares and contrasts two activities from two different periods of Emperor Xuanzong's life: the moment when Yang Guifei was being executed and the moment when they were happily together. The last two lines taunt Emperor Xuanzong for his inability to protect Yang Guifei, unlike Mochou's commoner husband.

Had this poem been merely a satire on Emperor Xuanzong and Yang Guifei, as most critics seem to think, it would have been just like other poems on history by Li Shangyin that we discussed earlier. But its popularity since the Song dynasty suggests that it contains something not found in them. Its straightforward style may be a factor in this, but I believe the main reason is that the poet is not simply recounting and satirizing a past event. Instead, he uses it as an occasion to reflect on the meaning of life in general; he is therefore directly involved. This is precisely what we expect poetry on history to be: not simply a stage for drama, as in the case of Wen Tingyun, but a meaningful experience that can shed light on one's own life.

This melancholy, even pessimistic feeling explains why Li Shangyin is so attracted to those historical events that demonstrate the fragility and vanity of humankind. In this sense the Southern Dynasties and Emperor Xuanzong are only the most handy examples, because they were repeatedly treated by other poets as well. Li Shangyin's interest in human vanity and decline leads him into other periods of Chinese history, as in the next poem:

| 楚宮 | CHU PALACES | |
|---|---|---|
| 複壁交青瑣 | Green patterns are inscribed on double walls, | |
| 重簾掛紫繩 | Purple ropes hang from multiple curtains. | |
| 如何一柱觀 | How come that the one-column temple | |
| 不礙九枝燈 | Did not prevent hanging nine lanterns? | 4 |
| 扇薄常規月 | The fan is thin, always imitating the moon, | |
| 釵斜只鏤冰 | And hairpins are slanting, only carved from ice. | |
| 歌成猶未唱 | The completed songs are not yet sung, | |
| 秦火入夷陵[127] | The fire of Qin has already burned ancestral tombs. | 8 |

The first seven lines of this eight-line regulated verse build a grand, luxurious palace with delicate, pretty women within, only to destroy it by the last line, which brings in the fire of the Qin troops. The structure of the poem seems to indicate that magnificent palaces with their beautiful court ladies represent human vanity and desire for sensual pleasures; they are constructed for the purpose of being destroyed. Not only that, they are made to be destroyed before one has the chance to enjoy them, just as the completed songs have not yet been performed. The slowness of construction (seven lines) and the rapidity of destruction (just one line) seem to convey a sense of disillusionment with human vanity and a *carpe diem* attitude that is widely condemned as decadent by modern Chinese critics.[128] It is disturbing to them because it reflects a loss of faith in society and life.[129] But Li Shangyin's poetry has been so successful precisely because of its ability to convey so effectively this sense of loss. The following is one of his best-known poems:

樂遊原　　　THE TRAVEL-LOVING PLATEAU

向晚意不適　Late during the day I feel disconsolate,
驅車登古原　I take a chariot to the ancient plateau.
夕陽無限好　The setting sun is infinitely beautiful,
只是近黃昏[130]　Only it is too close to the dusk.

The diction and syntax of this short poem very much resemble those of High Tang poetry, and in that matter it satisfies the canonical demand: it is transparent and straightforward, and it points to a poetic state that goes far beyond the linguistic medium. But the mood of the poem is without question the mood of Late Tang. The poet's melancholy comes from his keen awareness of his personal decline and the approaching end of an era. The setting sun, with all its beauty and transience, can be read as a symbol of the Tang dynasty and its glorious culture.[131] The greatness of this brief poem is that it catches a fleeting yet beautiful moment in nature and transforms it into an objective correlative of a poignant human phenomenon, thus sublimating a heartrending historical fact (the poet's personal decline and the decline of the Tang dynasty) to one of natural, universal significance and adding a touching beauty to it. In these four lines the poet successfully brings together the personal, the social, and the natural.

The Song critic Fan Wen 范溫 once remarked that "people only know the clever and ornate aspects Yishang's [Li Shangyin's] poetry, which is why they juxtapose his poetry with that of Wen Tingyun. What this demonstrates is that ordinary readers merely see the surface. The noble feelings and far-reaching ideas [in Li Shangyin's poetry] they simply fail to detect."[132] "The Travel-Loving Plateau" is perhaps one of the best illustrations of what Fan Wen means by "noble feelings and far-reaching ideas." What is most remarkable about this poem is that it has rid itself of all the rhetoric and ornament that one often associates with decadent poetry, while retaining the vague feeling of loss, melancholy, and nostalgia that are also typical of decadent literature.[133] Thus, in Li Shangyin's oeuvre Chinese decadent poetry has at last managed a successful negotiation with the canonical tradition.

# Conclusion

The close analysis in the previous chapters has demonstrated that there is a continuity and development from the much condemned Palace Style poetry of Xiao Gang to the much admired poetry of Li Shangyin. It is a matter of great significance that Chinese decadent poetry was first launched as a deliberate challenge to the canonical tradition but was later able to make canonical tradition accept it through a process of negotiation and integration. I would like to stress again that the influence of decadent poetry on the Chinese poetic tradition is pervasive, although in many cases the mutual integration between the two is so thorough that one often fails to notice their coexistence. Contrary to the conventional notion that regards decadent poetry as a marginal trend, decadent poetry is a vital part of the classical tradition, and the Chinese canon relies on this decadent component for its completeness, richness, and complexity.

Indeed, the often criticized Palace Style diction has become a vital part of Chinese poetic language and is frequently adopted by canonical poets of different periods. The violent condemnation of Palace Style poetry from the Sui dynasty on did succeed in marginalizing it, but only on a very superficial level; namely, it fostered the powerful impression that Palace Style poetry is a poetry of surface and, more sinister, that it signals political and moral corruption. But ironically the influence of this "poetry of surface" is felt most strongly on a deeper level in the poetry produced during the Tang dynasty, because from the Southern Dynasties on few poets could write about amorous topics or describe feminine beauty without consciously or unconsciously using the diction and imagery associated with Palace Style poetry. Even Du Fu, the great pillar of the Tang canon, succumbed. Stranded in the captured capital Chang'an during the An Lushan rebellion, Du Fu expressed his longing for his wife and children in these words:

| 月夜 | THE MOONLIT NIGHT | |
|---|---|---|
| 今夜鄜州月 | Tonight at Fuzhou the moon is out in sky, | |
| 閨中只獨看 | Alone in her boudoir she looks at it. | |
| 遙憐小兒女 | What a pity that our children are still small, | |
| 未解憶長安 | They have not learned to think of their father in Chang'an. | 4 |
| 香霧雲鬟濕 | Her cloud hair is damp in the fragrant mist, | |
| 清輝玉臂寒 | Her jade arms are cold in the limpid light. | |
| 何時倚虛幌 | When will we lean by the transparent curtains | |
| 雙照淚痕乾[1] | Together to watch tears dry on each other's face? | 8 |

In this, one of Du Fu's most famous poems, we see the poet's passionate love and deep anxiety for his wife and family during the chaos caused by the civil war. As in many of his other poems, the longing for reunion with his wife expressed in the last couplet can be read at a higher level as the poet's longing for the return of peace to the whole troubled land. But in lines 5 and 6 the poet's imagination of his wife is expressed in some quintessential Palace Style diction and imagery: "fragrant mist" (*xiangwu* 香霧), "cloud hair" (*yunhuan* 雲鬟), and "jade arms" (*yubi* 玉臂). Although these clichés have been thoroughly transformed by the context in which they appear, their presence in this intimate poem suggests that Palace Style poetry can function in ways that directly contradict the clichéd notions and expectations of the genre. In this poem, for example, it lends a vivid sensuality that enhances the poignancy of the poet's feelings, but without the artificial mannerism of many Palace Style poems.

Beside lending a necessary but transcendent sensuality and elegance to distinctly nondecadent works like this highly personal piece by Du Fu, decadent diction and imagery constituted a reflexive verbal system in the development of Chinese poetry. This reflexive system not only explains its resilience in the face of constant criticism and denunciation, but it also helps in interpreting poems that employ its distinctive idioms. It sheds light on an otherwise incomprehensible work because it puts us in an appropriate reading mode. For example, an obscure work like Li He's "Self-Mocking" becomes readable when we situate it within the reflexive linguistic system of decadent poetry. This is not only because many of its phrases and expressions evoke the works of earlier decadent poets like Xiao Gang, but also because the abundant presence of Palace Style elements cautions us to read it, not as a record of the poet's personal experience as we would in dealing with a canonical piece, but as a verbal play that derives its meaning and significance mostly from the pleasures and frustrations created by its highly crafted and deliberately baffling textual strategies. Understood in such way, the poem becomes intelligible. The same is also true of Li Shangyin's "In Imitation of a Thought."

However, this reflexive system is by no means monotonous. Our discussion has showed in detail that while the four poets included in this study share a descriptive system, they use it in very different ways. The fastidious sense of decorum in Xiao Gang could not be more different from Li He's obsession with the grotesque that deliberately disrupts decorum. Although Li Shangyin and Wen Tingyun have been named together as the representatives of the amorous "Wen-Li" style, our analysis has shown that the tantalizing elusiveness and intense personal engagement in Li Shangyin's poetry is a far cry from Wen Tingyun's superficial sensuality and dandified detachment. Thus in terms of textuality each poet in this study is unique, and it would be a mistake, or at least inadequate, to place them all under a general rubric like *tuifei* or decadent *without* pointing out the uniqueness of each of them. The only way to avoid this mistake is by a close and critical analysis of their complete poetic output, rather than repeating long-cherished conventional wisdoms that, like some images and metaphors in decadent poetry, have themselves become clichés.

Thus throughout this study I have tried to analyze as closely as possible individual poems of individual poets, in the hope that the strategies *in* the texts will make clear their individual agendas and therefore the nature of decadent poetry. Such close reading is certainly what is needed most in the study of traditional Chinese poetry, where "conventional wisdoms" may be repeated without critical investigation into the presumptions underlying them, and where general conceptualization has often replaced specific textualization. Like decadent poetry, which is a critique of canonical tradition, my study is a critique of conventional wisdom in this matter. As has been shown, the scope of Chinese poetic tradition has been greatly broadened by the challenge of decadent poetry. It is my hope that the present study will also bring some fresh air into conventional wisdom with regard to the issue in question.

Finally, the present study should help us reconsider some larger cultural issues and the methodologies we adopt to study them. We should no longer take for granted what has been taken for granted in the classical tradition; rather we should approach the materials that formed such tradition with a critical spirit. Instead of taking at face value concepts and theories articulated in canonical documents like the Great Preface, we should inquire into the validity and soundness of these concepts and theories, into how they are presented, and what their relevance and limitations are. Then we will be more wary about the problematic nature of some most revered parts of the canonical tradition. For example, the canonical concept of *shi yanzhi* is without question a noble ideal, but as an ideal it naturally falls far short of accounting for all poetry in practice. It cannot, for example, account for poetry that concentrates on its artistic skill and aesthetic appeal rather than on expressing the poet's personal feelings and thoughts, but in Chinese society there have been plenty of good reasons for poets to produce highly artistic, sophisticated, and technical poetry. This should have been obvious, because the sublime position that poetry enjoyed in Chinese culture guaranteed, ironically, that enormous amounts of energy and resources would be invested in perfecting its technical skills.

For a candidate in the civil service examinations during the Tang dynasty, for example, *yanzhi* or expressing his will, could not possibly be the most crucial factor to bear in mind, because he had a set of rules, often fastidiously technical and mechanical, to conform to, and his success and failure, which often determined his entire life, were mostly judged by his talent and ability to adapt to these rules.[2] Thus, except for the tensions within classical tradition that are discussed at length in chapter 1, in traditional Chinese culture there was at least one institutionalized social power that worked to undercut the canonical concept of poetry and expose its vulnerabilities.[3] Viewed from this perspective, the so-called decadent poetry, with its emphasis on poetic craftsmanship, should not have caused much uproar. The flourish of practical and technical poetry manuals since Late Tang should have convinced people of its right to existence. But the extreme uneasiness about decadent poetry expressed by various critics and scholars throughout the Chinese tradition shows that this is not the case at all, and this in turn shows how blinding and restrictive a convention-alized and dogmatized presumption could be. If this study can make us more aware of this, and if this book can not only help us appreciate a neglected but important subject, but also shed some light on the nature of the classical tradition in general, I will have achieved my goal.

---

$\mathcal{N}$otes

## INTRODUCTION

1. "Intertextuality" has been used differently by different critics. In this book it refers primarily to the relations between one particular text and other text(s); by text(s) I mean specifically poem(s). I am especially interested in the effect that earlier poem(s) might have on the meaning production of a later poem, in how our reading of the later poem might be affected by the interactions between them, and finally in the potential insights that such relations and interactions might shed on our understanding, not only of the specific poem in question, but of decadent poetry as a genre. For an introduction to the theory and practice of intertextuality, see Michael Worton and Judith Still, eds., *Intertextuality: Theories and Practices* (Manchester: Manchester University Press, 1990); for a practice of intertextual theory in the study of poetry, see Michael Riffaterre, *Semiotics of Poetry* (Bloomington: Indiana University Press, 1978).

2. Southern Dynasties, also known as Six Dynasties, is a loose historical term. It is generally used to refer to the Wu 吳, Eastern Jin 東晉, Liu Song 劉宋, Qi 齊, Liang 梁, and Chen 陳 dynasties (A.D. 222–589). Because all these dynasties had their capitals in Nanjing, they are referred to as Southern Dynasties. In the present study I use it mainly for the late Southern Dynasties period from 420 to 589, which covers the times of Song, Qi, Liang, and Chen, for it was during this era, especially during Qi, Liang, and Chen, that the great majority of

Palace Style poetry was produced. According to various historical records and the public perception, it was a period notorious for court corruption, and, at least in the minds of later generations, for short-lived dynasties. But as we shall see in this monograph, it was also a period of fervent literary production and innovation. As for the periodization of Tang poetry, there is no precise agreement. Here I am following the periodization in Luo Zongqiang's 羅宗強 *Sui-Tang Wudai wenxue sixiangshi* 隋唐五代文學思想史 (Shanghai: Shanghai guji, 1986), which in turn follows the periodization by the Southern Song (1127–1279) critic Yan Yu 嚴羽 in his *Canglang shihua* 滄浪詩話 (ed. Guo Shaoyu 郭紹虞, Beijing: Renmin wenxue, 1983), and by the Ming critic Gao Bing 高棅 (1350–1423) in his *Tangshi pinhui* 唐詩品匯 (Taipei: *Siku quanshu* edition, 1976). This periodization refers to Mid Tang as running from the first year of Da Li 大曆 (766) to the second year of Bao Li 寶曆 (826), and Late Tang as from the second year of Bao Li to the last year of Tian You 天祐 (904) when the Tang Dynasty ceased to exist. Like most periodizations in literary history, such demarcation is to some degree arbitrary. For instance, A. C. Graham's *Poems of the Late T'ang* (New York: Penguin, 1965) includes the late poems of Du Fu, whose life and career actually overlap with the periods of High and Mid Tang, not the Late Tang at all.

3. George Ross Ridge, *The Hero in French Decadent Literature* (Atlanta: University of Georgia Press, 1961), vii. See also the following description by Paul Verlaine:

> I like the word "decadent. . . . All shimmering with purple and gold. . . . it throws out the brilliance of flames and the gleam of precious stones. It is made up of carnal spirit and unhappy flesh and of all the violent splendors of the Lower Empire; it conjures up the paint of the courtesans, the sports of the circus, the breath of the tamers of animals, the bounding of wild beasts, the collapse among the flames of races exhausted by the power of feeling, to the invading sound of enemy trumpets. (Quoted in Richard Gilman, *Decadence: The Strange Life of an Epithet* [New York: Farrar Straus Giroux, 1975], 5–6.)

Verlaine's characterization echoes strongly the numerous historical descriptions and artistic representations of the activities in the court of Chen dynasty when the southern part of China was being invaded by its enemies to the north. See our discussions in the following chapters. Gilman also gives a brief account of the popular notion of decadence at our time; see pp. 16–21, and 169–79. For colorful accounts of such anecdotes, see A. E. Carter, *The Idea of Decadence in French Literature 1830–1900* (Toronto: University of Toronto Press, 1958); William Butler Yeats, *The Autobiography of William Butler Yeats* (New York: Macmillan, 1953), esp. the chapter "The Tragic Generation"; and Arthur Symons, "Ernest Dowson," in Richard Aldington, ed., *The Religion of Beauty: Selections from the Aesthetes* (Melbourne: William Heinemann, 1950), 264–77.

4. See "Yinyuezhi" 音樂志 in *Sui shu* 隋書 (Beijing: Zhonghua, 1973), vol. 2, chap. 3, 309.

5. See "Wenyuanzhuan" 文苑傳 in *Tang shu* 唐書 (Beijing: Zhonghua, 1975), vol. 14, chap. 19, 5078; Liu Sihan 劉斯翰 ed., *Wen Tingyun shicixuan* 溫庭筠詩詞選 (Hong Kong: Sanlian, 1986), 5.

6. For numerous simple condemnations of Southern Dynasties Palace Style poetry on moral grounds, see our discussion in chap. 2, and Wen Yiduo 聞一多, "Gongtishi de zishu" 宮體詩的自贖, in *Wen Yiduo quanji* 聞一多全集 (Taipei: Kaiming, 1967), 3:11–22. As early as the Song dynasty (960–1279) Late Tang poetry had been conceived as "trivial and delicate, devoid of the flavor of *feng* and *sao*" 晚唐人詩多小巧，無風騷氣味; see Wei Qingzhi 魏慶之 ed., *Shiren yuxie* 詩人玉屑 (Shanghai: Shanghai guji, 1978), chap. 16, 358. For a general, simplified picture of the Late Tang cultural milieu and its reflection in poetry, see Li Zehou 李澤厚, *Mei de licheng* 美的歷程 (Beijing: Wenwu, 1981), 141–60, and Wu Tiaogong 吳調公, "'Qiuhua' de 'wanxiang': Wan Tang de shigemei" 秋花的晚香: 晚唐的詩歌美, in his *Gudian wenlun yu shenmei jianshang* 古典文論與審美鑒賞 (Jinan: Qilu shushe, 1985), 213–33. See also Graham, *Poems of the Late T'ang*, 141–42,

7. "而頃者〔太學〕頹廢，至爲園採芻牧之處。" Fan Ye, *Hou Han shu* 後漢書 (Beijing: Zhonghua, 1975), vol. 6, chap. 48, 1602. It should be noted that while the compound *tuifei* 頹廢 appeared first in Fan Ye's writing (as far as we know), the single word *tui* 頹, which carries most of the weight of the compound, is of a much earlier origin. *Ci yuan* 辭源 (Beijing: Shangwu, 1988) records that *tui*, which means "to collapse, to fall down" had already appeared in *Li ji* 禮記, a Confucian classic collected from pre-Qin materials by Dai Sheng 戴聖 of the early Han period (140 B.C.–A.D. 8). Even in that context the transition from

the literal to the metaphorical level had already been made clear: "Mount Tai is collapsing (*tui* 頹); the pillars are decaying (*huai* 壞); the sages are withering (*wei* 萎)." Physical collapse in nature is accompanied by the physical and spiritual decline of human beings.

8. Carter, *Decadence in French Literature*, 165. For an investigation of the evolution of "decadence" as a cultural and literary term, see Gilman, *Decadence: The Strange Life*; for the various meanings of "decadence" in different contexts in late nineteenth-century France and England, see R. K. R. Thornton, *The Decadent Dilemma* (London: Edward Arnold, 1983), chaps. 1, 3, and Murray G. H. Pittock, *Spectrum of Decadence* (London and New York: Routledge, 1993), chap. 1.

9. See the essay on "Decadence" by Alfred Garwin Engstrom and Clive Scott, in Alex Preminger and T. V. F. Grogan, eds, *New Princeton Encyclopedia of Poetry and Poetics* (Princeton: Princeton University Press, 1993), 275–76.

10. This becomes more apparent in the following commentary by Havelock Ellis:

A society should be like an organism. Like an organism, in fact, it may be resolved into a federation of cells. The individual is the social cell. In order that the organism should perform its functions with energy it is necessary that the organisms composing it should perform their functions with energy, but with a subordinated energy, and in order that these lesser organisms should perform their functions with energy, it is necessary that the cells comprising them should perform their functions with energy, but with a subordinated energy. If the energy of the cells becomes independent, the lesser organisms will likewise cease to subordinate their energy to the total energy and the anarchy which is established constitutes the decadence of the whole. The social organism does not escape this law and enters into decadence as soon as the individual life becomes exaggerated beneath the influence of acquired well-being, and of heredity. A similar law governs the development and decadence of that other organism which we call language. A style of decadence is one in which the unity of the book is decomposed to give place to the independence of the page, in which the page is decomposed to give place to the independence of the phrase, and the phrase to give place to the independence of the word. (See "A Note on Paul Bourget," quoted in R. K. R. Thornton, "'Decadence' in Late Nineteenth-Century England," in Ian Fletcher and Malcolm Bradbury, eds., *Decadence and the 1890s* (New York: Holmes & Melier, 1980), 19–20.)

11. For a study of *xuanxue*, see Tang Yongtong 湯用彤, *Wei-Jin xuanxue lungao* 魏晉玄學論稿, in *Tang Yongtong xueshu lunwenji* 湯用彤學術論文集 (Beijing: Zhonghua, 1983), 193–308; see also Li Zehou 李澤厚 and Liu Gangji 劉綱紀, *Zhongguo meixueshi* 中國美學史 (Beijing: Zhongguo shehui kexue, 1987), 2:106–53.

12. For examples of such cyclic vision of Chinese poetic history, see Yan, *Canglang shihua*, 1–46; Luo, *Sui-Tang Wudai*, 447–76. It is worth pointing out that this vison functions only as a general framework for our discussion, and that the Mid and Late Tang eras are actually the most rich and diverse periods in the history of Chinese poetry. Different schools coexisted with each other. For instance, the socially and politically oriented poetry of Bai Juyi 白居易 (772–864) and Yuan Zhen 元稹 (779–831) existed alongside the grotesque, obscure works of Meng Jiao 孟郊 (751–814), Han Yu 韓愈 (768–824), and Li He 李賀. Even in the works of individual poets the situation is by no means uniform. Both Han Yu and Li He wrote many pieces that directly contradict the general perception of their poetry. Yan Yu and Luo Zongqiang are not unware of this, as is shown by their discussions of these poets.

13. Zhu Ziqing 朱自清 has commented on Li He's connection with the Palace Style convention; see his *Li He nianpu* 李賀年譜, in Chen Zhiguo 陳治國, ed., *Li He yanjiu ziliao* 李賀研究資料 (Beijing: Beijing shifan daxue, 1983), 64. Wen Tingyun and Li Shangyin's poetry has been labeled "amorous songs" (*yanqu* 艷曲), which is similar to the term *yange* 艷歌 that Xu Ling 徐陵 (507–83) once used to characterize the poems collected in his *Yutai xinyong* 玉台新詠 (Chendu: Chendu guji, n.d.); see Xin Wenfang 辛文房, *Tangcaizi zhuan [jiaozheng]* 唐才子傳〔校正〕, ed. by Zhou Benchun 周本淳 (Taipei: Wenjin, 1988), 238, and Xu Ling's preface to *Yutai xinyong*, 2. For an English translation of *Yutai xinyong*, see Anne Birrel, trans., *New Songs from a Jade Terrace* (New York: Penguin, 1986). *Yan* 艷 was also used by Tang historians to describe the works of Chen Houzhu; see my discussion in chap. 2.

14. See Guo Shaoyu 郭紹虞, *Zhongguo wenxue pipingshi* 中國文學批評史 (Shanghai: Shanghai guji, 1979), 6–8.

15. This approach was also adopted by those contemporary critics who stress the role of reading in poetry studies. See for example Ye Jiaying 葉嘉瑩, *Jialing lunshi conggao* 迦陵論詩叢稿 (Beijing: Zhonghua, 1984); Pauline Yu, *The Reading of Imagery in the Chinese Poetic Tradition* (Princeton: Princeton University Press, 1986).

16. London: Faber and Faber, 1948.

17. New York: Alfred Knopf, 1972.

## CHAPTER 1

1. For a discussion of the origin and evolution of "canon," see the essay "Canon" by John Guillory in Frank Lentricchia and Thomas McLaughlin, eds., *Critical Terms for Literary Study* (Chicago: University of Chicago Press, 1990), 233–49. In a secular context like that of Chinese culture, canonical works may be viewed as a set of texts that, because they were thought to represent the ultimate values in society, have been singled out for institutional preservation, dissemination, and reproduction, such as the Confucian classics. In this sense "canon" is equivalent to *jing* 經 in the Chinese tradition.

2. Poetry enjoys a special position in the Chinese literary tradition. Because of its early canonization by Confucius (it makes up one of the five Confucian classics: *The Book of Songs* 詩, *The Book of History* 書, *The Book of Rites* 禮, *The Book of Changes* 易, and *Spring and Autumn Annals* 春秋), poetry in classical tradition is used loosely to refer to literature as a whole. Therefore the Chinese theory of poetry can be safely regarded as a theory of literature in general. To some extent the same can be said of the Western tradition. Aristotle's *Poetics* can be viewed as a study of literature in the general sense as well, although he is mainly concerned with tragedy or drama, and his concept of poetry is very different from that of Confucius.

3. *The Book of Historical Documents* (this is Legge's rendering) in its authentic parts is the earliest written document of Chinese history, although its precise date of composition is unknown. Confucius is said to have edited it. The text I am using is in James Legge, ed. and trans., *Chinese Classics* (Hong Kong: Hong Kong University Press, 1960), vol. 3, *The Shoo King, or The Book of Historical Documents*, 48. Also in Guo Shaoyu, ed., *Zhongguo lidai wenlunxuan* 中國歷代文論選 (Shanghai: Shanghai guji, 1979), 1:1, and Stephen Owen, ed. and trans., *Readings in Chinese Literary Thought* (Cambridge: Harvard

University Press, 1992), 26, but he includes only the first six characters of the quotation. My translation.

4. Although Aristotle regards artistic imitation as coming from human instinct, his mimetic theory nevertheless focuses on the product of imitation rather than on the agent who does the imitation. In other words, the inner response of the writer is of little relevance for the success or the failure of a literary work. Sincerity, which is the ultimate criterion implied by the above remark from *Shang shu*, is simply not an issue. But it should also be noted that his discussion on rhetoric does place some emphasis on the psychological factors of both the orator and his audience. Still, Aristotle's mimetic theory of literature (more specifically drama and epic) is generally speaking a formalistic one that emphasizes the importance of artistic rules, rather than the will (*zhi* 志) of the artist. For a text of *Poetics*, see Hazard Adams, ed., *Critical Theory since Plato* (San Diego: Harcourt Brace Jovanovich, 1971).

5. Earl Miner calls this poetic theory "affective-expressive," as distinct from Aristotle's mimetic poetics. He further points out that the former is based on lyric, whereas the latter is founded on drama, that are "foundation genres" in East Asian and Western European literary traditions, respectively. See his *Comparative Poetics* (Princeton: Princeton University Press, 1990), 24 and passim.

6. See Kong Yingda 孔穎達 (574–648), ed., *Maoshi zhengyi* 毛詩正義, in *Shisanjing zhushu* 十三經注疏 (Beijing: Zhonghua, 1980), 1:269–70, and Legge, *Chinese Classics*, vol. 4, *The She King or The Book of Poetry*, 34; English translation in Owen, *Chinese Literary Thought*, 40–41, with modifications. For a brief discussion about the debate on authorship of this preface, see Guo, *Lidai wenlunxuan*, 1:64.

7. The Great Preface does not elaborate at all on the meaning and significance of *fu* 賦, *bi* 比 , and *xing* 興, that are regarded by later critics as technical terms, and its discussion of *feng* 風, *ya* 雅, and 頌 *song*, that refer to three kinds of poems and are therefore generic, is completely political and social. This absence is all the more remarkable if we compare the Great Preface, that is the first systematic treatise of poetry in the Chinese tradition, with the similar document in the Western tradition, Aristotle's *Poetics*, for Aristotle's main concerns are plot, style, characterization, and other technical aspects of drama.

8. See Yang Bojun 楊伯峻, ann. and trans., *Lunyu yizhu* 論語譯注 (Beijing: Zhonghua, 1965), 46, and Legge, *Chinese Classics*, vol. 1, *Confucian Analects, The Great Learning, The Doctrine of the Mean*, 174.

9. Yang, *Lunyu yizhu*, 192; Legge, *Chinese Classics*, 1: 323. My translation. There is much disagreement about the meaning of this quotation, a problem that is compounded by the lack of grammatical objects in the Chinese sentence. I interpret *xing* (to stimulate), *guan* (to observe), *qun* (to hold together), and *yuan* (to voice grievance) as functions of poetry, but some critics have taken them to be technical terms. See Donald Holzman, "Confucius and Ancient Chinese Literary Criticism," in Adele Austin Rickett, ed., *Chinese Approaches to Literature from Confucius to Liang Ch'i-ch'ao* (Princeton: Princeton University Press, 1978), 21–42.

10. In Guo, *Lidai wenlunxuan*, 1:63; Legge, *Chinese Classics*, vol. 4:34; Owen, *Chinese Literary Thought*, 41. My translation.

11. The research of many scholars has shown that in ancient times *si* 寺 (temple) and *zhi* 志 (will) are actually the same character or exchangeable. Since the character for poetry (*shi* 詩) is composed of *yan* 言 (to speak or to express) and *si* 寺, the etymological meaning of poetry in Chinese is then "to speak of will" or "will expressed in words." See Zhu Ziqing 朱自清, *Shi yanzhi bian* 詩言志辯, in *Zhu Ziqing gudian wenxue lunwenji* 朱自清古典文學論文集 (Shanghai: Shanghai guji, 1980), 1:193–94.

12. Ibid, 190.

13. Owen, *Chinese Literary Thought*, 37.

14. Yang, *Lunyu yizhu*, 142; Legge, *Chinese Classics*, 1:265.

15. Confucius once said that in personal cultivation "one is stimulated by poetry, established by rites, and consummated in music" 興於詩，立於禮，成於樂 (Yang, *Lunyu yizhu*, 87; Legge, *Chinese Classics*, 1:211). It is significant that all three means leading to self-fulfillment are highly aesthetic or artistic activities. For a study of the importance of rite and its implications to the Confucian ethical and aesthetic system, see Li Zehou 李澤厚, *Zhongguo gudai sixiangshi lun* 中國古代思想史論 (Beijing: Renmin, 1986), 7–51, and Li Zehou and Liu Gangji 劉綱紀, *Zhongguo meixueshi* 中國美學史 (Beijing: Renmin, 1984), 1:113–60.

16. Yang, *Lunyu yizhu*, 65; Legge, *Chinese Classics*, 1:190. Confucius once said that rid of its fur, the body of a beautiful leopard will be the

same as that of ordinary sheep or dog. What differentiates the former from the latter is its beautiful fur, which is essential to its nature. See Yang, *Lunyu yizhu*, 133–34; Legge, *Chinese Classics*, 1:254–55.

17. See *Chunqiu Zuozhuan zhengyi* 春秋左傳正義, in *Shisanjing zhushu*, 2:1985; Legge, *Chinese Classics*, vol. 5, *The Ch'un Ts'ew with the Tso Chuen*, 512.

18. Since poetry is viewed as an expression of the poet's will, to know the nature of such will and the conditions in which such will is formed is thought to be the most effective, and sometimes the only, means of discovering the meaning of a poem. This is why compiling an author's chronicle (*nianpu* 年譜) is a perennial industry in Chinese literary studies.

19. "Is it possible to recite their [the ancients'] poems and read their books without knowing what kind of persons they were? Therefore one considers the age in which they lived." Yang Bojun, ann. and trans., *Mengzi yizhu* 孟子譯注 (Beijing: Zhonghua, 1960), 1:251; Legge, *Chinese Classics*, vol. 2, *The Works of Mencius*, 392; English translation in Owen, *Chinese Literary Thought*, 34. It is not hard to tell the linkage between this exegetical principle and the concept of poetry as a spontaneous expression of one's will. Because meaning is located in the author's heart or mind, to know fully the author's motivation in writing and the milieu that has produced that motivation is a crucial, and to many, the only way to understand the content of his work.

20. For example, the poetry of Wei and Jin (220–420) is canonized more on the basis of its content; the often cited *Wei-Jin fenggu* 魏晉風骨 (the wind and bone of Wei and Jin) clearly slants toward content. The real balance is struck perhaps only during the High Tang period, especially in the poetry of Du Fu, where a deep concern for society is manifested in a highly complex, sometimes dazzling, linguistic medium.

21. In Guo, *Lidai wenlunxuan*, 1:63; Legge, *Chinese Classics*, 4:35; English translation in Owen, *Chinese Literary Thought*, 47, with modifications.

22. Among the numerous rebuttals of this theory of inevitable decline of poetry that of the Qing critic Ye Xie 葉燮 (1627–1703) deserves special attention. In his *Yuan shi* 原詩 he observes:

It is said that poems (*feng* and *ya* 風雅) can be either in correct or mutated forms, and that their being in correct or mutated forms depends upon the particular periods [in which they are written] because political customs lose what they once enjoy and therefore decline—this is to judge poetry according to the times; [according to this view] when the times become mutated, poetry follows. [But one can say that ] when the times become mutated, they cease to be correct. However, poetry does not lose its correct form. There is only gain, no decline—this is the fountainhead of poetry. (In Wang Fuzhi 王夫之 et al., *Qing shihua* 清詩話 [Shanghai: Shanghai guji, 1963], 2:569.)

Ye Xie dates from the seventeenth century. By then the authority of the Great Preface had been challenged for a long time, and the concept of literature had already undergone some changes. While it is necessary to point out that the view in the Great Preface is by no means the ultimate authority in this issue, it would be an anachronism to use a rebuttal like Ye Xie's to discount its influence during a much earlier period, for example, the period of Southern Dynasties, without which Ye Xie's somewhat radical theory would have been unlikely. For other challenges to the Great Preface in this issue, see Zhu Ziqing, *Shi yanzhi bian*, esp. the section "Shiti zhengbian" 詩體正變 (The norm and change in poetic styles), in his *Lunwen ji*, 1:335–55.

23. *Shi yanzhi bian*, in *Lunwenji*, 1:322–23.

24. 發乎情，止乎禮義. See Guo, *Lidai wenlunxuan*, 1:63; Legge, *Chinese Classics*, 4:35; Owen, *Chinese Literary Thought*, 47.

25. It should be noted that in *The Book of Songs*, especially in the "Xiaoya" 小雅 section, there are numerous poems that express a similar sentiment. For instance, a poem entitled "Du renshi" 都人士 is interpreted by Zheng Xuan as "lamenting that the ancient people [and their customs] no longer existed." See Legge, *Chinese Classics*, 4:72. But Confucius is certainly the most instrumental force in shaping this mentality among Chinese literati.

26. Yang, *Lunyu yizhu*, 30; Legge, *Chinese Classics*, 1:160. It is worth noting that such a mentality also pervaded in the writings of Western writers during the ancient periods. The following passage is by Cicero:

Before our time the customs of our people produced outstanding individuals, and ancient customs and traditional institutions were preserved by eminent personalities. In our age, however, the state has come to be like a painting which is remarkable but already fading because of old age, and people neglect not only to restore original colors in it, but even to preserve its shape and outline. (Quoted in Richard Gilman, *Decadence, The Strange Life of an Epithet*, 43.)

27. Yang, *Lunyu yizhu*, 171; Legge, *Chinese Classics*, 1:298.

28. Yang, *Lunyu yizhu*, 72; Legge, *Chinese Classics*, 1:196. The Duke of Zhou 周公 is Confucius's model of morality and statesmanship.

29. Among the ones contending for equal or superior status of "modern" literature over the ancient writings are Han philosopher Wang Chong 王充 (27–97), Jin Daoist writer Ge Hong 葛洪 (284–363), and Emperor Jianwen of Liang, Xiao Gang, one of the leading decadent writers of late Southern Dynasties period.

30. Owen, *Chinese Literary Thought*, 47.

31. Again for a more detailed discussion of this matter, see Zhu Ziqing, *Shi yanzhi bian*, esp. the chapter "Zheng bian" 正變, in *Lunwen ji*, 1:319–55.

32. Chen Guying 陳鼓應, ann. and trans., *Laozi zhushi ji pingjie* 老子注釋及評介 (Beijing: Zhonghua, 1984), 194. English translation in Wm. Theodore De Bary et al., *Sources of Chinese Tradition* (New York: Columbia University Press, 1960), 1:57; also in Arthur Waley, *The Way and Its Power* (New York: Grove Weidenfeld, 1958), 183.

33. In Guo, *Lidai wenlunxuan*, 1: 91.

34. For studies of cultural and ideological background of the Han period, see Li Zehou and Liu Gangji, *Meixueshi*, 1:439–603, and Kung-chuan Hsiao, *A History of Chinese Political Thought*, vol. 1, *From the Beginning to the Sixth Century A.D.*, trans. F. W. Mote (Princeton: Princeton University Press, 1979), 469–548.

35. For a study of the changes that occurred in Chinese culture during this time, see Li Zehou and Liu Gangji, *Meixueshi*, vol. 2, esp. chap. 1.

36. The Chinese text I am using is Zhou Zhenfu 周振甫, ann., and trans., *Wenxin diaolong jinyi* 文心雕龍今譯 (Beijing: Zhonghua, 1986). For a complete English translation of this text, see Vincent Yu-chung Shih, trans., *The Literary Mind and the Carving of Dragons* (Taipei: Chung Hwa Book Company, 1975); Stephen Owen's *Readings in Chinese Literary Thought* contains several chapters from Liu Xie's work and a brief account of different renderings of its title.

37. For a brief discussion of the symbolic significance of the dragon in Chinese culture, see Li Zehou, *Mei de licheng*, 2–15.

38. Wen 文 originally means "pattern" or "ornament." Thus when it is used to refer to writing it can be loosely translated as "literature," or "belles lettres," with the attendant emphasis on formal quality. The usage and meaning of the word may change with the different contexts and historical periods in which it appeared; therefore it poses great difficulties for the translator. I have adopted various versions, some of them may look awkward, in rendering this word so as to adhere as closely as possible to its contextual meaning. For a brief account of the various meanings of the word from antiquity to the Tang period, see Guo Shaoyu, *Zhongguo wenxue pipingshi*, 63–74, and Peter K. Bol, *This Culture of Ours: Intellectual Transitions in T'ang and Sung China* (Stanford: Stanford University Press, 1992), chap. 3.

39. Owen, *Chinese Literary Thought*, 185.

40. According to Guo Shaoyu, the phrase *wenzhang* first appeared during the Han period; it was used to refer to what we now call "literary works" (*wenxue zuopin* 文學作品).See his *Pipingshi*, 70.

41. Zhou, *Wenxin diaolong*, 22; English translation in Shih, *The Literary Mind*, 19, with considerable modifications.

42. Zhou, *Wenxin diaolong*, 317; English translation in Shih, *The Literary Mind*, 274, with modifications.

43. Yang, *Lunyu yizhu*, 153; Legge, *Chinese Classics*, 1: 276.

44. *Zhouyi zhengyi* 周易正義, in *Shisanjing zhushu*, 1:37; English translation in James J. Y. Liu, *Chinese Theories of Literature* (Chicago: University of Chicago Press, 1975), 17, with modifications.

45. *Zhouyi zhengyi*, in *Shisanjing zhushu*, 1:86; English translation in James Liu, *Chinese Theories of Literature*, 18, with modifications.

46. Zhou, *Wenxin diaolong*, 11; English translation in Shih, *The Literary Mind*, 10, with my modifications. Also in Owen, *Chinese Literary Thought*, 189–90.

47. Zhou, *Wenxin diaolong*, 10; English translation in Shih, *The Literary Mind*, 10, with my modifications. Also in Owen, *Chinese Literary Thought*, 188–89.

48. Zhou, *Wenxin diaolong*, 12; English translation in Shih, *The Literary Mind*, 11, with modifications. Also in Owen, *Chinese Literary Thought*, 191.

49. This chapter is entitled "Yuandao" 原道, "On the Origin of the Way [of literature]."

50. For example, one of the classic denunciations of Palace Style poetry by Wei Zheng 魏徵 (580–643) describes it as "[written in] clear diction and clever form, interested only in what happens on the sleeping mat; it carves and chisels (*diaozhuo* 雕琢) its elaborate style to exhaust what happens within women's bedrooms." See "Jingjizhi" 經籍志 in *Sui shu* 隋書 (Beijing: Zhonghua, 1973), vol. 4, chap. 35, 1090.

51. This is my rendering. Knechtges uses "writing" to translate *siwen* 斯文.

52. Xiao Tong, ed., *Wen xuan* 文選 (Beijing: Zhonghua, 1977), ann. Li Shan 李善 (630–89), 1:1; English translation in David R. Knechtges, trans., *Wen xuan: or Selections of Refined Literature* (Princeton: Princeton University Press, 1982), 1:73. For another translation and commentary on this preface, especially on its significance in the formation of genre theory in Chinese literature, see James Robert Hightower, "The *Wen Hsuan* and Genre Theory," in John L, Bishop, ed., *Studies in Chinese Literature* (Cambridge: Harvard University Press, 1966), 142–65.

53. *Wen xuan*, 1: 2; Knechtges, *Selections of Refined Literature*, 1: 87–88.

54. In his preface he cited nearly verbatim the opening sentence of the Great Preface. See *Wen xuan*, 1:1.

55. Knechtges, *Selections of Refined Literature* , 1:18.

56. Some scholars had related this new awareness of the musical quality of Chinese language to the translation of Buddhist sutras, which were meant to be read aloud. See for example Liu Dajie 劉大杰, *Zhongguo wenxue fazhanshi* 中國文學發展史 (Shanghai: Shanghai Guji, 1982), 1:288–90. Although the institutionalization of rhyme and metrical pattern in Chinese poetry was not established until the High Tang period, the energetic study on this subject made by the Southern Dynasties scholars and poets like Shen Yue is the necessary first step in transforming metrical pattern in poetry from the category of natural to the category of artificial: the former relies on the sound of oral speech, the latter on the sound regulation of the rhyme book. See Wang Li 王力, *Hanyu shilüxue* 漢語詩律學 (Shanghai: Shanghai Jiaoyu, 1979), 1.

57. *Song shu* 宋書 (Beijing: Zhonghua, 1974), vol. 6, chap. 67, 1779. Quoted and translated in Richard B. Mather, *The Poet Shen Yüeh* (Princeton: Princeton University Press, 1988), 43, with slight modifications.

58. In the context of Western culture this is easier to comprehend, because the Western view of poetry as something made, the emphasis on rhetoric, all lead "naturally" to the position taken by Shen Yue.

59. 立身之道，與文章異。立身先須謹重，文章且須放蕩. Xiao Gang made this statement in a letter to his son; see "Jie Dangyanggong Daxin shu" 誡當陽公大心書, in Zhang Pu 張溥, ed., *Han-Wei Liuchao Baisanjia ji* 漢魏六朝百三家集 (Taipei: Xinxing shuju, 1963), 2625 (hereafter cited as *Baisanjia ji*). Xiao Gang's view that literature should be unrestrained was later elaborated by his brother Xiao Yi 蕭繹, Emperor Yuan of the Liang dynasty 梁元帝 (508–55). In his *Jinlou zi* 金樓子 he said that "literature should be colorful and ornate to the eye, charming and melodious to the ear; its refined diction should intoxicate the reader's heart." In Guo Shaoyu, *Lidai wenlunxuan*, 1: 340.

60. Yang Xiong once said that "words are the sound of the heart; writing is the picture of the heart. When sound and picture are formed, a gentleman or a villain is revealed." In *Zhongguo meixueshi ziliao xuanbian* 中國美學史資料選編 (Beijing: Beijing daxue, 1980), 1: 116.

61. In *Baisanjia ji*, 2625.

62. For a detailed discussion of Xiao Gang's revisionist interpretation of the principle that poetry must express one's will, see chap. 2 of the present study; for the role that politics played in Xiao Gang's writing, see John Marney, *Liang Chien-Wen Ti* (Boston: Twayne, 1976), passim.

63. "Jianwendi ji" 簡文帝紀 in *Nan shi* 南史 (Beijing: Zhonghua, 1975) records that "[Emperor Jianwen] enjoyed tirelessly to entertain literary scholars. . . . He had a passion for writing poetry; he said that he had composed some pieces when he was seven years old and never got tired of it when he grew up. But his poetry was frivolous and was known as 'Palace Style'" (vol.1, chap. 8, 232–33).

64. Besides Palace Style poetry which form the main body of this anthology, this anthology also includes some anonymous *yuefu* poems and poems by early poets such as Cao Zhi 曹植 (192–232) and Ruan Ji 阮籍 (210–63). These works are distinctively different from Palace Style poetry, although they also deal with love and separation. Some Chinese scholars have argued that Xu Ling included these traditionally acclaimed pieces in order to legitimize the otherwise unacceptable practice of Palace Style poetry. See Wang Zhongluo 王仲犖, *Wei-Jin Nanbeichao shi* 魏晉南北朝史 (Shanghai: Shanghai renmin, 1980), 2: 971.

65. You Yu 由余 is a diplomat and persuader during the Warring States period. His advice helped the state of Qin to conquer the western part of China. See "Qinbenji" 秦本紀 in Sima Qian 司馬遷 (c. 145–87 B.C.), *Shi ji* 史記 (Beijing: Zhonghua, 1972). vol. 1, chap. 5, 192 3.

66. Zhang Heng 張衡 (78–139) is an Eastern Han writer and poet. He is particularly known for his "Xijing fu" 西京賦 and "Dongjing fu" 東京賦, both of which are collected in *Wen xuan*, 1: 36–68.

67. "East neighbor" 東鄰 alludes to the beautiful woman in Song Yu's 宋玉 "Dengtuzi haose fu" 登徒子好色賦; she is said to have flirted with Song Yu; see *Wen xuan*, 1: 268–69.

68. *Yutai xinyong*, 1; Anne Birrel, *New Songs from a Jade Terrace*, 337–38. I have consulted Birrel's version, but the translation is mine.

69. Artificiality is also one of the most salient trademarks of decadent literature in the Western tradition. This point is beautifully and subtly elaborated in Gautier's following remark on Baudelaire's poetry, which has remained the most often cited definition of decadent literature in the West:

The style of decadence . . . . is nothing else than art arrived at the extreme point of maturity produced by those old civilizations which are growing old with their oblique suns, style that is ingenious, complicated, learned, full of shades of meaning and research, always pushing further the limits of language, borrowing from all technical vocabularies, taking colors from all palettes, notes from all keyboards, forcing itself to express in thought that which is most ineffable, and in form the vaguest and most fleeting contours; listening, that it may translate them, to the subtle confidences of the neuropath, to the avowals of aging and depraved passion, and to the singular hallucinations of the fixed idea verging on madness. This style of decadence is the effort of the Word (*Verbe*), called upon to express everything, and pushed to the utmost extremity. We may remind ourselves, in connection with it, of the language of the late Roman Empire, already mottled with the greenness of decomposition, and, as it were, gamy (*faisandée*), and of the complicated refinement of the Byzantine school, the last form of Greek art fallen into delinquescence. Such is the inevitable and fatal idiom of peoples and civilizations where factitious life has replaced natural life, and developed in man unknown wants. Besides, it is no easy matter, this style despised of pedants, for it expresses new ideas with new forms and words that have not yet been heard. In opposition to the classic style, it admits of shading, and these shadows teem and swarm with the larvae of superstitions, the phantoms of insomnia, nocturnal terrors, remorse which starts and turns back at the slightest noise, monstrous dreams stayed only by impotence, obscure fantasies at which the day-light would stand amazed, and all the soul conceals of the dark, the unformed, and the vaguely horrible, in its deepest and finest recesses. (Quoted and translated in R. K. R. Thornton, *The Decadent Dilemma* [London: Edward Arnold, 1983], 19.)

70. Birrel, *New Songs*, 6.
71.*Yutai xinyong*, 2; Birrel, *New Songs*, 341.
72. "Dianlun: Lunwen" 典論: 論文, in Guo, *Lidai wenlunxuan*, 1:158–62.
73. According to Confucian ethical theory, there are three means to achieve immortality: by establishing deeds of merit (*ligong* 立功), by establishing one's virtue (*lide* 立德), and by establishing one's words (*liyan* 立言). See *Chunqiu Zuozhuan zhengyi*, in *Shisanjing zhushu*, 2:1979; Legge, *Chinese Classics*, 5:505.
74. Such deliberate challenge to canonical or classical tradition is also true of Western decadent literature, but in the Western context this is often more explicitly spelled out. The following passage is by Arthur Symons, one of the leading decadent writers and critics in late nineteenth-century England:

. . . taken frankly as epithets which express their own meaning, both Impressionism and Symbolism convey some notion of that new kind of literature which is perhaps more broadly characterized by the word Decadence. The most representative literature of the day—the writing which appeals to, which has done so much to form, the younger generation—is certainly not classic, nor has it any relation with that old antithesis of the Classic, the Romantic. After a fashion it is no doubt a decadence; it has all the qualities that we find in the Greek, the Latin, decadence: an intense self-consciousness, a restless curiosity in research, an over-subtilizing refinement upon refinement, a spiritual and moral perversity. If what we call the classic is indeed the supreme art—those qualities of perfect simplicity, perfect sanity, perfect proportion, the supreme qualities—then this representative literature of today, interesting, beautiful, novel as it is, is really a new and beautiful and interesting disease. (See R. V. Holdsworth, ed., *Arthur Symons: Poetry and Prose* [London: Carcanet Press, 1974], 72.)

75. Another contemporary criticism of the new literary trend of the time was voiced by Yan Zhitui 顏之推 (531–90), the author of *Yanshi jiaxun* 顏氏家訓, an important book about the social and cultural milieu of the Southern Dynasties period. In the chapter on literature "Wenzhang" 文章, he charged that the writings of his time were "frivolously ornate; its style competes with substance and reason" ( 率多浮艷，辭與理競). Like Pei Ziye, he regarded this literature as a definite falling away from the writings of the ancient times. In *Zhuzi jicheng* 諸子集成 (Shanghai: Shanghai shudian, 1986), 8:21.

76. I.e., *song* 頌(ode), *daya* 大雅 (big hymn), *xiaoya* 小雅 (small hymn), and *feng* 風 (air). Zheng Xuan explains that "shi 始 (beginning) is what the kingly way depends upon for its success and failure." See *Maoshi zhengyi* in *Shisanjing zhushu*, 1:272. Other scholars have taken *shi* to be a generic term, but Pei Ziye here clearly follows Zheng Xuan's lead in that he seems to be exclusively interested in the moral and political implications of the word. For a discussion of this, see Pauline Yu, *The Reading of Imagery in the Chinese Poetic Tradition*.

77. I.e., *feng* 風 (air), *ya* 雅 (hymn), *song* 頌 (ode), *fu* 賦 (enumeration), *bi* 比 (comparison), *xing* 興 (evocation). The Great Preface has 義 instead of 藝. For a study on this subject, see Guo Shaoyu, 郭紹虞, "Liuyi-shuo kaobian" 六義說考辨, in his *Zhaoyushi gudian wenxue lunji* 照隅室古典文學論集 (Shanghai: Shanghai guji, 1983), 2: 355–89.

78. *Zuo zhuan* records that Jizi was able to tell the political situation of a nation by listening to its music. See Legge, *Chinese Classics*, 5: 545–46.

79. Guo, *Lidai wenlunxuan*, 1: 324–26. Also in *Quan Liang wen* 全梁文, chap. 53, in Yan Kejun 嚴可均, ed., *Quan Shanggu Sandai Qin-Han Sanguo Liuchao wen* 全上古三代秦漢三國六朝文 (Beijing: Zhonghua, 1958), 4:3262;

80. Zhou, *Wenxin diaolong*, 270; English translation in Shih, *The Literary Mind*, 233, with my modifications.

81. "Wenxuezhuan xu" 文學傳序, in *Sui shu*, vol. 6, chap. 76, 1730.

82. "Yu Shinan zhuan" 虞世南傳 in Ouyang Xiu 歐陽修 et al., *Xin Tang shu* 新唐書 (Beijing, Zhonghua, 1975), vol. 13, chap. 102, 3972. Quoted and translated by Stephen Owen in *The Poetry of the Early T'ang* (New Haven: Yale University Press, 1977), 43.

83. This view is pervasive in Sui and early Tang writings. Besides consulting Chen Zi'ang's letter that will be quoted below, interested readers might look at the polemical letter to Emperor Gaozu of Sui by Li E 李諤 "Shang Sui Gaozu gaige wenhua shu" 上隋高祖改革文華書, Wang Bo 王勃 "Shang Libu Pei Shilang qi" 上吏部裴侍郎啓, Yang Jiong 楊炯 "Wang Bo ji xu" 王勃集序, all in Guo, *Lidai wenlunxuan*, 2: 5, 8, 11–13, respectively. For an account of this issue, see Owen, *The Poetry of the Early T'ang*, pt. 1, "Court Poetry and Its Opposition."

84. The idea that Tang poetry took a sharp turn with Chen Zi'ang's work is a myth that has been perpetuated by poets and critics like Han Yu and Yuan Haowen 元好問 (1190–1257), especially the often cited quatrain poem of the latter:

| 沈宋橫馳翰墨場 | Shen Chuanqi and Song Zhiwen dashed over the field of literature, |
|---|---|
| 風流初不廢齊梁 | Courtly men who at first couldn't abandon the Qi and Liang style. |
| 論功若準平吳例 | But if we judge whose is the credit in conquering Wu, |
| 合著黃金鑄子昂 | They ought to compose the shining gold to cast a Chen Ziang. |

(Chinese text in Guo, *Lidai wenlunxuan*, 2: 449; quoted and translated in Owen, *The Poetry of the Early T'ang*, 153.)

Many scholars have argued that the transition in early Tang poetry from the influence of Qi and Liang to the authentic Tang style is a very gradual one. See Owen, *The Poetry of the Early T'ang*, chaps. 1, 2; and Luo Zongqiang, *Sui-Tang Wudai*, chap. 2.

85. "Yu Dongfang Qiu Zuoshi xiuzhupian xu" 與東方虯左史修竹篇序, in Guo, *Lidai wenlunxuan*, 2:55; quoted and translated in Owen, *The Poetry of the Early T'ang*, 166, with modifications.

86. The word *feng* is translated by others as "Air," especially when it refers to a type of poetry in *The Book of Songs*.

87. Zhou, *Wenxin diaolong*, 262; English translation in Shih, *The Literary Mind*, 227, with my modifications; also in Owen, *Chinese Literary Thought*, 219.

88. The term *fenggu* has generated much discussion and debate among scholars of the past and present. For explanations and discussions of the term, see Guo, *Lidai wenlunxuan*, 1: 252–58, Owen, *Chinese Literary Thought*, 218–23, and Lin Wen-yüeh, "The Decline and Revival of *Feng-ku* (wind and bone): On the Changing Poetic Styles from Chien-an Era through the High T'ang Period," in Shuen-fu Lin and Stephen Owen, eds., *The Vitality of Lyric Voice: Shih Poetry from the Late Han to the T'ang* (Princeton: Princeton University Press, 1986), 130–66.

89. Jian'an period (196–219), the last reign period of Han, coincided with the founding of the Wei state. In the periodization of Chinese literature, the term is now loosely used to refer to the period when the Cao family reigned and gathered nearly all well-known writers of the time under their patronage. For a detailed discussion of this topic, see Lin Wen-yüeh, "The Decline and the Revival of *Feng-ku*."

90. Zhou, *Wenxin diaolong*, 399; English translation in Shih, *The Literary Mind*, 339, with my modifications.

91. See *Shi pin [zhu]* 詩品〔注〕, ann. Chen Yanjie 陳延傑 (Hong Kong: Shangwu, 1959), 3.

92. The remark was made in his essay "On Insect Carving."

93. 建安骨 "Jian'an bone." See his "Xuanzhou Xie Tiao lou jianbie Jiaoshu Shuyun" 宣州謝眺樓餞別校書叔雲, in *Quan Tang shi* 全唐詩 (Beijing: Zhonghua, 1960), vol. 5, chap. 177, 1809.

94. See "Gufeng wushi-jiu shou: qiyi" 古風五十九首: 其一 : "After Jian'an era, /The overrefined literature is worth nothing" 自從建安來, 綺麗不足珍; ibid, vol. 5, chap. 161, 1670.

95. Ed. Wang Liqi 王利器 (Beijing: Zhongguo shehui kexue, 1983), 279.

96. See Yan, *Canglang shihua*, 1, and Owen, *Chinese Literary Thought*, 394.

## CHAPTER 2

1. I pointed out in chap. 1 that the official biography of Xiao Gang in *Nan shi* takes the writing of Xiao Gang to be the beginnings of Palace Style poetry. But the biography of Xu Chi in *Nan shi* (vol. 5, chap. 52, 1521) also contains the following passage, which clearly regards Xu Chi as its originator:

Xu Chi liked to be innovative in his writing and loathed to be confined within old styles. . . . His distinctive style was imitated

by everyone in the Crown Prince's Palace. Hence the beginning
of the so-called 'Palace Style [Poetry]'.

As Xiao Gang's literary mentor, Xu Chi obviously had tremendous
influence in the formation of Xiao Gang's literary style and taste.
Unfortunately, very little of Xu Chi's poetry has survived; *Xian Qin
Han-Wei-Jin Nanbeichao shi* 先秦漢魏晉南北朝詩, ed. Lu Qinli 逯欽
立 (Beijing: Zhonghua, 1983), contains only six poems by him. For
studies on the origin of Palace Style poetry, see Shen Yucheng 沈玉成,
"Gongtishi yu *Yutai xinyong*" 宮體詩與玉台新詠, *Wenxue yichan* 文
學遺產 6 (1988): 55–65, and Ronald C. Miao, "Palace Style Poetry:
The Courtly Treatment of Glamour and Love," in Ronald C. Miao,
ed., *Studies in Chinese Poetics* (San Francisco: Chinese Materials
Center, 1978), 1: 1–42. Some critics have related the emergence of
Palace Style Poetry to the influence of Buddhism; see Wang Chunhong
汪春泓, "Lun Fojiao yu Gongtishi de chansheng" 論佛教與梁代宮體
詩的產生, *Wenxue pinglun* 文學評論 5 (1991): 40–56. To define Palace Style poetry will be the task of this chapter. But readers who are
interested in "handy" or conventional definitions of this genre may
consult Cao Daoheng 曹道衡 and Shen Yucheng 沈玉成, *Nanbeichao
wenxueshi* 南北朝文學史 (Beijing: Renmin wenxue, 1991), Ronald C.
Miao's aforementioned article, and Lin Wenyue 林文月, "Nanchao
Gongtishi yanjiu" 南朝宮體詩研究, *Wen-shi-zhe xuebao* 文史哲學報
15 (1966): 407–58. Cao and Shen define Palace Style Poetry from three
aspects: in metrical pattern it becomes even more sophisticated than
the earlier *Yongming* (永明) style; in language it shows an increasingly more extravagant and often frivolous tendency; and in content
it usually treats amorous matters, objects, and social occasions (p.
241). Miao's definition is much narrower: "'palace-style poetry' is a
thematic designation for Chinese verse centered on the life of the
imperial residence, and may include such varied but related subject
matters as court functions and ceremonies, objects of palace art and
architecture, landscape, as well as that most glamorous of fixtures
within the harem or 'forbidden interior,' the palace lady" (p. 1). Lin
defines Palace Style poetry mainly from its subject matter: in the narrow sense, it treats women and amorous love; in the broad sense, it
includes other aspects of the aristocrats' life, such as sightseeing and
partying, etc. Readers interested in other works on Palace Style poetry
may consult the following articles: Shang Wei 商偉, "Lun Gongtishi"

論宮體詩, *Beijing daxue xuebao* 北京大學學報 4 (1984): 66–74; Cao Daoheng 曹道衡, "Guanyu *Yutai xinyong* de banben ji bianzhe wenti" 關于玉台新詠的版本及編者問題, in *Zhongguo gudian wenxue luncong* 中國古典文學論叢 (Beijing: Renmin wenxue, 1985), 307–11; Cao Xu 曹旭, "Lun Gongtishi shenmei yishi xinbian" 論宮體詩審美意識新變, *Wenxue yichan* 文學遺產 6 (1988); and Wu Yun 吳雲 and Dong Zhiguang 董志廣, "Liangdai Gongtishi xinlun" 梁代宮體詩新論, *Wenxue yichan* 4 (1990): 25–30.

2. I. e., "The Code of Administration" (*zhidian* 治典), "The Code of Instruction" (*jiaodian* 教典), "The Code of Rites" (*lidian* 禮典), "The Code of Correction" (*zhengdian* 政典), "The Code of Penalty" (*xingdian* 刑典), and "The Code of Business" (*shidian* 事典); see *Zhouli zhushu* 周禮注疏, in *Shisanjing zhushu*, 1: 645.

3. I. e., *Zhouli* 周禮, *Yili* 儀禮, *Liji* 禮記; all three are Confucian classics.

4. This line alludes to the poem "Qiyue" 七月 in *The Book of Songs*. See *Maoshi zhengyi*, in *Shisanjing zhushu*, 1:389, and Legge, *Chinese Classics*, vol. 4, *The She King or The Book of Poetry*, 228.

5. This line alludes to a line in Song Yu's "Zhao hun" 召魂. See Wang Yi 王逸 (fl. early first century A.D.) and Hong Xingzu 洪興祖 (1090–1155), eds., *Chuci buzhu* 楚辭補注 (Taipei: Zhonghua, *Sibu beiyao* edition, 1965), chap. 9, 15.

6. "Yu Xiangdong Wang shu" 與湘東王書, in Zhang Pu, ed., *Han-Wei Liuchao baisanjia ji*, hereafter cited as *Baisanjia ji*, 2625; also in Guo Shaoyu, ed., *Zhongguo lidai wenlunxuan*, hereafter cited as *Lidai wenlunxuan*, 1: 327. Unless otherwise noted, all translations of Chinese materials in this chapter are mine.

7. Guo, *Lidai wenlunxuan*, 63; Legge, *Chinese Classics*, 4: 35–36; English translation in Stephen Owen, *Readings in Chinese Literary Thought*, 47, with slight modifications; emphasis mine.

8. "Da Zhang Zan xieji shu" 答張纘謝集書, in *Han-Wei Liuchao Baisanjia ji*, 2628.

9. See *Shi pin*, 13–14.

10. I have mentioned that Yang Xiong gave up his rhyme-prose writing late in his life because he came to consider it trivial and not worthy of a gentleman. Cao Zhi once also called poetry writing "trivial" (辭賦小道) and voiced his agreement with Yang Xiong on this issue. See his "Yu Yang Dezu shu" 與楊德祖書, in *Cao Zhi ji zhu* 曹植集注, ed. and ann. Zhao Youwen 趙幼文 (Beijing: Renmin wenxue, 1984),

154. Xiao Gang's accusation must have been directed against comments like this on the part of Cao Zhi.

11. Changmen Palace (長門宮) is where Empress Chen of Han lived after she fell out favor with Emperor Wu. Sima Xiangru wrote "Changmen fu" 長門賦 on her story. She later became an archetype of the deserted court lady. For the text of Sima Xiangru's *fu*, see *Wen xuan*, 1: 227–28.

12. "Da Xinyuhou heshi shu" 答新渝侯和詩書, in *Baisanjiaji*, 2628.

13. In his preface Xu Ling calls these poems *yange* 艷歌 (amorous poems). See *Yutai xinyong*, 1.

14. The Tang poet and writer Yuan Zhen 元稹 (779–831) described the poetry of Liang and Chen as "excessively ornate, overly carved and decorated" (*yingyan keshi* 淫艷刻飾), see "Tang gu Gongbu Yuanwailang Dujun muzhiming bing xu" 唐故工部員外郎杜君墓銘銘並序, in Guo, *Lidai wenlunxuan*, 2: 65; in both "Yinyue zhi" 音樂志 in *Sui shu* (vol. 2, chap. 13, 309) and "Zhang Guifei zhuan" 張貴妃傳 in *Nan shi* (vol. 2, chap. 12, 348), Chen Houzhu's poetry was portrayed as *yanli* 艷麗.

15. See Xing Wenfang, *Tangcaizi zhuan*, 238. In this case the term used was *ceci yanqu* 側詞艷曲 (frivolously amorous and ornate poetry).

16. "宋華父督見孔父之妻于路，目逆而送之，曰：美而艷。" Recorded in *Zuo zhuan* 左傳; see Legge, *Chinese Classics*, vol. 5, *The Ch'un Ts'ew with the Tso Chuen*, 35. On another occasion this word was also applied to a man; see ibid., 273. But such usage is rare, and as Qian Zhongshu 錢鍾書 pointed out, when words like *yan* 艷 and *li* 麗 were used to describe a man in later periods, they tend to convey negative meanings; see *Guanzhuibian* 管錐編 (Beijing: Zhonghua, 1979), 1:173.

17. It should be noted that this word, especially when it is used in the context of Southern Dynasties and Late Tang poetry, carries a derogatory tone. Chen Houzhu's poetry "strives at ornateness and is extremely frivolous" 艷麗相高，極于輕薄; see "Yinyuezhi" in *Sui shu*. Wen Tingyun and Li Shangyin's poetry is said to be "frivolously ornate" *ceyan* 側艷; see *Tang caizi zhuan*.

For a study on this topic, see Kang Zhengguo 康正果, *Fengsao yu yangqing* 風騷與艷情 (Zhengzhou: Henan renmin, 1988), 130–61, and passim.

18. For a study on this subject, see Anne Birrel, "The Dusty Mirror: Courtly Portraits of Woman in Southern Dynasties Love Poetry," in

Robert E. Hegel and Richard C. Hessney, eds., *Expressions of Self in Chinese Literature* (New York: Columbia University Press, 1985), 33–69.

19. It is noteworty that Xiao Gang regarded poetry produced in such an environment to be "distinctively new" (*xinqi* 新奇). This emphasis on the "newness" was repeated by Xu Ling in the title of *Yutai xinyong*: the poems colleted in this anthology are called "new songs" *xinyong* 新詠.

20. For a text of this poem, see *Chuci buzhu*, 1–47; for a translation and study of Qu Yuan's work, see David Hawkes, *The Songs of the South* (New York: Penguin, 1985). For Chinese scholarship on this topic, see Jiang Liangfu 姜亮夫, *Qu Yuan fu jiaozhu* 屈原賦校注 (Beijing: Shangwu, 1964); Tan Jiefu 譚介甫, *Qufu xinbian* 屈賦新編 (Beijing: Zhonghua, 1978); Zhu Jihai 朱季海, *Chuci jiegu* 楚辭解故 (Shanghai: Zhonghua, 1963); and You Guo'en 游國恩, *Chuci lunwenji* 楚辭論文集 (Hongkong: Wenchang, n.d.).

21. See Guo Maoqian 郭茂倩, *Yuefu shiji* 樂府詩集 (Taipei: Xinxing, 1968), 745. There are a number of studies on Music Bureau poetry. Interested readers may consult Xiao Difei 蕭滌非, *Han-Wei Liuchao yuefu wenxueshi* 漢魏六朝樂府文學史 (Beijing: Renmin wenxue, 1984); Yu Guanying 余冠英, *Han-Wei Liuchao shi luncong* 漢魏六朝詩論叢 (Shanghai: Zhonghua, 1962); Luo Genze 羅根澤, *Yuefu wenxueshi* 樂府文學史 (Taipei: Wen-shi-zhe, 1972); Chen Yicheng 陳義成, *Han-Wei Liuchao yuefu yanjiu* 漢魏六朝樂府研究 (Taipei: Chia Hsin Foundation, 1976); Wang Yunxi 王運熙, *Han-Wei Liuchao yuefushi* 漢魏六朝樂府詩 (Shanghai: Zhonghua, 1986); Hans H. Frankel, "Yueh-fu Poetry," in Cyril Birch, ed., *Studies in Chinese Literary Genres* (Berkeley: University of California Press, 1974); and Joseph R. Allen, *In the Voices of Others: Chinese Music Bureau Poetry* (Ann Arbor: University of Michigan Press, 1992).

22. The "Yiwenzhi " 藝文志 in *Han shu* 漢書 (Beijing: Zhonghua, 1962) notes that "The Music Bureau was established to collect folk songs during the reign of Xiaowu; since then there were poems of Dai and Zhao, poems of Qin and Chu. All of them were motivated by sorrows and delight and occasioned by specific events. This is why one can observe the conditions of local customs from them" (vol. 6, chap. 38, 1756). Liu Xie's *Wenxin diaolong* has a chapter on Music Bureau poetry where he made similar remarks. See Zhou Zhenfu, *Wenxin diaolong jinyi*, 64–72.

23. I am aware of the differences between the Chinese *bi, xing,* or
*yuyan* 寓言 and the Western "allegory," but this is a very complex
issue and it is impossible to discuss it in any detail here. In the present
context I am using "allegorical reading" to refer to a reading that
aims to discover in or confer to a text meanings that do not exist on
the textual level. The Han exegesis of *The Book of Songs* is a good
example of this practice because nearly all poems in that anthology
are interpreted as having a larger moral and political significance.
For a study on this subject see Pauline Yu, *The Reading of Imagery in
the Chinese Poetic Tradition,* chaps. 1, 2, and passim.

24. *Yuefu shiji,* chap. 63, 745; for an annotated text of this poem,
see Beijing daxue Zhongwenxi 北京大學中文系, ed., *Wei-Jin Nanbeichao wenxueshi cankao ziliao* 魏晉南北朝文學史參考資料 (Beijing:
Zhonghua, 1962), 1: 87–89.

25. *Yuefu shiji,* 745.

26. For example, in *Maoshi zhengyi* there is a rather far-fetched
reading of one of the pieces describing a woman picking mulberries.
Part of the poem reads:

| | |
|---|---|
| 彼汾一方 | There on a stretch by the Fen |
| 言采其桑 | I was plucking mulberry-leaves; |
| 彼其之子 | There came a gentleman |
| 美如英 | Who is beautiful as a flower, |
| 美如英 | Who is beautiful as a flower, |
| 殊異乎公行 | More splendid than any that escort |
| | The duke in his coach. |

This poem was read by the Han scholar Zheng Xuan 鄭玄 (127–
200), who compiled the influential *Maoshi zhengjian* 毛詩鄭箋, as
"an allegory of the diligence [of the king]. The king is modest and
industrious; this provides a lesson for those who fail to adhere to the
rites." See *Shisanjing zhushu*; 1:357; Legge, *Chinese Classics,* 4: 164;
English translation by Arthur Waley, *The Book of Songs* (New York:
Grove Press, 1937), 24; I have made some minor changes in my citation. The accuracy of this reading is not our concern here. What is
important is this strong tendency in Chinese poetic criticism to interpret poems, especially poems with a folk (later Music Bureau) origin,
allegorically.

27. Unfortunately this poem is too long to be quoted here. See Guo,
*Yuefu shiji,* chap. 28, 338; for an annotated text of this poem, see

Beijing daxue Zhongwenxi 北京大學中文系, ed., *Liang Han wenxueshi cankao ziliao* 兩漢文學史參考資料 (Beijing: Zhonghua, 1962), 515–20; for an English translation, see Hans Frankel, "Yueh-fu Poetry," in Birch, ed., *Studies in Chinese Literary Genres*, 71–81.

28. Guo Maoqian records another critic's commentary on this poem:

"The Mulberry Trees by the Road" is by a woman from a certain Qin family. The Qins, who were natives of Handan, had a daughter named Luo Fu. She was married to a man named Wang Ren who enjoyed a fief of a thousand carriages. Wang Ren later became the manager for the family of one Governor Zhao. When Luo Fu was out picking mulberry leaves, Governor Zhao saw her from the platform and took a fancy to her. He prepared some wine to entrap her, but with tact Luo Fu began to play her zither and composed this "Mulberry Trees by the Road" to make clear her will. The governor stopped upon hearing it. (See *Yuefu shiji*, chap. 28, 338.)

29. *Han-Wei yuefu fenjian* 漢魏樂府風箋 (Hong Kong: Shangwu, 1961), 203.

30. Modern critics generally accept this allegorical reading of the poem, although they are careful not to try to allegorize every aspect of it. See *Wei-Jin Nanbeichao wenxueshi cankao ziliao*, 87–88, *Cao Zhi ji jiaozhu*, 386, and the essay on this poem by Mou Shijin 牟世金 in *Han-Wei Liuchao shige jianshangji* 漢魏六朝詩歌鑒賞集 (Beijing: Renmin wenxue, 1985), 180–84.

31. For example, Confucius's remark that the poems in *The Book of Songs* can be characterized by one phrase: no evil thought (思無邪), and his comment on the well known "Guan Ju" (關雎) poem that it fits perfectly into the ideal of the golden mean (樂而不淫, 哀而不傷); all this is an attempt to treat the poems as the illustration of a preconceived ideology. See Yang Bojun, *Lunyu yizhu*, 13, 32; Legge, *Chinese Classics*, 1: 146, 161.

32. For texts of these two works, see *Maoshi zhengyi* and *Chuci buzhu*.

33. See note 26.

34. Chinese text in *Chuci buzhu*, chap. 1, 4–5; English translation in Hawkes, *Songs of the South*, 68.

35. *Chuci buzhu*, chap 1, 5.

36. Scholars disagree with regard to the identity of this Fair One. Some take it to refer to the Chu King, to whom Qu Yuan remained loyal until his suicide. But others consider the Fair One to be the poet himself, and I agree with this interpretation, for I think Qu Yuan is continuing using the trope on the feminine quality of flowers in the previous lines and develops it further into a figure for human being, to whom he of course has an even more natural link. This becomes more perceptible in the next few lines, where he directly compares his situation to that of a beautiful woman who is slandered by other jealous women. See You Guoen, "Chuci nüxing zhongxin shuo" 楚辭 女性中心說, in his *Chuci lunwenji*, 191–204. For a brief account of different interpretations of the image of Fair One (*meiren* 美人), see Beijing daxue Zhongwenxi 北京大學中文系 ed., *Xian Qin wenxueshi cankao ziliao* 先秦文學史參考資料 (Beijing: Zhonghua, 1962), 512; and Hawkes, *Songs of the South*, 82.

37. *Chuci buzhu*, chap. 1, 12; Hawkes, *Songs of the South*, 70.

38. Jonathan Culler, *Structuralist Poetics* (Ithaca, N.Y.: Cornell University Press, 1975), 151.

39. There is no modern annotated edition of Xiao Gang's poetry. The complete collection of his poetry can be found in *Han-Wei Liuchao baisanjia ji*, ed. Zhang Pu; *Quan Han Sanguo Jin Nanbeichao shi* 全 漢三國晉南北朝詩 (Taipei: Yiwen, 1975), ed. Ding Fubao 丁福保; and Lu Qinli, ed., *Xian Qin Han-Wei-Jin Nanbeichao shi*, 先秦漢魏晉南 北朝詩 (Beijing: Zhonghua, 1983), hereafter cited as *Shi*, which I am using in the present study. A large portion of Xiao Gang's poetry was translated into English by John Marney in a collection entitled *Beyond the Mulberries: An Anthology of Palace-Style Poetry by Emperor Chienwen of the Liang Dynasty (503–551)* (Taipei: Chinese Materials Center, 1982). Unless otherwise noted, all cited poems in the chapter are translated by me. For the text of this poem, see Lu, *Shi*, 3: 1908.

40. Her description of her residence—"Our green mansion faces the big road,/The high gate is locked with several bolts"—is a metaphor for both her noble social status and her carefully protected virtue.

41. Paul Rouzer commented that Palace Style poetry was written as a commentary on the *yuefu* tradition. "The author of a palace poem no longer addresses and woos a lover but instead addresses his fellow poets in an extended commentary on an object they all observe and seek to capture in language; if such a poet writes in a female persona, it is still commentary, both on the *yuefu* tradition he imitates and on

the feminine psychology he believes he is capturing in a convincing and subtle manner." See his "Watching the Voyeurs: Palace Poetry and *Yuefu*," *Chinese Literature: Essays, Articles, Reviews* 11 (1989): 11–34.

42. According to Wen Yiduo, *chenfeng* 晨風 is the name for pheasant. It is thought that the pheasant often seeks its mate in the morning. See *Liang Han wenxueshi cankao ziliao*, 508.

43. Lu, *Shi*, 1:160. For an annotated text, see *Liang Han wenxueshi cankao ziliao*, 507–8; there are slight textual variations between the two versions.

44. There are some allegorical readings of this poem. *Yuefu shiji* records the following version of the Song Dynasty critic He Chengtian 何承天 (d.n.): "'My Beloved' is about longing for the ancients. Zeng [Sheng] and Min [Sun] [two students of Confucius who were known for their filial piety] were both very filial to their parents; they talked about encountering sufferings in life and not being able to see their loving parents" (chap. 16, 198). *Liang Han wenxueshi cankao ziliao* mentions another two readings; one claims the poem to be a satire on elopers, the other regards it to be the work of a banished government official; 507.

45. Lu, *Shi*, 3: 1910.

46. See, for example "Mang" 氓, *Maoshi zhengyi*, in *Shisanjing zhushu*, 1: 324; Legge, *Chinese Classics*, 4: 97–101; and Arthur Waley, *The Book of Songs*, 96–97.

47. See "Yuan shi" 怨詩, in *Yutai xinyong*, 14–15; Birrel, *New Songs*, 43

48. For a text of this poem, see *Yutai xinyong*, 1; Birrel, *New Songs*, 30.

49. 長跪問故夫　She knelt down and asked her former husband,
新人復何如　"What is your new wife like?"
新人雖言好　"Even though my new wife is good,
未若故人姝　She is not as pretty as the old one.
顏色類相似　In looks they are similar to each other,
手爪不相如　But her hands cannot be compared with those of the old."
新人從門入　"Your new wife came in through the main gate,
故人從閣去　While the old one left by the back door."
新人工織縑　"The new one is skilled at weaving finespun,
故人工織素　The old one was skilled at weaving homespun.

織縑日一匹　Finespun is made one *pi* a day,
織素五丈余　Homespun is made more than five *zhang*.
將縑來比素　Comparing finespun and homespun,
新人不如故　I think the new one won't match the old."

(In *Yutai xinyong*, 1, and Birrel, *New Songs*, 30.)

50. In Lu, *Shi*, 3:1923.

51. Ibid.

52. Jonathan Culler says that parody "is an imitation and that by making its model explicit it implicitly denies that it is to be read as a serious statement of feelings about real problems or situations, thus freeing us from one type of *vraisemblance* used to enforce metaphorical readings of poems" (*Structuralist Poetics*, 153). In other words, to understand Xiao Gang's poem one must abandon the metaphorical reading required by the earlier poem; our understanding can not take place in the *vraisemblance* or generic expectations of a poetry dealing with "feelings about real problems or situations"; quite the contrary, we must treat it as mere verbal play.

53. "Liang Jianwendi zhuan" 梁簡文帝傳, in *Liang Shu* 梁書 (Beijing: Zhonghua, 1973), vol. 1, chap. 4, 109.

54. John Marney, *Liang Chien-Wen Ti*, 89. Also on page 79: "Xiao Gang was concerned with the free voicing of sentiment in the Odes [*The Book of Songs*], untrammeled by artificial rhetoric." But he later contradicts: "In the competitive atmosphere of the salons, poetry was a game. The urgency of poetic composition was not a compulsion to express one's mind but a social obligation to display one's wit"; 108. I agree with this view, although it seems to me that this compulsion to display one's poetic wit is not confined to Xiao Gang's occasional poetry alone.

55. Liqiu is a place well-known for its honey. See *Yutai xinyong*, 164.

56. The valley of the Zhongtai Mountain is said to produce the best musk, and its smell is supposed to be beneficial to health. Ibid.

57. A kind of rug that was once used by Yin Lihua 陰麗華, the Emperess of Emperor Guangwu of Han Dynasty 漢光武帝 (r. 25–57). Ibid.

58. In Lu, *Shi*, 3:1939, *Yutai xinyong*, 163–64, and Birrel, *New Songs*, 193–94.

59. According to Bernhard Karlgren's reconstruction in his *Gram-*

*mata Serica Recensa* (Stockholm, 1957), these two characters were both pronounced around A.D. 600 as "miêt." See 114–15, ref. no. 405.

60. For courtly decorum and its effect upon Palace Style poetry, see Cao Daoheng and Shen Yucheng, *Nanbeichao wenxueshi*, chaps. 1 and 13; Stephen Owen, *The Poetry of the Early T'ang*, pt. 1, and Marney, *Liang Chien-Wen Ti*, chaps. 3, 4, 5.

61. For illustrations of this pervasive view, see Wen Yiduo, "Gongtishi de zishu," Liu Dajie, *Zhongguo wenxue fazhanshi*, 1: 303–6, Li Zehou and Liu Gangji, *Zhongguo meixueshi*, 2: 537–60, and Wang Zhongluo, *Wei Jin Nanbeichao shi*, 2: 971–72.

62. Lu, *Shi*, 3: 1941–42.

63. Verbal parallelism is clearly a fashion in the Southern Dynasties period, in line with the general aesthetic tendency of the literature of the time. Liu Xie even claims that this is how the universe works and links this linguistic structure with the structure of humankind, viewing the former as a reflection of the latter. As he writes:

Nature, creating living beings, endows them with limbs and pairs. The divine reason operates in such a way that nothing stands alone. The mind creates literary language, and in doing this it organizes and shapes one hundred different thoughts, making what is high supplement what is low, and spontaneously producing linguistic parallelism.(See Zhou, *Wenxin diaolong*, 314; English translation in Vincent Yu-chung Shih, *The Literary Mind and the Carving of Dragons*, 270.)

64. A. E. Carter, *The Idea of Decadence in French Literature 1830–1900*, 57.

65. William K. Wimsatt Jr., and Cleanth Brooks, *Literary Criticism: A Short History* (Chicago: University of Chicago Press, 1957), 243.

66. Lu, *Shi*, 3:1905.

67. Naturalization can be carried out only within a convention because it depends on conventional expectations and rules to determine if a work is "natural"; if it conforms to these expectations and rules it is natural, and if it does not conform to them, it is unnatural. For a discussion of the relationship between naturalization and convention see Culler, *Structuralist Poetics*, chap. 2.

68. For the numerous examples of such poetry, interested readers might consult *"Feifeng"* 匪風 and *"Dongshan"* 東山 from *The Book of*

*Songs* (in *Shisanjing zhushu*, 1: 382–83, 395–96; Legge, 4: 218, 235), and *"Xingxing fu xingxing"* 行行復行行 from "Nineteen Ancient Poems" (in Lu, *Shi*, 1:329).

69. Xiao Gang's other poems of this kind are *"Deng Fenghuotai"* 登烽火台, *"Deng cheng"* 登城, *"Jing Pipaxia"* 經琵琶峽, all in Lu, *Shi*, 193–94.

70. In Lu, *Shi*, 3:1952; and *Yutai xinyong*, 168.

71. Such usage of this word is frequent in Xiao Gang's poetry. For example, 羅裙宜細簡 "Her silken skirt is fittingly slender" ("Xizeng liren" 戲贈麗人詩); 一種細腰身 "Their slender waists are precisely the same" ("Yong meiren kanhua" 詠美人看畫). In Lu, *Shi*, 3: 1939, 1953.

72. Lu, *Shi*, 3:1959.

73. "Gold wind" (*jinfeng* 金風) refers to "autumn wind," but I have decided to retain the word "gold" in my translation because the physical quality of *jin* 金 is not only highlighted by its contextual language, which is loaded with words for hard, precious objects such as *manao* 瑪瑙 (agate) and *yu* 玉 (jade), it is also implied by the parallelism in the last two lines: jade is meant to be paralleled by gold because both belong to the same category of precious, artificial objects. Although this requirement in parallelism did not become written regulation until the Tang period, we must remember that the later regulation is a theorization of the earlier practice, of which this quatrain by Xiao Gang is a good example.

74. Lu, *Shi*, 1972.

75. For a study of peculiar descriptive characteristics in *fu*, see Dore J. Levy, "Constructing Sequences: Another Look at the Principle of *Fu* 賦 'Enumeration,'" *Harvard Journal of Asiatic Studies* 46 (December 1986): 471–93; Burton Watson, *Chinese Rhyme-Prose* (New York: Columbia University Press, 1977); for Chinese scholarship on this subject see Cheng Tingzuo 程廷祚, *Sao-fu lun* 騷賦論 (Taipei: Li hang, 1970); Jiang Shuge 姜書閣, *Pianwenshi lun* 駢文史論 (Beijing: Renmin wenxue, 1986).

76. For detailed discussion of this issue, see chap. 1.

77. An annotated text of this *fu* can be found in *Wen xuan*, chap. 17, 239–44, and *Wei-Jin Nanbeichao wenxueshi cankao ziliao*, 252–75. For English translations of this work, see Cyril Birch, ed., *Anthology of Chinese Literature* (New York: Grove Press, 1965), 1: 204–14, and Stephen Owen, *Readings in Chinese Literary Thought*, 73–181.

78. Translated by Owen, *Chinese Literary Thought*, 130, with slight modifications.

79. For instance, "Guitian fu" 歸田賦 by Zhang Heng, and "Denglou fu" 登樓賦 by Wang Can 王粲 (177–217) can be cited as typical examples of this change. See *Wen xuan*, chap 15, 317–18, and chap. 11, 221–23.

80. Many critics have pointed out the revisionist nature in this rephrasing of Lu Ji because in the ancient maxim of *shi yanzhi* the emphasis is on the political and social aspect of *zhi* 志 (will); by replacing it with *qing* 情 (feelings) Lu Zhi successfully broadens the scope of this maxim and, what is more, shifts the emphasis to the personal aspect of poetic experience. This shift in subject matter corresponds to his view that the appropriate style of poetry should be colorful (*qimi* 綺靡). This reflects the change of attitude toward literature in general that took place in the Southern Dynasties period. As Stephen Owen pointed out, some Confucian scholars of later ages found this change too radical and disturbing. See *Chinese Literary Thought*, 131.

81. The exegetical history of these three key terms in Chinese poetic theory is long and extremely complicated; it is impossible for me to rehearse them here. Generally speaking, however, they are regarded as technical principles used to bring the poem from a somewhat objective description into a subjective response or meditation. Thus the purpose of *fu* is thought to be "describing objects to express will" (體物寫志); *bi* and *xing* are united in their symbolic and allegorical functions, although the former is thought to be explicit, while the latter works in a more implicit way (比顯而興隱). See Guo, *Lidai wenlunxuan*, 1: 63–76; Xu Fuguan 徐復觀, "*Shi shi de bi-xing: chongxin dianding Zhongguoshi de xinshang jichu*" 釋詩的比興：重新奠定中國詩的欣賞基礎, in his *Zhongguo wenxue lunji* 中國文學論集 (Taipei: Xuesheng shuju, 1985), 91–117; Yu, *The Reading of Imagery*, chaps. 1, 2, and passim; Owen, *Chinese Literary Thought*, 37–48; Shih-hsiang Chen, "The *Shih-ching*: Its Generic Significance in Chinese Literary History and Poetics," in Birch, ed., *Studies in Chinese Literary Genres*, 8–41, especially 16–27.

82. For example, Liu Dajie's *Zhongguo wenxue fazhanshi* completely ignores this genre.

83. For example, the Song dynasty critic Zhang Jie 張戒 (fl. 1124–38) accuses the poetry of objects during Southern Dynasties period of "exclusively focusing on describing objects and becoming increasingly chiseled and carved; thus it had lost all the fundamental functions of

poetry." See *Suihantang shihua* 歲寒堂詩話, in Ding Fubao 丁福保, ed., *Lidai shihua xubian* 歷代詩話續編 (Beijing: Zhonghua, 1983), 1: 450. Wang Fuzhi 王夫之 voiced similar criticism of the poetry on objects of Qi and Liang and charged that it was too much like a craft (*jiangqi* 匠氣). See his *Jiangzhai shihua* 薑齋詩話, in *Qing shihua*, 1: 22. This is a crucial difference between poetry on objects of the Southern Dynasties and that of the Tang period. Li Shangyin's "On a Patterned Zither" 錦瑟, for example, differentiates itself from the former by a feeling of melancholy and loss which is widely interpreted as coming from the poet's own experience. See my discussion in chap. 5.

84. Lu, *Shi*, 1953.

85. There are other poetic subgenres that adopt this word, such as *yonghuai* 詠懷 (poems of the heart) or *yongshi* 詠史 (poems on history). But as Palace Style poetry has carefully avoided these two genres because of the seriousness of their topics, they will not be recalled in reading Xiao Gang's poetry.

86. Kang-i Sun Chang, *Six Dynasties Poetry* (Princeton: Princeton University Press, 1986), 156.

87. See Cao Pi, "Dianlun: lunwen" 典論：論文, in Guo, *Lidai wenlunxuan*, 1: 158–59, Owen, *Chinese Literary Thought*, 57–72.

88. Frederic Jameson, "Baudelaire as Modernist and Postmodernist: The Dissolution of the Referent and the Artificial 'Sublime,'" in Chaviva Hosek and Patricia Parker, eds., *Lyric Poetry beyond New Criticism* (Ithaca: Cornell University Press, 1985), 260.

89. Li Zehou and Liu Ganji, *Zhongguo meixueshi* 中國美學史 (Beijing: Zhonggu shehui kexue, 1987), vol. 2, chap. 16.

90. Zhou, *Wenxin diaolong*, 61; English translation in Shih, *The Literary Mind*, 48, with modifications.

91. See *Zhuangzi jishi* 莊子集釋, ed. Guo Qingfan 郭慶藩 (Beijing: Zhonghua, 1978), 944.

92. "Books are no more than language; there is something valuable in language, and this something is idea. Idea points at something else, and this something else can never be conveyed by language." Ibid., 488.

93. This has been noted by some critics in the classical tradition. Yan Yu once said that the poets of Southern Dynasties "valorized the diction but did poorly in [conveying] thought" (南朝人尚詞而病於理); see his *Canglang shihua*, 148. The Qing critic Chen Zuoming 陳祚明 (1623–74) made a similar comment: "The shortcoming of [the poetry of] Liang and Chen is that it ignored the meaning to seek after

the word" (梁陳之弊, 在舍意問辭); quoted in Cao Daoheng and Sheng Yucheng, *Nanbeichao wenxueshi*, 243.

## CHAPTER 3

1. "Huan zi Kuaiji ge" 還自會稽歌, in Wang Qi 王琦, ed., *Sanjia pingzhu Li Changji geshi* 三家評注李長吉歌詩 (Hong Kong: Zhonghua, 1976), hereafter cited as *Sanjia pingzhu*, 12; Ye Congqi 葉蔥奇, ed. and ann., *Li He Shiji* 李賀詩集 (Beijing: Remin wenxue, 1959), hereafter cited as *Shiji*; 6; J. D. Frodsham, trans., *The Poems of Li He* (Oxford: Clarendon Press, 1970), hereafter cited as *Poems*, 13. My translation.

2. "Wenxuezhuan" 文學傳, in *Nan shi*, chap. 72, 1762.

3. "Li Changji xiaozhuan" 李長吉小傳, in Chen Zhiguo 陳治國, ed., *Li He yanjiu ziliao* 李賀研究資料 (Beijing: Beijing shifan daxue, 1983), here after cited as *Yanjiu ziliao*, 4.

4. Traditionally scholars have attributed this centrifugal tendency in Mid and Late Tang culture to the devastating effect of the An Lushan rebellion (755–63), from which the Tang dynasty never fully recovered. See Li Zehou, *Mei de licheng*, 147, and David McMullen, *State and Scholars in T'ang China* (Cambridge: Cambridge University Press, 1988), 234–49.

5. Some critics see the emergence of the highly personal, grotesque poetry in the Mid and Late Tang eras as a reaction to the increasingly superficial, pragmatic, and dogmatic concepts of literature advocated by Bai Juyi and Yuan Zhen, and the so-called new *yuefu* poetry, which considers political and social criticism to be the sole function of poetry. See Luo Zongqiang, *Sui-Tang Wudai wenxue sixiangshi*, 355–61.

6. In Wang, *Sanjia pingzhu*, 12; English translation in Frodsham, *Poems*, 2, with my modifications.

Qian Zhongshu 錢鐘書 contends that Du Mu's characterization is inaccurate in some parts: "[The poetry of ] Changji [Li He] is marked by grotesque diction, sharp tone, and very dense colors; how can these be described by 'meandering,' 'verdure,' and 'clarity'?" See his *Tanyilu* 談藝錄 (Beijing: Zhonghua, 1984), 47. For a reading of this preface, see Michael B. Fish, "The Tu Mu and Li Shang-yin Prefaces to the Collected Works of Li Ho," in Ronald C. Miao, ed., *Studies in Chinese Poetics*, 231–86.

7. 求取情狀，離絕遠去筆墨畦徑間，亦殊不能知之。 Cited in Wang, *Sanjia pingzhu*, 12.

8. "辭尙奇詭，所得皆警邁，絕去翰墨畦逕，當時無能效者。"
*Xin Tang shu,* vol. 18, chap. 203, 5788. This biographical sketch also says that very few of Li He's works were passed on to posterity, thanks to their strangeness and Li He's untimely death. The *Taiping guangji* 太平廣記 (Beijing: Zhonghua, 1961), compiled by the Song writer Li Fang 李昉 and others during 977–98, records a story to the effect that one of Li He's cousins was assigned by an official to collect Li He's poetry; but he threw the poems he collected into the privy because he disliked Li He as a person (chap. 265). This may explain the later myth that Li He's poetry was neglected until the modern period. A. C. Graham claims that Li He was only recently rediscovered by contemporary criticism (see his *Poems of the Late T'ang,* 89); Naotaro Kudo, in his *The Life and Thought of Li Ho* (Tokyo: Waseda University Press, 1972), says that "there has never been much critical controversy about his works" (p. 8). One certainly gets a similar impression reading Frodsham's preface to his *The Poems of Li Ho,* later reprinted as *Goddesses, Ghosts and Demons: The Collected Poems of Li He* (San Francisco: North Point Press, 1983). As a matter of fact, Li He's poetry had been edited soon after his death. Du Mu's well known preface is a hard proof of this activity. The earliest extant edition of Li He's poetry was collected and annotated by the Southern Song Dynasty (1127–1279) scholar Wu Zhengzi 吳正子. Wang Qi's edition was completed in 1761; Ye Congqi's edition was first published in 1959. Compared with many other Tang poets for whom annotated editions of their works are not yet available, Li He has not been neglected. In terms of the availability of critical materials, I would also like to point out that critical debate of Li He's poetry has been very consistent from his own time to the present. This is demonstrated by *Li He yanjiu ziliao,* edited by Chen Zhiguo. For a general study of Li He's life and work, see Kuo-ch'ing Tu, *Li Ho* (Boston: Twayne, 1979), Zhou Chengzhen 周誠眞, *Li He lun* 李賀論 (Hong Kong: Wenyi, 1972), and Fu Jingshun 傅經順, *Li He zhuanlun* 李賀傳論 (Xi'an: Shanxi renmin, 1981).

9. See Yan Yu, *Canglang shihua,* 178–79. Guo Shaoyu, quoting *Hailu suishi* 海錄碎事, comments that this nickname of Li He was already used in Tang dynasty; see *Canglang shihua,* 179.

10. It is said that Confucius himself declined to talk about such things. See Yang Bojun, *Lunyu yizhu,* 77; James Legge, *Chinese Classics,* 1: 201.

11. *Li He nianpu* 李賀年譜 in Chen, *Yanjiu ziliao,* 64.

12. The critical editions of Li He's poetry used in this study are Wang Qi's *Sanjia pingzhu Li Changji geshi*, and Ye Congqi's *Li He shiji*. All of Li He's poetry has been translated into English by Frodsham in his *The Poems of Li Ho*, updated and republished as *Goddesses, Ghosts, and Demons: The Collected Poems of Li He*. In doing my translation I have consulted Frodsham's versions, but unless otherwise noted, all cited poems are translated by me. Wang, *Sanjian pingzhu*, 117; Ye, *Shiji*, 203; Frodsham, *Poems*, 154.

13. See my discussion in chap. 1.

14. For a detailed discussion of this issue, see chap. 4.

15. Lu Qinli, *Xian Qin Han-Wei-Jin Nanbeichao shi*, 3: 1953.

16. "The color of old rook's plumage" 老鴉色 is a metaphor for the woman's dark hair. I have kept this metaphor in my translation because it deliberately confuses our sensual perceptions: normally we simply do not say that our hands could "pile up" (tactile) a "color" (visual).

17. Wang, *Sanjian pingzhu*, 165; Ye, *Shiji*, 305; Frodsham, *Poems*, 240–41.

18. *Li He nianpu*, in Chen, *Yanjiu ziliao*, 64.

19. "The Life of Cowley," in Bertrand H. Bronson, ed., *Samuel Johnson: Rasselas, Poems and Selected Prose* (New York: Holt, Rinehart and Winston, 1958), 471.

20. Cited in Wang, *Sanjia pingzhu*, 15. The Song critic Zhou Yigong 周益公 made a similar remark:

Before it was thought that poetry could impoverish people, but actually it can not only impoverish, it can kill as well. To carve and grind one's five viscera [for words] is already unhealthy, let alone mocking the myriad phenomena [of nature]—how can one presume that this is what nature likes? This is why Li He of Tang . . . died of untimely death. (In Chen, *Yanjiu ziliao*, 17.)

21. It would be pointless to argue whether this anecdote is historical. In citing it I do not mean to suggest that all of Li He's poems were composed in such manner. Rather, the anecdote should be taken as a metaphor for Li He's poetic practice, with its implied disconnectedness and inconsistency.

22. See his "Batong da" 巴童答, in Wang, *Sanjia pingzhu*, 104; Ye, *Shiji*, 175; Frodsham, *Poems*, 130.

23. This is an allusion to a poem in *The Book of Songs*. See Legge,

*Chinese Classics*, 4: 303-7. The dreams of bears are thought to be "the auspicious intimations of sons" (維熊維羆，男子之祥).

24. Wang, *Sanjia pingzhu*, 90-94; Ye, *Shiji*, 138-50; Frodsham, *Poems*, 106-12.

25. This notion of poetry was pervasive during Mid and Late Tang. In addition to Li Shangyin's account of Li He's story, another well known anecdote of such poetic practice concerns the Mid Tang poet Jia Dao 賈島 (799-843). It is said that once when he was riding on a donkey, the following couplet suddenly came to him: 鳥宿池邊樹，僧敲月下門 (birds rest in the trees by the pond,/monk knocks at the doors under the moon). He was not sure whether he should choose *tui* 推 (to push) instead of *qiao* 敲 (to knock) for the second character in the second line. Completely absorbed in his thought, he began to imitate the acts of *tui* and *qiao* on his donkey, and accidentally bumped into the retinue of Han Yu, another famous Mid Tang poet. He was arrested and brought to Han Yu. Jiao Dao told Han Yu how he came to commit his offense, and instead of punishing him, Han Yu endorsed his choice for the word *qiao*. Now *tuiqiao* has become a proverbial phrase for meticulous and painstaking practice in writing or thinking. See Wu Jingxu 吳景旭, ed., *Lidai shihua* 歷代詩話 (Taipei: Shijie shuju, 1961), 2: 732-33.

For more detailed discussion on this subject, see Stephen Owen, *The End of the Chinese Middle Ages: Essays in Mid-Tang Literary Culture* (Stanford: Stanford University Press, 1996), 107-29.

26. The occasional poems in Li He's collection could be used as such examples. See "Huan zi Kuaiji ge" 還自會稽歌, "Mian'ai xing ershao song Xiaoji zhi Lushan" 勉愛行二首送小季之盧山, and many other pieces. See Wang, *Sanjia pingzhu*, 36-37, 85, and Ye, *Shiji*, 6, 125, respectively.

27. Cited in Wang, *Sanjia pingzhu*, 94.

28. See Ye, *Shiji*, 150. He calls this poem a "narrative of a romantic affair" ( 狎遊的紀事詩).

29. Wang, *Sanjia pingzhu*, 94.

30. For the texts of these three poems, see *Wen xuan*, 1: chap. 19, 265-69. Significantly, Xiao Tong categorizes these as works about *qing* 情 (feelings, particularly amorous feelings in this context). This entire section consists of the above-mentioned three pieces by Song Yu and "Luoshen fu" 洛神賦 by Cao Zhi. For a discussion of Song Yu's above mentioned *fu* poems, especially of their place and significance in the

development of Chinese amorous literature, see Wai-yee Li, *Enchantment and Disenchantment: Love and Illusion in Chinese Literature* (Princeton: Princeton University Press, 1993), 23–41.

31. Both Ye (*Shiji*, 140) and Frodsham (*Poems*, 106) interpret this allusion along this line. Wang Qi takes this line as an allusion to "Jiu bian" 九辯, another poem attributed to Song Yu (*Sanjia pingzhu*, 90).

32. For a text of this poem, see *Yutai xinyong*, 15.

33. See Ye, *Shiji*, 146. Frodsham's endorsement of this view is also reflected by his translation of the title of the poem. Instead of "Self-mocking" which is the literal meaning of *naogong* 惱公 (see Ye, *Shiji*, 140 n. 1), he translates it into "She Steals My Heart," which is clearly a decision based on his interpretation of the content of the poem. Like other Chinese critics (Wu Yanmu and Ye Congqi), Frodsham believes this poem to be Li He's account of his own personal experience. "She Steals My Heart" presupposes a story that involves two characters and an act that connects them. See Frodsham, *Poems*, 106. Wang Qi's interpretation is more flexible; he regards Song Yu as a substitute figure for the man involved. See Wang, *Sanjia pingzhu*, 90.

34. This is also Frodsham's reading; see Frodsham, *Poems*, 106–7.

35. This is also Ye Congqi's reading; see Ye, *Shiji*, 141 n. 21. Frodsham explains that lines 25 and 26 refer to two activities: "The red nets were to catch birds, the green to catch fish." See Frodsham, *Poems*, 107n.8.

36. Qian Zhongshu criticizes Li He's passion for florid poetic diction and his neglect of commonplace vocabulary; he quotes the following words of the Song critic Zhang Jie 張戒 (fl. 1124–38): "[The poetry of Li He] writes only about flowers, grass, bees and butterflies; he did not know that everything in the world can be poetry." See Qian, *Tanyilu*, 57. Such criticism apparently comes from an urge to encompass all of Li He's poetry into a few clichés of Li He studies. The present example is an excellent illustration of the inaccuracy of this accusation.

37. Ye, *Shiji*, 147. This is also Frodsham's reading; see Frodsham, *Poems*, 107n.7. Wang Qi reads line 29 as a description of her putting on makeup, but he does not seem to be bothered by the inconsistency in this couplet.

38. Dore Levy has observed that in Chinese narrative poetry temporal sequence is "not conceived to be the primary focus of poetic composition and execution," because such sequence tends to be manipulated by the expressive intent of the poet. See her *Chinese Narrative Poetry:*

*The Late Han through T'ang Dynasties*, 106. The "expressive intent" of Li He's "Self-Mocking," it seems to me, is the desire to put on a masterful display of poetic skill, not to provide an account of a specific historical event. This is proved by the fact that most of the poem consists of descriptive units.

39. Qian Zhongshu has also noticed this: "Changji [Li He] [in writing his poetry] moves in and out of the obscure and the unexpected areas. He takes pains to cultivate diction and its color. As for the meaning of the poem, it is only of secondary importance." (長吉穿幽入仄，慘淡經營，都在修辭設色，舉凡謀篇命意，均落第二意). See Qian, *Tanyilu*, 46.

40. Recorded in *Shanhai jing* 山海經, cited in Ye, *Shiji*, 142.

41. For such information, see *Ci yuan*, 506. Kongdong Mountain also appears in another two poems by Li He: "*Renheli zaxu Huangfu Shi*" 仁和里雜敘皇甫湜, and "*Chucheng bie Zhang Youxin chou Li Han*" 出城別張又新酬李漢 (Ye, *Shiji*, 119–20, 315–16; Frodsham, *Poems*, 90–92, 250–52). According to Ye's interpretation, in the first poem "Kongdong" refers to a mountain in Henan, but in the second poem the phrase is used adjectivally, describing the majestic height of Zhongnan Mountain near Chang'an.

42. See Frodsham, *Poems*, 107, and n. 12. This story is from chap. 5 of *Liezi* 列子, but in that context the two mountains mentioned are Taixing 太形, also refered to as Taihang 太行 and Wangwu 王屋. Frodsham did not explain why he related the one in Li He's poem to this story.

43. Ye, *Shji*, 147.

44. Frodsham, *Poems*, 107.

45. Ye, *Shiji*, 148.

46. For a discussion of narrative and lyrical experience, see Levy, *Chinese Narrative Poetry*, 3–4.

47. 洛陽城東路，桃李生路旁。 See *Yutai xinyong*, 15.

48. To further illustrate this change, we might cite Cao Zhi's "On a Beautiful Woman" where the heroine is located "At the southern end of the town./Our green house faces the big road,/The high gate is locked with several bolts." See my discussion in chap. 2.

It is noteworthy that the isolation that the heroine in Cao Zhi's poem (or according to the the allegorical reading, the poet himself) feels is not an isolation from society at large, but from a group of villains who have betrayed the interests of society. The fact that she is seen as living by the big road is the indication that she is eager to serve society, if the opportunity presents itself. Therefore, Cao Zhi's beautiful woman symbolizes frustrated political ambition, whereas in the poetry of Xiao Gang and Li He, a beautiful woman embodies detatchment from such political ambition.

49. Wang Qi takes this couplet as describing the beautiful flowers from different geographical locations. This is a more plausible interpretation, although it still leaves unanswered the question why they are inserted into the middle of two couplets (lines 49–50, and 53–54) that portray various activities in the woman's bedroom. Another possibility is to treat them as flowers planted in the woman's boudoir, although it makes the couplet no less strange because of the abrupt shift of descriptive point of view.

50. I incline to regard this couplet (and others as well) as an excellent illustration that in some of Li He's poems form, instead of content, is the determining factor. The various items in this couplet are brought together by the formal requirement of the metrical pattern of the poem *pailü* or extended regulated verse, which strictly prescribes parallelism within the couplet. As the rule requires that parallel items be taken from the same category, "the lanes of Chu" 楚巷 inevitably demands another place term that might not necessarily have any geographical relationship with it. Frodsham writes that "the lanes of the Chu were the streets in the Golden Wall quarter in the northwest of Luoyang, where the singing girls lived" (*Poems*, 108), thus making them refer to one geographical location. In either case the interpretations reflect a desire to find a historical base for the poem, which to me is an inappropriate way to approach a work like this one.

51. See "Wei Guan zhuan" 魏瓘傳 in *Jin shu*, vol. 4, chap. 36, 1055–66.

52. "[The woman?] takes out brush and paper to entertain the guest;" Ye, *Shiji*, 148. Wang Qi does not make this clear either.

53. "The girl is writing a letter in a hand as vigorous as that in which Wei Guan transcribed the Yellow Courtyard classic." Frodsham, *Poems*, 109 n. 19.

54. Recorded in Gan Bao 干寶 (?–336), *Soushen ji* 搜神記, cited in Ye, *Shiji*, 143 n. 43.

55. Frodsham, *Poems*, 109n.19.

56. For studies on regulated verse, see Wang Li, *Hanyu shilüxue*, 142–62; and Yu-kung Kao, "The Aesthetics of Regulated Verse," in

Lin Shuen-fu and Stephen Owen, eds., *The Vitality of the Lyric Voice*, 320–87.

57. In fact, this technique dates back to Qu Yuan's "Li Sao," in which the poet repeatedly uses the dawn/dusk antithesis to suggest the constancy of his moral cultivation (for instance, 朝搴阰之木蘭兮，夕攬洲之宿莽 "In the morning I gathered the angelica on the mountains,/In the evening I plucked the sedges of the isles"). But Qu Yuan is certainly not talking about narrative sequence here; rather, he is using this time antithesis freely to illustrate a concept and a practice. Therefore, when such technique was later adopted in a supposedly narrative context, it tended to undermine it for precisely this reason.

58. In Song Yu's "*Gaotang fu*" a goddess at Wu Gorge told the king of Chu after their sexual encounter in his dream that "in the morning I will be the cloud, in the evening I will be the rain." Later "cloud and rain" (*yunyu* 雲雨) become permanently related to lovemaking. This is even more noticeable here because besides the word *yu* (rain), the poet also mentions the specific location where the king of Chu and the goddess met. Ye Congqi avoided explaining this obvious euphemism for sexual intercourse. Ye identifies the allusion to Song Yu's *fu*, but prefers to take it as a description of the curtains and covers in the woman's bedroom. See Ye, *Shiji*, 148.

59. For the text of this book see Liu Yiqing 劉義慶 (403–44), *Shishuo xinyu [jiaojian]* 世說新語〔校箋〕, ed. Xu Zhen'e 徐震堮 (Beijing: Zhonghua, 1984).

60. Ibid., chap. 27, 458.

61. Ibid., chap 35, 491–92.

62. Frodsham, *Poems*, 110, n. 29.

63. Ye, *Shiji*, 149.

64. Wang Qi's reading of these two lines is more open. He acknowledges the difficulty and leaves us with two other interpretations, although he does not agree with either of them: "some consider the water [in the first line] to be tears; some regard horse's mane to be human hair." Wang, *Sanjia pingzhu*, 93.

65. David Lattimore suggests that the abundant use of allusions in Chinese poetry, especially of the Tang era, is motivated by a desire to participate in a long, established, and continuing tradition. It is an effort on the part of the poet to achieve a literary immortality because unlike "Roman and Renaissance poets [who] envisaged chiefly the

Notes

immortality of their own literary 'monuments,' whereas the Chinese envisaged chiefly a corporate immortality, devolving upon the individual poet from his participation. . . in a continuing tradition." See his "Allusions and T'ang Poetry," in Arthur F. Wright and Denis Twitchett, eds., *Perspectives on the T'ang* (New Haven: Yale University Press, 1973), 405–39.

66. For a text of this poem, see *Yuefu shiji*, chap. 28, 338–39.

67. See Sima Qian, *Shi ji*, vol. 9, chap. 117, 3000.

68. For such examples, see his "Yonghuai ershou" 詠懷二首, no. 1, and "Nanyuan shisan shou" 南園十三首, no. 7; in Wang, *Sanjia pingzhu*, 42, 62 and Ye, *Shiji*, 17, 67.

69. Ye, *Shiji*, 149.

70. Frodsham, *Poems*, 110 n. 31.

71. This is Wang Qi's reading; see *Sanjia pingzhu*, 93. Ye Congqi takes 王子 as a reference to the legendary Prince Jin 王子晉; see *Shiji*, 145.

72. Another Qing scholar, Dong Maoce 董懋策 regards this poem to be an account of a dream, which might better explain the inconsistencies. Cited in Ye, *Shiji*, 149.

73. See Ye, *Shiji*, 149. Ye Conqi also regards these two lines as Li He's answer to the girl.

74. Recorded in *Hanwu gushi* 漢武故事. See *Ci yuan*, 1824. This is my reading. Wang Qi and Ye Congqi prefer to take this line as alluding to another story in *Soushen ji*, that tells that a man named Wu Meng 吳猛 wrote a message on an amulet and put it on the roof; the amulet was then taken away by a blue bird. See Wang, *Sanjia pingzhu*, 94; Ye, *Shiji*, 146.

75. This is Ye Congqi's reading; see *Shiji*, 149. Wang Qi takes this couplet to be a followup to the previous two lines: that because he is not in a good health, he needs to take some protective measures. Blue bird's amulet and the silk-sewn bag can perform such functions. *Sanjia pingzhu*, 94.

76. This is also Ye Congqi's reading. Frodsham translated *zhongfu* 中婦 as "middle-aged maid;" see *Poems*, 112.

77. Wang, *Sanjia pingzhu*, 94; Ye, *Shiji*, 149.

78. Luo Zongqiang says that High Tang poetry strives at a limpid beauty, a lingering effect beyond the linguistic medium. See his *Sui-Tang Wudai wenxue sixiangshi*, 87–110.

79. The Southern Song critic Wu Zhengzi thought this was what

happened to "Changgu shi" 昌谷詩, another difficult poem by Li He. See Wang, *Sanjia pingzhu*, 133.

80. Wang, *Sanjia pingzhu*, 46–47; Ye, *Shiji*, 28–29; Frodsham, *Poems*, 31.

81. Li He's love of synesthetic images has been pointed out by some critics; see, for example, Tu, *Li Ho*, 108–9. However, few have pointed out the disorienting effect of this device. In this sense the use of synesthetic images is part of Li He's eccentric, unconventional poetic practice. Although such images are common throughout Chinese poetic history, especially during the Tang period, in those cases it seldom arouses feelings of strangeness because the transition from one sense to another is not forced. For instance, Du Fu's couplet 香霧雲鬢濕，清輝玉臂寒 (her cloud hair is damp in the fragrant mist; her jade arms are cold in the limpid light) combines olfactory, tactile, and visual senses. But it sounds "natural" in that we expect the woman's hair to be wet if she stands in the mist during night; the same is true for her arms, which are inevitably cold on a moonlit night. Li He's forcing the color of sky to be wept out by the hare presents a very different case.

82. Sikong Tu 司空圖 *Shi pin* 詩品 (Beijing: Renmin wenxue, 1981), 21; English translation by Yang Xianyi and Gladys Yang, *Poetry and Prose of the Tang and Song* (Beijing: Chinese Literature, 1984), 198. For the philosophical origin of this aesthetic standard, see my discussion in chap. 1. This aesthetic standard was later canonized by Yan Yu; see his *Canglang shihua*, 26.

83. "李長吉詩，字字欲傳世，顧過于劌鉥，無天眞自然之趣。" Cited in Chen, *Yanjiu ziliao*, 29.

84. "篇章以含畜天成爲上，破碎雕鎪爲下⋯以平夷恬淡爲上，怪險蹶趨爲下。如長吉錦囊句，非不奇也，而牛鬼蛇神太甚，所謂施之廊廟則駴也。" Zhang Biaochen 張表臣, *Shanhugou shihua* 珊瑚鈎詩話, in ibid., 21.

85. Lady Ban once declined to ride together with Emperor Cheng because she thought it was improper; she was later praised by the emperor for this virtuous act. See "Ban Jieyu zhuan" 班婕妤傳 in *Han shu*, vol. 12, chap. 67, 3983–84.

86. Wang, *Sanjia pingzhu*, 176; Ye, *Shiji*, 330; Frodsham, *Poems*, 260. Yao Wenxie interprets this poem as a political satire; see Wang, *Sanjia pingzhu*, 282–83.

87. For a text of this poem, see *Yutai xinyong*, 14; English translation in Birrel, *New Songs*, 43.

88. Donne's "The Relique," for example, writes about betrayed love, but sets his poem in a graveyard. The next line is strikingly similar to line 7 in Li He's present poem: "A bracelet of bright hair about the bone." See Edwin Honig and Oscar Williams, eds., *The Major Metaphysical Poets of the Seventeenth Century* (New York: Washington Square Press, 1969), 80. As the editors note, Donne's poetry was reviled by Dryden and Johnson, two major representatives of neoclassical tradition, for offending literary decorum.

89. For a comparative study of Li He and Baudelaire, see Frances Ann LaFleur, "The Evolution of a Symbolist Aesthetic in Classical Chinese Verse: The Role of Li Ho Compared with That of Charles Baudelaire in Nineteenth-Century French Poetry" (Ph.D. diss., Princeton University, 1993).

90. Wang, *Sanjia pingzhu*, 96; Ye, *Shiji*, 154; Frodsham, *Poems*, 116.

91. Wang and Ye refer to the following line of Xie Lingyun in their annotations: 白楊信裊裊 (The while poplars are tossing gently indeed).

92. Wang, *Sanjia pingzhu*, 46; Ye, *Shiji*, 27; Frodsham, *Poems*, 30.

93. See *Yuefu shiji*, chap. 85, 974.

94. This descriptive system is also called "hypogram" by Riffaterre. For a discussion of how a hypogram functions in poetry, see Riffaterre, *Semiotics of Poetry*, passim.

95. *Youlan* 幽蘭 (lonely or subtle orchids) was first used in Qu Yuan's "Li Sao:" 時曖曖其將罷兮，結幽蘭而延佇 (The day was getting dark and drawing to its close,/Knotting the subtle orchids, I waited in indecision); 戶服艾以盈要兮，謂幽蘭其不可佩 (For they wear mugwort and cram their waistbands with it,/But the subtle orchids they deem unfit to wear). Chinese text in *Chuci buzhu*, chap. 1, 23, 28; English translation in Hawkes, *The Songs of the South*, 73, 74. Through the association with Qu Yuan this expression has become a standard trope for virtue and virtuous gentleman. As for the other terms one can easily locate them in the works of Xiao Gang and other Palace Style poets.

96. For example, in "Shangxin xing" 傷心行 he says, "Mournfully chanting, I study the songs of Chu" 咽咽學楚吟. See Wang, *Sanjia pingzhu*, 77; Ye, *Shiji*, 105; Frodsham, *Poems*, 80.

97. Tu, *Li Ho*, 107.

98. See Kudo, *The Life and Thoughts of Li He*, esp. chap. 7; David

Chen, "Li Ho and Keats: A Comparative Study of Two Poets" (Ph.D. diss., Indiana University, 1962).

99. See John Keats, *Selected Poems and Letters*, ed. Douglas Bush (Boston: Houghton Mifflin Company, 1959), 205–8.

100. See Liu Dajie, *Zhongguo wenxue fazhanshi*, 1: 215–20, Ye Jian-ying, "Tan gushi shijiushou zhi shidai wenti" 談古詩十九首之時代問題, in *Jialing lunshi conggao*, 8–17, and Jean-Pierre Dieny, *Les dix-neuf poémes anciens* (Paris: Centre de Publication Asie Orientale, 1974). Chinese texts in Lu, *Shi*, 329–34.

101. For example, no. 15:

| | |
|---|---|
| 生年不滿百 | One's life cannot last a hundred years, |
| 常懷千歲憂 | Yet one always has a thousand years of sorrow. |
| 畫短苦夜長 | The days are short, but the nights are long, |
| 何不秉燭游 | Why not then hold a candle to roam? |

102. Wang, *Sanjia pingzhu*, 55; Ye, *Shiji*, 50–51; Frodsham, *Poems*, 48–49.

103. The following two lines from the "The Nine Persuasions" attributed to Song Yu are genereally considered the origination of this genre: "How sad is the autumn air; desolately the tree leaves fall and wither" 悲哉秋之爲氣也，蕭瑟兮草木搖落而變衰; see *Chuci buzhu*, chap. 8, 2. During the Han and Wei periods it became one of the most popular subjects of poetry, but its apex was reached during the Tang era. Practically every major poet wrote at least one poem in this genre. The most famous example of this is probably Du Fu's "Autumn Meditations: Eight Poems" 秋興八首, in which Du Fu characteristically combines the lament over his personal decline with the lament for nature's seasonal fading and the social disturbance that the country was facing at that time. For numerous other poems treating this topic, readers might consult Li Fang 李昉 (925–96) et al., eds., *Wenyuan yinghua* 文苑英華 (Taipei: Xinwenfeng, 1979), vol. 2.

104. Even Meng Jiao 孟郊 (751–814), who is known for his dark mood and description, is able to avoid sinking into sheer despair in his long series "Autumn Feelings" 秋懷. In Meng's poems the misery and pain he feels in autumn are explained as having been caused by the slander of vicious people. The poet consoles himself that although he is in physical decline, he has never given up the pursuit of virtue represented by the ancient sages. For Meng, integrity and virtue are redeeming powers that make his personal decline and change in nature

bearable. But it is precisely these powers that we find lacking in Li He's poem. For the text of this series see *Quan Tang shi*, vol. 11, chap. 375, 4206–8. Stephen Owen's *The Poetry of Meng Chiao and Han Yu* (New Haven: Yale University Press, 1975) contains a complete translation and detailed discussion of this series of poems; see 161–85.

105. See, for example, Li Bai's "Shenye duzuo huai gushan" 深夜獨坐懷故山. In *Quan Tang shi*, vol. 6, chap. 182, 1855.

106. See Du Fu, "Denggao" 登高, in *Quan Tang shi*, vol. 7, chap. 227, 2467. Du Fu did not state this belief explicitly, but the couplet "Unlimited number of trees are losing their leaves,/The infinite Yangtze flows on in its tremendous power" 無邊落木蕭蕭下，不盡長江滾滾來 certainly has the effect of sublimating the personal decline described in the next four lines.

107. See Wang Wei, "Qiuye duzuo" 秋夜獨坐, in *Wang Youcheng ji jianzhu* 王右丞集箋注, ed. Zhao Diancheng 趙殿成 (Shanghai: Shanghai guji, 1961), 158.

108. This is actually a cliché, but its structural position in the poem gives it a fresh meaning because when read together with its antithetical term in the next line, it has a special effect, particularly in terms of color, as "green" 青 and "flowery" 花 combine to produce a very strong visual impression.

109. Yang, *Lunyu yizhu*, 32; Legge, *Chinese Classics*, 1: 161.

110. See *Liji zhengyi* 禮記正義, in *Shisanjing zhushu*, 2: 1609.

111. A. C. Graham noted briefly this characteristic of Li He: "He seems quite uninterested in any of the common recipes for reconciliation with death, Confucian, Taoist, or Buddhist, with the result that he is equally far from the serenity of the greatest Chinese poets and the facile melancholy of the more commonplace." See *Poems of the Late T'ang*, 90.

112. Wang, *Sanjia pingzhu*, 149–50; Ye, *Shiji*, 271–73; Frodsham, *Poems*, 210–11.

113. For the Chinese text of this poem, see *Chuci buzhu*, chap. 9. English translation in Hawkes, *Songs of the South*, 219–30.

114. *Chuci buzhu*, chap. 9, 1.

115. This phrase alludes to a line in Qu Yuan's "Li sao" where Qu Yuan describes his love of wearing the orchid girdle: "[I] wear the autumn orchid as girdle" 紉秋蘭以爲佩. Wang Yi read this as a symbolic act of moral cultivation. See *Chuci buzhu*, chap. 1, 5.

116. The story of Bao Jiao is recorded in Ying Shao 應劭 (l. 168–

89), *Fengsu tongyi* 風俗通義, cited in Ye, *Shiji*, 272; as for the story on Yan Hui, see Sima Quian, *Shi ji*, vol. 7, chap. 67, 2188.

117. This is because in the Chinese poetic tradition a poem is regarded as a historical person's response to a historical experience (see my discussion of the Great Preface to *The Book of Songs* in chap. 1). It is different from the Western poetic theory, which presumes fictionality and thus a disjunction between the empirical subject (the poet) and the lyrical subject (the "I" in the poem). The use of poetic persona is therefore not as widely practiced in the Chinese poetic tradition as it is in the West, but it has been used, especially in *yuefu* poems to which the present piece belongs. Thus it is possible to read *wo* 我 (I) in this poem as referring to a persona, although as I have noted the connection between the *peilanke* (orchid-wearing man) and *wo* (I) strongly suggests that *wo* refers to a poet like Qu Yuan, and this will be Li He himself. For more discussion of this issue, see chap. 5. Some critics have discussed the tendency in Chinese exegetical tradition to allegorize all texts, in particular, by historicizing poetic events. See Stephen Owen, *Traditional Chinese Poetry and Poetics: Omen of the World* (Madison: University of Wisconsin Press, 1985), passim; Yu, *The Reading of Imagery*, passim. For the Western notions of disjunction and fictionality in lyric poetry, see Northrop Frye, "Approaching the Lyric," in *Lyric Poetry Beyond New Criticism*, 31–37, and Jonathan Culler, *Structuralist Poetics*, chap. 8.

118. Line 12, with its unusual words, reminds one of some of Han Yu's poetry, such as "*Ye Hengyuemiao suisu Yuesi ti menlou*" 謁衡岳廟遂宿岳寺題門樓. Han Yu had personal relations with Li He and was once his patron. His poetic practice and his theory that in poetry one must "get rid of clichés" (惟陳言之務去) might have influenced Li He's work, at least works like the present piece. For a study of Han Yu's poetry, see Owen, *The Poetry of Meng Chiao and Han Yu*, and Charles Hartman, *Han Yu and the T'ang Search for Unity* (Princeton: Princeton University Press, 1986).

119. "Questions to Heaven" is a poem attributed to Qu Yuan. Wang Yi says:

> "Questions to Heaven" was written by Qu Yuan. . . .When Qu Yuan was in exile, he was full of sorrows and anxieties. He wandered among mountains and rivers; looking up at heaven he gave out long sighs. In the Chu state there were temples for ancestors

and ministers. On the walls of these buildings there were paintings of heaven and earth, mountains and rivers, gods and goddesses, and ancient saints and grotesque creatures. They were all in grand and colorful style. [Qu Yuan] would rest under them when he was tired. When he saw these paintings, he would write on them and shout his questions in order to release his anger and sadness. (See *Chuci buzhu*, chap. 3, 1–2.)

Frodsham's interpretation of these two lines that "If you doubt the truth of my words, think of Qu Yuan, who found inspiration in despair" (*Poems*, 210) is not only forced but seems not to fit the context of the poem. The reference to Qu Yuan, like the references to Yan Hui and Bao Jiao, serves to illustrate the abnormal, and hence incomprehensible nature of the world, not as the source of poetic inspiration.

120. Li Shangyin's "Biographical Sketch of Li He" records that when Li He was dying, he dreamed of an immortal who told him that the god in heaven had constructed a "white jade-tower" for him and was waiting for him to come. I do not intend to draw a far-fetched comparison between Li He's "white jade-tower" and the "ivory tower" of Oscar Wilde or Mallarmé, but the coincidence in their use of such a refined, artificial metaphor clearly reveals a coincidence in their aesthetic tastes and attitudes toward their art. Monroe Beardsley comments on the rich implications of this metaphor in the following passage:

The implications of the metaphor are extremely rich, and have not been exhausted to our own day. Most of the standards in the theme of alienation are comprised in it, including the artist's need for protection, for solitude, for special care; his self-imposed or at least resignedly accepted uniqueness, carrying his curse as a pride; the transcendent importance of his calling; and something of Mallarmé's view that the artist practices a mystery, which cannot be revealed to the masses who are not initiated into the rites. (See his *Aesthetics from Classical Greek to the Present* [Tuscaloosa: University of Alabama Press, 1966], 285.)

121. Wang, *Sanjia pingzhu*, 150.

122. Ibid., 269.

123. Yao Wenxie's remark, cited in Wang, *Sanjia pingzhu*, 192. Also see the introduction to *Li He shige shangxiji* 李賀詩歌賞析集, ed. Fu Jingshun 傅經順 (Chengdu: Bashu shushe, 1988), 1–6.

124. For example, Yao interprets "Six Satirical Poems: No. 5," that is apparently a Palace Style piece, as a "satire to the Wang Shuwen 王叔文 clan." See Wang, *Sanjia pingzhu*, 283. In a more general remark he says that "Li He's poetry, in its use of diction, its choice of meaning and title, all satirizes the evils of society and exposes the dark side of the world." Ibid.

125. Yan, *Canglang shihua*, 1.

126. Ibid., 180.

127. See You Guoen 游國恩 et al., *Zhongguo wenxueshi* 中國文學史 (Beijing: Renmin wenxue, 1963), 173; Luo, *Sui-Tang Wudai wenxue sixiangshi*, 359–60.

## CHAPTER 4

1. Following *Wen Feiqing shiji jianzhu*; *Quan Tang shi* has 湖亭 instead of 澧湖.

2. "Apricot Garden" 杏花園 in Chang'an is the place where the successful candidates of civil service examination first met to celebrate. For the text of this poem, see *Wen Feiqing shiji jianzhu* 溫飛卿詩集箋注, eds. Zeng Yi 曾益, Gu Yuxian 顧予咸, and Gu Sili 顧嗣立 (Taipei: Zhonghua, *Sibu beiyao* edition, 1965), hereafter cited as *Shiji jianzhu*; chap. 9, 1; *Quan Tang shi*, vol. 17, chap. 583, 6753; and *Wen Tingyun shicixuan* 溫庭筠詩詞選, ed. Liu Sihan 劉斯翰 (Hong Kong: Sanlian, 1986), hereafter cited as *Shicixuan*; 135. Except Liu Sihan's book, which contains only a small portion of Wen Tingyun's *shi* and *ci*, there is no modern annotated edition of his poetry. The book by the above-mentioned Ming and Qing scholars Zeng Yi, Gu Yuxian, and Gu Sili remains the only complete annotated edition of Wen Tingyun's poetry. Paul Rouzer's *Writing Another's Dream: The Poetry of Wen Tingyun* (Stanford: Stanford University Press, 1993) contains sixty-two translations of Wen Tingyun's poetry. I have consulted his versions of the poems I cite, but unless otherwise noted, all translations in this chapter are mine.

3. See *Yuefu shiji*, chap. 49, 587.

4. It is worth noting that this echoes loudly Xiao Gang's separation of one's personal cultivation and one's literary production, especially since Wen Tingyun is explicitly referring to the Palace Style poetry of the Southern Dynasties. See my discussion in chap. 1.

5. All his life Wen Tingyun held only minor posts, despite his reputedly brilliant poetic talents, which at that time could be a key to a

successful official career. Ji Yougong's 計有功 *Tangshi jishi* 唐詩紀事 (Taipei: Shangwu, *Guoxue jiben congshu* edition, 1968) records that his notoriety was such that for a period he had to hide his real name to avoid being insulted (p. 671).

6. See the official biography of Wen Tingyun in *Xin Tang shu*, vol. 12, chap. 19, 3787, and Xing Wenfang, *Tangcaizi zhuan*, 238. Significantly, unlike *Jiu Tang shu*, that was composed during the Five Dynasties period (907–60), the biographical sketch of Wen Tingyun is not included in the section of "Yiwenzhi" 藝文志 in *Xin Tang shu* written during the Song dynasty, the section that records the lives of renowned literati. Instead it is listed together with other members of the Wen family under the biography of an ancestor called Wen Daya 溫大雅. This different arrangement in *Xin Tang shu* may suggest that by early Song dynasty Wen Tingyun's fame as a poet had already declined. This is further shown in another important Song document written later than *Xin Tang shu*, Yan Yu's *Canglang shihua*. In the chapter on poetic styles (*shiti* 詩體) he named various styles after poets whom he considered important in the development of poetry up to his time. Among these he included Li He, Li Shangyin, and other Late Tang poets, but ignored Wen Tingyun (p. 59). The popularity of Wen Tingyun's poetry in his lifetime is seen in the large number of his works collected in the Late Tang anthology *Caidiao ji* 才調集, ed. Wei Hu 韋 縠 (fl. 940 A.D.), in *Tangren xuan Tangshi* 唐人選唐詩 (Shanghai: Zhonghua, 1958). Of the thousand poems selected there are sixty-one by Wen Tingyun, compared with two by Wang Wei, twenty-eight by Li Bai, and forty by Li Shangyin.

7. See the official biography of Wen Tingyun in *Jiu Tang shu*, vol. 14, chap. 19, 5078; *Tangcaizi zhuan*, 238–39, and *Tangshi jishi*, 671–72.

8. Liu, *Shicixuan*, 3.

9. *Ci* or song lyric is a subgenre of Chinese poetry with very different generic rules and functions from *shi*, which has been the subject of my discussion. I have decided to exclude Wen Tingyun's *ci* from the present study because the framework I have established so far will be largely irrelevant if his *ci* poems were included. For instance, "femininity" and "sensuality" are the most salient decadent qualities in *shi*, but in *ci* they are considered "as intrinsic properties of the genre." See Shuen-fu Lin, "The Formation of a Distinct Generic Identity for Tz'u," in Pauline Yu, ed., *Voices of the Song Lyric in China* (Berkeley: University of California Press, 1994), 19. In other words, what is considered as a

deviation in *shi* is considered as a norm in *ci*. For a brief study of Wen Tingyun's *ci* poetry, see Ye Jiaying 葉嘉瑩, "Wen Tingyun ci gaishuo" 溫庭筠詞概說, in *Jialing lunci conggao* 迦陵論詞叢稿 (Shanghai: Shanghai guji, 1980), 1–38; for general studies in this genre, interested readers may consult Yang Haiming 楊海明, *Tang-Song cishi* 唐宋詞史 (Jiangsu: Jiangsu guji, 1987), Kang-i Sun Chang, *The Evolution of Chinese T'zu Poetry: From the Late T'ang to the Northern Sung* (Princeton: Princeton University Press, 1980), and Pauline Yu's book cited above. Wen Tingyun's extant sixty-six *ci* poems are collected in *Huajianji* 花間集, a collection of amorous and often erotic song lyrics edited by Ouyang Jiong 歐陽炯 (896–971). For a text of this anthology, see *Huajianji zhushi* 花間集注釋, ed. and ann. Li Yi 李誼 (Chengdu: Sichuan wenyi, 1986).

10. Following *Quan Tang shi*; *Shiji jianzhu* has 芳意.

11. Zeng et al., *Shiji jianzhu* , chap. 1, 9; *Quan Tang shi*, vol. 17, chap. 575, 6697.

12. Zeng et al., chap. 1, 4–5; *Quan Tang shi*, vol. 17, chap. 575, 6695; Liu, *Shicixuan* , 10–11.

13. See Liu An 劉安 (179–122 B.C.) et al., *Huainanzi* 淮南子, reprinted as *Huainan honglie jishi* 淮南鴻烈集釋 (Taipei: Shangwu, *Guoxue jiben congshu* edition, 1968), vol. 2, chap. 19, 17.

14. For the texts of these two poems, see *Quan Tang shi*, vol. 13, chap. 435, 4821–22, and vol. 10, chap. 340, 3813, respectively. For a discussion of such a theme in Bai Juyi's poem, see Dore J. Levy, *Chinese Narrative Poetry*, 70–75.

15. See Wang Qi, *Sanjia pingzhu Li Changji geshi*, 35–36; Ye Congqi, *Li He shiji*, 3.

16. Paul Rouzer claims that the sensual descriptions in Wen Tingyun's poem "are atmospheric phenomena that may be expected to arise sympathetically from the playing of a 'watery' instrument" (*Writing Another's Dream*, 57). But he does not provide any supporting information as to how such descriptions derive from listening to the performance of this specific instrument—namely, "earthen jars" (*ou* 甌). I tend to think that there is no "natural" connection between Wen Tingyun's erotic fantasy and the music of this instrument. That he produced such a poem at all can only be explained in the context of his poetic practice in general.

17. See "Xiang jun" 湘君 ("The Goddess of the Xiang") and "Xiang

furen" 湘夫人 ("The Lady of the Xiang") in *Chuci buzhu*, chap. 2, 9–14; David Hawkes, *The Songs of the South*, 104–9.

18. Paul Rouzer also points out the eroticism of these two lines; see *Writing Another's Dream*, 56.

19. Zeng et al., *Shiji jianzhu*, chap. 3, 6; *Quan Tang shi*, vol. 17, chap. 577, 6711.

20. See Xiao Gang, "Yongwushi ershou" 詠舞詩二首, and "Ye ting-jishi" 夜聽妓詩, in Lu Qingli, *Xian Qin Han-Wei-Jin Nanbeichao shi*, 3:1942, 1954.

21. Zeng et al., *Shiji jianzhu*, chap. 3, 6.

22. For example, see Wang Changling 王昌齡, "Congjunxing qishou" 從軍行七首, and Wang Han 王翰, "Liangzhouci" 涼州詞, in *Quan Tang shi*, vol. 4, chap. 143, 1443–44, and vol. 5, chap. 156, 1605.

23. Lu, *Shi*, 3: 1954; *Yutai xinyong*, 177.

24. Zeng et al., *Shiji jianzhu*, chap. 4, 12–13; *Quan Tang shi*, vol. 17, chap. 578, 6723; Liu, *Shicixuan*, 78–79.

25. Following *Shiji jianzhu*; *Quan Tang shi* has 和道溪君別業.

26. *Quang Tang shi* has 風.

27. *Quan Tang shi* has 雙飛.

28. Zeng et al., *Shiji jianzhu*, chap. 4, 10; *Quan Tang shi*, vol. 17, chap. 577, 6721.

29. An example that most readily comes to mind is Wang Wei's "Bie Wangchuan bieye" 別輞川別業; see *Wang Youcheng ji jianzhu*, 251.

30. See *Han shu*, vol. 12, chap. 67, 3951.

31. For a text of this poem, see *Quan Tang shi*, vol. 13, chap. 435, 4816–20. For a discussion on this issue, see Levy, *Chinese Narrative Poetry*, 70–75.

32. Paul Rouzer has discussed this in some detail; see his *Writing Another's Dream*, passim.

33. Zeng et al., *Shiji jianzhu*, chap. 9, 15–16; *Quan Tang shi*, vol. 17, chap. 583, 6761–62; Liu, *Shicixuan*, 149.

34. See *Han shu*, vol. 12, chap. 67, 395.

35. Following *Quan Tang shi*; *Shiji jianzhu* has 欺.

36. Zeng et al., *Shiji jianzhu*, chap. 6, 14–16; *Quan Tang shi*, vol. 17, chap. 580, 6736.

37. See Wang Pu 王浦, *Tanghuiyao* 唐會要 (Taipei: Shangwu, 1968, *Guoxue jiben congshu* edition), chap. 33.

38. "Yinyuezhi" 音樂志 in *Xin Tang shu*, vol. 2, chap. 12, 476.

39. Bai Juyi has also described this in his "Song of Everlasting Sorrow":

春寒賜浴華清池　In cold spring she was given the privilege of bathing in Huaqing pool,

溫泉水滑洗凝脂　So she could wash her creamy skin with the smooth hot spring water.

侍兒扶起嬌無力　Serving girls held her up, she was indolently strengthless—

始是新承恩澤時　That was when she first enjoyed the imperial favor.

40. This is how Paul Rouzer interprets these two lines; see *Writing Another's Dream*, 147.

41. For the text of this poem, see Lu, *Shi*, 2: 1161.

42. *Wei-Jin Nanbeichao wenxueshi cankao ziliao*, 467–68.

43. His reason for this interpretation is the following anecdote recorded in *An Lushang shiji* (安祿山事跡), or *The Life of An Lushan*:

Xuanzong often invited [An] Lushan over to have dinner at night. When Lushan was drunk, he laid himself down and turned into a black pig with a dragon head. People who witnessed this told it to Xuanzong, who said: "This pig is a dragon. No one else can do this." Before Lushan was to enter the imperial court, [Xuanzong] had a mansion built for him by the hot spring and gave him the privilege of bathing in it. (Cited in Zeng et al., *Shiji jianzhu*, chap. 4, 15.)

44. Rouzer, *Writing Another's Dream*, 148.

45. *Xian Qin wenxueshi cankao ziliao*, 8–9.

46. *Jiu Tang shu*, vol. 7, chap. 51, 2181.

47. This and the next few lines describe the capturing of Nanjing by the invading Sui troops.

48. Following *Shiji jianzhu*; *Quan Tang shi* has 容.

49. Zeng et al., *Shiji jianzhu*, chap. 1, 1–2; *Quan Tang shi*, vol. 17, chap. 575, 6694; Liu, *Shicixuan*, 3–6.

50. Wen Tingyun's extant poems number about 340. According to the counting done by Paul Rouzer, there are seventy-five *yuefu* poems. See *Writing Another's Dream*, 46.

51. See Joseph Allen, *In the Voices of Others: Chinese Music Bureau Poetry*, passim.

52. See Pauline Yu, *The Reading of Imagery in the Chinese Poetic Tradition*, passim.

53. See "Wumu Huanghou zhuan" 武穆皇后傳, in *Nan shi*, vol. 2, chap. 11, 330.

54. "Chen Houzhu zhuan" in *Nan shi*, vol. 1, chap. 10, 309.

55. *Quan Tang shi*, vol. 11, chap. 365, 4117.

56. Ye, *Li He shiji*, 77–78, Frodsham, *The Poems of Li Ho*, 65–67.

57. According to "Yinyuezhi" 音樂志 in *Jiu Tang shu* (vol. 4, chap. 9, 1069), "Jade-Tree and Rear-court Flower" was a song composed by Chen Houzhu for entertainment at his court.

58. Rouzer, *Writing Another's Dream*, 128.

59. *Zhengqin* 正寢 is where the monarch resides and works, hence a metaphor for the monarch.

60. The book of *Zhuangzi* mentions three kinds of sounds (*lai* 籟): the sound of earth (*dilai* 地籟), the sound of humankind (*renlai* 人籟), and the sound of heaven (*tianlai* 天籟); see Chen Guying, *Zhuangzi jinzhu jinyi*, 33.

61. For the sources and significance of these two allusions, see the following discussion of this poem.

62. Zeng et al., *Shiji jianzhu*, chap. 6, 11–12; *Quan Tang shi*, vol. 17, chap. 580, 6735.

63. *Shishuo xinyu*, chap. 14, 333.

64. Following *Shiji jianzhu*; *Quan Tang Shi* has 澄 .

65. Following *Shiji jianzhu*; *Quan Tang shi* has 飄 .

66. Following *Shiji jianzhu*; *Quan Tang shi* has 頗黎.

67. Following *Shiji jianzhu*; *Quan Tang shi* has 寫.

68. Zeng et al., *Shiji jianzhu*, chap. 2, 13; *Quan Tang shi*, vol. 17, chap. 576, 6707; Liu, *Shicixuan*, 38–41.

69. "Yinyuezhi" 音樂志 in *Jiu Tang shu* (vol. 4, chap. 9, 1069) records that "'The Night of Spring River and Flowery Moon,' 'The Jade Tree and Rear-court Flower' . . . were composed by Chen Houzhu. Houzhu often wrote poems with his literarily talented court ladies and courtiers. . . . He selected the most ornate and amorous pieces and set them to this tune."

70. Lu, *Shi*, 3: 2663.

71. Unfortunately this poem is too long to be quoted here. It is worth pointing out that this poem does not mention a single historical event, although it was composed after the falls of Chen and Sui dynasties. For a text of this poem, see *Yuefu shiji*, chap. 47, 557–58.

72. "The music of a defeated nation is sorrowful, and its people are in trouble" (亡國之音哀以思，其民困). See The Great Preface to *The Book of Songs*, in Guo Shaoyu, *Zhongguo lidai wenlunxuan*, 1: 63; Legge, *Chinese Classics*, 4: 34.

73. *Quan Tang shi*, vol. 16, chap. 523, 5980.

74. Zeng et al., *Shiji jianzhu*, chap. 9, 5–6; *Quan Tang shi*, vol. 17, chap. 583, 6755–56.

75. See Yang Bojun, *Lunyu yizhu*, 99; Legge, *Chinese Classics*, 1: 222.

76. See "Yonghuai guji wushou" 詠懷古跡五首, in *Quan Tang shi*, vol. 7, chap. 230, 2510–11.

77. See note 6 in this chapter. I mentioned Liu Dajie's complete disregard of Wen Tingyun's *shi* at the beginning of this chapter. Another way to demonstrate this is to check the number of Wen Tingyun's poems collected in the numerous Tang poetry anthologies composed during the later imperial periods and compare it with that of Li Shangyin, who was named together with Wen Tingyun as the representatives of the "Wen-Li" style. In *Tangshi biecaiji* 唐詩別裁集 (Taipei: Shangwu, 1968), one of the better-known selections edited by the Qin Confucian scholar Shen Deqian 沈德潛 (1673–1769), only eighteen poems by Wen Tingyun were selected, compared with forty by Li Shangyin. And in *Tangshi sanbaishou* 唐詩三百首, the most widely read anthology of Tang poetry edited by the Qing scholar Sun Zhu 孫洙(1711–78), only four poems by Wen Tingyun were included, compared with twenty-four by Li Shangyin.

## CHAPTER 5

1. *Jiu Tang shu*, vol. 14, chap. 190, 5077.

2. See *Tangcaizi zhuan*, 238.

3. See *Tangren xuan Tangshi*.

4. For statistical evidence of this reversal of fortune, see note 77 in chap. 4.

5. Cai Juhou 蔡居厚, *Cai Kuanfu shihua* 蔡寬夫詩話, cited in Ye Congqi 葉蔥奇, ed. and ann., *Li Shangyin shiji shuzhu* 李商隱詩集疏注 (Beijing: Renmin wenxue, 1985), 2: 728; hereafter cited as *Shiji shuzhu*.

6. Lu Shiyong 陸時雍, *Shijing zonglun* 詩鏡總論, in Ding Fubao 丁福保, ed., *Lidai shihua xubian* 歷代詩話續編 (Beijing: Zhonghua, 1983), 3:1422.

7. *Yipiao shihua* 一瓢詩話, cited in Ye, *Shiji shuzhu*, 2:768.

8. For a brief account of Li Shangyin's influence and later criticism of his poetry, see Wu Tiaogong 吳調公, *Li Shangyin yanjiu* 李商隱研究 (Shanghai: Shanghai guji, 1982), chap. 8 and 9.

9. An excellent example of such work is "Xingci xijiao zuo yibaiyun" 行次西郊作一百韻. There are a number of critical editions of Li Shangyin's poetry. The ones used in the present study are Ye Congqi, *Li Shangyin shiji shuzhu*, cited above; and Liu Xuekai 劉學鍇 and Yu Shucheng 余恕誠, eds., *Li Shangyin shige jijie* 李商隱詩歌集解 (Beijing: Zhonghua, 1988), hereafter cited as *Shige jijie*; it collects all important previous interpretations of individual poems. For a brief account of the textual history of Li Shangyin's poetry, see Liu and Yu, *Shige jijie*, 1:1–4. James J. Y. Liu has translated one hundred poems by Li Shangyin into English in a collection called *The Poetry of Li Shang-yin* (Chicago: University of Chicago Press, 1969); A. C. Graham's *Poems of the Late T'ang* includes twenty-five poems by Li Shangyin. Unless otherwise noted, all translations in this chapter are mine. For the text of this poem, see Ye, *Shiji shuzhu*, 2:661–69; Liu and Yu, *Shige jijie*, 1:232–58.

10. Liu Kezhuang 劉克莊 (1187–1269), *Houcun shihua* 後村詩話, cited in Ye, *Shiji shuzhu*, 2: 746. Yu Xin's later poetry transcends Palace Style convention, which marked his early works, but Liu Kezhuang's comparision is probably made with his early poetry in mind.

11. Ye, *Shiji shuzhu*, 1:407; Liu and Yu, *Shige jijie*, 4:1751.

12. See *Yuefu shiji*, chap. 94, 1071.

13. See "Ma Liao zhuan" 馬廖傳 in *Hou Han shu*, vol. 3, chap. 24, 853.

14. Ye, *Shiji shuzhu*, 2:519; Liu and Yu, *Shige jijie*, 5:1841.

15. 細腰宜窄衣; see his *"Nanyuan kanrenhuan"* 南苑看人還, in Lu Qinli, *Xian Qin Han-Wei-Jin Nanbeichao shi*, 3:1995.

16. Wu Tiaogong complains in commenting on the first of these two verses that "the rebirth of Palace Style poetry under Li Shangyin's pen is reflected only in his repeated use of clichés like 'pearl nets,' 'kingfisher-feather clothes,' 'Chu waist,' and 'palace brows'" (*Li Shangyin yanjiu*, 169). This is an exaggeration of another kind. I will show in what follows that Li Shangyin actually revitalized Palace Style poetry. In this sense Li Shangyin did not simply conform to this genre, but transformed it.

17. Ye, *Shiji shuzhu*, 1:173; Liu and Yu, *Shige jijie*, 4:1461.

18. The "Xiyuzhuan zan" 西域傳贊 in *Han shu* records a precious horn whose two ends are connected. See vol. 8, chap. 96, 3928–29 n. 3.

19. These are two guessing games that people play after finishing their drinking. The players are usually divided into two teams.

20. "Orchid Terrace" *lantai* 蘭臺 is usually used to refer to the governmental secretariat. *Shiji shuzhu* has 斷蓬 instead of 轉蓬. Ye, *Shiji shuzhu*, 1:136; Liu and Yu, *Shige jijie*, 1:389.

21. Li Zehou, *Mei de licheng*, 155.

22. For example, Cao Cao's "Que dongxi-men xing" 卻東西門行, Cao Zhi's "Yujue pian" 吁嗟篇, and "Zashi qishou " 雜詩七首, no. 2; all in Lu, *Shi*, 1: 354, 423, 465.

23. See Zhou Zhenfu, *Wenxin diaolong jinyi*, 399; Shih, *The Literary Mind and the Carving of Dragons*, 339.

24. Ye, *Shiji shuzhu*, 1:137. Similar views are also given by some Ming and Qing scholars; see Liu and Yu, *Shige jijie*, 1:390–98. There are also those who believe that this poem, like other of Li Shangyin's untitled poems, are simply poems on an amorous topic. They include the Qing scholar Ji Yun 紀昀 ( cited in Liu and Yu, *Shige jijie*, 1:397), and Liu and Yu themselves, 1:399–400. Since nearly every poem in Li Shangyin's oeuvre is controversial and the views of his works are too many to rehearse, I will cite or discuss only those that are most representative and relevant to our present study. Readers who are interested in more thorough accounts of the poems discussed in this chapter may consult Liu and Yu's very helpful collection of different interpretations of each poem.

25. Cited in Liu and Yu, *Shige jijie*, 4:1751. Here I would like to provide a brief account of an aspect of Li Shangyin's life that has served as the framework of much of the biographical study of his poetry. When still young Li Shangyin won the favor of a powerful government official, Linghu Chu 令狐楚, who encouraged him in his literary career. But later he married the daughter of Wang Maoyuan 王茂元, who happened to belong to a rival political clan of Linghu Chu. Li Shangyin's behavior was viewed by people on Linghu Chu's side as an act of betrayal and was never completely forgiven by Linghu Chu's son, Linghu Tao 令狐綯, who later became one of the prime ministers of the country. Li Shangyin's life was thus caught up in the fierce political rivalry of two powerful groups. He tried throughout his life to reconcile with Linghu Tao, which resulted in some very obsequious

poems. Many critics view Li Shangyin's poetry from this perspective, of which this far-fetched interpretation by Yao Peiqian is one of the extreme examples. See *Jiu Tang shu*, vol. 14, chap. 190, 5077, and *Xin Tang shu*, vol. 18, chap. 203, 5792. For biographical studies of Li Shangyin's poetry, see Zhang Caitian 張采田, *Yuxi Sheng nianpu huijian* 玉溪生年譜會箋 (Beijing: Zhonghua, 1963); Su Xuelin 蘇雪林, *Yuxi shimi* 玉溪詩迷 (Taipei: Shangwu, 1969); and Lan Yu 藍于, *Li Shangyin shi lungao* 李商隱詩論稿 (Hong Kong: Zhonghua, 1975).

26. Ye, *Shiji shuzhu*, 1:396; Liu and Yu, *Shige jijie*, 4:1460.

27. Ye Congqi thinks the woman is sewing a wedding-net, *baizizhang* 百子帳. See Ye, *Shiji shuzhu*, 1:396.

28. The alluded lines are "雷殷殷而響起兮，聲象君之車音" (the deep rumbling of thunder arises; it is like the of sound my lord's carriage). See *Wen xuan*, chap. 16, 227–28.

29. Huang Jie, *Han-Wei yuefu fengjian*, 162.

30. Ibid., 162–63.

31. Cited in Liu and Yu, *Shige jijie*, 4:1456.

32. Ye Congqi says that this poem uses the unmarried woman as a metaphor for the poet's failure at the civil service examination; see Ye, *Shiji shuzhu*, 1:396.

33. Ye, *Shiji shuzhu*, 2:571, Liu and Yu, *Shige jijie*, 1:79.

34. *Yuxi Sheng nianpu huijian*, cited in Liu and Yu, *Shige jijie*, 1:96.

35. *The Poetry of Li Shang-yin*, 69.

36. For example, Ye Congqi and James Liu. It should be noted that as in most cases in classical poetry, both interpretations are grammatically acceptable.

37. One critic, while acknowledging these associations, asks us to disregard them, calling them "clichéd prejudices." She would rather read them as describing the lush beauty of spring. See Ye Jiaying, "Jiushi xinyan" 舊詩新演, in her *Jialing lunshi conggao*, 163. Contemporary literary theory and criticism tell us that it is impossible to disregard clichéd associations because they play an essential role in the meaning production of a text, especially in poetry. For very often it is against these clichéd associations that a fresh meaning emerges. In addition, to interpret a metaphor or image in spite of its linguistic history is to distort its meaning and significance. See Riffaterre, *Semiotics of Poetry*, passim.

38. Again I am following Liu and Yu; Ye Congqi and James Liu

regard the woman as the player of this part. In fact, they have greatly reduced the complexity of this poem by giving it a uniform perspective and voice—namely, that of the woman.

39. *The Poetry of Li Shang-yin*, 70.

40. Ye congqi and James Liu's reading solves this difficulty by taking the woman as the subject of these two acts. Liu regards this couplet as describing the woman waking up and is "still half-dreaming and talking (or listening) to her lover, who has appeared to her in her dream." Ibid., 70.

41. For example, in the famous *"Jinse"* 錦瑟 ("Patterned Zither"), that will be discussed later.

42. This is what is implied in James Liu's reading, see *The Poetry of Li Shang-yin*, 70.

43. *Yuxi Sheng nianpu huijian*, cited in Liu and Yu, *Shige jijie*, 1:97.

44. Cited in Liu and Yu, *Shige jijie*, 1:92

45. See Ye, *Shiji shuzhu*, 2:572. For a summary of different readings of this and other poems in the series, see Liu and Yu, *Shige jijie*, 1:91–99.

46. Ye, *Shiji shuzhu*, 1:268; Liu and Yu, *Shige jijie*, 2:531–32.

47. For instance, Tao Yuanming's *"Lianyu duzhuo"* 連雨獨酌, Wang Wei's *"Qiuye duzuo huai neidi Cui Xingzong"* 秋夜獨坐懷內弟崔興宗, in Lu, *Shi*, 1:693, and *Wang Youcheng ji jianzhu*, 26.

48. *Chuci buzhu*, chap. 9, 1.

49. *Yuxi Sheng shishuo* 玉溪生詩說, cited in Liu and Yu, *Shige jijie*, 2:534.

50. Liu and Yu, *Shige jijie*, 2:534.

51. This interpretation is adopted by most commentators. See Ye, *Shiji shuzhu*, 1:268–69; Liu and Yu, *Shige jijie*, 2:533–34.

52. 芙蓉爲帶石榴裙, see "Wuyi qu" 烏衣曲, in Lu , *Shi*, 3:2036.

53. 風搖翡翠簪, see Liu and Yu, *Shige jijie*, 2:532.

54. "In the simplest terms, allegory says one thing and means another. It destroys the normal expectations we have of language, that our words 'mean what they say.'" Angus Fletcher, *Allegory: The Theory of a Symbolic Mode* (Ithaca, N.Y.: Cornell University Press, 1964), 2.

55. Ye, *Shiji shuzhu*, 1:268.

56. 南登灞陵岸, see *"Qi'ai shi sanshou: qisan"* 七哀詩三首：其三, in Lu, *Shi*, 365.

57. See, for example, *"Qiugui yesi"* 秋閨夜思 by Xiao Gang, in *Yutai*

*xinyong*, 165; *"Daoyi"* 搗衣 by Xiao Yan 蕭衍, ibid., 151. This image is also popular during the Tang period. For example, one of the poems by Li Bai begins 長安一片月，萬戶搗衣聲 (The whole Chang'an is covered by bright moonlight,/ From tens of thousands houses comes the sound of clothes beating); see *"Ziye Wuge: qiuge"* 子夜吳歌：秋歌, in *Quan Tang shi*, vol. 5, chap. 165, 1711.

58. *Li Yishan shi bianzheng* 李義山詩辨正, cited in Liu and Yu, *Shige jijie*, 2:534.

59. Ye, *Shiji shuzhu*, 1:268.

60. Ye, *Shiji shuzhu*, 1:1; Liu and Yu, *Shige jijie*, 3:1420. In translating this poem, I have consulted A. C. Graham's version; see his *Poems of the Late T'ang*, 169–73.

61. Of the numerous complaints about the obscurity of this poem, the best known is by the Jin critic Yuan Haowen 元好問, who observed:

| | |
|---|---|
| 望帝春心託杜鵑 | Wang Di bequeathed his spring heart to the nightjar, |
| 佳人錦瑟思華年 | The fair one's brocade zither laments the youthful years. |
| 詩家總愛西崑好 | Poetry scholars love the style of Xi Kun, |
| 獨恨無人作鄭箋 | I only regret that no one could write a Zheng Xuan commentary. |

See *"Lunshi sanshi shou: qi shier"* 論詩三十首：其十二, in Guo Shaoyu, *Zhongguo lidai wenlunxuan*, 2: 450.

62. For a detailed account of the different interpretations of this poem, see Liu and Yu, *Shige jijie*, 1422–38. James J.Y. Liu sums up various interpretations as five theories: (1) that it is a love poem; (2) that it is about music; (3) that it was written in memory of the poet's deceased wife; (4) that it is a lamentation of the poet's unfortunate life and career; and (5) finally that it is an introduction to the poet's collected poems. James Liu himself views this poem as "a variation on the common theme that life is a dream. The poet meditates on the apparently unreal nature of life in general and of love in particular." See his *The Poetry of Li Shang-yin*, 51–57.

63. See Chen Guying, *Zhuangzi jinzhu jinyi*, 92.

64. Recorded in *"Shuwang benji"* 蜀王本紀 and *"Chengduji"* 成都紀, cited in Liu and Yu, *Shige jijie*, 3:1421–22.

65. "To George and Thomas Keats," in *Selected Poems and Letters by John Keats*, 261.

66. *"Zhongguo yunwen nei suo biaoxian de qinggan"* 中國韻文內

所表現的情感, in his *Yinbing shi heji* 飲冰室合集 (Shanghai: Zhonghua, 1936), vol. 13, chap. 37, 119–20.

67. New York: Columbia University, 1971, 192.

68. For a discussion of imagistic and propositional language in Tang poetry, see Kao Yu-kung and Mei Tsu-lin, "Syntax, Diction, and Imagery in T'ang Poetry," *Harvard Journal of Asiatic Studies* 31(1971): 49–136.

69. *Yuxi Sheng shiji jianzhu* 玉溪生詩集箋注, cited in Liu and Yu, *Shige jijie*, 3:1422.

70. To further demonstrate this difference, I refer interested readers to Xiao Gang's "Yong xinyan" 詠新燕 (in Lu, *Shi*, 3: 1974) and Li Shangyin's "Liuying" 流鶯 (in Ye, *Shiji shuzhu*, 1:361; Liu and Yu, *Shige jijie*, 2:891). Xiao Gang's piece focuses exclusively on the feminine and the erotic associations of the bird, while Li Shangyin's poem makes the uncertain, fragile life of the the bird an objective correlative of his own experience.

71. One of such readers is the Song writer and poet Su Shi 蘇軾 (1037–1101). See Hu Zi 胡仔 (1095–1170), ed., *Tiaoxi yuyin conghua* 苕溪漁引叢話 (Taipei: Shijie shuju, 1961), vol. 1, chap. 22, 146.

72. *Yang Wengong tanyuan* 楊文公談苑, cited in Ye, *Shiji shuzhu*, 2:727.

73. He used this expression on several occasions. See "Xixi" 西溪 (Ye, *Shiji shuzhu*, 1:55, Liu and Yu, *Shige jijie*, 3:1191), and "Xiti Shuyan caoge sanshieryun" 戲題樞言草閣三十二韻 (Ye, *Shiji shuzhu*, 2:636, Liu and Yu, *Shige jijie*, 3:999).

74. Following *Shige jijie*; *Shiji shuzhu* has 屏.

75. Following *Shige jijie*; *Shiji shuzhu* has 若.

76. Ye, *Shiji shuzhu*, 2:694–95; Liu and Yu, *Shige jijie*, 4:1723–24.

77. Still, Ye Congqi regards this poem as being based on the poet's personal experience. To him the word "imitation" merely indicates that Li Shangyin's involvement with the woman in question is not deep. See Ye, *Shiji shuzhu*, 2: 697–98.

78. For "The girl of Zhang" 張女, see Pan Yue's "Sheng fu" 笙賦, in *Wen xuan*, chap. 18, 261 and Jiang Zong's 江總 (519–94) "Zaiqu sanshou: qisan" 雜曲三首：其三, in Lu, *Shi*, 3:2574. For "A Hou" 阿侯 see Xiao Yan's 蕭衍, Xiao Gang's father or Emperor Wu of Liang dynasty 梁武帝 (464–549) "*Hezhong zhishuige*" 河中之水歌, in ibid., 3:1511. It should be noted that "A Hou" in Xiao Yan's poem is the name of Mo Chou's 莫愁 son, but Li Shangyin apparently uses it to refer to Mo Chou and, by extension, to young women in general. The

same usage also occurs in another poem of his; see "Untitled" 無題 ("She is known as A Hou in the neighbourhood" 近知名阿侯), in Ye, *Shiji shuzhu*, 109.

79. That is, the circle symbolizes union or reunion. See Wu Jing 吳競, *Yuefu guti yaojie* 樂府古題要解, cited in Ye, *Shiji shuzhu*, 2:695.

80. These two images come from the following two lines by Zhang Zhengxian 張正見, a poet at Chen Houzhu's court: "並卷茱萸帳，爭移翡翠床。" See his "Yange xing" 艷歌行, in Lu, *Shi*, 3:2472.

81. See "Waiqizhuan" 外戚傳 in *Han shu*, vol. 8, chap. 97, 3988, and "Yang Kan liezhuan" 楊侃列傳 in *Nan shi*, vol. 5, chap. 63, 1547.

82. See "Waiqizhuan" 外戚傳 in *Han shu*, vol. 8, chap. 67, 3951.

83. "Wei Jie zhuan" 衛玠傳 in Fang Xuanling 房玄齡 et al., *Jin shu* 晉書 (Beijing: Zhonghua, 1974), vol. 4, chap. 36, 1067.

84. "Wenyuanzhuan" 文苑傳 in *Bei shi* 北史 (Beijing: Zhonghua, 1974), vol. 9, chap. 83, 2778.

85. Recorded in Wang Jia 王嘉, *Shiyi ji* 拾遺記; cited in Liu and Yu, *Shige jijie*, 4:1727.

86. Liu and Yu pointed out the "indecent" suggestion of the couplet but did not elaborate on it. See *Shige jijie*, 4:1727.

87. See Beijing daxue Zhongwenxi 北京大學中文系, ed., *Tao Yuanming shiwen huiping* 陶淵明詩文匯評 (Beijing: Zhonghua, 1961), 338–39.

88. See *Chuci buzhu*, chap. 2, 12.

89. This is the reading of Ye Congqi, with which I agree. Other commentators take this to be an allusion. See Liu and Yu, *Shige jijie*, 1728.

90. *Wen xuan*, chap. 19, 268.

91. See *Wen xuan*, chap. 19, 269–72.

92. "願作石尤風，四面斷行旅;" 尤 and 郵 are interchangeable homophones in this case; see *Yuefu shiji*, chap. 45, 537.

93. This story is recorded in *Jianghu jiwen* 江湖紀聞; cited in Liu and Yu, *Shige jijie*, 4:1730 n. 35.

94. Recorded in Liu Xiang 劉向 (79–8 B. C.), *Liexian zhuan* 列仙傳; cited in Liu and Yu, *Shige jijie*, 4:1730 n. 37.

95. For the treatment of this story in Cao Zhi and Ruan Ji's works, see "Luoshen fu" by Cao Zhi and poem no. 2 in the series called "Yonghuaishi" 詠懷詩 by Ruan Ji. Both are in *Wen xuan*, chap. 19, 270–72, and chap. 23, 321–23.

96. "凌波微步", see *Wen xuan*, chap. 19, 322.

97. For example, Zhong Rong ranks this series the first in his *Shi pin* and says that "each word of these poems is worth a thousand gold." See *Shi pin*, 11.

98. See Lu, *Shi*, 1:331.

99. *Yuxi Sheng shishuo*, cited in Liu and Yu, *Shige jijie*, 4:1731.

100. *Yuxi Sheng shiji jianzhu*, cited in ibid., 1731.

101. Ye, *Shiji shuzhu*, 1:112; Liu and Yu, *Shige jijie*, 4:1679.

102. Liu and Yu, *Shige jijie*, 4:1679.

103. Ye, *Shiji shuzhu*, 113.

104. Recorded in *Hanwu neizhuan* 漢武內傳, cited in Liu and Yu, *Shige jijie*, 4:1680 n. 3.

105. See Li Shan's note on the following sentence from Ji Kang's 嵇康 (223–63) *"Yangshenglun"* 養生論: "The supreme medicine nourishes life" 上藥養命; in *Wen xuan*, chap. 53, 729.

106. Recorded in *Fayuan zhulin* 法苑珠林, cited in Liu and Yu, *Shige jijie*, 4:1680–81 n. 6.

107. As Liu and Yu noted, this allusion actually combines two stories in *Shishuo xinyu*; see ibid., 4:1681 n. 7.

108. The Qing scholar Zhu Yizun 朱彝尊 said that "both the title and the poem are incomprehensible." Cited Liu and Yu, *Shige jijie*, 4:1681.

109. Liu and Yu, *Shige jijie*, 4:1683.

110. Ye Congqi, *Shiji shuzhu*, 1:113.

111. Ibid.

112. *Li Yishan shi bianzheng*, cited in Liu and Yu, *Shige jijie*, 4:1683.

113. *Yuxi Sheng shiji jianzhu*, cited in ibid., 1683.

114. This critic is Wang Dajin 王達津. See Liu and Yu, *Shige jijie*, 4:1683.

115. Cited Liu and Yu, *Shige jijie*, 4:1681.

116. Ye, *Shiji shuzhu*, 1:50–51; Liu and Yu, *Shige jijie*, 1:11.

117. "Wudiji" 武帝紀, in *Jin shu*, vol. 1, chap. 3, 69.

118. Such direct criticism, although rare in Li Shangyin's poetry, does exist. See his "On History" ("Yongshi" 詠史), in Ye, *Shiji shuzhu*, 1:134; Liu and Yu, *Shige jijie*, 1:347.

119. Cheng Mengxing believes that this poem is a satire against Emperor Jingzong of Tang 唐敬宗 (r. 825–27). The reason he gives is that none of the events referred to in the poem, especially the last line, which alludes to another Southern Dynasties ruler, Qi Houzhu 齊後主 (r. 565–77), actually happened in the Chen dynasty. See *Li*

*Yishang shiji jianzhu*, cited in Liu and Yu, *Shige jijie*, 1:14. Whatever the case is, the satirical tone of the poem is unmistakable.

120. Ye, *Shiji shuzhu*, 1:261; Liu and Yu, *Shige jijie*, 3:1370.

121. "Liang Yuandi Xufei zhuan" 梁元帝徐妃傳, in *Nan shi*, vol. 2, chap. 12, 341.

122. For instance, see Ye, *Shiji shuzhu*, 1:261.

123. *Yuxi Sheng shishuo*; cited in Liu and Yu, *Shige jijie*, 1:1371.

124. Ye, *Shji shuzhu*, 1:227; Liu and Yu, *Shige jijie*, 1:307. There is a play on the phrase *mochou* 莫愁 in the last line. In this context it both refers to the household name of a young woman and is used in its literal meaning, which means "carefree."

125. For a summary of different interpretations of this poem, see Liu and Yu, *Shige jijie*, 310–15.

126. For more information on this story, see Chen Hong 陳鴻, "*Changhenge zhuan*" 長恨歌傳, cited in Liu and Yu, *Shige jijie*, 1:309 n. 5.

127. Ye, *Shiji shuzhu*, 1:61; Liu and Yu, *Shige jijie*, 2:695.

128. For example, see Wu, *Li Shangyin yanjiu*, 184.

129. I do not intend to get into political argument with these critics. But to demand that one should have faith in society when society does not provide the grounds for doing so is to disregard social reality, which is ironically what these critics value most. The melancholy, even pessimism, in Li Shangyin's poetry is in this sense more realistic than a groundless faith because it reflects the social and intellectual conditions of Late Tang.

130. Ye, *Shiji shuzhu*, 1:31; Liu and Yu, *Shige jijie*, 5:1942–43.

131. This is only one of a number of possible readings of the poem. For a summary of different readings of this piece, see Liu and Yu, *Shige jijie*, 5:1943–45.

132. *Qianxi shihua* 潛溪詩話, cited in Liu and Yu, *Shige jijie*, 2:728.

133. One of the characteristics of decadent literature is "a pervasive sense of something lost—a nostalgic semi-mysticism without clear direction or spiritual commitment." See *New Princeton Encyclopedia of Poetry and Poetics*, 275.

## CONCLUSION

1. *Quan Tang shi*, vol. 7, chap. 224, 2403.

2. For a study on the mutual relationship between literature and the examination system in the Tang period, see Fu Xuancong 傅玄琮,

*Tangdai keju yu wenxue* 唐代科舉與文學 (Xi'an: Shanxi renmin, 1986).

3. As has been shown in chap. 2, the cultural atmosphere at court during the Southern Dynasties also discourages intense personal engagement in poetry, because this might disrupt decorum, the ultimate standard for judgment. To a lesser extent, this is also true for the social occasions on which numerous poems were written. To match a friend or colleague's poem one must not merely focus on his own feelings and thoughts, but he must also abide by the rules, technical and social, demanded of the particular occasion. The *"lianju"* 聯句, or linked poetry that flourished during the Southern Dynasties and Tang periods illustrates this point. The succeeding poet is confined by the preceding poet's work, both in his choice of metrical pattern, diction, imagery, and in his vision and experience of the occasion. He must twist his experience to fit into them.

# Selected Bibliography

## Chinese Sources

Ban Gu 班固. *Han shu* 漢書. Beijing: Zhonghua, 1962.

Cao Daoheng 曹道衡 and Shen Yucheng 沈玉成. *Nanbeichao wenxueshi* 南北朝文學史. Beijing: Renmin wenxue, 1991.

Cao Zhi 曹植. *Cao Zhi ji zhu* 曹植集注. Edited and annotated by Zhao Youwen 趙幼文. Beijing: Renmin wenxue, 1984.

Chen Yicheng 陳義成. *Han-Wei Liuchao yuefu yanjiu* 漢魏六朝樂府研究. Taipei: Chia Hsin Foundation, 1976.

Chen Zhiguo 陳治國, ed. *Li He yanjiu ziliao* 李賀研究資料. Beijing: Beijing shifan daxue, 1983.

Ding Fubao 丁福保, ed. *Quan Han Sanguo Jin Nanbeichao shi* 全漢三國晉南北朝詩. Taipei: Yiwen, 1975.

Dong Naibin 董乃斌. "Li Shangyin de yuxiang fuhao xitong fenxi" 李商隱的語象符號系統分析. *Wenxue yichan* 文學遺產 1(1989): 59–70.

Fan Ye 范曄. *Hou Han shu* 後漢書. Beijing: Zhonghua, 1975.

Fang Yu 方喻. *Zhongwan Tang sanjiashi xilun* 中晚唐三家詩析論. Taipei: Muniu, 1975.

Fu Jingshun 傅經順. *Li He zhuanlun* 李賀傳論. Xi'an: Shanxi renmin, 1981.

———, ed. *Li He shige shangxiji* 李賀詩歌賞析集. Chengdu: Bashu shushe, 1988.

Gao Bing 高棅, ed. *Tangshi pinhui* 唐詩品匯. *Siku quanshu* edition. Taipei: 1976.

Guo Shaoyu 郭紹虞. "Lun zhongguo wenxue zhong de yinjie wenti" 論中國文學中的音節問題, in Zheng Zhenduo 鄭振鐸 et al. *Zhongguo wenxue yanjiu congbian* 中國文學研究叢編, vol. 2. Hong Kong: Longmen shu-dian, 1967.

————, ed. *Zhongguo lidai wenlungxuan* 中國歷代文論選, in four volumes. Shanghai: Shanghai guji, 1979–1980.

————. *Zhongguo wenxue pipingshi* 中國文學批評史. Shanghai: Shanghai guji, 1979.

————. *Zhaoyushi gudian wenxue lunji* 照隅室古典文學論集. Shanghai: Shanghai guji, 1983.

Guo Maoqian 郭茂倩, ed. *Yuefu shiji* 樂府詩集. Taipei: Xinxing,1968.

*Han-Wei Liuchao shige jianshanji* 漢魏六朝詩歌鑒賞集. Beijing: Renmin wenxue, 1985.

Hu Zi 胡仔, ed. *Tiaoxi yuyin conghua* 苕溪漁引叢話. Taipei: Shijie shuju, 1961.

Huang Jie 黃節, ed. *Han-Wei yuefu feng jian* 漢魏樂府風箋. Hong Kong: Shangwu, 1961.

Huang Kunyao 黃坤堯. *Wen Tingyun* 溫庭筠. Taipei: Guojia, 1984.

Ji Yougong 計有功. *Tangshi jishi* 唐詩紀事. Taipei: Shangwu, 1968.

*Jin shu* 晉書. By Fang Xuanling 房玄齡 et al. Beijing: Zhonghua, 1974.

Kang Zhengguo 康正果. *Fengsao yu yanqing* 風騷與艷情. Zhengzhou: Henan renmin, 1988.

Kong Yingda 孔穎達. *Maoshi zhengyi* 毛詩正義. In *Shisanjing zhushu* 十三經注疏. Beijing: Zhonghua, 1980.

Kongzi 孔子. *Lunyu [yizhu]* 論語〔譯注〕. Annotated and translated by Yang Bojun 楊伯峻. Beijing: Zhonghua, 1965.

Lan Yu 藍于. *Li Shangyin shi lungao* 李商隱詩論稿. Hong Kong: Zhonghua, 1975.

Laozi 老子. *Laozi [zhushi ji pingjie]* 老子〔注釋及評介〕. Edited and trans-lated by Chen Guying 陳鼓應. Beijing: Zhonghua, 1984.

*Lidai shihua* 歷代詩話. Edited by Wu Jingxu 吳景旭. Taipei: Shijie shuju, 1961.

*Lidai shihua* 歷代詩話. Edited by He Wenhuan 何文煥. Beijing: Zhonghua, 1981.

*Lidai shihua xubian* 歷代詩話續編. Edited by Ding Fubao 丁福保. Beijing: Zhonghua, 1983.

Li He 李賀. *Li He shiji* 李賀詩集. Edited and annotated by Ye Congqi 葉蔥奇. Beijing: Renmin wenxue, 1959.

————. *Sanjia pingzhu Li Changji geshi* 三家評注李長吉歌詩. Edited by Wang Qi 王琦. Hong Kong: Zhonghua, 1976.

Li Yanshou 李延壽. *Liang shu* 梁書. Beijing: Zhonghua, 1973.

————. *Nan shi* 南史. Beijing: Zhonghua, 1975.

————. *Bei shi* 北史. Beijing: Zhonghua, 1974.

Li Zehou 李澤厚. *Mei de licheng* 美的歷程. Beijing: Wenwu, 1981.

———. *Zhongguo gudai sixiangshi lun* 中國古代思想史論. Beijing: Renmin, 1986.

———. and Liu Ganji. 劉綱紀. *Zhongguo meixueshi* 中國美學史. Beijing: Zhongguo shehui kexue: 2 volumes, 1984–1987.

Li Shangyin 李商隱. *Li Shangyin shiji shuzhu* 李商隱詩集疏注. Edited and annotated by Ye Congqi 葉蔥奇. Beijing: Renmin wenxue, 1985.

———. *Li Yishan shiwen quanji* 李義山詩文全集, ed. Feng Hao 馮浩, *Wangyou wenku huiyao* edition. Taipei: Shangwu, 1965.

———. *Li Shangyin shige jijie* 李商隱詩歌集解. Edited by Liu Xuekai 劉學鍇 and Yu Shucheng 余恕誠. Beijing: Zhonghua, 1988.

*Lian Han wenxueshi cankao ziliao* 兩漢文學史參考資料. Edited by Beijing daxue Zhongguo wenxue jiaoyan shi. Beijing: Zhonghua, 1962.

Liang Qichao 梁啓超. *Yinbing shi heji* 飲冰室合集. Shanghai: Zhonghua, 1936.

*Liang shu* 梁書. By Yao Silian 姚思廉. Beijing: Zhonghua, 1973.

Lin Wenyue 林文月. "Nanchao gongti shi yanjiu" 南朝宮體詩研究. *Wen-shizhe xuebao* 15(1966): 407–58.

Lin Bangjun 林邦鈞. "Lun Wen Tingyun he ta de shi" 論溫庭筠和他的詩. *Wenxue yichan* (4) 1981: 132–44.

Liu An 劉安. *Huainanzi* 淮南子. Rpt. as *Huainan honglie jishi* 淮南鴻烈集釋. Taipei: Shangwu, *Guoxue jiben congshu* edition, 1968.

Liu Dajie 劉大杰. *Zhongguo wenxue fazhanshi* 中國文學發展史. Shanghai: Shanghai guji, 1982.

Liu Xie 劉勰. *Wenxin diaolong [jinyi]* 文心雕龍〔今譯〕. Edited and translated by Zhou Zhenfu 周振甫. Beijing: Zhonghua, 1986.

Liu Xuekai 劉學鍇. "Li Shangyin yu Song Yu" 李商隱與宋玉. *Wenxue yichan* 1 (1987): 51–58.

Liu Yiqing 劉義慶. *Shishuo xinyu [jiaojian]* 世說新語〔校箋〕. Edited by Xu Zhen'e 徐震堮. Beijing: Zhonghua, 1984.

Lu Ji 陸機. "Wen fu" 文賦. In Guo Shaoyu, ed., *Zhongguo lidai wenlunxuan* 中國歷代文論選. Shanghai: Shanghai guji, 1979. 1: 170–75.

Lu Qinli 逯欽立, ed. *Xian Qin Han-Wei-Jin Nanbeichao shi* 先秦漢魏晉南北朝詩. Beijing: Zhonghua, 1983.

Luo Zongqiang 羅宗強. *Sui-Tang Wudai wenxue sixiangshi* 隋唐五代文學思想史. Shanghai: Shanghai Guji, 1986.

Luo Genze 羅根澤. *Yuefu wenxueshi* 樂府文學史. Taipei: Wenshizhe, 1972.

Mengzi 孟子. *Mengzi [yizhu]* 孟子〔譯注〕. Annotated and translated by Yang Bojun 楊伯峻. Beijing: Zhonghua, 1963.

Ouyang Jiong 歐陽炯, ed. *Huajianji* 花間集. Edited and annotated by Li Yi 李誼. Chengdu: Sichuan wenyi, 1986.

Ouyang Xiu 歐陽修 et al. *Xin Tang shu* 新唐書. Beijing: Zhonghua, 1975.

Qian Zhongshu 錢鍾書. *Guanzhuibian* 管錐編. Beijing: Zhonghua, 1979.

———. *Tangyilu* 談藝錄. Beijing: Zhonghua, 1984.

*Quan Shanggu Sandai Qin-Han Sanguo Liuchao wen* 全上古三代秦漢三國六朝文. Edited by Yan Kejun 嚴可均. Beijing: Zhonghua, 1958.

*Quan Tang shi* 全唐詩 Beijing: Zhonghua, 1960.

Shang Wei 商偉. "Lun gongtishi" 論宮體詩. *Beijing daxue xuebao* 7(1984): 66–74.

Shen Yue 沈約. *Song shu* 宋書. Beijing: Zhonghua 1975.

Sheng Yucheng 沈玉成. "Gongtishi yu *Yutai xinyong*" 宮體詩與玉台新詠. *Wenxue yichan* 6 (1988): 55–65.

Sima Qian 司馬遷, *Shi ji* 史記. Beijing: Zhonghua, 1972.

Sikong Tu 司空圖. *Shipin* 詩品. Beijing: Renmin wenxue, 1981.

Su Xuelin 蘇雪林. "Li He de geshi" 李賀的歌詩. In *Xuelin zixuanji* 雪林自選集. Taipei: Xinlu, 1954.

———. *Yuxi shimi* 玉溪詩迷. Taipei: Shangwu, 1969.

*Sui shu* 隋書. By Linghu Defen 令狐德棻 et al. Beijing: Zhonghua, 1975.

*Tangren xuan Tangshi* 唐人選唐詩. Shanghai: Zhonghua, 1958.

*Tang shu* 唐書, also known as *Jiu Tang shu* 舊唐書. By Liu Xu 劉昫 et al. Beijing: Zhonghua, 1975

*Taiping guanji* 太平廣記. By Li Fang 李昉 et al. Beijing: Zhonghua, 1961.

Tao Yuanming 陶淵明. *Tao Yuanming shiwen huiping* 陶淵明詩文匯評. Edited by Beijing daxue Zhongwenxi. Beijing: Zhonghua, 1961.

Wang Wei 王維. *Wang Youcheng ji [jianzhu]* 王右丞集〔箋注〕. Edited and annotated by Zhao Diancheng 趙殿成. Shanghai: Shanghai guji, 1961.

Wang Yi 王逸 and Hong Xingzu 洪興祖. *Chuci buzhu* 楚辭補注. Beijing: Zhonghua, 1983.

Wang Li 王力. *Hanyu shilüxue* 漢語詩律學. Shanghai: Shanghai jiaoyu, 1979.

Wang Chunhong 汪春泓. "Lun Fojiao yu gongtishi de chansheng" 論佛教與梁代宮體詩的產生. *Wenxue pinglun* 5 (1991): 40–56.

Wang Dajin 王達津. "Wen Tinyun shengnian zhi ruogan wenti" 溫庭筠生年之若干問題. *Nankai daxue xuebao* 2 (1982): 48–53.

Wang Zhongluo 王仲犖. *Wei-Jin Nanbeichao shi* 魏晉南北朝史. Shanghai: Shanghai renmin, 1980.

*Wei-Jin Nanbeichao wenxueshi cankao ziliao* 魏晉南北朝文學史參考資料. Edited by Beijing daxue Zhongguo wenxue jiaoyanshi. Beijing: Zhonghua, 1961.

Wei Qingzhi 魏慶之 ed. *Shiren yuxie* 詩人玉屑. Shanghai: Shanghai guji, 1978.

*Wenjing mifulun* 文鏡秘府論. Compiled by Kukai 空海, edited and annotated by Wang Liqi 王利器. Beijing: Zhongguo shehui kexue, 1983.

Wen Yiduo 聞一多. "Gongtishi de zishu" 宮體詩的自贖. In *Wen Yiduo quanji* 聞一多全集. Taipei: Kaming, 1967. 3:11–22.

Wen Tingyun 溫庭筠. *Wen Feiqing shiji [jianzhu]* 溫飛卿詩集〔箋注〕. Edited by Zeng Yi 曾益, Gu Yuxian 顧予咸, and Gu Sili 顧嗣立, the *Sibu beiyao* edition. Taipei: Zhonghua, 1965.

———. *Wen Tingyun shicixuan* 溫庭筠詩詞選. Edited by Liu Sihan 劉斯翰. Hong Kong: Sanlian, 1986.

*Wenyuan yinghua* 文苑英華. Edited by Li Fang 李昉 et al. Taipei: Xin wenfeng, 1979.

Wu Qiming 吳企明. *Li He yanjiu ziliao huibian* 李賀研究資料匯編. Beijing: Zhonghua, 1994.

Wu Tiaogong 吳調公. *Li Shangyin yanjiu* 李商隱研究. Shanghai: Shanghai guji, 1982.

———. *Gudian wenlun yu shenmei jianshang* 古典文論與審美鑒賞. Jinan: Qilu shushe, 1985.

Wu Yun 吳雲 and Dong Zhiguang 董志廣. "Liangdai gongtishi xinlun" 梁代宮體詩新論. *Wenxue yichan* 4 (1990): 25–30.

*Xian Qin wenxueshi cankao ziliao* 先秦文學史參考資料. Edited by Beijing daxue Zhongguo wenxue jiaoyanshi. Beijing: Zhonghua, 1962.

Xiao Tong 蕭統, ed. *Wen xuan* 文選, annotated by Li Shan 李善. Beijing: Zhonghua, 1977.

Xing Wenfang 辛文房. *Tangcaizi zhuan [jiaozheng]* 唐才子傳〔校正〕. Edited by Zhou Benchun 周本淳. Taipei: Wenjin, 1988.

Xu Fuguan 徐復觀. *Zhongguo wenxue lunji* 中國文學論集. Taipei: Xuesheng shuju, 1985.

Xu Ling 徐陵, ed. *Yutai xinyong* 玉台新詠. Chengdu: Chengdu guji, n.d..

Yan Yu 嚴羽. *Canglang shihua [jiaoshi]* 滄浪詩話〔校釋〕. Edited and annotated by Guo Shaoyu. Beijing: Renmin wenxue, 1983.

Yan Zhitui 顏之推. *Yanshi jiaxun* 顏氏家訓. In *Zhuzi jicheng* 諸子集成. Shanghai: Shanghai shudian, 1986.

Yang Haiming 楊海明. *Tangsongci shi* 唐宋詞史. Jiangsu: Jiangsu guji, 1987.

Ye Jiaying 葉嘉瑩. *Jialing lunci conggao* 迦陵論詞叢稿. Shanghai: Shanghai guji, 1980.

———. *Jialing lunshi conggao* 迦陵論詩叢稿. Beijing: Zhonghua, 1984.

You Guoen 游國恩 et al. *Zhongguo wenxueshi* 中國文學史. Beijing: Renmin wenxue, 1963.

———. *You Guoen xueshu lunwenji* 游國恩學術論文集. Beijing: Zhonghua, 1989.

Yuan Xingpei 袁行霈. *Zhongguo shige yishu yanjiu* 中國詩歌藝術研究. Beijing: Beijing daxue, 1987.

Zhang Caitian 張采田. *Yuxi Sheng nianpu huijian* 玉溪生年譜會箋. Shanghai: Shanghai guji, 1963.

Zhang Shuxiang 張淑香. *Li Yishan shi xilun* 李義山詩析論. Taipei: Yiwen, 1974.

Zhang Pu 張浦, ed. *Han-Wei Liuchao baisanjia ji* 漢魏六朝百三家集. Taipei: Xinxing shuju, 1963.

Zhong Rong 鍾嶸. *Shi pin* 詩品. Beijing: Renmin wenxue, 1961.

*Zhongguo meixueshi ziliao xuanbian* 中國美學史資料選編. Edited by Beijing daxue zhexuexi meixue jiaoyanshi. Beijing: Beijing University Press, 1980.

Zhou Chengzhen 周誠眞. *Li He lun* 李賀論. Hong Kong: Wenyi, 1972.

Zhu Ziqing 朱自清. *Zhu Ziqing gudian wenxue lunwenji* 朱自清古典文學論文集. Shanghai: Shanghai guji, 1980.

Zhuangzi 莊子. *Zhuangzi [jinzhu jinyi]* 莊子〔今注今譯〕. Edited and translated by Chen Guying 陳鼓應. Beijing: Zhonghua, 1983.

## WESTERN SOURCES

Adam, Paul. *Symboilstes et Décadents*. Exter: University of Exter Press, 1989.

Adams, Hazard, ed. *Critical Theory Since Plato*. San Diego: Harcourt Brace Jovanovich, 1971.

Aldington, Richard, ed. *The Religion of Beauty: Selections from the Aesthetes*: Melbourne: William Heinemann, 1950.

Allen, Joseph R. *In the Voices of Others: Chinese Music Bureau Poetry*. Ann Arbor: University of Michigan Press, 1992.

Aristotle. *The Rhetoric of Aristotle*. Translated by Richard C. Jebb. Cambridge University Press, 1909.

———. Aristotle's *Theory of Poetry and Fine Art*. Translated by S. H. Butcher. New York: Dover Publications, 1955.

Baudelaire, Charles-Pierre. *Selected Writings on Art and Artists*. Baltimore: Penguin Classics edition, 1972.

Beardsley, Monroe. C. *Aesthetics From Classical Greek to the Present*. Tuscaloosa: The University of Alabama Press, 1966.

Beckson, Karl, ed. *Aesthetes and Decadents of the 1890s: An Anthology of British Poetry and Prose*. New York: Vintage, 1966.

Birch, Cyril, ed. *Studies in Chinese Literary Genres*. Berkeley: University of California Press,1974.

Birrel, Anne. "Courtly Portraits of Woman in Southern Dynasties Love Poetry." In *Expressions of Self in Chinese Literature*. Edited by Robert E. Hegel and Richard C. Hessney. New York: Columbia University Press, 1985.

———, trans. *New Songs from a Jade Terrace: An Anthology of Early Chinese Love Poetry*. Baltimore: Penguin Classics edition, 1986.

Bol, Peter K. *This Culture of Ours: Intellectual Transitions in T'ang and Sung*. Stanford: Stanford University Press, 1992.

Carter, A..E. *The Idea of Decadence in French Literature 1830–1900*. Toronto: University of Toronto Press, 1958.

Chang, Kang-i Sung. *The Evolution of Chinese T'zu Poetry: From the Late T'ang to the Northern Sung*. Princeton: Princeton University Press, 1980.

————. *Six Dynasties Poetry*. Princeton: Princeton University Press, 1986.

Chen, David. "Li Ho and Keats: A Comparative Study of Two Poets." Ph.D. dissertation. Indiana University, 1962.

Clayton, Jay and Eric Rothstein, eds. *Influence and Intertextuality in Literary History*. Madison: University of Wisconsin Press, 1991.

De Bary, Theodore W. M et al. *Sources of Chinese Tradition*. New York: Columbia University Press, 1960.

Diény, Jean-Pierre. *Aux Origines de la Poésie Classique en Chine*. Leiden: E. J. Brill. 1968

————. *Les dix-neufs poémes anciens*. Paris: Centre de Publicayion Asie Orientale, 1974.

Dowling, Linda C. *Aestheticism and Decadence: A Selected Bibliography*. New York: Garland Publishing, 1977.

————. *Language and Decadence in the Victorian Fin de Siècle*. Princeton: Princeton University, 1986.

Fish, Michael. "Mythological Themes in the Poetry of Li Ho (791–817)." Ph.D. dissertation. Indiana University, 1973.

————. "The Tu Mu and Li Shang-yin Prefaces to the Collected Works of Li Ho." In *Studies in Chinese Poetry and Poetics*. Edited by Ronald C. Miao. San Francisco: Chinese Materials Center, 1978. 1: 231–86.

Fletcher, Ian and Malcolm Bradbury, eds. *Decadence and the 1890s*. New York: Holmes & Meir, 1980.

Fletcher, Angus. *Allegory: The Theory of a Symbolic Mode*. Ithaca, N.Y.: Cornell University Press, 1964.

Frankel, Hans H. "Yueh-fu Poetry." In *Studies in Chinese Literary Genres*. Edited by Cyril Birch. Berkeley: University of California Press, 1974. 69–107.

Frodsham, J. D, trans. *The Poems of Li Ho*. Oxford, England: Claredon Press, 1970.

————. *Goddesses, Ghosts and Demons: The Collected Poems of Li He*. San Francisco: North Point Press, 1983.

Gibbon, Edward. *The Decline and Fall of the Roman Empire*. New York: Wise, 1943.

Gilman, Richard. *Decadence, The Strange Life of an Epithet*. New York: Farrar, Straus, and Giroux, 1979.

Gourmont, Remy De. *Decadence and Other Essays on the Culture of Ideas*. New York: Harcourt, Brace and Company, 1921.

Graham, A.C., trans. *Poems of the Late T'ang*. Baltimore: Penguin Classics Edition, 1965.

Hartman, Charles. *Han Yu and the T'ang Search for Unity*. Princeton: Princeton University Press, 1986.

Hawkes, David. *The Songs of the South*. Baltimore: Penguin Classics edition, 1985.

———. "The Supernatural in Chinese Poetry." *University of Toronto Quarterly* 3 (1961): 311–24.

Henderson, John B. *Scripture, Canon, and Commentary: A Comparison of Confucian and Western Exgesis*. Princeton: Princeton University Press, 1991.

Hightower, James Robert. "The Wen Hsuan and Genre Theory." In *Studies in Chinese Literature*. Edited by John L. Bishop. Cambridge: Harvard University Press, 1966.

Honig, Edwin and Oscar Williams, eds. *The Major Metaphysical Poets of the Seventeenth Century*. New York: Washington Square Press, 1969.

Horace. "Art of Poetry." In *Horace for English Readers*. Edited by E. C. Wicham. Oxford: Oxford University Press, 1908.

Hsiao, Kun-chuan. *A History of Chinese Political Thought*. Volume I: *From the Beginning to the Sixth Century A.D.* Translated by F. W. Mote. Princeton: Princeton University Press, 1979.

Huysmans, J. K. *A Rebours*. English translation *Against the Grain*. New York: Illustrated New Editions, 1931.

Iser, Wolfgan. *Walter Pater: The Aesthetic Moment*. London: Cambridge University Press, 1987.

Jackson, Holbrook. *The Eighteen Nineties: A Review of Art and Ideas at the Close of the Nineteenth Century*. New York: Alfred Knopf, 1972.

Jameson, Fredric. "Baudelaire as Modernist and Postmodernist: The Dissolution of the Referent and the Artificial 'Sublime.'" In *Lyric Poetry beyond New Criticism*. Edited by Chaviva Hosek and Patricia Parker, 247–63. Ithaca, N.Y: Cornell University Press.

Joad, C. E. M. *Decadence: A Philosophical Inquiry*. London: Faber and Faber, 1948.

Johnson, Samuel. *Samuel Johnson: Rasselas, Poems and Selected Prose*. Edited by Bertrand Bronson. New York: Holt, Rinehart and Winston, 1958.

Kahn, Gustave. *Symbolistes et Décadents*. Paris: Librairie Banier, 1902.

Kao, Yu-kung and Mei Tsu-lin. "Meaning, Metaphor, and Allusion in T'ang Poetry." *Harvard Journal of Asiatic Studies* 38.2 (December 1978): 281–356.

———. "Syntax, Diction, and Imagery in T'ang Poetry." *Harvard Journal of Asiatic Studies* 31(1971): 49–136.

Kayser, Wolfgan. *The Grotesque in Art and Literature*. Translated by Ulrich Weisstein. New York: McGraw-Hill, 1966.

Keats, John. *Selected Poems and Letters*. Edited by Douglas Bush. Boston: Houghton Mifflin, 1959.

Knechtges, David, trans. *Wen Xuan or Selections of Refined Literatur*. Princeton: Princeton University Press, 1982–1987.

Kudo, Naotaro. *The Life and Thought of Li Ho*. Tokyo: Waseda University Press, 1972.

Lafleur, Frances Ann. "The Evolution of a Symbolist Aesthetic in Classical Chinese Verse: The Role of Li Ho Compared with that of Charles Baudelaire in Nineteenth-Century French Poetry." Ph.D. dissertation. Princeton University, 1993.

Lattimore, David. "Allusions and T'ang Poetry." In *Perspectives on the T'ang*. Edited by Arthur F. Wright and Denis Twitchett, 405–40. New Haven: Yale University Press, 1973,

Legge, James, trans. *The Chinese Classics*, in five volumes. Hong Kong: Hong Kong University Press, 1982.

Levy, Dore J. "Constructing Sequences: Another Look at the Principle of Fu 賦 'Enumeration.'" *Harvard Journal of Asiatic Studies* 46 (December 1986): 471–93.

———. *Chinese Narrative Poetry: The Late Han through T'ang Dynasties*. Durham: Duke University Press, 1988.

Li, Wai-yee. *Enchantment and Disenchantment: Love and Illusion in Chinese Literature*. Princeton: Princeton University Press, 1993.

Lin, Shuen-fu and Stephen Owen, eds. *The Vitality of Lyrical Voice: Shih Poetry from the Late Han to the T'ang*. Princeton: Princeton University Press, 1986.

Liu, James Y. *The Art of Chinese Poetry*. Chicago: University of Chicago Press, 1962.

———. *The Poetry of Li Shang-yin*. Chicago: University of Chicago Press, 1969.

———. *Chinese Theories of Literature*. Chicago: University of Chicago Press, 1975.

Marney, John. *Liang Chien-Wen Ti*. Boston: Twayne Publishers, 1976.

———, trans. *Beyond the Mulberries: An Anthology of Palace-Style Poetry by Emperor Chien-wen of the Liang Dynasty (503–551)*. San Francisco: Chinese Materials Center, 1982.

Marqueze-Pouey, Louis. *Le Movement décadent en France*. Paris: Press Universitaires de France, 1986.

Mather, Richard B. *The Poet Shen Yueh*. Princeton: Princeton University Press, 1988.

McMullen, David. *State and Scholars in Tang China*. Cambridge: Cambridge University Press, 1988.

Miao, Ronald C. "Palace Style Poetry: The Courtly Treatment of Glamour and Love." In *Studies in Chinese Poetics*. Edited by Ronald C. Miao, 1: 1–42. San Francisco: Chinese Materials Center, 1978.

Miner, Earl. *Comparative Poetics*. Princeton: Princeton University Press, 1990.

Munro, John M. *The Decadent Poetry of the Eighteen-Nineties*. Beruit: American University of Beirut Press, 1970.

Owen, Stephen. *The Poetry of Meng Chiao and Han Yu*. New Haven: Yale University Press, 1975.

———. *The Poetry of the Early T'ang*. New Haven: Yale University Press, 1977.

———. *The Great Age of Chinese Poetry: The High T'ang*. New Haven: Yale University Press, 1981.

———. *Traditional Chinese Poetry and Poetics: Omen of the World*. Madison: University of Wisconsin Press, 1985.

———. *Remembrances: The Experience of the Past in Classical Chinese Literature*. Cambridge: Harvard University Press, 1986.

———. *Readings in Chinese Literary Thought*. Cambridge: Harvard University Press, 1992.

———. *The End of the Chinese "Middle Ages": Essays in Mid-Tang Literary Culture*. Stanford: Stanford University Press, 1996.

Pater, Walter. *Appreciations*. London: Macmillan, 1924.

———. *Marius the Epicurean*. London: Macmillan, 1910.

Pittock, Murray G. H. *Spectrum of Decadence: The Literature of the 1890s*. London and New York: Routledge, 1993.

Praz, Mario. *The Romantic Agony*. Translated by Angus Davison. London and New York: Oxford University Press, 1970.

Preminger, Alex and T. V. F. Brogan, eds. *The New Princeton Encyclopedia of Poetry and Poetics*. Princeton: Princeton University Press, 1993.

Richare, Noel. *Le Movement décadent: Dandys, esthètes et quintessents*. Paris: Nizet, 1968.

Rickett, Adele Austin, ed. *Chinese Approaches to Literature from Confucius to Liang Ch'i-ch'ao*. Princeton: Princeton University Press, 1978.

Ridge, George Ross. *The Hero in French Decadent Literature*. Athens: University of Georgia Press, 1961.

Riffaterre, Michael. *Semiotics of Poetry*. Bloomington: Indiana University Press, 1978.

Rouzer, Paul. "Waching the Voyeurs: Palace Poetry and Yuefu." In *Chinese Literature: Essays, Articles, Reviews* 11 (1989): 11–34.

———. *Writing Another's Dream: The Poetry of Wen Tingyun*. Stanford: Stanford University Press, 1993.

Ryals, Clyde de L. "Towards a Definition of Decadent as Applied to British Literature of the Nineteenth Century." *Journal of Aesthetic and Art Cricism* 17 (1958): 85–92.

Saussy, Haun. *The Problem of a Chinese Aesthetic*. Stanford: Stanford University Press, 1993.

Shih, Vincent Yu-chung, trans. *The Literary Mind and The Carving of Dragons*. Taipei: Chung Hwa Book Company, 1975.

Symons, Arthur. *The Symbolist Movement in Literature*. New York: E. P. Dutton and Company, 1908.

———. *Poetry and Prose*. Edited by R. V. Holdsworth. Carcanet Press (Paul and Co., Concord, Mass.), 1972.

Thornton, R. K. R. *The Decadent Dilemma*. London: Edward Arnold, 1983.

Tu, Kuo-ch'ing. *Li Ho*. Boston: Twayne Publishers, 1979.

Waley, Arthur, trans. *The Book of Songs*. New York: Grove Press, 1937.

———. *The Way and Its Power*. New York: Grove Weidenfeld, 1958.

Watson, Burton. *Chinese Lyricism: Shih Poetry from the Second to the Twelfth Century*. New York: Columbia University Press, 1971.

———. *Chinese Rhyme-Prose*. New York: Columbia University Press, 1977.

Weir, David. *Decadence and the Making of Modernism*. Amherst: University of Massachusetts Press, 1995.

Wellek, René. *A History of Modern Criticism 1750–1950*. Volume 4, *The Later Nineteenth Century*. New Haven: Yale University Press, 1965.

Wilde, Oscar. *The Portable Oscar Wilde*. Edited by Richard Aldington. New York: Viking Press, 1946.

Wilson, Edmund. *Axel's Castle: A Study in the Imaginative Literature of 1870 to 1930*. New York: Charles Scribner's Sons, 1931.

Wimsatt, William K. Jr. and Cleanth Brooks. *Literary Criticism: A Short History*. Chicago and London: The University of Chicago Press, 1983.

Worton, Michael and Judith Still, eds. *Intertextuality: Theories and Practices*. Manchester: Manchester University Press, 1990.

Wu, Fusheng. "Decadence in Chinese Literature: Xiao Gang's Palace Style Poetry" in *Chinese Studies* XV, no. 1 (1997): 351–95.

———. "The Concept of Decadence in the Chinese Poetic Tradition" in *Monumenta Serica* XLV (1997): 39–62.

Yang, Xianyi and Gladys Yang, trans. *Poetry and Prose of the Tang and Song*. Beijing: Chinese Literature, 1984.

Yeats, W. B. *The Autobiography of William Butler Yeats*. New York: Macmillan, 1953.

Yoshio, Kawakatsu. "La décadence de l'aristocratie chinoise sous les Dynasties du sud." *Acta Asiatica* 21(1871):13–38.

Yu, Pauline. *The Reading of Imagery in the Chinese Poetic Tradition*. Princeton: Princeton University Press, 1986.

———. "Poems in their Place: Collections and Canons in Early Chinese Literature." *Harvard Journal of Asiatic Studies* 50.1 (1990): 163–96.

———, ed. *Voices of the Song Lyric in China*. Berkeley: University of California Press, 1994.

Zoren, Steven Van. *Poetry and Personality: Reading, Exegesis and Hermeneutics in Traditional China*. Stanford: Stanford University Press, 1991.

Hightower, James, 207n. 52
Holzman, Donald, 202n. 9
Hu Zi, 254n. 71
*huaigu* (recalling the antiquity),
140, 148
Huang Jian, 171
Huang Jie, 48

immortality, in Confucian thinking, 30, 210n. 73
intertextuality, 1, 72, 195n. 1
ivory tower, 115, 153, 241n. 120

Jackson, Holbrook, 8
Jameson, Frederic, 73, 226n. 88
Ji Yougong, 243n. 5
Jia Dao, 230n. 25
Jiang Zong, 254n. 78
Ji Yun, 164, 177, 185, 250n. 24
Jin Wudi (Emperor Wu of Jin
Dynasty), 183
"Jiuge" ("Nine Songs"), 175
Joad, C. E. M., 8
Johnson, Samuel, 85, 107, 109,
237n. 88

Kang Zhengguo, 216n. 17
Kao Yu-kung, 233–34 n. 56; and
Mei Tsu-lin, 254n. 68
Karlgren, Bernard, 222n. 59
Keats, John, 109, 169
Knechtges, David, 25, 207n. 52
Kudo, Naotaro, 228n. 8
*kuyin* (painstaking composition),
86, 89, 171, 230n. 25

LaFleur, Ann, 237n. 89
Lan Yu, 250n. 25
language, Daoist concept of, 5, 74
Late Tang, and periodization of
Tang poetry, 1, 2, 196n, 2
Late Tang poetry, conventional
perception of, 2, 197n. 6
*Laozi*, 16–17
Lattimore, David, 234n. 65
Legge, James, 200n. 3

Levy, Dore J., 224n. 75, 231n. 38,
232n. 46, 244n. 14, 245n. 31
Li Bai, 38, 213nn. 93, 94, 239n.
105, 253n. 57
Li Dongyang, 105, 236n. 83
Li E, 212n. 83
Li He, 1, 6, 75, 77–116, 125, 138,
147, 151–52, 158, 160, 169, 173,
191
Li He poems cited: "Excursion
Among Flowers: A Song" 花游
曲, 81; "A Lovely Woman Combing Her Hair: A Song" 美人梳頭
歌, 83; "Self-Mocking" 惱公, 86–
89; "A Dream of Heaven" 夢天,
103–104; "Six Satirical Poems:
No. 5" 感諷六首: 其五, 105;
"Five Satirical Poems: No. 3"
感諷五首: 其三, 105; "Su Xiao-
xiao's Tomb" 蘇小小墓, 108;
"The Coming of Autumn" 秋來,
110; "Do not Go Out of Your
Gate, Sir!" 公無出門, 112–13
Li Ling, 31
"Li Sao" ("Encountering Sorrow"). *See* Qu Yuan
Li Shangyin, 1, 6, 46, 75, 77, 79,
116, 149–93, 191, 216n. 17,
248n. 77
Li Shangyin poems cited: "In Imitation of Xu Ling's Style: To a
Court Maid in Charge of Changing Clothes" 效徐陵體贈更衣,
150; "In Imitation of Changji"
效長吉, 151–52; "Untitled: Last
Night's Stars" 無題: 昨夜星辰,
153; "Two Untitled Poems, No.
1: Phoenix Tail Like Scented
Silk" 無題二首: 鳳尾香羅, 155–
56; "Yan Terrace, Four Poems:
Spring" 燕臺四首: 春, 159–60;
"Feelings of Solitary Living" 獨
居有懷, 163–64; "Patterned
Zither" 錦瑟, 167–68; "In Imitation of a Thought" 擬意, 171–73;
"Refining Elixir" 藥轉, 177–78;